GAYLORD			PRINTED IN U.S.A.

HANDBOOK OF

WOMEN, STRESS, AND TRAUMA

BRUNNER-ROUTLEDGE PSYCHOSOCIAL STRESS SERIES
Charles R. Figley, Ph.D., Series Editor

1. *Stress Disorders among Vietnam Veterans*, Edited by Charles R. Figley, Ph.D.
2. *Stress and the Family Vol. 1: Coping with Normative Transitions*, Edited by Hamilton I. McCubbin, Ph.D. and Charles R. Figley, Ph.D.
3. *Stress and the Family Vol. 2: Coping with Catastrophe*, Edited by Charles R. Figley, Ph.D., and Hamilton I. McCubbin, Ph.D.
4. *Trauma and Its Wake: The Study and Treatment of Post-Traumatic Stress Disorder*, Edited by Charles R. Figley, Ph.D.
5. *Post-Traumatic Stress Disorder and the War Veteran Patient*, Edited by William E. Kelly, M.D.
6. *The Crime Victim's Book, Second Edition*, By Morton Bard, Ph.D., and Dawn Sangrey.
7. *Stress and Coping in Time of War: Generalizations from the Israeli Experience*, Edited by Norman A. Milgram, Ph.D.
8. *Trauma and Its Wake Vol. 2: Traumatic Stress Theory, Research, and Intervention*, Edited by Charles R. Figley, Ph.D.
9. *Stress and Addiction*, Edited by Edward Gottheil, M.D., Ph.D., Keith A. Druley, Ph.D., Steven Pashko, Ph.D., and Stephen P. Weinsteinn, Ph.D.
10. *Vietnam: A Casebook*, by Jacob D. Lindy, M.D., in collaboration with Bonnie L. Green, Ph.D., Mary C. Grace, M.Ed., M.S., John A. MacLeod, M.D., and Louis Spitz, M.D.
11. *Post-Traumatic Therapy and Victims of Violence*, Edited by Frank M. Ochberg, M.D.
12. *Mental Health Response to Mass Emergencies: Theory and Practice*, Edited by Mary Lystad, Ph.D.
13. *Treating Stress in Families*, Edited by Charles R. Figley, Ph.D.
14. *Trauma, Transformation, and Healing: An Integrative Approach to Theory, Research, and Post-Traumatic Therapy*, By John P. Wilson, Ph.D.
15. *Systemic Treatment of Incest: A Therapeutic Handbook*, By Terry Trepper, Ph.D., and Mary Jo Barrett, M.S.W.
16. *The Crisis of Competence: Transitional Stress and the Displaced Worker*, Edited by Carl A. Maida, Ph.D., Norma S. Gordon, M.A., and Norman L. Farberow, Ph.D.
17. *Stress Management: An Integrated Approach to Therapy*, by Dorothy H. G. Cotton, Ph.D.
18. *Trauma and the Vietnam War Generation: Report of the Findings from the National Vietnam Veterans Readjustment Study*, By Richard A. Kulka, Ph.D., William E. Schlenger, Ph.D., John A. Fairbank, Ph.D., Richard L. Hough, Ph.D., Kathleen Jordan, Ph.D., Charles R. Marmar, M.D., Daniel S. Weiss, Ph.D., and David A. Grady, Psy.D.
19. *Strangers at Home: Vietnam Veterans Since the War*, Edited by Charles R. Figley, Ph.D., and Seymour Leventman, Ph.D.
20. *The National Vietnam Veterans Readjustment Study: Tables of Findings and Technical Appendices*, By Richard A. Kulka, Ph.D., Kathleen Jordan, Ph.D., Charles R. Marmar, M.D., and Daniel S. Weiss, Ph.D.
21. *Psychological Trauma and the Adult Survivor: Theory, Therapy, and Transformation*, By I. Lisa McCann, Ph.D., and Laurie Anne Pearlman, Ph.D.
22. *Coping with Infant or Fetal Loss: The Couple's Healing Process*, By Kathleen R. Gilbert, Ph.D., and Laura S. Smart, Ph.D.
23. *Compassion Fatigue: Coping with Secondary Traumatic Stress Disorder in Those Who Treat the Traumatized*, Edited by Charles R. Figley, Ph.D.
24. *Treating Compassion Fatigue*, Edited by Charles R. Figley, Ph.D.
25. *Handbook of Stress, Trauma and the Family*, Edited by Don R. Catherall, Ph.D.
26. *The Pain of Helping: Psychological Injury of Helping Professionals*, by Patrick J. Morrissette, Ph.D., RMFT, NCC, CCC
27. *Disaster Mental Health Services: A Primer for Practitioners*, by Diane Myers, R.N., M.S.N, and David Wee, M.S.S.W.
28. *Empathy in the Treatment of Trauma and PTSD*, by John P. Wilson, Ph.D. and Rhiannon B. Thomas, Ph.D.
29. *Family Stressors: Interventions for Stress and Trauma*, Edited by Don. R. Catherall, Ph. D.

Editorial Board

HANDBOOK OF
WOMEN, STRESS, AND TRAUMA

EDITED BY

KATHLEEN A. KENDALL-TACKETT

Brunner-Routledge
Taylor & Francis Group
NEW YORK AND HOVE

Published in 2005 by
Brunner-Routledge
Taylor & Francis Group
270 Madison Avenue
New York, NY 10016
www.brunner-routledge.com

Cover design: Pearl Chang
Cover photos: Clockwise from upper left:
©LarryWilliams/CORBIS, © Royalty-free/CORBIS, ©Tim Wright/CORBIS, © Royalty-free CORBIS.
Copyright © 2005 by Taylor & Francis Group, a Division of T&F Informa.
Brunner-Routledge is an imprint of the Taylor & Francis Group.

Printed in the United States of America on acid-free paper.

10 9 8 7 6 5 4 3 2 1

Library of Congress Cataloging-in-Publication Data
    The handbook of women, stress, and trauma / edited by Kathleen
Kendall-Tackett.
        p.; cm.— (Brunner-Routledge psychosocial stress series ; 30)
    Includes bibliographical references and index.
    ISBN 0-415-94742-1 (hardback : alk. paper)
    1. Women—Mental health—Handbooks, manuals, etc. 2. Women—Psychology—Handbooks,
    manuals, etc. 3. Stress (Psychology)—Handbooks, manuals, etc. 4. Post-traumatic stress
    disorder—Patients—Handbooks, manuals, etc. 5. Psychic trauma—Patients—Handbooks,
    manuals, etc. 6. Stress management for women—Handbooks, manuals, etc.
    [DNLM: 1. Stress, Psychological. 2. Stress Disorders, Traumatic. 3. Women's Health.
    WM 172 H2396 2005] I. Kendall-Tackett, Kathleen A. II. Title. III. Series.

RC451.4W6H365 2005
616.85'21'0082—dc22   2004011604

Contents

SECTION III: STRESS AND TRAUMA IN THE LIVES OF
WOMEN OF COLOR, WOMEN WITH DISABILITIES,
AND LESBIAN WOMEN

Contributors

Rosalie J. Ackerman, PhD
ABackans Diversified Computer Processing, Inc.
Akron, Ohio

Martha E. Banks, PhD
ABackans Diversified Computer Processing, Inc.
Akron, Ohio
and
Department of Black Studies
College of Wooster
Wooster, Ohio

Kathleen C. Basile, PhD
Division of Violence Prevention
Centers for Disease Control and Prevention
Atlanta, Georgia

L. Rene Bergeron, MSW, PhD
Social Work Department
University of New Hampshire
Durham, New Hampshire

J. Douglas Bremner, MD
Departments of Psychiatry and Radiology
Emory University School of Medicine
Atlanta, Georgia

Rebecca P. Cameron, PhD
Department of Psychology
California State University, Sacramento
Sacramento, California

Jacquelyn C. Campbell, PhD, RN, FAAN
Johns Hopkins University
School of Nursing
Baltimore, Maryland

Danette Crawford, BA
Alliant University
Alameda, California

Stephanie J. Dallam, RN, MS, FNP
Leadership Council for Mental Health, Justice, and the Media
Spring Hill, Kansas

Jasmine Eliav, MA
Department of Human Development and Applied Psychology
Ontario Institute for Studies in Education
University of Toronto
Toronto, Ontario
Canada

Batya Hyman, MSW, PhD
Department of Social Work
Salisbury University
Salisbury, Maryland

Kathleen A. Kendall-Tackett, PhD, IBCLC
Family Research Laboratory/Crimes against Children
   Research Center
University of New Hampshire
Durham, New Hampshire

Linda R. Mona, PhD
Veterans' Administration Hospital
Long Beach Healthcare System
Long Beach, California

Jane A. Rysberg, PhD
Department of Psychology
California State University, Chico
Chico, California

Katreena Scott, PhD, CPsych
Department of Human Development and Applied Psychology
Ontario Institute for Studies in Education
University of Toronto
Toronto, Ontario
Canada

Carolyn M. West, PhD
Interdisciplinary Arts and Sciences Program
University of Washington, Tacoma
Tacoma, Washington

Barbara W. K. Yee, PhD
Department of Family and Consumer Sciences
University of Hawaii
Honolulu, Hawaii

Series Editor's Foreword

I am very fortunate to be the father of two daughters, Jessica and Laura. The contents of this book will help me understand them better. I have enjoyed experiencing every age and stage of their lives as they became extraordinary women. As a social scientist, I knew that most studies are gender biased toward males; that our understanding of women's growth and development was inadequate; and that sexism, sexual harassment, and sexual assault made the world more hostile for females. Being blessed with a loving and intelligent mother, Geni Figley, and sister, Sandy Elliott, assured me that everything would work out. Certainly it did for my wife, Kathy, in spite of setbacks in life.

My first two books focused mostly on men. My next two focused on family stress and included writings by female authors and addressed issues important to women. However, it was not until I became editor of the *Journal of Family Psychotherapy*, now ably edited by Dr. Terry Trepper, that I was afforded an opportunity to begin to close the gap in our knowledge of women. I commissioned several special issues devoted to new knowledge about women. It is with considerable pleasure, therefore, that I write this Series Foreword for another book on women. This book is the first of its kind.

This is a book of firsts. Dr. Kathleen Kendall-Tackett's *Handbook of Women, Stress, and Trauma* is the first book in this series to address the special challenges of women coping with stress, particularly traumatic stress. There have been other books on stress written or edited by women, of course. And this series has had other handbooks on stress and trauma, such as the recently published *Handbook of Stress, Trauma, and the Family*, edited by Dr. Don Catherall. Like his book, Dr. Kendall-Tackett's book brings needed attention to the special challenges faced by women exposed to stress and trauma. Also, this is the first book to review what is known about the stress of women generally and, especially, traumatized women and to discuss what and who women need to manage and eliminate in order to avoid the unwanted consequences of stress. This is also the first book that devotes considerable attention to often neglected topics: women of color, women with disabilities, and lesbian women.

Who would be the best person to be responsible for so many firsts? Kathleen Kendall-Tackett, PhD, IBCLC, is a University of New Hampshire research associate professor of psychology at the Family Research Lab and Crimes against Children Research Center. Currently, she is a cochair of the International Family Violence Research Conferences and works with students and postdocs who are interested in women's issues. Dr. Kendall-Tackett has had a long-standing interest in women's health. As a woman with a chronic illness (lupus), she was able to observe firsthand the challenges for women facing the American health care system. As a result, she has considerable sensitivity for women who have experienced traumatic events, because they often experience vague health symptoms that can be incapacitating but are sometimes brushed off as "not real" by health care providers. It was only natural for her to migrate toward this area of research on women, stress, and trauma.

In her impressive career, Dr. Kendall-Tackett's work with depressed mothers, especially during the postpartum period, has led to important contributions. Due, in part, to her efforts, those who care for these women are more sensitive to screening mothers for depression and insuring that medications and other treatments are compatible with breast feeding. She has also been a pioneer in linking childhood abuse with adult health problems. Several different groups of researchers and practitioners have documented health problems that were more common in adult survivors of childhood abuse. In her book, *Treating the Lifetime Health Effects of Childhood Abuse*, Dr. Kendall-Tackett took the first step in trying to account for this phenomenon by linking the findings of the health psychology and childhood abuse literatures. Together with her other book, *The Health Consequences of Abuse in the Family*, practitioners as well as scholars in both fields are more prepared to study and treat women's health and mental health challenges.

In her introduction, Professor Kendall-Tackett discusses several important questions. Among them is the question, why focus exclusively on women? And why focus on the stress and trauma of women?

The book is divided into three sections. Section I, *Women's Stress and Trauma in Life-Span Perspective*, includes four chapters that describe the intersections of stress and trauma for women in childhood, adolescence, in young- and middle-adulthood, and in old age. Section II, *The Specter of Violence against Women*, includes five chapters that describe the range of violence against women. Unfortunately, rape, intimate partner violence, and elder abuse are common experiences for women and disproportionately affect women. Section III, *Stress and Trauma in the Lives of Women of Color, Women with Disabilities, and Lesbian Women*, includes three powerful chapters that focus on stress and trauma in the lives of three specific populations of women: women of color, women with disabilities, and lesbian women.

The topic discussed in chapter 11 by Linda R. Mona, Rebecca P. Cameron, and Danette Crawford breaks new ground not only in traumatology but also in the field of disability studies. Although the latter field has existed for more than 40 years, research and theory tended to focus on men, even though there are more females with disabilities (21.3%) than males with disabilities (19.8%) in the United States. At the same time, the field of disability studies has long neglected trauma, either as a stressor or stress reaction, despite the fact that a large number of women are disabled as a result of traumatic events. The authors conclude their chapter by urging more research that focuses on these women in order to establish

> a foundation to reach a better understanding of this population, provide better services for women with disabilities, and serve to launch new research directions to help inform future investigators as to how to comprehensively explore this topic (p. 242).

By bringing into focus the struggles women have with stress and trauma—in all of life's circumstances—Professor Kendall-Tackett and I hope that researchers and practitioners will devote far more time, energy, and publications to understanding these struggles and to being more a part of the solution.

Charles R. Figley, Ph.D., Series Editor
Fulbright Fellow, Kuwait University, Kuwait

Acknowledgments

This book would not have been possible without the efforts of many people. First, I would like to thank Charles Figley. He has made so many contributions to the trauma field, and to my work. Thanks for inviting me to take part in this exciting project. It has been an honor to work with you. I would also like to thank Susan Reynolds, from the American Psychological Association, for introducing us and making my participation possible.

The chapter authors have contributed so much to making this volume a success. Thank you for your excellent contributions to this book and for your work on behalf of women and families.

My editors at Brunner-Routledge—Emily Epstein Loeb, Dana Bliss, and Shannon Vargo—have helped at every step of the process. Thank you for sharing your expertise with me.

And finally, I would like to thank my husband, Doug, and sons, Ken and Chris, for being my constant source of support as I worked on this book. I could not have done it without you.

Introduction: Women's Experiences of Stress and Trauma

KATHLEEN A. KENDALL- TACKETT

In the musical *My Fair Lady*, the character Henry Higgins asks: "Why can't a woman be more like a man?" It is a comical song about the differences between men and women. Unfortunately, life has imitated art, and for decades, clinical researchers seemed to approach their work with a similar lament. For years, women were excluded from clinical trials, and findings based on studies of men were applied uncritically to women.

The massive oversight of women in health research had a negative impact on their health and eventually led to the women's health movement. In the United States, the federal government opened the Office on Women's Health (U.S. Department of Health and Human Services). Various advocacy groups furthered the cause and demonstrated what might seem obvious: men and women are different in significant ways, and these differences influence their health.

The study of trauma was also, initially, based on the experiences of men. There is a logical explanation for this: traumatic stress was first recognized and extensively studied among combat veterans. Even today, much of what is known about trauma comes out of the Veteran's Administration hospitals. This information has been extremely valuable, but researchers have recognized that, although there is some overlap, trauma models based on men's experiences do not completely describe the experiences of women.

1

1 WHY WOMEN'S STRESS AND TRAUMA

It is becoming increasingly clear that men and women have *different sources* of stress and trauma in their lives and *respond to* stressful and traumatic events differently. From the women's health movement, we learned that women's health must be considered in the context of their lives. Australian psychologist Christina Lee (1998) noted:

> The psychology of women's health ... must be approached as an integrated perspective ... from the traditional issues of childbirth and menopause through contemporary issues such as violence, harassment and the division of household labor. (p. 175)

As we consider stress and trauma in the lives of women, each of these contextual elements will be considered.

In this book, the chapter authors and I focus on women's experiences of stress and trauma. In doing so, we do not wish to minimize men's experiences. But, we want to recognize that there are differences, and if we are to intervene effectively with women clients, we must understand what these differences mean in their lives. Below is an overview of the differences to which I referred. These ideas will be described in detail in subsequent chapters, and a general description follows in the next section.

1.1 Women's Stress and Trauma is Often Relationally Based

Women often suffer from stress and trauma because of their relationships. Starting in childhood, girls and boys are vulnerable to abuse and neglect from primary caregivers. They are vulnerable to peer-group victimization and dating violence. Although each of these can affect boys, girls are often overrepresented among victim groups—especially in child sexual abuse and dating violence. As they mature, women are more susceptible to rape and intimate partner violence than their male counterparts. As older women, they are more likely to be victims of elder abuse. In each of these cases, the abuser is, more often than not, a family member or intimate partner.

Women's sources of stress are also often relationally based. For example, women have stronger stress reactions to marital strife than men, as demonstrated in cardiovascular reactivity, lipid profiles, blood pressure, and other measures of cardiovascular health (see chapter 2). Cardiovascular disease is the number one killer of women, so anything that increases the risk of cardiovascular disease is especially germane to women's health.

Several of the chapters in this book describe various aspects of caregiving. Although caregiving can be protective of mental and physical health (see chapter 4), being a caregiver can also be a source of stress at various stages of women's lives. Mothering and grandmothering are described in several chapters, as is taking care of partners. The centrality of relationships as potential sources of stress and trauma is one way that women's experiences can be vastly different from those of men.

1.2 Women are More Vulnerable to Depression and Possibly PTSD

Women have twice the lifetime rate of depression compared to men (Mazure, Keita, & Blehar, 2002). Many possible explanations for this have been offered: genetic differences between males and females; or biological factors, such as fluctuations in female sex hormones (Burt & Stein, 2002; Mazure et al., 2002). Others point out that sexism and violence against women are to blame. No doubt, there is truth in each of these suppositions (Mazure et al., 2002).

Women also appear to be more vulnerable to posttraumatic stress disorder (PTSD) after exposure to traumatic events. In a Canadian community sample ($N = 1,007$), women were more likely to develop PTSD than men, even when men and women had experienced the same number of traumatic events. This was especially true if they were exposed to traumatic events in childhood (Breslau, Davis, Andreski, & Peterson, 1997; Kendall-Tackett, 2003). In another study of men and women who had experienced motor vehicle accidents, women had more symptoms of PTSD. They were 4.7 times more likely to meet avoidance and numbing criteria and 3.8 times more likely to meet arousal criteria than were men (Fullerton et al., 2001). However, this sex difference has not consistently appeared in all studies.

Findings of sex differences in some studies raise interesting questions about why they might occur. Yehuda (1999), in discussing possible sex differences in PTSD, indicated that we really do not know whether biological factors account for this difference or whether women are simply more vulnerable to trauma-producing events overall. That remains a question.

1.3 Women are More Vulnerable to Stress-Related Physical Illnesses

Although men and women both have physical sequelae in the wake of traumatic events, women seem more susceptible to certain types. One example is chronic pain. According to a recent review, even when they do not experience trauma, women are at higher risk for a number of pain syndromes and have higher levels of clinical pain relative to men (Fillingim, 2003).

There also appears to be a relationship between trauma and chronic pain. One example of a condition with a probable trauma connection is irritable bowel syndrome (IBS). A high percentage of patients with IBS are survivors of physical or sexual abuse (Drossman et al., 2000; Kendall-Tackett, 2003), and two thirds of IBS patients are women (Society for Women's Health Research, 2002). Other types of chronic pain have also been related to traumatic events, including headaches, chronic pelvic pain, and fibromyalgia (Kendall-Tackett, 2003). Each of these conditions disproportionately affects women.

2 ABOUT THIS BOOK

The book you are about to read represents some of the latest thinking on women's experiences of stress and trauma. Even if you are familiar with the trauma and stress literatures, you will likely find information in this book that is new. In section I, the authors provide a developmental framework to describe the intersections of stress and trauma for women in childhood and adolescence, in young and middle adulthood, and in old age. These chapters cover a wide range of experiences, from childhood relationships, to division of household labor, to nursing home placement. The stresses and traumas that women experience—from the mundane to the severe—are described in detail.

In section II, the authors describe current research on violence against women. Unfortunately, rape, intimate partner violence, and elder abuse are common experiences and disproportionately affect women. No book on women's experiences of trauma would be complete without these chapters. This section also includes two chapters that present cutting-edge research on the physical health and neuropsychiatric outcomes of violence against women.

In section III, you will be introduced to stress and trauma in the lives of three specific populations of women: women of color, women with disabilities, and lesbian women. Unfortunately, these populations have been understudied in the trauma field—something that we sincerely hope will change. These chapters provide insight into the worlds of women of color, who must contend with not only sexism but also racism (chapter 10). Some of the unique stressors, such as historical stressors, for women of color are also presented. Similarly, women with disabilities must contend with sexism and ableism. And they have stresses unique to their disability status, such as depending on their abusers for care. The title of one of the articles cited in this chapter says it all: "Bring my scooter so I can leave you" (Saxton et al., 2001). Finally, lesbian women face discrimination based on sexual orientation. They are often victimized in their families and by peers because of their sexual orientation, and because they are women. Lesbian women face the dual prejudices of sexism and heterosexism.

The chapter authors and I hope that you will find this book enlightening and useful. We wish you great success in your work.

REFERENCES

Breslau, N., Davis, G. C., Andreski, P., & Peterson, E. L. (1997). Sex differences in post-traumatic stress disorder. *Archives of General Psychiatry, 54,* 1044–1048.

Burt, V. K., & Stein, K. (2002). Epidemiology of depression throughout the female life cycle. *Journal of Clinical Psychiatry, 63 (Suppl. 7),* 9–15.

Drossman, D. A., Leserman, J., Li, Z., Keefe, F., Hu, Y. J. B., & Toomey, T. C. (2000). Effects of coping on health outcome among women with gastrointestinal disorders. *Psychosomatic Medicine, 62,* 309–317.

Fillingim, R. B. (2003). Sex-related influences on pain: A review of mechanisms and clinical implication. *Rehabilitation Psychology, 48,* 165–174.

Fullerton, C. S., Ursano, R. J., Epstein, R. S., Crowley, B., et al. (2001). Gender differences in posttraumatic stress disorder after motor vehicle accidents. *American Journal of Psychiatry, 158,* 1486–1491.

Kendall-Tackett, K. A. (2003). *Treating the lifetime health effects of childhood victimization.* Kingston, NJ: Civic Research Institute.

Lee, C. (1998). *Women's health: Psychological and social perspectives.* Thousand Oaks, CA: Sage.

Mazure, C. M., Keita, G. P., & Blehar, M. C. (2002). *Summit on women and depression: Proceeding and findings.* Washington, DC: American Psychological Association.

Saxton, M., Curry, M. A., Powers, L. E., Maley, S., Eckels, K., & Gross, J. (2001). "Bring my scooter so I can leave you": A study of disabled women handling abuse by personal assistance providers. *Violence Against Women, 7,* 393–417.

Society for Women's Health Research. (2002). *Irritable bowel syndrome more than an irritation.* Retrieved December 7, 2002, from http://www.womens-health.org/health/ibs.htm

Yehuda, R. (1999). Biological factors associated with susceptibility to posttraumatic stress disorder. *Canadian Journal of Psychiatry, 44,* 34–39.

Section I

WOMEN'S STRESS AND TRAUMA IN LIFE-SPAN PERSPECTIVE

1

Relational Stress and Trauma in the Lives of Girls and Teens

KATREENA SCOTT AND JASMINE ELIAV

Childhood is often considered an idyllic period of development. The reality, as increasingly recognized, is that girls and boys are exposed to a relatively large number of difficult and potentially traumatic situations. A recent survey of children and youth from a fairly poor, predominantly rural area of the United States found that one in four children experienced a high-magnitude traumatic event—one that involved experiencing, witnessing, or learning about a close family member's experience of actual or threatened death or serious injury (Costello, Erkanli, Fairbank, & Angold, 2002). Other statistics confirm this finding. In 2000, for example, an estimated 99,630 children under 15 years of age were treated in hospital emergency rooms for burn-related injuries (National Safe Kids Campaign, 2002). Rates of rape, robbery, and simple and aggravated assault are two to three times higher for juveniles (ages 12 to 19 years) than adults, yielding an estimated 116 victims in every 1,000 youth (Hashima & Finkelhor, 1999). Children under the age of 12 also come to the attention of the justice system with traumatic experiences, most commonly by being kidnapped or experiencing a sexual assault (Finkelhor & Ormrod, 2000).

Unfortunately, the above statistics are likely a vast underestimate of exposure to traumatic events among children and adolescents in less developed nations, where war and terrorism are ongoing, and natural disasters are common. The International Save the Children Alliance reported that currently 20 million children have been forced from their homes by war, and more than four million children have been disabled by armed conflict or political violence (International Save the Children Alliance, 2001). Researchers also investigated the effects of natural events, such as floods (Green et al., 1994), hurricanes (Shannon, Lonigan, Finch, & Taylor, 1994), and earthquakes (Pynoos et al., 1993), all of which have greater potential impact in nations lacking the infrastructure to predict and respond to natural disasters.

1 CHRONIC RELATION- BASED TRAUMA

The traumatic events just highlighted, and those that are most often considered when discussing trauma and associated psychological difficulties, are single, sudden, unexpected, and severe events. Ironically, some of the most common and problematic are not sudden, single events, but rather relationally based and chronic. Traumas come from key relationships. Included in this category are experiences such as abuse from a family member, bullying in the school yard, and violence in adolescent dating relationships.

In this chapter, we highlight girls' and female adolescents' experiences of these relationship-based chronic and abusive traumatic events. We will begin by reviewing the important characteristics of chronic relational traumas. Then, we consider common relational traumas in peer and adolescent relationships and review evidence of their impact on children's development and functioning. From this, we develop an argument for a relational path to trauma continuity across the life span. As much of existing literature on trauma in childhood is not gender specific, reference is made to children and adolescents of both genders, with experiences of girls highlighted when possible.

2 CHARACTERISTICS AND IMPACT OF CHRONIC AND ABUSIVE TRAUMAS

Acute Versus Chronic Trauma

Acute trauma: Eight-year-old Alisa was playing outside on the school grounds with her friend Vanessa. The girls knew that after school they were supposed to go directly home, but Vanessa was taking gymnastics and wanted to show Alisa how she had learned to swing from the bars. As the girls were playing, they heard a group of adolescent boys yelling angrily at each other. The girls froze in fear as half of the boys ran past them. Then Alisa heard a terrible noise. Vanessa had been shot with a bullet aimed at one of the boys running past. Alisa was terrified and stood screaming and crying until an adult from the neighborhood ran over and called the police.

Chronic trauma: By the age of 8 years, Sara had been walking home from school by herself for 4 months. Sarah would beg and plead with her father to walk her to school, because she was tormented by a group of neighborhood children. Every day she would come home terrified and would cry to her father about the mean kids who would tease and hurt her. Her father was frustrated with her continued complaints and what he saw as whining. When Sara complained about walking to school, he would react by telling her that she was a baby and blaming her for provoking the other kids. As a result, not only was Sara terrified to go to and from school each day, but she was also vigilant in never showing fear or hurt in front of her father.

Terr (1991) first drew the distinction between acute, nonabusive stressors, and chronic or abusive stressors. She noticed that a number of children presenting with trauma-like reactions had not experienced a single, severe, life-threatening event, such as a car accident. Instead, these children were presenting with repeated experiences of stressful events in the context of close relationships. She characterized these children as experiencing "chronic" trauma and differentiated them from those who experienced "acute" trauma. The difference between these types of traumas is illustrated in "Alisa's and Sara's stories." Alisa's horror, terror, and feelings of helplessness in response to witnessing her friend get shot are clearly traumatic. It is also an acute, one-time event, in that it is unlikely that a similar shooting will take place at Alisa's school. Sara, in contrast, is experiencing chronic trauma. She is repeatedly terrified for her life on her way home from school, with this trauma compounded by fear of her father's anger and disdain.

Acute and chronic traumas have significant negative impacts on children and adolescents. Among children and youth, the most common emotional responses to trauma include emotional numbness, loss of interest in activities, difficulty concentrating, generalized anxiety, low self-esteem, dissociation, and feelings of guilt (Fletcher, 1996). Stress-related reactions are also commonly connected to aspects of the traumatic experience, such as daydreaming about the event, reenacting the event, having bad dreams and intrusive memories, developing trauma-specific fears, and finding reminders of the event distressing. Symptoms such as hypervigilance, regressive behavior, somatic complaints, and aggressive or antisocial behavior are less common but still occur relatively frequently (Fletcher, 2003).

3 THE IMPACT OF TRAUMA ON CHILDREN

As recently as 15 to 20 years ago, professionals believed that there was little impact from stressful and traumatic events on children. We now know that the opposite is true. The impact of stressful and traumatic events is greater for children and adolescents than it is for adults. This occurs for a number of reasons. First, because younger children have less control over their physiological and emotional functioning than do older children and adults, distressing events are more likely to overwhelm them (American Psychiatric Association, 1994; Cicchetti, 1989). This is clearly demonstrated by rates of posttraumatic symptoms in children and adults. Following exposure to a traumatic event, approximately 36% of children develop PTSD, as compared to 24% of adults. In addition, the overall incidence rates for almost all symptoms of trauma listed in the *Diagnostic and Statistical Manual of Mental Disorders (fourth edition)* ([*DSM-IV*] American Psychiatric Association, 1994) are higher in children than in adults following exposure to traumatic events (Fletcher, 2003).

Second, due to the rapid and demanding pace of child development, traumatic experiences that occur early in life can significantly disrupt children's progress toward developmental goals, and thus, they have rippling negative effects over time. For example, a key task of middle childhood is the establishment of a sense of competence in independent activities. If a traumatic event is experienced at this age, children may numb to social interactions and withdraw from others. Sara and Alisa, from the case examples, may begin to avoid being with other children from their classes. They may also want to avoid school to minimize reminders of their traumatic experiences. As a consequence, they are likely to engage in fewer independent activities and may fail to develop an age-appropriate sense of competence.

3.1 Differential Impact of Acute and Chronic Traumas

Although there are clear similarities in the negative effects of acute and chronic traumas on children, there are also a number of important differences. To begin, the short-term impact of acute and chronic stresses differs. Fletcher (2003) compared the incidence rates of children's posttraumatic stress responses to acute and chronic stressors. He found that although children exposed to both types of stressors were equally likely to be diagnosed with PTSD (36% in each case), children exposed to chronic trauma were more likely to experience avoidance or numbing and to actively avoid reminders of the traumatic event. For example, about 55% of children exposed to chronic trauma made efforts to forget about the event and avoid reminders compared to about 20% of children who experienced acute traumas. Children who experienced chronic trauma were also more likely to be distressed by reminders of their experiences (74% versus 51%), and to reexperience their traumas in bad dreams (61% versus 23%). Elevated levels of arousal in survivors of chronic or abusive stress are also more common, as evidenced by symptoms such as exaggerated startle response, general irritability, and negative affect.

3.2 Making Meaning from Traumatic Experiences

Increased incidence of symptoms of negative affect and irritability may relate to children's ability to make meaning out of traumatic experiences. Individuals able to attribute external, controllable causes to their traumas and to find ways to see dignity and virtue in the ways they handled their experiences are more likely to recover from traumatic events (Herman, 1992). For children experiencing chronic traumas, their ability to use external attributions and create "healing" stories of their traumas is limited by the continued context of fear and potential trauma. As a result, rather than seeing virtue in their experiences, these children often develop a "sense of foreshortened future"—an attitude that life can end at any moment, so the future cannot be planned for or anticipated. This pessimistic attitude is not prevalent among children exposed to acute stressors (12% on average) but characterizes about one third of children exposed to chronic trauma (Fletcher, 2003).

3.3 Relational Aspects of Chronic Trauma

Chronic, abusive stressors are also distinguished from acute traumatic experiences in terms of the relational contexts in which they generally occur. In approximately 80% of cases that come to the attention of child protection and welfare agencies, parents are the alleged perpetrators of child abuse and neglect. In the other 20% of cases, maltreatment is most often perpetrated by relatives and adult friends of the family (Trocmé et al., 2001). Even in later adolescence, youth are more likely to be victimized by acquaintances, friends, or dating partners than by strangers (Finkelhor & Ormrod, 2000). For example, only 11% of crimes against youth are perpetrated by strangers—most are known to the victim as either a family member or acquaintance (Finkelhor & Ormrod, 2000). Thus, with the exception of stresses that occur in war-torn countries, chronic traumatization of children and youth almost always occurs within important relationships.

This has two important implications. First, the trauma is likely to be magnified by associated damage to the relationship. Consider, for example, a girl's experience of severe physical abuse from her mother. The potential for trauma exists both in the fear of the attack and in the impact of the mother's betrayal of her role in keeping the child safe and protected from harm. Second, the relational context of trauma forces children and adolescents to deal with unresolvable conflict. In the case of child abuse, for example, the child must preserve a sense of trust in his or her parents, who have now shown that they are unpredictable and dangerous.

Abuse and trauma that occur in other relationships carry that same conflict. To adapt to this situation, chronically traumatized children and adolescents generally make several cognitive, affective, and social adaptations. These include cognitive hypervigilance to potential indicators of danger from loved ones (Hennessy, Rabideau, Cicchetti, & Cummings, 1994; Pollak, Cicchetti, Klorman, & Brumaghim, 1997), dissociative experiences (Friedrich, Jaworski, Huxsahl, & Bengtson, 1997; Macfie, Cicchetti, & Toth, 2001; Tricket, Noll, Reiffman, & Putnam, 2001), and diminished recognition of internal affective states (Cicchetti & Beeghly, 1987). To the extent that these adaptations are successful, chronically traumatized children and adolescents are able to preserve trust in relationships. However, the costs of such adaptations in terms of self-worth and adaptation to future relationships are high.

In summary, the impact of chronic, abusive trauma on children and adolescents is more severe and detrimental to children's relational functioning than acute trauma. Moreover, due to the severity and lengthened duration of symptoms, disruptions in development associated with chronic trauma are potentially more severe. In the following sections, we highlight three chronic stressors experienced by girls in early and middle childhood and adolescence: child maltreatment, bullying, and adolescent dating violence. Following this, findings are integrated along a developmental continuum to advance understanding of the context and course of trauma (Williams, 2003).

4 CHILD MALTREATMENT AS A CHRONIC TRAUMA IN CHILDHOOD

CHRONIC TRAUMA IN CHILDHOOD

Cathy was removed from her parent's home at the age of three as a result of neglect and emotional abuse. At home, Cathy's parents rarely interacted with her. For the most part, they would ignore her cries of hunger and would leave her diaper unchanged. When they interacted with Cathy, it was usually to scream about the mess she had made or about her crying. A few weeks after her removal from home, Cathy's parents went to visit her in foster care. When they entered the room, Cathy did not move toward them. When her mother tried to give her a toy,

Cathy was uninterested and looked away. When her father spoke to her, she got up and ran around the room yelling the word "no." Her parents, angered by their inability to engage their daughter, got up to go. As they went to leave, Cathy began to cry inconsolably. She ran toward the door trying to grab onto her mother's leg. Her parents were confused about Cathy's changing behavior and pulled away. Cathy moved into a corner to sob after they left and could not be calmed by her foster parents.

Child maltreatment is one of the most prevalent and concerning forms of chronic trauma experienced by children. National incidence studies from the United States and Canada indicate that more than 20 children in every 1,000 are reported to child protection agencies each year for concerns about child abuse and neglect (Trocme et al., 2001; U.S. Department of Health and Human Services, 2001). Prevalence rates in retrospective community surveys indicate even higher rates, with 10% to 25% of adults reporting experiences of physical abuse in childhood (MacMillan et al., 1997; Straus & Gelles, 1986), and one in four women reporting sexual abuse as a child or adolescent (World Health Organization, 1999). Girls and female adolescents are alleged victims in about half of cases overall but are overrepresented as alleged victims of sexual abuse (Trocme et al., 2001). Put in context, children and youth in North America are more likely to be sexually abused or severely physically maltreated by age 16 than to be victims of serious accidents, natural disasters, and fires, or to experience violence from a nonfamily member (Costello et al., 2002).

4.1 Trauma and Child Maltreatment

The traumatic impact of childhood maltreatment is clear. In the immediate aftermath of child maltreatment, an estimated 36% of sexually abused children and 39% of physically abused children meet criteria for PTSD (Famularo, Fenton, & Kinscherff, 1994; McLeer et al., 1998). Lifetime rates of PTSD are also elevated for individuals with experiences of maltreatment in childhood or youth. One third of adults who were victims of childhood maltreatment meet criteria for lifetime PTSD, compared to 20% of individuals with similar backgrounds who were not maltreated (Widom, 1999). There is some evidence that girls and women are more vulnerable than men to developing PTSD as a result of childhood maltreatment. Kessler, Sonnega, Bromet, and Hughes (1995) reported that lifetime rates of PTSD were higher for women than for men with respect to reports of childhood physical abuse (48.5% of women versus 22.3% of men) and molestation (26.5% versus 12.2%), though the rates were similar for childhood neglect (19.7% versus 23.9%).

The negative impact of maltreatment-related trauma is also apparent across other domains of functioning. Fascinating research is demonstrating that chronic trauma takes a significant toll on children's developing brains (see chapter 9). For example, Beers and De Bellis (2002) found that children with maltreatment-related PTSD demonstrated significant deficits within domains of attention, abstraction, reasoning, and executive function as compared to nonmaltreated children. This finding may underlie, at least partially, the relationship between child maltreatment and poor achievement at school (Barahal, Waterman, & Martin, 1981; Erickson, Egeland, & Pianta, 1989; Hoffman-Plotkin & Twentyman, 1984; Salzinger, Kaplan, Pelcovitz, Samit, & Krieger, 1984). Other research outlines the impact of chronic relational trauma on the development of self, beliefs, and attributions about the world and on the learning of skills for social interaction (Wekerle & Wolfe, 2002). In particular, there is evidence that traumatized children become "honed" to indicators of potential trauma. For maltreated children, this means hypervigilance to cues of aggression (Dodge, 1980; Dodge, Lochman, Laird, Zelli, & the Conduct Problems Prevention Research Group, 2002; Hennessy et al., 1994; Zelli & Dodge, 1999), especially quick recognition of negative emotion in others (Pollak & Sinha, 2002; Pollak & Tolley-Schell, 2003), and a tendency to attribute hostile intent to actors in ambiguous circumstances (Bugental, Lewis, Lin, Lyon, & Kopeikin, 1999; Bugental, Lyon, Lin, McGrath, & Bimbela, 1999).

The experience of chronic trauma in the context of a parent–child relationship also has significant implications for a child's relational capacities. As previously mentioned, when children are traumatized by their parents, they are placed in the impossible situation of needing support, comfort, and security from the people who have traumatized them. For Cathy, in the examples provided, this resulted in significant disruptions in her ability to trust and rely on her mother, as well as on other adults in her life. Cathy has not been able to find a consistent way to preserve closeness with her mother in times of stress, and so she tries and then abandons strategies of showing and inhibiting distress, seeking and then avoiding her mother's attempts to comfort her.

This pattern of insecure and disorganized attachment (Main & Solomon, 1990) characterizes as many as 80% of young children abused by their caretakers (Cicchetti & Beeghly, 1987; Cicchetti, Toth, & Bush, 1988). As Cathy gets older, she will likely develop strategies to gain control of the interaction between her and her caregiver, potentially becoming demanding and rigid to ensure predictability in her caregivers' responses (Crittenden, 1992). She has a much higher chance than a nonmaltreated child of displaying aggression and hostility to others, especially authority figures (for reviews, see Kolko, 1992, 2002). Alternatively, she may become anxious, withdrawn, and isolated (Hartman & Burgess, 1989).

In summary, in addition to the "common" symptoms of trauma (i.e., avoidance, reexperience, and increased arousal), chronic maltreatment-related traumatic experiences interfere with girls' ability to establish solid foundations for developing relationships with others. Although young boys and girls are both negatively affected by maltreatment, girls may be more vulnerable to developing symptoms of trauma and PTSD. Due to the relational nature of maltreatment-related trauma, children also need to make adaptations in their individual and social functioning to maintain relationships with their parents. The adaptations needed to compensate for this early relational deficit, along with the perturbations in functioning caused by symptoms of trauma, have implications that go well beyond early childhood.

5 CONTINUITY OF RELATIONAL TRAUMA IN MIDDLE CHILDHOOD

CHRONIC RELATIONAL TRAUMA IN MIDDLE CHILDHOOD

Julie is 11 years old and is one of five children. In order to support the children, both of Julie's parents work two jobs. They return home at night exhausted and with little patience. They are easily angered and are likely to yell at the children for the smallest disturbance. Julie and her siblings are sensitive and try to be on their best behavior in front of their parents. But sometimes, their parents still become angry and abusive. Julie's restraint at home is not carried into the school environment. At school, Julie is known to be a bully. She has few friends, and she is always getting into trouble and spending time in the office. Other children are quick to tease Julie and to gang up on her when the teachers are not watching. Julie's classroom teacher describes her as always on the defensive, ready to fight. She has noticed that Julie automatically assumes that her peers are trying to hurt her, and she thinks that Julie calls them names and physically hurts them in anticipation of being teased.

As children get older, the potential for experiencing trauma in relationships expands to include peers. Although relatively rare, a small number of children and adolescents are exposed to, or are victims of, deadly forms of violence at school. During the 1998 to 1999 school year, there were 29 school homicides in the United States, down from 54 in 1992 to 1993 (Shafii & Shafii, 2001). Moreover, on the basis of administrator reports (i.e., teachers and principals), an estimated 4.2% of adolescents ages 12 to 19 are victims of violent crimes at school (Shafii & Shafii, 2001). Incidents such as stabbings and criminal assaults are mostly confined to inner-city schools, but in that context, they are potent sources of trauma (Pynoos et al., 1987). For example, one survey of 6th to 8th grade students in inner-city schools in the United States found that 41% of these students reported witnessing a shooting or stabbing in the past year (Schwab-Stone et al., 1995).

6 BULLYING

Bullying, a less deadly but far more common form of peer victimization, can result in elevated rates of trauma symptoms and PTSD. Bullying may be defined as a type of aggression in which the behavior is intended to harm or disturb, is repeated over time, and in which there is an imbalance of power with a more powerful person or group attacking a less powerful person or group (Olweus, 1999). Estimates of the prevalence of bullying vary depending on the criteria used for definition and the reporter of the event. In a recent survey of almost 5,000 Canadian children, Craig and Pepler (1997) found that 15% of children reported being bullied, and 6% reported bullying "more than twice" during the term. Incidence rates from countries around the world are similarly concerning. The World Health Organization's study of children across 28 countries found that rates of victimization ranged from 13% to 55%, with 25% of U.S. students reporting having been bullied at school during their last term (World Health Organization, 2000).

6.1 Sex Differences in Bullying

Differences were noted in the types of bullying most common among girls and boys. Girls are more likely to experience, engage in, and be distressed by relational or indirect forms of bullying, such as the spread of rumors, social exclusion, and social manipulation; whereas among boys, physical and verbal aggression are more common (Crick & Nelson, 2002; Oesterman et al., 1998; Paquette & Underwood, 1999). Due to differences in forms of bullying, it is difficult to compare rates of victimization across genders. However, it has been argued that when relational forms of aggression are included, girls are as likely as boys to be perpetrators and victims of bullying (Bjoerkqvist, 1994; Paquette & Underwood, 1999; Solberg & Olweus, 2003).

6.2 Impact of Bullying

Initial work on the impact of bullying examined its effects on general emotional distress. This research established that victims of bullying are more likely to report symptoms of depression, anxiety, and distress and to display behavioral and conduct problems (Craig, 1998; Crick & Nelson, 2002; Olweus, 1991; Slee, 1995). To date, one published study specifically examined posttraumatic stress reactions to peer victimization in a large sample. Mynard, Joseph, and Alexander (2000) surveyed 331 English girls and boys in grades 8 through 11. Of these students, 40% reported being bullied, and of these, 40% of boys and 43% of girls reported clinically significant symptoms of posttraumatic stress. Despite these findings, bullying has only recently been recognized as an important source of stress for children, and it is still inconsistently included in lists of potential traumatic events.

It is again important to consider the interface of bullying and trauma reactions for children's development, and in particular, for their growing capacity to relate to others. In childhood, friends and peers are important sources of companionship and support. It is within peer relationships that children learn strategies for negotiation and amicable conflict resolution. These relationships also serve to promote social competence and provide companionship and social support (Shaffer, 1994). Children involved in bullying, as victims, as perpetrators, or as both, are more likely to be rejected by their peers and to be lonely (Crick & Nelson, 2002; Warden & MacKinnon, 2003). When bullied children have friends, their friendships are likely to be characterized by relational, verbal, and occasional physical aggression (Crick & Nelson, 2002). As a result, children like Julie, in "Chronic Relational Trauma in Middle Childhood," have few opportunities to develop the social skills needed for effective negotiation of difficult interpersonal situations and for development of healthy interpersonal relationships.

Symptoms of trauma also impede the ability of bullied children to develop relationships with others. Bullied and bullying children show high levels of social avoidance and withdrawal and are more likely than other children to attribute hostile intent to others (Camodeca, Goossens, Schuengel, & Terwogt, 2003; Crick & Dodge, 1994; Crick & Nelson, 2002). Although these behaviors were initially thought to result from deficits in social skills, they may instead couple with generally high levels of arousal and dysregulation associated with chronic trauma and with trauma-related hypervigilance. Children who have been repeatedly traumatized are likely to experience qualitatively higher levels of distress and anger in response to negative peer interactions than are nontraumatized children. The resulting challenge of regulating this increased arousal adaptively, rather than remediating deficits in social skills, may explain children's quick and hostile overreactions to others. For example, Julie ("Chronic Relational Trauma in Middle Childhood") may react negatively toward her peers, in part, because she is especially likely to notice any small indication that peers might be preparing to tease her or to engage in other hurtful behavior and, in part, due to the high level of trauma-related arousal caused by this attribution.

In summary, symptoms of trauma may be related to the initiation or continuance of a cycle of repeat victimization in peer relationships. Children who have been traumatized in relationships may be expected to be hypervigilant to signs of interpersonal aggression and to experience increased arousal to relational stresses. These trauma-based reactions may make children "brittle" playmates who easily move into the roles of bullies or victims. Such experiences can be expected to interfere with children's ability to progress toward age-appropriate developmental goals, resulting in further social isolation and greater potential for continued traumatic relationship experiences.

7 CONTINUITY OF RELATIONAL TRAUMA IN ADOLESCENCE

RELATIONAL TRAUMA IN ADOLESCENCE

Fifteen-year-old Lynn and her boyfriend of 1 year, Bobby, were at her high school dance. Bobby suggested that they go for a walk outside to get some time alone. Once outside and in a secluded area, they started kissing. Bobby was more forward than he had been in the past, and he attempted to unbutton Lynn's shirt and pants. Lynn was startled and upset by Bobby's behavior and pulled away, looking back toward the dance. Bobby grabbed Lynn's arm, preventing her from returning, and made a joke about his "caveman" behavior and his inability to control himself. Lynn smiled at his antics, relaxed, and returned to Bobby's embrace. However, instead of smiling back, Bobby began to kiss her again in an aggressive manner, forcing his hand down her pants. Lynn was scared, and she pulled away forcefully. Just then, a group of Lynn's friends came outside and noticed that something seemed to be wrong. They asked Lynn if everything was okay. Lynn stared blankly at her friends. Bobby grabbed Lynn's hand, kissed her cheek, and said that everything was fine. With a gentle tug, Bobby pulled Lynn away into a crowd of other teenagers milling around outside the dance.

Adolescence represents an important period for continuity or discontinuity in patterns of relationships with others, and potentially for relationship-based chronic trauma. A key developmental task in adolescence is establishment of autonomous relationships outside the family of origin. After experience in mixed-peer relationships, and a period of experimentation in multiple casual partnerships, youth generally progress to more serious, exclusive dating relationships (Brown, 1999). By age 14 or 15, about half of all adolescents have had some experience dating (Connolly & Johnson, 1996; Feiring, 1996), and by 18 years of age, only a small number of adolescents have not had at least one "steady" relationship (Thornton, 1990).

7.1 Violence in Dating Relationships

Unfortunately, verbal, physical, and sexual abuses are relatively common in adolescent dating relationships. Considering only the more severe forms of physical aggression and sexual coercion, approximately 1 in 10 to 1 in 5 high-school-aged teens (boys as well as girls) report being hit, slapped, or forced to have sex by a dating partner (Centers for Disease Control, 2000; Coker et al., 2000; Grunbaum et al., 2002; Silverman, Raj, Mucci, & Hathaway, 2001). When the definition is extended to include acts of verbal and psychological intimidation, close to half of youth report experiences as victims, perpetrators, or both (Malik, Sorenson, & Aneshensel, 1997; Wolfe, Scott, Wekerle, & Pittman, 2001). Although the prevalence of physical and psychological abuse in dating violence is comparable for adolescent girls and boys, the consequences of these behaviors are more severe for girls in terms of physical injury and psychological distress (Wolfe, Scott, & Crooks, scheduled for 2005 release). Moreover, although girls and boys tend to report comparable rates of perpetuating and sustaining physical violence in relationships, more adolescent girls report being victims of sexual violence (Bergman, 1992; Jezl, Molider, & Wright, 1996), and more adolescent boys report perpetrating such acts (O'Keefe, 1997).

Research with adults clearly established that victimization by a dating or marital partner is strongly associated with development of PTSD. In a review of the literature, Jones, Hughes, and Unterstaller (2001) concluded that 31% to 84% of battered women across various samples (e.g., shelters, hospitals, community agencies) exhibited PTSD symptoms. Similarly, in studies of "date rape" in college-aged women, elevated rates of PTSD and distress in victims were found (Molidor & Tolman, 1998; Shapiro & Chwarz, 1997).

7.2 Links Between Trauma and Relational Difficulties

Fewer studies examined the potentially traumatic effects of dating violence on adolescents. Our research in this area explored the interrelationships of child maltreatment, adolescent dating violence, and trauma symptomatology. Using a sample of over 1,400 youth, we found that among youth who reported dating violence, 36% reported clinically significant symptoms of trauma, compared to 22% of youth reporting no victimization (Scott, Wolfe, & Wekerle, 2003). In addition, symptoms of trauma appeared to mediate the relationship between childhood maltreatment and adolescent dating violence for girls (Wekerle et al., 2001).

Reciprocal links between trauma symptomatology and difficulties in relationships are relatively well conceptualized and documented. Three processes, in particular, are thought to contribute to a pattern of revictimization: (a) hypervigilance, (b) arousal, and (c) avoidance of trauma-related stimuli.

In adolescence, as in early and middle childhood, hypervigilance is recognized as both a symptom of trauma and a potential contributor to further traumatic-relationship experiences. Traumatized adolescents and adults have an agitated, highly reactive style of responding to ambiguous or negative behaviors from partners (Dutton, 1995, 1999; Holtzworth-Munroe & Smutzler, 1996; Dutton & Holtzworth-Munroe, 1997). In the context of an intimate relationship, this response style can contribute to the development of a "controlled/controller" relationship dynamic and set the foundation for abusive behavior.

Elevated levels of arousal derived from traumatic experiences are also associated with violence and victimization in intimate relationships. Davis, Petretic-Jackson, and Ting (2001) found that trauma-related anger and irritability mediated relationships between childhood maltreatment and dysfunction in adult intimate relationships. Similarly, in our research, we found that rates of hostility and interpersonal sensitivity are especially high among high-school-aged girls who reported a history of childhood maltreatment and experiences of victimization in their dating relationships (Scott et al., 2003). The mechanism of this association has yet to be elucidated. Perhaps when one member of a couple is highly aroused, there is a higher frequency or intensity of conflict and a correspondingly higher risk of abuse. Alternatively, individuals with histories of trauma may react to potentially dangerous situations in their intimate relationships with overwhelming shock that limits their ability to problem solve escape strategies. In the situation outlined earlier, Lynn's high arousal may have interfered with her ability to problem solve ways to gather support and protection from nearby peers.

Finally, research has identified a contribution of posttraumatic avoidance symptoms to subsequent victimization. Chu (1992) proposed that women with histories of trauma (specifically, childhood sexual abuse) tend to "tune out" or fail to integrate significant information that would otherwise signal danger of a potential reassault. In support of this proposition, studies have shown that a tendency toward dissociation is negatively correlated with the extent to which people actively process significant and meaningful stimuli in a rape scenario and to their judgments of the overall dangerousness of that scenario (Sandberg, Lynn, & Matorin, 2001). In the Lynn example, she may have avoided awareness of cues of potential danger in Bobby's actions.

In summary, victimization in intimate relationships is clearly associated with trauma. Research continues to uncover ways that elevations in symptoms of avoidance, arousal, and hypervigilance make youth more vulnerable to subsequent traumatic experiences. Moreover, as adolescents move into dating relationships, it is girls who may become more vulnerable to victimization than boys.

8 RELATIONAL PATHS TO STRESS AND TRAUMA: REPEATING RELATIONSHIP CYCLES

A theoretical model that integrates the three experiences of trauma discussed in this chapter—child maltreatment, peer victimization, and dating violence—is presented in Figure 1.1. The model outlines the impact of chronic trauma and stress on girls and women across developmental stages, illustrates how prior and concurrent victimization experiences interact, and underscores the reciprocal connections between trauma and relational stress over time.

First, this model illustrates the connection between different forms of chronic relational trauma and stress. Research clearly shows that childhood maltreatment increases the likelihood of bullying and peer victimization (Shields & Cicchetti, 2001; Streeck-Fischer & Van Der Kolk, 2000), and both childhood maltreatment and peer victimization predict the emergence of coercive romantic relationships in adolescents. Children who are chronically abused are less liked by their peers and report greater difficulties in forming and maintaining peer relationships (Bolger, Patterson, & Kupersmidt, 1998; Parker & Herrera, 1996; Salzinger,

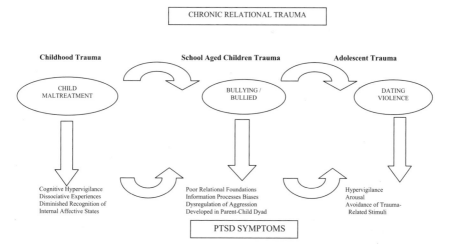

FIGURE 1.1. Theoretical model integrating experiences of chronic trauma at different stages of development.

Feldman, Hammer, & Rosario, 1993). Childhood maltreatment is also strongly associated with the development of adolescent dating violence. In a study of over 1,400 high-school students, Wolfe and colleagues found that girls who reported experiencing moderate to severe childhood maltreatment were 1.8 times as likely to report experiencing sexual abuse and 2.8 times as likely to report being threatened by a dating partner than girls without childhood maltreatment histories (Wolfe et al., 2001). Finally, peer bullying provides a proximal route to understanding romantic aggression. Childhood friendships provide models for the types of romantic relationships that develop in adolescence (Furman, 1999), and as such, problems in establishing friendships influence the quality of later romantic relationships (Connolly, Craig, Pepler, & Taradesh, 2000; Feiring, 1999; Noll, Trickett, & Putnam, 2000).

The second link illustrated by this model is the strong relationship between chronic experiences of relational stress and symptoms of trauma. Clearly, child abuse, peer victimization, and adolescent dating violence are associated with elevations in trauma symptoms. Individuals who experienced relational abuse reported avoidance of trauma-related stimuli, heightened arousal, and reexperiencing. In addition, due to the relational context of these chronic traumas, girls make significant adaptations in their cognitive, affective, and social functioning. Some of these adaptations include cognitive hypervigilance, dissociative experiences, chronic hyperarousal, and diminished recognition of potentially dangerous situations.

These adaptations and symptoms further perpetuate developmental disruptions, as illustrated in the final aspect of this model—paths linking trauma symptoms at one developmental stage to traumatic experiences in the next stage. Unfortunately, symptoms of trauma associated with chronic relational stress and abuse increase individuals' susceptibility to future traumatic experiences. The poor relational foundations and dysregulation of aggression developed in the abusive parent–child dyad extend to peer relationships and can lead to bullying or to being a victim of peer harassment. Cyclical patterns in aggression and trauma are also likely to promote patterns of revictimization in dating relationships. At this stage, specific trauma processes include hypervigilance and increased trauma-related anger, which may contribute to a victim–victimizer abuse dynamic and dissociation or avoidance of trauma-related stimuli, which in turn, may lead individuals to overlook important warning signs of impending abuse.

This cyclic pattern of relationship trauma and abuse has a number of important implications for prevention and intervention. First, due to the lasting pattern of trauma and relational dysfunction associated with chronic relational trauma, prevention is essential. Parents and families need societal support to ensure that the stress of child rearing does not become overwhelming. Single parents of low socioeconomic status, young age, and who were victims of relational trauma, are particularly in need of support. Studies have shown that these parents benefit significantly from receiving pre- and postnatal home visitation services to learn about their children's developmental needs, establish resource links, and gain support for their parenting efforts (e.g., Olds et al., 1997). Families continue to need support as children get older. Involvement in community and neighborhood activities, parenting-support programs, and high-quality children's activities are likely important to the promotion of healthy family relationships, as is the availability of employment with reasonable pay and working hours. Schools, as well, need support to promote healthy peer and dating relationships and to ensure that children are safe while at school. Finally, clear societal laws and norms around nonabusive behavior in all relationships are needed for effective prevention efforts.

Although prevention may be the ultimate goal, there are still those children and adolescents who will suffer from chronic relational trauma. With recognition of the cyclical pattern of relationship trauma and abuse, it becomes clear that these individuals need a long-term commitment from society for intervention support. Children who have been abused by their families need aid in developing healthy peer relationships. Children and adolescents who are bullied by their peers need direction in choosing dating partners. Adolescents involved in dating violence need guidance to ensure that they do not proceed to violent and abusive marriages. Developing relationship skills takes commitment over a long period of time to shape children and adolescents as they cycle through healthy and less healthy relationships.

Finally, if a relational path underlies trauma continuity, then learning new skills or developing different attitudes about family, peer, and dating relationships is likely to be insufficient for promoting change. Skill-based interventions need to be coupled with treatment targeting the amelioration of symptoms of trauma and stress. Treatment should include opportunities for children and youth to share their traumatic experiences and to process their feelings associated with these events. These exposure-based models of treatment have been shown to lead to reductions in trauma symptomatology (Rothbaum, Meadows, Resick, & Foy, 2000), which for chronically traumatized children and youth, may translate to lesser risk of revictimization.

9 SUMMARY AND CONCLUSIONS

In the past 25 years, important advances in our understanding of stress and trauma in the lives of girls and female adolescents were made.

Since the diagnosis of PTSD was first applied to children and adolescents in 1987, conceptual models of trauma in children have developed rapidly. We are now aware that children's and adolescents' coping resources are more easily overwhelmed by traumatic experiences than those of adults. In addition, we realize that symptoms of trauma and, in particular, the development of PTSD, seriously hinder children's ability to keep up with the rapid pace of development. As a result, experiencing stressful and traumatic events can have rippling effects on children's physical, cognitive, social, and relational development.

Chronic, as opposed to acute, experiences of trauma have particularly severe negative effects on children's development. Chronic traumas are repeated stressful experiences, such as those that occur in the context of an abusive parent–child, peer bullying, or violent adolescent dating relationship. Developmental disruptions associated with these forms of trauma are particularly severe due to the duration of stress, the increased magnitude of trauma symptoms, and the accommodations children and adolescents necessarily make to preserve important relationships in the face of abuse and trauma.

Another reason to be concerned about experiences of chronic relational trauma is the reciprocal relationship that develops between experiences of abuse in relationships and symptoms of trauma. As illustrated in Figure 1.1, abuse in close relationships sets into motion a series of relationship events and resultant trauma that is mutually reinforcing of both subsequent abuse and PTSD symptoms. Specifically, trauma-related symptoms, such as hypervigilance, hyperarousal, and avoidance, put children and youth at greater risk for subsequent experiences of traumatic abuse, which in turn, predicts increases in trauma symptomatology.

Due to this cyclical pattern, it is particularly important that greater attention be paid to the incidence of chronic relational traumas and to their implications for development. In addition, prevention and treatment programs need to augment relational-skills training with interventions to ameliorate symptoms of trauma. Through greater understanding of the course of chronic trauma, and through well-conceptualized prevention and intervention programs, we will be able to prevent revictimization and promote meaningful change in the relationships of chronically traumatized girls and adolescents.

REFERENCES

American Psychiatric Association. (1994). *Diagnostic and statistical manual of mental disorders* (4th ed.). Washington, DC: American Psychiatric Press.

Barahal, R., Waterman, J., & Martin, H. P. (1981). The social cognitive development of abused children. *Journal of Consulting and Clinical Psychology, 49,* 508–516.

Beers, S. R., & De Bellis, M. D. (2002). Neuropsychological function in children with maltreatment-related posttraumatic stress disorder. *American Journal of Psychiatry, 159,* 483–486.

Bergman, L. (1992). Dating violence among high school students. *Social Work, 37,* 21–27.

Bjoerkqvist, K. (1994). Sex differences in physical, verbal and indirect aggression: A review of recent research [Special issue: On aggression in women and girls: Cross-cultural perspectives]. *Sex Roles, 30,* 177–188.

Bolger, K. E., Patterson, C. J., & Kupersmidt, J. B. (1998). Peer relations and self-esteem among children who have been maltreated. *Child Development, 69,* 1171–1197.

Brown, B. (1999). "You're going out with who?" Peer group influences on adolescent romantic relationships. In W. Furman, B. Brown, & C. Feiring (Eds.), *The development of romantic relationships in adolescence* (pp. 291–329). London: Cambridge University Press.

Bugental, D. B., Lewis, J. C., Lin, E., Lyon, J., & Kopeikin, H. (1999). In charge but not in control: The management of teaching relationships by adults with low perceived power. *Developmental Psychology, 35,* 1367–1378.

Bugental., D. B., Lyon, J. E., Lin., E., McGrath, E. P., & Bimbela, A. (1999). Children "tune out" in response to ambiguous communication style of powerless adults. *Child Development, 70,* 214–230.

Camodeca, M., Goosens, F. A., Schuengel, C., & Terwogt, M. (2003). Links between social informative processing in middle childhood and involvement in bullying. *Aggressive Behavior, 29,* 239–268.

Centers for Disease Control and Prevention. (2000, June 9). Youth risk behavior surveillance— United States 1999. *Morbidity and Mortality Weekly Report, 49*(5), 1–96.

Chu, J. A. (1992). The revictimization of adult women with histories of childhood abuse. *Journal of Psychotherapy Practice and Research, 1,* 259–269.

Cicchetti, D. (1989). How research on child maltreatment has informed the study of child development: Perspectives from developmental psychopathology. In D. Cicchetti & V. Carlson (Eds.), *Child maltreatment: Theory and research on the causes and consequences of child abuse and neglect* (pp. 377–431). London: Cambridge University Press.

Cicchetti, D., & Beeghly M. (1987). Symbolic development in maltreated youngsters: An organizational perspective. *New Directions for Child Development, 36,* 5–29.

Cicchetti, D., Toth, S., & Bush, M. (1988). Developmental psychopathology and incompetence in childhood: Suggestions for intervention. In B. B. Lahey & A. E. Kazdin (Eds.), *Advances in clinical child psychology* (Vol. 11, pp. 1–77). New York: Plenum.

Coker, A. L., McKeown, R. E., Sanderson, M., Davis, K. E., Valois, R. F., & Huebner, E. S. (2000). Severe dating violence and quality of life among South Carolina high school students. *American Journal of Preventive Medicine, 19,* 220–227.

Connolly, J., Craig, W., Pepler, D., & Taradesh, A. (2000). Dating experiences and romantic relationships of bullies in adolescence. *Child Maltreatment, 5,* 297–308.

Connolly, J. A., & Johnson, A. M. (1996). Adolescents' romantic relationships and the structure and quality of their close interpersonal ties. *Personal Relationships, 3,* 185–195.

Costello, E. J., Erkanli, A., Fairbank, J. A., & Angold, A. (2002). The prevalence of potentially traumatic events in childhood and adolescence. *Journal of Traumatic Stress, 15,* 99–112.

Craig, W. (1998). The relationship among bullying, depression, anxiety and aggression among elementary school children. *Personality and Individual Differences, 24,* 123–130.

Craig, W. M., & Pepler, D. J. (1997). Observations of bullying and victimization in the school yard. *Canadian Journal of School Psychology, 13,* 41–59.

Crick, N. R., & Dodge, K. A. (1994). A review and reformulation of social information- processing mechanisms in children's social adjustment. *Psychological Bulletin, 115,* 74–101.

Crick, N. R., & Nelson, D. A. (2002). Relational and physical victimization within friendships: Nobody told me there'd be friends like these. *Journal of Abnormal Child Psychology, 30,* 599–607.

Crittenden, P. M. (1992). Children's strategies for coping with adverse home environments: An interpretation using attachment theory. *Child Abuse and Neglect, 16*, 329–343.

Davis, J. L., Petretic-Jackson, P. A., & Ting, L. (2001). Intimacy dysfunction and trauma symptomatology: Long term correlates of different types of child abuse. *Journal of Traumatic Stress, 14*, 63–79.

Dodge, K. A. (1980). Social cognition and children's aggressive behavior. *Child Development, 51*, 162–170.

Dodge, K. A., Lochman, J. E., Laird, R., Zelli, A., & the Conduct Problems Prevention Research Group. (2002). Multidimensional latent-construct analysis of children's social information processing patterns: Correlations with aggressive behavior problems. *Psychological Assessment, 14*, 60–73.

Dutton, D. G. (1995). Intimate abusiveness. *Clinical Psychology: Science and Practice, 2*, 207–224.

Dutton, D. G. (1999). Traumatic origins of intimate rage. *Aggression and Violent Behavior, 4*, 431–447.

Dutton, D. G., & Holtzworth-Munroe, A. (1997). The role of early trauma in males who assault their wives. In D. Cicchetti & S. L. Toth (Eds.). *Developmental perspectives on trauma: Theory, research and intervention. Rochester Symposium on Developmental Psychopathology, 8*, 379–401.

Erickson, M. F., Egeland, B., & Pianta, R. (1989). The effects of maltreatment on the development of young children. In D. Cicchetti & V. Carlson (Eds.), *Child maltreatment: Theory and research on the causes and consequences of child abuse and neglect* (pp. 647–684). London: Cambridge University Press.

Famularo, R., Fenton, T., & Kinscherff, R. (1994). Maternal and child posttraumatic stress disorder in cases of maltreatment. *Child Abuse and Neglect, 18*, 27–36.

Feiring, C. (1996). Concepts of romance in 15-year-old adolescents. *Journal of Research on Adolescence, 6*, 181–200.

Feiring, C. (1999). Other-sex friendship networks and the development of romantic relationships in adolescence. *Journal of Youth and Adolescence, 28*, 495–512.

Finkelhor, D., & Ormrod, R. K. (2000). Juvenile victims of property crimes. *Juvenile Justice Bulletin—NCJ184740*, 1–12.

Fletcher, K. E. (1996). Childhood posttraumatic stress disorder. In E. J. Mash & R. A. Barkley (Eds.), *Child psychopathology* (1st ed., pp. 242–276). New York: Guilford.

Fletcher, K. E. (2003). Childhood posttraumatic stress disorder. In E. J. Mash & R. A. Barkley (Eds.), *Child psychopathology* (2nd ed., pp. 330–371). New York: Guilford.

Friedrich, W. N., Jaworski, T. M., Huxsahl, J. E., & Bengtson, B. S. (1997). Dissociative and sexual behaviors in children and adolescents with sexual abuse and psychiatric histories. *Journal of Interpersonal Violence, 12*, 155–171.

Furman, W. (1999). Friends and lovers: The role of peer relationships in adolescent heterosexual romantic relationships. In W. A. Collins & B. Laursen (Eds.), *Relationships as developmental context: Minnesota Symposium on Child Development* (Vol. 30). Hillsdale, NJ: Lawrence Erlbaum.

Green, B. L., Grace, M., Vary, M. G., Kramer, T., Gleser, G. C., & Leonard, A. (1994). Children of disaster in the second decade: A 17-year follow-up of Buffalo Creek survivors. *Journal of the American Academy of Child and Adolescent Psychiatry, 33*, 71–79.

Grunbaum, J. A., Kann, L., Kinchen, S., Williams, B., Ross, J., Lowry, R., & Kolbe, L. (2002). Youth risk behavior surveillance, United States, 2001. *Morbidity and Mortality Weekly Report, 51 (SS-4)*, 1–68.

Hartman, C. R., & Burgess, A. W. (1989). Sexual abuse of children: Causes and consequences. In D. Cicchetti & V. Carlson (Eds.), *Child maltreatment: Theory and research on the causes and consequences of child abuse and neglect* (pp. 95–128). London: Cambridge University Press.

Hashima, P., & Finkelhor, D. (1999). Violent victimization of youth versus adults in the National Crime Victimization Survey. *Journal of Interpersonal Violence, 14*, 799–820.

Hennessy, K. D., Rabideau, G. J., Cicchetti, D., & Cummings, E. M. (1994). Responses of physically abused and nonabused children to different forms of interadult anger. *Child Development, 65*, 815–828

Herman, J. L. (1992). *Trauma and recovery: The aftermath of violence—From domestic abuse to political terror.* New York: Basic Books.

Hoffman-Plotkin, D., & Twentyman, C. T. (1984). A multimodal assessment of behavioral and cognitive deficits in abused and neglected preschoolers. *Child Development, 55*, 794–802.

Holtzworth-Munroe, A., & Smutzler, N. (1996). Comparing the emotional reactions and behavioral intentions of violent and nonviolent husbands to aggressive, distressed, and other wife behaviors. *Violence and Victims, 11*, 319–339.

International Save the Children Alliance. (2001). *Children's rights: A second chance.* London: Author.

Jezl, D. R., Molider, C. E., & Wright, T. L. (1996). Physical, sexual and psychological abuse in high school dating relationships: Prevalence rates and self-esteem issues. *Child and Adolescent Social Work Journal, 59*, 69–87.

Jones, L., Hughes, M., & Unterstaller, U. (2001). Post-traumatic stress disorder (PTSD) in victims of domestic violence: A review of the research. *Trauma, Violence and Abuse, 2*, 99–119.

Kessler, R., Sonnega, A., Bromet, E., & Hughes, M. (1995). Posttraumatic stress disorder in the National Comorbidity Survey. *Archives of General Psychiatry, 52*, 1048–1060.

Kolko, D. J. (1992). Characteristics of child victims of physical violence: Research findings and clinical implications. *Journal of Interpersonal Violence, 7*, 244–276.

Kolko, D. J. (2002). Child physical abuse. In J. E. B. Myers, L. Berliner, J. Briere, C. T. Hendrix, C. Jenny, & T. A. Reid (Eds.), *The APSAC handbook on child maltreatment* (pp. 21–54). Thousand Oaks, CA: Sage.

Macfie, J., Cicchetti, D., & Toth, S. L. (2001). The development of dissociation in maltreated preschool-aged children. *Developmental Psychopathology, 13*, 233–254.

MacMillan, H. L., Fleming, J. E., Trocme, N., Boyle, M. H., Wong, R., Racine, Y. A., Beardslee, W. R., & Offord, D. R. (1997). Prevalence of child physical and sexual abuse in the community: Results from the Ontario Health Supplement. *Journal of the American Medical Association, 278*, 131–135.

Malik, S., Sorenson, S. B., & Aneshensel, C. S. (1997). Community and dating violence among adolescents: Perpetration and victimization. *Journal of Adolescent Health, 21*(5), 291–302.

McLeer, S. V., Dixon, J. F., Henry, D., Ruggiero, K., Escovitz, K., Niedda, T. et al. (1998). Psychopathology in non-clinically referred sexually abused children. *Journal of American Academy of Child and Adolescent Psychiatry, 37*, 1223–1229.

Molidor, C., & Tolman, R. M. (1998). Gender and contextual factors in adolescent dating violence. *Violence Against Women, 4*, 180–194.

Mynard, H., Joseph, S., & Alexander, J. (2000). Peer-victimization and posttraumatic stress in adolescents. *Personality and Individual Differences, 29*, 815–821.

National Safe Kids Campaign. (2002). *Injury facts: Burn injury.* Retrieved from http://www.safekids.org

Noll, J. G., Trickett, P. K., & Putnam, F. W. (2000). Social network constellation and sexuality of sexually abused and comparison girls in childhood and adolescence. *Child Maltreatment, 5*, 323–337.

Oesterman, K., Bjoerkqvist, K., Lagerspetz, K., Kaukiainen, A., Landau, S. F., Fraczek, A., & Caprara, G. V. (1998). Cross-cultural evidence of female indirect aggression. *Aggressive Behavior, 24*, 1–8.

O'Keefe, M. (1997). Predictors of dating violence among high school students. *Journal of Interpersonal Violence, 12*, 546–568.

Olds, D., Eckenrode, J., Henderson, C. R., Jr., Kitzman, H., Powers, J., Cole, R., Sidora, K., Morris, P., Pettitt, L. M., & Luckey, D. (1997). Long-term effects of home visitation on maternal life course and child abuse and neglect: Fifteen year follow-up of a randomized trial. *Journal of the American Medical Association, 278,* 637–643.

Olweus, D. (1991). Bully/victim problems among school children: Some basic facts and effects of a school-based intervention program. In D. Pepler & K. Rubin (Eds.), *The development and treatment of childhood aggression* (pp. 411–438). Hillsdale, NJ: Erlbaum.

Olweus, D. (1999). Sweden. In P. K. Smith, Y. Morita, J. Junger-Tas, D. Olweus, R. Catalano, & P. Slee (Eds.), *The nature of school bullying: A cross-national perspective* (pp. 7–27). New York: Routledge.

Paquette, J. A., & Underwood, M. K. (1999). Gender differences in young adolescents' experiences of peer victimization: Social and physical aggression. *Merrill–Palmer Quarterly, 45,* 242–266.

Parker, J. G., & Herrera, C. (1996). Interpersonal processes in friendship: A comparison of abused and nonabused children's experiences. *Developmental Psychology, 32,* 1025–1038.

Pollak, S., Cicchetti, D., Klorman, R., & Brumaghim, J. T. (1997). Cognitive brain event-related potentials and emotion processing in maltreated children. *Child Development, 68,* 773–787.

Pollak, S. D., & Sinha, P. (2002). Effects of early experience on children's recognition of facial displays of emotion. *Developmental Psychology, 38,* 784–791.

Pollak, S. D., & Tolley-Schell, S. A. (2003). Selective attention to facial emotion in physically abused children. *Journal of Abnormal Psychology, 112,* 323–338.

Pynoos, R., Goenjian, A., Tashjian, M., Krakashian, M., Manjikian, A., Manoukian, G., Steinberg, A. M., & Fairbanks, L. A. (1993). Post-traumatic stress reactions in children after the 1988 Armenian earthquake. *British Journal of Psychiatry 163,* 239–247.

Pynoos, R. S., Frederick, C., Nader, K. et al. (1987). Life threat and posttraumatic stress in school-age children. *Archives of General Psychiatry, 44,* 1057–1063.

Rothbaum, B. O., Meadows, E. A., Resick, P., & Foy, D. W. (2000). Cognitive-behavioral therapy. In E. B. Foa, T. M. Keane et al. (Eds.), *Effective treatments for PTSD: Practice guidelines from the International Society for Traumatic Stress Studies* (pp. 60–83). New York: Guilford.

Salzinger, S., Feldman, R. S., Hammer, M., & Rosario, M. (1993). The effects of physical abuse on children's social relationships. *Child Development, 64,* 169–187.

Salzinger, S., Kaplan, S., Pelcovitz, D., Samit, C., & Krieger, R. (1984). Parent and teacher assessment of children's behavior in child maltreating families. *Journal of the American Academy of Child Psychiatry, 23,* 458–464.

Sandberg, D. A., Lynn, S. J., & Matorin, A. I. (2001). Information processing of an acquaintance rape scenario among high- and low-dissociating college women. *Journal of Traumatic Stress, 14,* 585–603.

Schwab-Stone, M. E., Ayers, T. S., Kasprow, W., Voyce, C., Barone, C., Shriver, T., & Weissberg, R. P. (1995). No safe haven: A study of violence exposure in an urban community. *Journal of the American Academy of Child and Adolescent Psychiatry, 34,* 1343–1352.

Scott, K. L., Wolfe, D. A., & Wekerle, C. (2003). Maltreatment and trauma: Tracking the connections in adolescence. *Child and Adolescent Psychiatric Clinics of North America, 12,* 211–230.

Shaffer, D. R. (1994). *Social and personality development.* Pacific Grove, CA: Brooks/Cole.

Shaffi, M., & Shaffi, S. L. (2001). *School and violence. Assessment, management and prevention.* Washington, DC: American Psychiatric Publications.

Shannon, M. P., Lonigan, C. J., Finch, A. J. Jr., & Taylor, C. M. (1994). Children exposed to disaster: I—Epidemiology of posttraumatic stress symptoms and symptom profiles. *Journal of the American Academy of Child and Adolescent Psychiatry, 33,* 80–93.

Shapiro, B. L., & Chwarz, J. C. (1997). Date rape: Its relationship to trauma symptoms and sexual self-esteem. *Journal of Interpersonal Violence, 12,* 407–419.

Shields, A., & Cicchetti, D. (2001). Parental maltreatment and emotion dysregulation as risk factors for bullying and victimization in middle childhood. *Journal of Clinical Child Psychology, 30,* 349–363.

Silverman, J. G., Raj, A., Mucci, L. A., & Hathaway, J. E. (2001). Dating violence against adolescent girls and associated substance use, unhealthy weight control, sexual risk behavior, pregnancy, and suicidality. *Journal of the American Medical Association, 286,* 572–579.

Slee, P. T. (1995). Bullying in the playground: The impact of inter-personal violence on Australian children's perceptions of their play environment. *Child Environment, 12,* 320–327.

Solberg, M., & Olweus, D. (2003). Prevalence estimation of school bullying with the Olweus Bully/Victim Questionnaire. *Aggressive Behavior, 29,* 239–268.

Straus, M. A., & Gelles, R. J. (1986). Societal change and change in family violence form 1975 to 1985 as revealed by two national surveys. *Journal of Marriage and the Family, 48,* 465–479.

Streeck-Fischer, A., & Van Der Kolk, B. A. (2000). Down will come baby, cradle and all: Diagnostic and therapeutic implications of chronic trauma on child development. *Australian and New Zealand Journal of Psychiatry, 34,* 903–918.

Terr, L. C. (1991). Childhood traumas: An outline and overview. *American Journal of Psychiatry, 148,* 10–20.

Thornton, A. (1990). The courtship process and adolescent sexuality. *Journal of Family Issues, 11,* 239–273.

Trickett, P. K., Noll, J. G., Reiffman, A., & Putnam, F. W. (2001). Variants of intrafamilial sexual abuse experience: Implications for short and long-term development. *Developmental Psychopathology, 13,* 1001–1019.

Trocmé, N., MacLaurin, B., Fallon, B., Daciuk, J., Billingsley, D., Tourigny, M., Mayer, M., Wright, J., Barter, K., Burford, G., Hornick, J., Sullivan, R., & McKenzie, B. (2001). *Canadian incidence study of reported child abuse and neglect.* Ottawa, ON: Minister of Public Works and Government Services Canada.

U.S. Department of Health and Human Services, National Center on Child Abuse and Neglect. (2001). *Child maltreatment 1999: Reports from the states to the National Center on Child Abuse and Neglect.* Washington, DC: U.S. Government Printing Office.

Warden, D., & Mackinnon, S. (2003). Prosocial children, bullies and victims: An investigation of their sociometric status, empathy and social problem-solving strategies. *British Journal of Developmental Psychology, 21,* 367–385.

Wekerle, C., & Wolfe, D. A. (2002). Child maltreatment. In E. J. Mash & R. A. Barkley (Eds.), *Child psychopathology* (2nd ed., pp. 632–684). New York: Guilford.

Wekerle, C., Wolfe, D. A., Hawkins, D. L., Pittman, A.-L., Glickman, A., & Lovald, B. E. (2001). Childhood maltreatment, posttraumatic stress symptomatology, and adolescent dating violence: Considering the value of adolescent perceptions of abuse and a trauma mediational model. *Development and Psychopathology, 13,* 847–871.

Widom, C. S. (1999). Posttraumatic stress disorder in abused and neglected children grown up. *American Journal of Psychiatry, 156,* 1223–1229.

Williams, L. M. (2003). Understanding child abuse and violence against women: A life course perspective. *Journal of Interpersonal Violence, 18,* 441–451.

Wolfe, D. A., Scott, K. L., & Crooks, C. V. (scheduled for 2005). Dating and relationship violence among adolescent girls. In D. Bell-Dolan, E. J. Mash, & S. Foster (Eds.), *Handbook of emotional and behavioral problems in girls.* New York: Kluwer Academic.

Wolfe, D. A., Scott, K., Wekerle, C., & Pittman, A.-L. (2001). Child maltreatment: Risk of adjustment problems and dating violence in adolescence. *Journal of the American Academy of Child and Adolescent Psychiatry, 40,* 282–289.

World Health Organization (WHO). (1999). *Report of the consultation on child abuse prevention.* Geneva: Author.

World Health Organization (WHO). (2000). The WHO Cross-National study on health behavior in school-aged children from 28 countries: Findings from the United States. *Journal of School Health, 70,* 227–228.

Zelli, A., & Dodge, K. A. (1999). Personality development from the bottom up. In D. Cervone & Y. Shoda (Eds.), *The coherence of personality: Social-cognitive bases of personality consistency, variability and organization* (pp. 94–126). New York: Guilford.

2

Caught in the Middle: Stress in the Lives of Young Adult Women[1]

KATHLEEN A. KENDALL- TACKETT

A reporter recently called me about a heartbreaking incident that had taken place in his community. A mother of two young children had been up all night with her 2-year-old, a child with special needs. The next morning, she loaded her 6-month-old in the car and left for work. In her sleep-deprived state, she forgot to drop the baby off at day care and left her in the car all day. Eight hours later, when she realized what she had done, she found that her baby had died.

In this tragic story, we see the potentially devastating impact of every-day stressors in the lives of young adult women. In this chapter, I describe some common stressors for women in their second, third, and fourth decades. This chapter focuses on day-to-day stressors, rather than more serious stressors, such as sexual assault and intimate partner violence, as these topics are described in separate chapters. What the story of the sleep-deprived mother amply demonstrates is that mundane

---

[1] Some of the material in this chapter was adapted from: Kendall-Tackett, K. A. (2001). *The hidden feelings of motherhood: Coping with stress, depression and burnout.* Oakland, CA: New Harbinger; and Kendall-Tackett, K. A. (2003). *Treating the lifetime health effects of childhood victimization.* Kingston, NJ: Civic Research Institute.

stressors can have devastating effects on women—and those around them. The first stressor I describe is caregiving.

1 CAREGIVING STRESS

In most families, caregiving is primarily the woman's responsibility (Lee, 1998). It can take many forms. Women care for children, aging parents, and sick partners and friends. Much of the caregiving at this age centers on childcare. According to the National Center on Health Statitics (Bramlett & Mosher, 2002), 81% of women ages 40 to 44 have children (although the number of women in this age range without children has doubled since 1970). But, women without children can also be subject to caregiver stress. Below are some examples.

1.1 Aging Parents

As our population ages, a higher percentage of women will find themselves caring for aging parents. Nearly one family in four is currently providing care for an elderly family member or friend—a number that is expected to increase (National Academy on an Aging Society, 2000; U.S. Department of Labor, 1998). According to the U.S. Department of Labor, 72% of caregivers are women, and women provide the majority of care for aging relatives. These women can be single or married, with or without children. They also spend more time in caregiving, providing an average of 19.9 hours per week in direct and indirect care. In contrast, male caregivers spend an average of 11.8 hours per week. The "typical" caregiver of an aging relative is a 46-year-old woman who is employed and also spends around 18 hours per week caring for her mother who lives nearby (U.S. Department of Labor, 1998).

Caregivers of both sexes are vulnerable to caregiver stress, and not only caregivers in the United States. In Japan, caregivers for elderly people in one recent study reported increased risk of depression when asked for their subjective evaluation of their caregiving experiences (Karasawa, Hatta, Gushiken, & Hasegawa, 2003). Some of the difficulties they reported included physical and economic strains, negative attitudes of the elders they were caring for, and unsupportive family members. All of these factors were related to depression.

Caregiver stress can be manifested in weight changes in those caring for elderly relatives. In a study of 200 people providing informal care for elderly people released from rehabilitation hospitals, 19% had gained or lost at least 10 pounds since becoming a caregiver (Fredman & Daly, 1997). Weight change was significantly associated with higher scores on measures of burden and stress and poorer self-rated health for the caregivers. Weight change was also more common in caregivers of patients who had a stroke compared to other types of rehabilitation problems (perhaps reflecting the seriousness of the condition and an increased need for care).

Young adult women may find themselves caring for children and parents at the same time. Approximately 41% of women caring for elderly relatives are also caring for children under age 18 (U.S. Department of Labor, 1998). Some have called women in this age group the "sandwich generation," in reference to their dual caregiving activities (Remennick, 1999; U.S. Department of Labor, 1998).

Women in other countries also experience the "sandwich-generation" phenomenon. In a study of Russian immigrants in Israel, Remennick (1999) described the stresses on women caring for children and tending to the needs of their elderly parents. As their parents' health deteriorated, these women felt significantly burdened. Needing to care for two generations hindered their occupational attainments and their social integration into their new culture. The women reported exhaustion, lack of time, poor self-care, and a host of somatic symptoms.

1.2 Complex Childcare

Childcare can be a challenging task, even under the best of circumstances. However, there are times when it is even more difficult. When looking at stress in women's lives, situations that are extra challenging are important to consider. Some of the more challenging childcare situations are listed below.

1.2.1 Single Mothering. Single mothering can be another form of stressful caregiving. According to the U.S. Census Bureau, there are 10 million single mothers in the United States, and single mothers head approximately 27% of all families (U.S. Census Bureau, 1998). Single mothers often report relentless childcare activities, with no downtime. Loneliness and isolation can also be challenges for the single mother.

Several recent studies documented the stress that single mothers feel. In a large national study, single and married mothers were compared. Single mothers were more likely to suffer from depression, report chronic stress, relate more stressful life events, and tell of a higher number of childhood adversities than their married counterparts (Cairney, Boyle, Offord, & Racine, 2003). They also reported less social support and contact with friends and family than married mothers. Stress and lack of social support accounted for 40% of the variance between single-parent status and depression in these mothers.

In a study of rural single mothers, mothering was at the center of their daily stress (Wijnberg & Reding, 1999). They reported numerous daily hassles and overwhelming childcare. They were overwhelmed with needing to discipline their children or dealing with their children's chronic illnesses. They reported negative social networks and difficulties securing childcare. The authors suggested that interventions aimed at reducing these mothers' daily hassles could lower their overall stress levels.

Economics makes a difference in how single mothers fare. Unfortunately, single mothers are more likely to be poor and are the fastest growing group of American poor, currently including 3.9 million families (Scoon-Rogers, 1999; U.S. Census Bureau, 1998). This is not simply a problem of being a single parent: female-headed households have twice the poverty rate of custodial fathers (Scoon-Rogers, 1999).

Even among poor families, however, support can make a difference. Support for single mothers can happen within the family or in the community at large. Ceballo and McLoyd (2002) examined the moderating effect of neighborhood on parenting strategies among 262 poor, African American single mothers. When the neighborhoods were better and provided social support, the women's parenting was also more positive. However, when the neighborhood was dangerous, the level of social and instrumental support the mothers received decreased, as did their nurturant behavior toward their children. The authors concluded that the effect of social support was attenuated in poorer, high-crime neighborhoods. But, neighborhoods with positive supports helped single mothers cope and be more effective with their children.

1.2.2 Children With Special Needs. Another factor that complicates childcare is when children have special needs. Caring for children with special needs requires more time and effort than ordinary childcare. Women without help and support may feel overwhelmed, as in the tragic case I described at the beginning of this chapter. Of course, the amount of caregiving varies considerably depending on the condition the child has and the number of other children at home. Mothers may feel isolated, because their experiences are so different from those of other mothers (Kerr & McIntosh, 2000). As described in Greenspan (1998):

> On a bad day, I feel like Sisyphus of the Greek myth…. Just when things seem to even out, a new set of daunting challenges presents itself…. At these times, I enter a state beyond fatigue that is akin to despair. (p. 42)

In a study comparing mothers of children with cerebral palsy and mothers of children with no diagnosis, Britner, Morog, Pianta, and Marvin (2003) found that mothers of children with cerebral palsy reported more parenting stress than mothers of children in the control group. However, there were no overall differences in the families' functioning as a result of the children's disabilities (Britner et al., 2003).

Women caring for children with special needs seem more susceptible to parenting stress than men. Little (2002) examined a sample of mothers and fathers of children with Asperger's syndrome and nonverbal learning disabilities. Compared with their husbands, mothers experienced more family stress, were more pessimistic about their children's futures, were more likely to be taking medication for depression, and were more likely to be seeking professional help than their spouses. However, the rates of antidepressant use were high for both mothers (45%) and fathers (26%) in this study.

Children with special needs are also at higher risk for abuse and neglect than children without special needs (Sullivan & Knutson, 1998). Maltreatment compounds these children's levels of impairment, further increasing the amount of care they require. Even if not abusive, stressed mothers may not be as nurturing as they could be. In a study of single African American mothers of children ages 3 to 5, the authors used structural equation modeling to construct a model of parenting stress and its relation to quality of parenting (Jackson & Huang, 2000). Children's behavioral problems set off a cascade of difficulties. The more behavioral problems the child had, the more depressed the mother. The more depression she had, the more she reported parental stress; and, the more depression and stress she felt, the lower her self-efficacy. Finally, the lower her self-efficacy, the less competent her parenting was.

Social support, however, can help these families cope. In a qualitative study of mothers whose children had disabilities, many reported feelings of isolation and concern about what the future would be like for their children. Parent-to-parent support was a great buffer for these families and provided much-needed practical, emotional, and social support (Kerr & McIntosh, 2000). The authors concluded that parents whose children had disabilities were in a unique position to help each other.

1.2.3 Closely-Spaced Children and Multiples. Twins, triplets, or children closely spaced in age can also lead to caregiving overload, because the caregiving tasks are unrelenting. Caregiving may be so intense that everything else goes on hold: relationships, house, job, and friends. It is not unusual for women with two or more small children to report that their lives are completely overwhelmed by child-rearing responsibilities (Gromada, 1999). For example, in a study of 17 families with triplets (ages 4 to 6 years old), the researchers found that parents described their lives as chaotic when their children were babies. The parents also reported that they spent more time organizing and arranging their day and less time on providing emotional care for their infants than did parents of singletons, or even twins (Akerman, Hovmoeller, & Thomassen, 1997).

Parenting stress was subject to some moderation, however. In a longitudinal study of parents of twins, mothers were interviewed at 27 weeks gestation (time 1) and at 1 year postpartum (time 2). At time 2, parenting stress was predicated by personal well-being and marital support at both time points. Social support and other children in the home did not predict stress in any significant way (Colpin, De Munter, Nys, & Vandemeulebroecke, 2000).

1.3 Overinvolvement and "Taking Care of the World"

Women are also prone to caregiver stress when they provide care to all within their circle of family and friends. Taylor and colleagues (Taylor et al., 2000) theorized that this occurs because men and women have different patterns of "survival mode" when faced with threats. Women under threat would not run or fight when threatened. Rather, they would protect and nurture their children. Taylor et al. (2000) characterized women's response to stress as "tending and befriending." This is an intriguing hypothesis and seems to explain some of women's affiliative and caregiving activities. Caregiving behavior can cross a line and become too much, however. When a woman takes care of everyone but never takes time for herself, she is endangering her own health and well-being.

Why do some women cross the line into too much involvement? To understand why this occurs, Helgeson and Fritz's (1999) research on interaction styles is useful. On the affiliative end of the spectrum, they compare the communion and unmitigated-communion interaction styles. Communion refers to a healthy involvement in the lives of others. Unmitigated communion is involvement with others to the detriment of self. Women are more likely than men to fall into the unmitigated-communion style (Fritz & Helgeson, 1998). (Men, in contrast, are more likely to fall into unmitigated agency, an extreme isolation from others.)

1.3.1 Communion Versus Unmitigated Communion. Below, the characteristics of healthy (communion) and unhealthy (unmitigated-communion) interaction styles are compared and contrasted. These relate to caregiving, attachment style, and relationships. Women in these studies were asked to indicate whether certain beliefs applied to them. Most women will have aspects of both styles but will lean more heavily toward one or the other.

Caretaking. Communion and unmitigated communion are both related to caretaking (Helgeson & Fritz, 1998). People with a communion style help others, because they are genuinely concerned and want to increase the other person's well-being. In contrast, those with an unmitigated-communion style help people in order to improve their status in the eyes of others (Helgeson & Fritz, 1998).

Attachment style. Unmitigated communion was associated with a preoccupied attachment style indicated by endorsement of items such as, "I worry that my partner doesn't really love me" (Helgeson & Fritz, 1998, p. 175). In contrast, communion was associated with secure attachments, as reflected in endorsement of items such as, "I find it easy to get close to others," and "I rarely worry about being abandoned by others."

Relationships. Communion is associated with empathy, a positive view of self and others, and the belief that other people are good and valuable. Unmitigated communion, in contrast, is associated with depression and a negative view of self. The person with the unmitigated style is outward focused, relies on others for esteem, perceives that others view them negatively, and has a high fear of the negative evaluation of others (Helgeson & Fritz, 1998). In addition, those with an unmitigated-communion style often have a history of problematic relationships (Hegleson & Fritz, 1998), are less comfortable receiving help and support from others, and have difficulties asserting themselves in relationships (Fritz & Helgeson, 1998; Helgeson & Fritz, 1998). They give lots of social support but rarely receive it from others.

1.4 Factors That Compound Caregiving Stress

Circumstances and interpersonal style can explain some of the differences in the coping abilities of women involved in caregiving. Two other factors that can compound caregiving stress include fatigue and sleep deprivation and unrealistic expectations.

1.4.1 Fatigue and Sleep Deprivation. Women overwhelmed by caregiving duties are often lacking sleep. According to the National Sleep Foundation's Omnibus survey (2000), there are striking sex differences in sleep deficits. Women are substantially more sleep-deprived than their male counterparts, especially if they are caring for others. Sleep deprivation can wreak havoc on a woman's emotional state. Many accidents on the job, on the highway, and at home are caused by the overly fatigued, as the example I shared at the beginning of the chapter so strongly illustrated. Sleep deprivation also compromises the immune system and increases the likelihood that women will get sick (National Sleep Foundation, 2000).

1.4.2 Unrealistic Expectations. Young adult women often labor under unrealistic expectations of what they can and need to do for others, particularly if they have an unmitigated-communion style of relating to

others. These expectations often take the form of "should" statements. Here are some examples:

"Women should anticipate all their families' needs."
"Women should be able to take care of everything."
"Women who take time off are lazy."

Women can knock themselves out trying to meet these expectations and feel guilty when they cannot. Women who are survivors of childhood abuse seem especially susceptible to unrealistic expectations, often because they are trying to rise above their past and parent better than they were parented (Kendall-Tackett, 2001). This is an admirable goal, but it is one that can lead to caregiving stress if not balanced with self-care.

1.5 Conclusion

In *Toward a New Psychology of Women*, Baker Miller (1995) described how women's identities and mental and physical well-being are directly related to their connections with others. Women's relationships are strengths, not weaknesses. However, when relationships are out of balance—as they can be in caregiving—they can be a source of stress. This does not mean that women should not be caregivers. It simply means that they need support, and realistic expectations for themselves, when they take on the role of caregiver. In the next section, I describe another source of relational stress—stress in adult relationships.

2 STRESS IN ADULT RELATIONSHIPS

Adult relationships can be gifts or major sources of stress. Sometimes, they are both. Of all types of relationships, marriage has been studied the most. According to the National Center for Health Statistics (Bramlett & Mosher, 2002), by age 30, 75% of women in the United States have been married, and approximately half have cohabitated outside marriage. Much of what these studies revealed about marriage can be applied to other relationships. These studies are described below.

2.1 The Impact of Marital Strife

When marriage is good, it can be very good, and both men and women benefit. Kiecolt-Glaser and Newton (2001), in their recent review, found that marital happiness contributes to global happiness more than any other variable, even friendships and satisfaction with work. Similarly, Myers (2000) found that happily married people had the lowest rates of depression of any group.

A happy marriage can also have a substantial impact on mortality. This effect is especially pronounced for men: married men have a 250% lower mortality rate than their nonmarried counterparts. Marriage benefits women as well, but not as much: married women, overall, have a 50% lower mortality rate compared to nonmarried women (Kiecolt-Glaser & Newton, 2001). Gallo and colleagues (Gallo, Troxel, Matthews, & Kuller, 2003) found that women who were married or cohabitating, and who were satisfied with those relationships, had significantly better cardiovascular profiles than women who were single, widowed, or divorced.

Conversely, people in "not-very-happy" marriages reported even lower levels of happiness than those who are divorced and those who never married (Myers, 2000). Later in this volume (in chapter 6), Campbell and I describe the impact of intimate partner violence—an extreme form of marital strife. What recent studies have revealed, however, is that even less severe forms of marital strife can have significant impact on women's health. Negative aspects of marriage directly influence health through cardiovascular, endocrine, immune, and neurosensory mechanisms (Kiecolt-Glaser & Newton, 2001). In one recent study, women who were less satisfied with their marriages or cohabitating relationships had an increase in cardiovascular risk over the 13-year study period. This was particularly true for their lipid profiles, including low levels of high-density lipoprotein (HDL) and high triglycerides, which are both risk factors for cardiovascular disease. Quality of the marital relationship was also related to differences in body mass index, blood pressure, depression, and anger, with poorer quality relationships being related to poorer quality of health (Gallo et al., 2003).

Kiecolt-Glaser and Newton (2001) found that high-stress marriages can neutralize or lessen the effectiveness of vaccines, slow wound healing, and increase the risk of infectious disease for both men and women. Marital conflicts increase blood pressure, which has obvious implications for hypertension and cardiovascular disease. Marital tension seems to have a particularly strong influence on women. In a recent Swedish study, Orth-Gomer and colleagues (Orth-Gomer, 2000) followed 292 women for 5 years after these women had heart attacks. Women with high levels of marital strife were nearly three times more likely to have another heart attack as women who were married but not distressed.

This finding could be due to sex differences in causes of cardiovascular reactivity. Smith and colleagues (Smith, Gallo, Goble, Ngu, & Stark, 1998) found that men and women responded to different types of threat. Women in the study had increased cardiovascular reactivity in response to perceived threats to their relationships, and men reacted to potential threats to their competence or dominance. Cardiovascular reactivity (CVR) is considered the link between people's beliefs and social connections, and their subsequent development of cardiovascular disease. Some of these changes associated with cardiovascular reactivity include enduring changes in heart rate and blood pressure (Miller, Smith, Turner, Guijarro, & Hallet, 1996). Women who feel threatened in their relationships may be at increased risk for cardiovascular disease.

One major source of relational strife for married or cohabitating partners is division of household labor. This is described below.

2.2 Domestic Work and Relational Strife

In most households, women still do the majority of domestic work. The type of work women do has dramatically changed over the past 100 years. However, the sheer number of hours that women devote to child-care and home care has remained constant: ranging from 49 to 56 hours per week (Schor, 1992). Even when women are employed outside the home, they do the majority of the housework and childcare—a phenomenon Hochshild (Hochshild, with Machung, 1989) describes as the "second shift." Some of the stress from women's work at home is reflected in their blood pressure levels. In one recent study, researchers compared blood pressures for employed men and employed women with children. For men, blood pressure was higher at work than at home. For women, blood pressure was the same at home as it was at work (Marco et al., 2000).

2.3 Chore Wars: The Gender Gap in Time Devoted to Household Tasks

Not surprisingly, there are large differences in the amounts of time men and women spend in domestic activities. Sometimes couples start out equally sharing the work, only to fall into rigid sex roles after having children. By current estimates, women at home full-time spend approximately 50 hours per week caring for children and home, whereas women employed outside the home spend about 35 hours per week in the same activities. In contrast, men spend approximately 11 to 14 hours per week, with husbands or partners of employed women spending approximately 10 minutes extra per day, and men with small children adding another 10 minutes (Hammonds, 1998; Schwartz Cowan, 1983). Of course, this is not true for all relationships. But these figures reflect an overall trend.

Women's ethnicity and cultural heritage can also impact the division of domestic labor. In some cultures, traditional sex roles are expected and are more common. Religious beliefs can also influence sex-role demarcations, as can social class. Even in gay and lesbian families, there can be an adherence to traditional sex roles when it comes to taking care of children or a household, with one partner following the "mother" role, and the other partner adhering to the "father" role (Benkov, 1998).

2.3.1 Partner Support and Depression. Partners' participation in domestic work is also directly related to women's emotional health. Several studies have found that when partners do not provide support or participate in childcare or household tasks, women are more likely to be depressed (e.g., Campbell, Cohn, Flanagan, Popper, & Meyers, 1992; Logsdon & Usui, 2001). The impact of partner support is so powerful that it can even cross ethnic and social-class lines. A recent study examined the importance of partner support with three samples of postpartum women: 105 middle-class white women, 37 middle-class mothers of premature babies, and 57 low-income African American mothers (Logsdon & Usui, 2001). The authors tested a causal model, using structural equation modeling, and found that women who had support and close relationships with their partners had greater self-esteem and fewer instances of depression. The commonalities of these experiences are striking; these predictors were the same for all three groups of mothers, even in different life circumstances.

2.4 Divorce and Separation

Marital strife may eventually lead to divorce. According to the National Center for Health Statistics (Bramlett & Mosher, 2002), in a 5-year time period, 20% of marriages and 49% of cohabiting relationships broke up. After 10 years, 33% of marriages and 62% of cohabiting relationships have ended. Fifty-four percent of divorced women will remarry, but the divorce rates are high for this group as well. For this group, after 5 years, 23% are divorced; and after 10 years, 39% are divorced.

Trauma history may also have a role to play in relationships ending in divorce. In several studies, women with histories of child sexual abuse were significantly more likely to be divorced or separated than their nonabused counterparts (Felitti, 1991; Finkelhor, Hotaling, Lewis, & Smith, 1989; Fleming, Mullen, Sibthorpe, & Bammer, 1999). This was especially true for those whose abuse experience involved intercourse or occurred at an older age. As described in chapter 1, marital strife may also be due to an abuse-related dysfunctional style of interacting that can include hostility (Teegen, 1999) or interpersonal sensitivity (Downey, Freitas, Michaelis, & Khouri, 1998). Interpersonal sensitivity occurs when one partner is hypervigilant about possible rejection.

The partner may respond to perceived rejection with hostility. This can cause real relationship problems and has also been related to increased risk of intimate partner violence in dating relationships (Downey, Feldman, & Ayduk, 2000).

Divorce, separation, and other marital difficulties can affect more than relational status, these instances can also affect income and socioeconomic status, which bring us to the third form of stress common for young adult women: work and money stresses.

3 WORK AND MONEY STRESSES

Work and money issues comprise the final form of stress that I discuss for women ages 20 to 40. For women who are employed, these three decades are approaching women's peak earning capacities. Work also takes place in the context of many other responsibilities. Chief among these is the balance between work and caregiving responsibilities.

3.1 Work and Family Issues

Another potential source of stress for young adult women is the balance of employment and family. Currently, 55% of women with infant children are in the workforce—the highest percentage in recent times. The percentage of employed mothers rises as the children become older (Bachu & O'Donnell, 2001). The media often portrays this as a "yuppie" issue, with two-income, high-earning partners juggling private schools, sports' teams, exotic vacations, and live-in nannies. But this portrayal does not capture the experience of many, if not most, families.

For many families, the decision for mothers to be employed is not a decision at all. For families with lower incomes, women's wages may mean the difference between "making it" and poverty. For example, according to the U.S. Department of Labor (1997a), the median income for Latina women alone was $13,474. For Latino families in which only the father was employed, the median was $22,257. For Latino married couples, where both partners were employed, the median family income was $29,861. The results are even more striking for African American families. When wives were employed, the median family income was $48,533; when the wife was not in the labor force, it was only $25,507. For female-headed households, the median income was $15,004 (U.S. Department of Labor, 1997b).

As described earlier, family caregiving can also mean taking care of aging relatives. This can also mean that women step out of the workforce, with its attendant loss of income (Rysberg, this volume, chapter 4; U.S.

Department of Labor, 1998). The pressures that families experience when both parents are employed have led to the implementation of family-friendly policies in many companies. But there has been another curious development. Recognizing that companies need to provide women with family-friendly options, such as flexible hours, telecommuting, and part-time employment, some companies are putting these policies into place, while providing subtle pressure on employees not to take advantage of them. Those who take advantage of these policies risk censure or risk being "mommy-tracked" (Hochshild, 1997).

3.2 Debt

Debt is something we do not often think of as a psychological variable. But it can have a direct impact on well-being, and can be a significant source of stress. Women with children may feel that they have no choice in whether they work because of debt. Families with large debt loads often have no financial safety net. Even families with middle-class lifestyles know that they are only one or two paychecks from the street.

Debt has been specifically related to depression. In a longitudinal study of 271 families with young children, worry about debt was the strongest predictor of depression in mothers at the initial and follow-up contacts (Reading & Reynolds, 2001). Worrying about debt at time 1 predicted depression at time 2, 6 months later. Other economic factors associated with depression in this study included overall family income, not being a homeowner, and lack of access to a car.

3.3 Poverty

Women who cannot work may find themselves living in poverty, and this can have a detrimental effect on their well-being. The American Psychological Association's Task Force on Women and Depression identified poverty as a risk factor for depression in women (McGrath, Keita, Strickland, & Russo, 1990). Two recent studies also found that depression is more common with low-income mothers. In these studies, the rates of maternal depression ranged from 23% (Hobfoll, Ritter, Lavin, Hulsizer, & Cameron, 1995) to 51% (McKee, Cunningham, Jankowski, & Zayas, 2001).

There are many problems related to poverty. Women of lower socioeconomic status tend to have fewer resources available and less support. They may live in neighborhoods that are unsafe. They may worry about their children's safety at day care or school. They may face the constant worry about whether child support payments will arrive. In a recent study examining factors related to "nervous breakdowns," women most at risk were poor, young, single mothers with no religious affiliation (Swindle, Heller, Pescosolido, & Kikuzawa, 2000).

Middle-class women may become poor once they divorce. They may be in financial positions where they need to move from their homes and are suddenly worried about whether they will be able to make ends meet. In one study, women whose incomes did not drop after divorce fared better than women whose divorces made them poor. The children of families with adequate financial resources also fared better after divorce. The authors speculated that these children were buffered from stress, because their mothers were less likely to be depressed (Murray, 2000). Poverty is a realistic concern for women contemplating divorce, and fear of impending poverty may keep women in abusive relationships.

3.3.1 Poverty and Trauma History. Poverty can also be related to trauma history. Some recent studies demonstrated that adult survivors of childhood abuse can have lower educational attainment and lower lifetime income than their nonabused counterparts (Hulme, 2000; Hyman, this volume, chapter 12; Jinich et al., 1998). This was true for men (Jinich et al., 1998), as well as women (Hulme, 2000; Hyman, this volume, chapter 12). The seeds for lower lifetime income may be sewn during childhood and can be tied to school performance. Not surprisingly, abuse survivors often have had trouble in school. Miller (1999) noted that child abuse can cause subtle brain damage that might not manifest itself immediately but could influence the child's performance in reading, writing, math, and reasoning—all basic and necessary skills for school success. Difficulties with any of these skills can have a detrimental impact on academic learning (see also Bremner, this volume, chapter 9; Dallam, this volume, chapter 8).

Other types of learning difficulties have also been documented. For example, a study of sexually abused women in a primary care practice found that abused women had problems with learning, memory loss, episodes of "your mind going blank," and keeping their minds on what they were doing (Hulme, 2000). In another study, learning disabilities were 3.5 times more likely to be found in women who had been sexually abused than in nonabused women (Springs & Friedrich, 1992). Higher rates of attention deficit/hyperactivity disorder (ADHD), learning problems, and repeated grades in school occurred among abuse survivors with posttraumatic stress disorder (PTSD) than abuse survivors without PTSD (Gurvits et al., 2000).

As adults, people with PTSD may also have employment difficulties. In a community sample from Canada, men and women reported that PTSD interfered with their jobs. Those with more severe symptoms had the most difficulties on the job (Stein, Walker, Hazen, & Forde, 1997). A similar finding was made for people with anxiety disorders. They were less likely to be working full time and were more likely to be receiving public assistance or disability payments than those without anxiety disorders (Warshaw et al., 1993). For women who experienced trauma as children or adults, the net result may be financial, unfortunately increasing the likelihood that they will end up living in poverty.

4 SOCIAL SUPPORT BUFFERS STRESS

The news from this time of life is not all negative. Young adult women can thrive if they have adequate social support (Seeman, 1996). For people in general, we know that supportive relationships can help people weather the storms of life. The benefits of social support have been demonstrated in a variety of settings. Social relationships can help people deal with physical symptoms, medical procedures, or traumatic events. In a recent review, Salovey and colleagues (Salovey, Rothman, Detweiler, & Steward, 2000) noted that social support boosts the immune system and lowers mortality rates. People with good social support experience a lower prevalence of coronary heart disease and recover more quickly following surgery. When faced with stress, those with few social resources are more vulnerable to illness and mood disorders than people with those resources.

Social support also predicts how well a woman will cope with serious trauma, such as rape as an adult. In one study, women who were isolated from others or had dysfunctional relationships experienced more depression and PTSD after being raped than women with good support. The authors speculated that women who fared poorly may have had trouble initiating and maintaining gratifying and reciprocal relationships (Regehr & Marziali, 1999).

Social support appears to be especially important for people with lower incomes. In one recent study, people with low incomes who had social support had better cardiovascular health (i.e., higher HDLs and lower mean arterial pressures) and natural-killer-cell activity than people with low incomes who did not have support. These findings did not occur for subjects with higher incomes (Vitaliano et al., 2001).

Women with support from their communities or within their kinship networks may find that they are buffered from the stressors described in this chapter. Even women at the poorest end of the spectrum have better lives if they do not need to face their stressors alone. The buffering influence of social support can be demonstrated by an incident that recently took place in my community. The 3-year-old son of a young couple was recently diagnosed with autism. He has a mild form, and his prognosis is good. But the news has hit this young family hard. As they shared this situation with their church, family after family spontaneously stood and pledged their support. It was amazing and moving to observe, and I know the members of this family left church that day feeling like they would not have to face this crisis alone.

Seeing this, I have to wonder: Would support have made a difference for the woman I described at the beginning of this chapter? If her company had family-friendly policies that were real, and not lip service, could she have come in late that day or taken the day off? Could a friend have helped with some of her day-to-day responsibilities? Could she have let others know that her responsibilities were overwhelming her? Of course, we will never know. Her experience demonstrates that the stresses women experience in their 20s, 30s, and 40s are real, and can be severe. We can also see that our culture still has a long way to go to support women at this stage of life.

REFERENCES

Akerman, B. A., Hovmoeller, M., & Thomassen, P. A. (1997). The challenges of expecting, delivering and rearing triplets. *Acta Geneticae Medicae et Gemllologiae, 46,* 81–86.

Bachu, A., & O'Donnell, M. (2001). *Fertility of American women: June 2000* (Pub. P-20-543RV). Washington, DC: U.S. Census Bureau.

Baker Miller, J. (1995). *Toward a new psychology of women.* Boston: Beacon.

Benkov, L. (1998). Yes, I am a swan: Reflections on families headed by lesbians and gay men. In C. Garcia Coll, J. L. Surrey, & K. Weingarten (Eds.), *Mothering against the odds: Diverse voices of contemporary mothers* (pp. 113–133). New York: Guilford.

Bramlett, M. D., & Mosher, W. D. (2002). *Cohabitation, marriage, divorce, and remarriage in the United States.* National Center for Health Statistics. Vital Health Stat 23(22).

Britner, P. A., Morog, M. C., Pianta, R. C., & Marvin, R. S. (2003). Stress and coping: A comparison of self-report measures of functioning in families of young children with cerebral palsy or no medical diagnosis. *Journal of Child and Family Studies, 12,* 335–348.

Cairney, J., Boyle, M., Offord, D. R., & Racine, Y. (2003). Stress, social support and depression in single and married mothers. *Social Psychiatry and Psychiatric Epidemiology, 38,* 442–449.

Campbell, S. B., Cohn, J. F., Flanagan, C., Popper, S., & Meyers, T. (1992). Course and correlates of postpartum depression during the transition to parenthood. *Development and Psychopathology, 4,* 29–47.

Ceballo, R., & McLoyd, V. C. (2002). Social support and parenting in poor, dangerous neighborhoods. *Child Development, 73,* 1310–1321.

Colpin, H., De Munter, A., Nys, K., & Vandemeulebroecke, L. (2000). Pre- and postnatal determinants of parenting stress in mothers of one-year-old twins. *Marriage and Family Review, 30,* 99–107.

Downey, G., Feldman, S., & Ayduk, O. (2000). Rejection sensitivity and male violence in romantic relationships. *Personal Relationships, 7,* 45–61.

Downey, G., Freitas, A. L., Michaelis, B., & Khouri, H. (1998). The self-fulfilling prophecy in close relationships: Rejection sensitivity and rejection by romantic partners. *Journal of Personality and Social Psychology, 75,* 545–560.

Felitti, V. J. (1991). Long-term medical consequences of incest, rape, and molestation. *Southern Medical Journal, 84,* 328–331.

Finkelhor, D., Hotaling, G. T., Lewis, I. A., & Smith, C. (1989). Sexual abuse and its relationship to later sexual satisfaction, marital status, religion and attitudes. *Journal of Interpersonal Violence, 4,* 379–399.

Fleming, J., Mullen, P. E., Sibthorpe, B., & Bammer, G. (1999). The long-term impact of childhood sexual abuse in Australian women. *Child Abuse and Neglect, 23,* 145–159.

Fredman, L., & Daly, M. P. (1997). Weight change: An indicator of caregiver stress. *Journal of Aging and Health, 9,* 43–69.

Fritz, H. L., & Helgeson, V. S. (1998). Distinctions of unmitigated communion from communion: Self-neglect and overinvolvement with others. *Journal of Personality and Social Psychology, 75,* 121–140.

Gallo, L. C., Troxel, W. M., Matthews, K. A., & Kuller, L. H. (2003). Marital status and quality in middle-aged women: Associations with levels and trajectories of cardiovascular risk factors. *Health Psychology, 22,* 453–463.

Greenspan, M. (1998). "Exceptional" mothering in a "normal" world. In C. Garcia Coll, J. L. Surrey, and K. Weingarten (Eds.), *Mothers against the odds: Diverse voices of contemporary mothers* (pp. 37–60). New York: Guilford.

Gromada, K. (1999). *Mothering multiples.* Schaumburg, IL: La Leche League International.

Gurvits, T. V., Gilbertson, M. W., Lasko, N. B., Tarhan, A. S., Simeon, D., Macklin, M. L., Orr, S. P., & Pitman, R. K. (2000). Neurologic soft signs in chronic posttraumatic stress disorder. *Archives in General Psychiatry, 57,* 181–186.

Hammonds, K. H. (1998, April 15). There really aren't enough hours in the day. *Business Week Online.* Retrieved from http://www.businessweek.com

Helgeson, V. S., & Fritz, H. L. (1998). A theory of unmitigated communion. *Personality and Social Psychology Review, 2,* 173–183.

Helgeson, V. S., & Fritz, H. L. (1999). Unmitigated agency and unmitigated communion: Distinctions from agency and communion. *Journal of Research in Personality, 33,* 131–158.

Hobfoll, S. E., Ritter, C., Lavin, J., Hulsizer, M. R., & Cameron, R. P. (1995). Depression prevalence and incidence among inner-city pregnant and postpartum women. *Journal of Consulting and Clinical Psychology, 63,* 445–453.

Hochshild, A., with Machung, A. (1989). *The second shift.* New York: Avon.

Hochshild, A. R. (1997). *The time bind: When work becomes home and home becomes work.* New York: Metropolitan.

Hulme, P. A. (2000). Symptomatology and health care utilization of women primary care patients who experienced childhood sexual abuse. *Child Abuse and Neglect, 24,* 1471–1484.

Jackson, A. P., & Huang, C. C. (2000). Parenting stress and behavior among single mothers of preschoolers: The mediating role of self-efficacy. *Journal of Social Service Research, 26,* 29–42.

Jinich, S., Paul, J. P., Stall, R., Acree, M., Kegeles, S., Hoff, C., & Coates, T. J. (1998). Childhood sexual abuse and HIV risk-taking behavior among gay and bisexual men. *AIDS and Behavior, 2,* 41–51.

Karasawa, K., Hatta, T., Gushiken, N., & Hasegawa, J. (2003). Depression among Japanese informal caregivers for elderly people. *Psychology, Health and Medicine, 8,* 371–376.

Kendall-Tackett, K. A. (2001). *The hidden feelings of motherhood: Coping with stress, depression and burnout.* Oakland, CA: New Harbinger.

Kerr, S. M., & McIntosh, J. B. (2000). Coping when a child has a disability: Exploring the impact of parent-to-parent support. *Child: Care, Health, and Development, 26,* 309–321.

Kiecolt-Glaser, J. K., & Newton, T. L. (2001). Marriage and health: His and hers. *Psychological Bulletin, 127,* 472–503.

Lee, C. (1998). *Women's health: Psychological and social perspectives.* Thousand Oaks, CA: Sage.

Little, L. (2002). Differences in stress and coping for mothers and fathers of children with Asperger's syndrome and nonverbal learning disorders. *Pediatric Nursing, 28,* 565–570.

Logsdon, M. C., & Usui, W. (2001). Psychosocial predictors of postpartum depression in diverse groups of women. *Western Journal of Nursing Research, 23,* 563–574.

Marco, C. A., Schwartz, J. E., Neale, J. M., Shiffman, S., Catley, D., & Stone, A. (2000). Impact of gender and having children in the household on ambulatory blood pressure in work and nonwork settings: A partial replication and new findings. *Annals of Behavioral Medicine, 22,* 110–115.

McGrath, E., Keita, G. P., Strickland, B. R., & Russo, N. F. (1990). *Women and depression: Risk factors and treatment issues.* Washington, DC: American Psychological Association.

McKee, M. D., Cunningham, M., Jankowski, K. R., & Zayas, L. (2001). Health-related functional status in pregnancy: Relationship to depression and social support in a multi-ethnic population. *Obstetrics and Gynecology, 97,* 988–993.

Miller, L. (1999). Child abuse brain injury: Clinical, neuropsychological, and forensic considerations. *Journal of Cognitive Rehabilitation* (Mar/April), 10–19.

Miller, T. Q., Smith, T. W., Turner, C. W., Guijarro, M. L., & Hallet, A. J. (1996). A meta-analytic review of research on hostility and physical health. *Psychological Bulletin, 119,* 322–348.

Murray, B. (2000). Family income predicts children's post-divorce well-being. *Monitor on Psychology* (June), 14.

Myers, D. G. (2000). The funds, friends, and faith of happy people. *American Psychologist, 55,* 56–67.

National Academy on an Aging Society. (2000). *Cargiving: Helping the elderly with activity limitations.* Retrieved from http://www.agingsociety.org

National Sleep Foundation. (2000). *2000 Omnibus sleep in America poll.* Retrieved from http://www.sleepfoundation.org

Orth-Gomer, K., Wamala, S. P., Horsten, M., Schenk-Gustafsson, K., Schneiderman, N., & Mittleman, M. A. (2000). Marital stress worsens prognosis in women with coronary heart disease: The Stockholm Female Coronary Risk Study. *Journal of the American Medical Association, 284,* 3008–3014.

Reading, R., & Reynolds, S. (2001). Debt, social disadvantage and maternal depression. *Social Science and Medicine, 53,* 441–453.

Regehr, C., & Marziali, E. (1999). Response to sexual assault: A relational perspective. *Journal of Nervous and Mental Disease, 187,* 618–623.

Remennick, L. I. (1999). Women of the "sandwich" generation and multiple roles: The case of Russian immigrants of the 1990s in Israel. *Sex Roles, 40,* 347–378.

Salovey, P., Rothman, A. J., Detweiler, J. B., & Steward, W. T. (2000). Emotional states and physical health. *American Psychologist, 55,* 110–121.

Schor, J. (1992). *The overworked American: The unexpected decline of leisure.* New York: Basic.

Schwartz Cowan, R. (1983). *More work for mother: The ironies of household technology from the open hearth to the microwave.* New York: Basic.

Scoon-Rogers, L. (1999). *Child support for custodial mothers and fathers: 1995.* Washington, DC: U.S. Department of Commerce, Economics, and Statistics Administration. Retrieved from http://www.census.gov

Seeman, T. E. (1996). Social ties and health. *Annals of Epidemiology, 6,* 442–451.

Smith, T. W., Gallo, L. C., Goble, L., Ngu, L. Q., & Stark, K. A. (1998). Agency, communion, and cardiovascular reactivity. *Health Psychology, 17,* 537–545.

Springs, F. E., & Friedrich, W. N. (1992). Health risk behaviors and medical sequelae of childhood sexual abuse. *Mayo Clinic Proceedings, 67,* 527–532.

Stein, M. B., Walker, J. R., Hazen, A. L., & Forde, D. R. (1997). Full and partial posttraumatic stress disorder: Findings from a community survey. *American Journal of Psychiatry, 154,* 1114–1119.

Sullivan, P. M., & Knutson, J. F. (1998). The association between child maltreatment and disabilities in a hospital-based epidemiological study. *Child Abuse and Neglect, 22,* 271–288.

Swindle, R., Heller, K., Pescosolido, B., & Kikuzawa, S. (2000). Responses to nervous breakdowns in America over a 40-year period. *American Psychologist, 55,* 740–749.

Taylor, S. E., Klein, L. C., Lewis, B. P., Gruenewald, T. L., Gurung, A. R., & Updegraff, J. A. (2000). Female responses to stress: Tend and befriend, not fight or flight. *Psychological Review, 107,* 421–429.

Teegen, F. (1999). Childhood sexual abuse and long-term sequelae. In A. Maercker, M. Schutzwohl, & Z. Solomon (Eds.), *Posttraumatic stress disorder: A lifespan developmental perspective* (pp. 97–112). Seattle, WA: Hogrefe & Huber.

U.S. Census Bureau. (1998). *The official statistics.* Retrieved from http://www.census.gov

U.S. Department of Labor. (1997a). *Women of Hispanic origin in the labor force.* Retrieved from http://www.dol.gov

U.S. Department of Labor. (1997b). *Black women in the labor force.* Retrieved from http://www.dol.gov

U.S. Department of Labor. (1998). *Work and elder care: Facts for caregivers and their employers.* Retrieved from http://www.dol.gov

Vitaliano, P. P., Scanlan, J. M., Zhang, J., Savage, M., Brummett, B., Barefoot, J., & Siegler, I. C. (2001). Are the salutogenic effects of social supports modified by income? A test of an "added value hypothesis." *Health Psychology, 20,* 155–165.

Warshaw, M. G., Fierman, E., Pratt, L., Hunt, M., Yonkers, K. A., Massion, A. O., & Keller, M. B. (1993). Quality of life and dissociation in anxiety disorder patients with histories of trauma or PTSD. *American Journal of Psychiatry, 150,* 1512–1516.

Wijnberg, M. H., & Reding, K. M. (1999). Reclaiming a stress focus: The hassles of rural, poor single mothers. *Families in Society, 80,* 506–515.

3

Trauma Associated with Perinatal Events: Birth Experience, Prematurity, and Childbearing Loss[1]

KATHLEEN A. KENDALL- TACKETT

I recently spoke at a large childbirth education conference on "Helping women make peace with their birth experiences." The topic resonated with the audience, and many waited afterwards to share their stories with me. Later that evening, a woman approached me when I was alone. She told me that her first birth had been like a rape, and that she had never discussed her experience with anyone. It had happened more than 20 years ago.

Perinatal[2] events can cause trauma in young adult women and influence them for the rest of their lives. Although these events would seem to occur only when women are of "childbearing age," traumatic perinatal experiences can impact women's lives well into their 70s and 80s (Smart, 2003). As common as these experiences are, however, they are usually

---

[1] Some of the material in this chapter is from Kendall-Tackett, K. A. (in press). *Depression in new mothers: Causes, consequences and treatment options.* Binghamton, NY: Haworth.

[2] The perinatal period includes pregnancy, birth, and the postpartum period.

missing from discussion of trauma in the lives of women. This chapter is an initial step in addressing that oversight.

According to the diagnostic criteria for posttraumatic stress disorder (PTSD), a traumatic experience is one that victims believe is life threatening or could cause great bodily harm to themselves or a loved one. This applies to many perinatal events, when women sincerely believe that they or their babies might die. Even if their risk of death is not strictly true in a medical sense, women's beliefs about impending harm can still affect them. In this chapter, I describe how perinatal events can cause trauma and leave a lifelong imprint on women's lives. The perinatal events I describe include negative birth experiences, having a premature baby, and childbearing loss (miscarriage, infertility, abortion, stillbirth, and neonatal death). These are described below.

1 NEGATIVE BIRTH EXPERIENCES

I broached the subject of negative birth experiences while working on my first book. So many women had related these types of experiences to me, but negative birth experiences were not acknowledged in the research literature. One of the first women I interviewed for my book had a cesarean section with failed epidural anesthesia. She was awake and could feel everything during the surgery, and the anesthesiologist did not believe her. She screamed throughout the procedure. Her birth was fairly recent, about a year before I interviewed her. Not surprisingly, she was deeply traumatized by her experience.

The situation I just described is, thankfully, relatively rare (although I know of several similar cases). Generally speaking, are negative birth experiences common? One national study addressed this question (Genevie & Margolies, 1987). It is an older study, but the only one of its kind. Women in this study comprised a nationally representative sample of 1,100 mothers, ages 18 to 80. Given the age range of the sample, a wide range of birth experiences was covered. Still, 60% of the mothers described their births in predominantly positive terms. This group also included mothers who described their experiences in terms such as "tough, but worth it." However, 40% of mothers in this sample described their births in predominantly negative terms. More concerning, 14% described their births as "peak negative experiences"—one of the worst experiences of their lives. In the qualitative accounts, women in this study expressed deep feelings about their births. Several of these women explained that their births had been so difficult that they had elected not to have any more children.

Another question then becomes the following: were their experiences sufficiently bad to cause psychological trauma? Two more recent studies found that some women developed PTSD following birth. The first of these was a prospective study of 289 women who were assessed while pregnant and when they were 6 weeks and 6 months postpartum. The authors found that at 6 weeks, 2.8% of women met full criteria for PTSD, and approximately half of these women still met criteria at 6 months (Ayers & Pickering, 2001). Women with preexisting PTSD or depression were not included in the analyses.

The second study assessed 264 women who had unassisted vaginal births at 72 hours and at 6 weeks postpartum (Czarnocka & Slade, 2000). Three percent of the women met full criteria for PTSD, and 24% had at least one symptom. The factors that predicted traumatic-stress symptoms included a low level of partner or staff support and low perceived control during labor.

The percentage of women who met full criteria for PTSD may, at first, seem small. But, there are some factors you should take into account when considering these results. First, the Ayers and Pickering (2001) study excluded all women who had previous episodes of PTSD or depression—the women most vulnerable to subsequent PTSD. If these women were included, the percentage would probably double. Second, in the weeks following the September 11, 2001, terrorist attacks on New York City, the rate of PTSD in Manhattan was 7.5%. People who suffered from previous episodes of depression and PTSD were not excluded from this analysis (Galea et al., 2003). This percentage is more than double the percentages in the previously cited birth studies, but is in reference to an event that killed thousands of their neighbors. Birth, in contrast, is supposed to be a happy event. The fact that there are *any* women who meet full criteria for PTSD, and 24% who have symptoms, should alert us that something is seriously amiss.

Findings such as these raise another important question—namely, what is it about birth that can turn it into a negative experience? Researchers have also examined this issue. For a long time, research was limited by a paradigm that designated cesarean births as "bad" and vaginal births as "good." This framework is somewhat helpful, but there are many experiences that do not fit neatly into these categories (e.g., women who are traumatized by vaginal births or women who feel positively about their cesarean births). These studies, however, were a starting place for understanding the psychological impact of negative birth experiences. Some of the more recent findings are cited below.

1.1 The Psychological Impact of Cesarean Births

In a prospective study of 272 Australian women, Fisher, Astbury, and Smith (1997) assessed the psychological outcomes of three types of birth: cesarean, assisted vaginal, and unassisted vaginal. As predicted, women who had cesareans were significantly more likely to have negative moods and low self-esteem following birth. In contrast, women who had unassisted vaginal deliveries had the most positive moods. Women with assisted vaginal deliveries were somewhere between the two groups. The authors concluded that operative childbirth carries "significant psychological risks rendering those who experience these procedures vulnerable to a grief reaction or to posttraumatic distress and depression" (p. 728). They noted that the prospective design allowed them to make causal inferences, and that the reactions of the women could not be attributed to preexisting symptoms.

These authors also conducted a study with women admitted to a private mother–baby unit for psychiatric care (Fisher, Feekery, Amir, & Sneddon, 2002; Fisher, Feekery, & Rowe-Murray, 2002). Thirty-six percent of mothers were disappointed with their birth experiences, but the percentage varied by type of birth (66% for cesarean, 45% for assisted vaginal, and 20% for unassisted vaginal).

Durik and colleagues (Durik, Hyde, & Clark, 2000) had contrasting findings. They compared women who had vaginal deliveries, women who had planned cesareans, and women who had unplanned cesareans. They assessed women at 1, 4, and 12 months postpartum. As predicted, women with unplanned cesareans described their deliveries more negatively than women in the other two groups. But they were not more likely to be depressed or have low self-esteem during the first year postpartum.

Another large study ($N = 1,596$) of planned cesareans versus vaginal deliveries for breech birth had similar findings to those of Durik et al. The authors found similar rates of postpartum depression in both groups—approximately 10% (Hannah et al., 2002). Breast-feeding rates were high in both groups and were not significantly different. Also, 78% of women found it "easy" or "very easy" to care for their infants, and approximately 82% of the total sample found adjusting to motherhood "easy" or "very easy." These findings on postpartum depression, breast feeding, and women's transition to motherhood are unusually good and strongly suggest that these women had an exceptional amount of support postpartum, perhaps because of participating in the study.

In summary, the results of the above-cited studies indicate that cesarean births can cause negative reactions for women who experience them. Women who received ample support following their cesareans, however, were significantly less likely to have negative reactions than those with no support. These variations in responses indicate that it is not the procedure of cesarean delivery per se that causes negative reactions. Women are less likely to have negative reactions to cesarean deliveries if they are provided with support and reassurance and are involved in decisions about their care.

1.2 Subjective Variables

If objective factors, such as type of delivery, do not consistently predict a negative reaction, what does? I found that women's subjective experiences of their births are often far better predictors. Three subjective variables have emerged from the literature: a woman's sense of control, how supportive she perceives the environment to be, and her prior vulnerabilities. These are described below.

1.2.1 Sense of Control. Women's subjective sense of control is one of the most consistent predictors of positive feelings after birth. It can be difficult for a woman to achieve a sense of control in a hospital setting. Hospital environments have many aspects and procedures that can disempower patients (American Medical Association, 1995; Rothman, 1982; Wertz & Wertz, 1989). Patients are stripped of their clothing and surrounded by strangers. Other people control their most basic functions, including eating, drinking, and going to the bathroom. They often have little say about what happens to them, and medical decisions may be made without their input. This is especially likely when there is a medical emergency. This lack of control can lead to a negative reaction to birth.

The importance of sense of control was recently demonstrated in the large clinical trial of planned cesarean versus vaginal deliveries for breech presentation described earlier. Sense of control predicted what women in both groups liked about their deliveries. Women in the planned-cesarean birth group liked the following: being able to schedule their deliveries, that their pain was well controlled, and that they felt reassured about the health of their babies. Women in the planned-vaginal group liked the following: being able to actively participate in their births, that their births were natural, and that recovery from childbirth was not difficult. Women in both groups felt reassured about their own health (Hannah et al., 2002).

Personal control also varied by type of delivery in a prospective study from Australia (Fisher et al., 1997). Fifty-six percent of women who had unassisted vaginal deliveries felt that they had personal control over their deliveries compared with 19% of the women who had cesarean births. For women in the cesarean group, it did not matter whether their births were emergency or planned cesareans—women in each group felt that they did not have control.

Simkin (1991), in her longitudinal study of women's reaction to birth, noted that being "in control" included two specific elements. The first was "self-control"; it included women's feelings that they conducted themselves with discipline and dignity. The second aspect was feeling that they had control over what was happening to them. Some of the women in the study were still angry and disappointed by what doctors and nurses did to them, even after 20 years had elapsed. Simkin noted, "the way a woman is treated by the professionals on whom she depends may largely determine how she feels about the experience for the rest of her life" (p. 210). This brings us to our next variable.

1.2.2 Supportive Environment. Another subjective variable is a mother's perceived level of care. When women perceived a lack of care, especially during labor and delivery, they were more likely to have negative reactions. In a study of 790 women at 8 to 9 months postpartum, Astbury and colleagues (Astbury, Brown, Lumley, & Small, 1994) found that women were more likely to be depressed if their caregivers were unkind, if they had unwanted people present during birth, if they were dissatisfied with their care during pregnancy, or if they felt that the doctors or nurses did not do enough to control their pain during labor.

A more recent study (Rowe-Murray & Fisher, 2001) found that lack of support during labor increased the risk for depression postpartum. The authors compared the experiences of 203 women after their first births. They found three variables related to postpartum depression at 8 months: a perceived lack of support during labor and birth, a high degree of postpartum pain, and a less-than-optimal first contact with their babies. These variables accounted for 35% of the variance in depression.

1.2.3 Prior Characteristics of the Mother. The mother's previous experiences may also influence how she felt about her birth experience. In a study from Finland (Saisto, Salmela-Aro, Nurmi, & Halmesmaki, 2001), the authors found that pain in labor and emergency cesarean sections were the strongest predictors of disappointment with delivery. Depression during pregnancy also made a difference; women who had been depressed during their pregnancies were significantly more likely to be disappointed with their deliveries and to become depressed after they had their babies.

In summary, these studies demonstrate that women who had poorly controlled pain in labor or during delivery felt out of control during their births, felt that the hospital was a hostile or unsupportive environment, or had preexisting depression were more likely to perceive their births negatively (Reynolds, 1997). In the next section are two birth stories from a woman named Kathy. Each birth was difficult, but for different reasons. These stories are described below.

1.2.3.1 Two Difficult Births: Kathy's Story *When Peter was born, the birth itself was pain free. He was small, especially his head and shoulders, and it truly didn't hurt at all. I kept insisting I wasn't really in labor up until 2 minutes before he was born, when the doctor told me to lay down, shut up and push! But afterwards, he was born at 9:30, they told us he had Down syndrome at noon,* *and by 4 p.m., I was hemorrhaging so badly that I came within 2 minutes of death. I had to have an emergency D & C[3] with no anesthesia (talk about PAIN!!) and a big blood transfusion.*

That night, they told us Peter needed immediate surgery and had to go to a hospital in another city. A very traumatic day, to say the least. And then they sent me home the next day with no mention at all that I might want to talk to somebody about any of this—the Down syndrome, the near-death experience, nothing. I can still call up those memories with crystal clarity. And whenever we hear about another couple, I have to reprocess those feelings. Interestingly, most of them relate to the hemorrhaging and D&C, not to the Down syndrome "news." They're all tied up together. Maybe it's good to remind myself, every so often, of how precious life is.

My third birth was excruciatingly painful—the baby was 9 lb 3 oz, with severe shoulder dystocia—his head was delivered 20 minutes before his shoulders. I had some Stadol in the IV line right before transition, but that's all the pain relief I had. I thought I was going to die, and lost all perspective on the fact that I was having a baby. I just tried to live through each contraction. Of course, I was flat on my back, with my feet up in stirrups, and watching the fetal monitor as I charted each contraction—I think those things should be outlawed! I know now that if I had been squatting, or on my hands and knees, I probably could have gotten him out much easier. I'm the one who has the giant shoulders and incredibly long arms, so I can't blame anyone else on my two babies with broad shoulders (Miranda, the first, also took several extra pushes to get her shoulders out, but she was "only" 8 lb 1 oz).

That night, after Alex was born (at 9 in the morning), I could not sleep at all because every time I tried to go to sleep, my brain would start rerunning the tape of labor, and I would feel the pain and the fright and the fears of dying all over again. I stayed up all that night and the next day, and didn't sleep until I was home in my own bed.

In Kathy's stories, we see some classic symptoms of a posttraumatic stress response: fear of dying, sleeplessness, and reexperiencing her birth, both immediately afterwards and when someone had a similar experience. There was also a lack of control and the perception that the hospital was not a supportive place. She eventually came to a place of peace over her experiences, but the memories of those two episodes have remained vivid.

1.3 Summary

A negative birth experience can exert an influence for years afterwards. Immediately afterwards, women may feel grateful to have simply survived. It is often later, when they can allow themselves to feel the anger, guilt, or sadness that accompanies their experiences, that they appraise

---

[3] D&C: dilation and curettage.

these experiences negatively. Unfortunately, this delayed reaction means that care providers are often completely unaware of the impact their actions have on their patients. Women rarely feel empowered to go back later and tell their care providers how they really felt.

The good news is that recovery is possible, and women can gain some closure on their experiences. First, women must allow themselves to be angry or upset. Then they must be given the opportunity to voice their concerns. Only then can they put these experiences behind them.

In the next section, I describe an experience with many similarities to a negative birth experience—giving birth to a premature baby. Women who have premature babies have often had difficult births. Their reactions are compounded, because their babies are medically fragile.

2 PREMATURE DELIVERY

My first child was premature. He was born at 35 weeks with severe Hyaline Membrane Disease .... He was in the hospital for 5 months; in the NICU[4] for 4 months and in intermediate care for 1 month.... The depression started around the time he was 3 or 4 weeks old.... Up until that time, everything had been so urgent. He had had a couple of arrests. It was overwhelming. Suddenly my son was doing better. Why was I feeling so bad? I had difficulties going to sleep. I was up several times during the night. It was difficult to wake up in the morning. I didn't want to do anything during the day except sleep and call the NICU to check in. I started not to eat well. I felt an impending sense of doom.

Premature birth can be a source of trauma for women. Every year in the United States, more than 400,000 premature babies are born. A premature baby born in the United States has a high chance of survival. However, babies born very early, or very small, are at risk for a number of serious complications, including brain hemorrhages, chronic lung disease, respiratory distress, blindness or visual impairment, cerebral palsy, and language delays (American Association for Premature Infants, 2000). These serious problems can cause mothers a great deal of worry. Mothers may carry these fears long after their children have recovered. Linda, whose son was born at 27 weeks and weighed 2 lb, described these feelings:

> When my son was about 16 months old, I began to have anxiety attacks. I don't think I ever dealt with all of the pain and heartache of the NICU.... No matter how old or big our babies get, they will always be preemies to us. (Kendall-Tackett, 2001, p. 172)

A preterm birth is one that occurs before 37 weeks of gestation. Although preterm babies have a high chance of survival, prematurity is

---

[4] NICU: neonatal intensive care unit.

the second leading cause of infant death in the United States. A problem related to premature birth is low birth weight (LBW), or a baby that weighs less than 5 lb (<2,500 g). Babies at highest risk are those classified as "very low birth weight," or less than 3 ½ lb (<1,500 g). Approximately 7% of babies are of LBW, and approximately 1.5% are very LBW. The highest mortality rates occur in babies born at the lowest weights or youngest gestational ages.

Premature delivery has been characterized as an "ambiguous loss," in that parents often feel the contradictory emotions of joy at the babies' birth, and grief over their fragile state. In a qualitative study of family members who experienced a premature delivery, the subjects experienced a range of reactions. They mourned the loss of a full-term pregnancy and feared for the baby's life and health. They also sometimes had difficulty communicating their grief to others, because the baby was still alive (Golish & Powell, 2003).

Some risk factors of premature birth have been identified. In a sample of African American women with low incomes, maternal depression during pregnancy was associated with spontaneous preterm birth and was an independent risk factor for prematurity (Orr, James, & Blackmore Prince, 2002). In a study of more than 100,000 women in Bavaria, Martius and colleagues (Martius, Steck, Oehler, & Wulf, 1998) found that preterm birth was associated with premature rupture of the membranes, treatment for infertility, previous induced abortion, a maternal age of greater than 35 or less than 18, cervical dilatation, history of stillbirth or previous preterm birth, malpresentation, preeclampsia (hypertension during pregnancy), uterine bleeding, preterm labor, or chorioamnionitis (infection of the amniotic fluid). The authors concluded that these risk factors fell into approximately four categories: obstetrical history, genital infections, preeclampsia, and maternal age.

Not surprisingly, degree of infant illness is related to how well mothers coped. Blumberg (1980) examined the direct relationship between neonatal illness and maternal depression. She found that neonatal risk was significantly causally related to depression: the sicker the baby, the more likely the mother was to be depressed. Mothers with babies who were most at risk had higher levels of anxiety and more negative perceptions of their newborns than mothers whose babies were not at risk. This finding was true regardless of ethnicity or socioeconomic status of the mothers, indicating that the effects of neonatal risk were independent of other characteristics within the sample.

In another study, mothers with sick, very LBW babies showed high levels of distress postpartum, and this influenced their interactions with their babies 1 year later. At 1 year, the mothers of babies at highest risk were less responsive, and the babies showed less cognitive growth.

The authors recommended interventions for maternal distress as a way to help both mother and baby (Singer et al., 2003).

A study of 67 mothers of medically fragile infants found that mothers can experience both distress and personal growth through the process of caring for their infants (Miles, Holditch-Davis, Burchinal, & Nelson, 1999). Measured at 6 months postpartum, these mothers were at risk for depression. However, by 16 months, some were reporting positive growth. Distress was influenced by a stressful and nonsupportive hospital environment, and the mothers' worry about their infants' health. Interestingly, maternal growth was influenced by the same characteristics.

2.1 Intervention With Mothers of Premature Infants

As noted previously, support can help mothers cope. In a recent study (Preyde & Ardal, 2003), mothers of babies who were preterm (less than 30 weeks) were randomly assigned to either a parent "buddy" who previously had a preterm infant or a control group. After 4 weeks, mothers in the peer-support group reported less stress than mothers in the control group. By 16 weeks, mothers in the peer-support group were less anxious and depressed and reported greater levels of social support than mothers in the control group.

Another popular intervention for prematurity is Kangaroo Care, where mothers or fathers have extensive skin-to-skin contact with their babies by "wearing" them in slings that are under their clothes. This technique has proven highly effective in helping mothers (and fathers) and babies. In a study by Feldman, Eidelman, Sirota, and Weller (2002), mothers and fathers who participated in Kangaroo Care had more positive interactions with their babies, were less depressed, and were less likely to perceive their babies as abnormal compared to mothers and fathers whose babies received standard incubator care. The babies also fare better with Kangaroo Care. As newborns, their respirations are consistently better, they gain more weight, and they are able to leave the hospital sooner than their counterparts who receive standard care (Anderson, 1991; Dombrowski, Anderson, Santori, & Burkhammer, 2001). At 6 months of age, the babies in the Kangaroo Care group also had higher scores on the Bayley Mental Development Index (Feldman et al., 2002).

Much of the above discussion assumes that the babies survived. In some sad cases, they do not. These babies may have died shortly after birth. Or they may have lingered for several weeks or months in the hospital before finally succumbing. In either case, the loss of one or multiple babies can influence women for the rest of their lives.

3 CHILDBEARING LOSS

In a moment's time, our world shatters like fine china. And the darkness comes. For some, it was a phone call from the doctor. Still others were all alone. Perhaps you found your precious baby lifeless in the crib, a heartbeat suddenly stopped. Or maybe, like me, it was in a cold, dark room that you felt life slip away as you watched a black, silent ultrasound. Our stories are all different, but our pain is the same. (DeYmaz, 1996, p. 1)

Childbearing loss is another common, and unacknowledged, source of trauma in the lives of women. Women of all nationalities and income levels have suffered from childbearing losses. Childbearing loss can strike a woman more than once. For example, treatment for infertility may have finally resulted in a pregnancy, which ended in miscarriage. Women may have one baby die, only to miscarry on a subsequent pregnancy. Or they may be unable to get pregnant again. The pain from each of these experiences is real, and can persist for years.

In this section, I describe some of the more common types of childbearing loss, including miscarriage, infertility, abortion, stillbirth, and neonatal death. Although the focus of this chapter is pregnancy and infant loss, much of what I share in this section can apply to the death of an older child as well.

3.1 Miscarriage

Miscarriage is the most common, and least acknowledged, form of infant loss. Each year, 600,000 to 800,000 women miscarry in the United States (Diamond, 1996). These numbers probably underestimate the true incidence. Women vary in the amount of grief they feel following a miscarriage. Some women seem to take miscarriage in stride and are ready to "try again" in relatively short order. Other women feel a deep sense of loss after a miscarriage, as several recent studies have documented. For example, in a cohort study of 229 women who miscarried and 230 women from the community, women who had miscarried had a relative risk of 5.2 for minor depression in the 6 months after a miscarriage. Risk did not vary by length of gestation or women's attitude toward their pregnancies (Klier, Geller, & Neugebauer, 2000).

The psychological and emotional impact of miscarriage is compounded for women who have had more than one. Each subsequent pregnancy is filled with fear, as women wonder whether this one will last. Diamond (1996) described her experience of multiple miscarriages this way:

> The mourning process became shorter after each miscarriage, because I was resigned to failure and did not actually think each pregnancy was real.... After each miscarriage, I went about business as usual. No one else could

possibly feel as badly as I did, and besides, I had a sense of terrible shame and failure. (p. 67)

Miscarriage might also occur in the midst of treatment for infertility (see "Infertility" section below). After months of hormone treatments, invasive exams, daily temperature charts, and one or more sessions of in vitro fertilization, women can still miscarry. With each miscarriage, the odds of having a baby are reduced. Women often feel an overwhelming sense of hopelessness. Getting and staying pregnant can become the driving force of their lives.

A qualitative study of eight women found that women who had this experience reported feeling like they were going back to "square one." They had an inner struggle between hope and hopelessness for their future fertility. They also reported feeling like they were running out of time, were angry and frustrated with others, felt alone and numb with their grief, guilty, and frustrated with others' lack of understanding of what they were going through. These women grieved intensely and felt profoundly alone. Some of the women reported that they were hospitalized for their miscarriages on postpartum units, and that this experience was unbearable for them (Freda, Devine, & Semelsberger, 2003).

The physical aspects of miscarriage can also be traumatic. A woman's first hint that she was about to miscarry may have been a small amount of blood. She may have frantically called her doctor's office, only to be told there was little that she can do. Or rather than a little blood, there may have been a lot. Gushing blood and passing large clots are frightening to most people. In the case of miscarriage, bleeding is the harbinger of impending pregnancy loss.

Many women I interviewed described the aftermath of miscarriage to be one of the most traumatic parts. It may have occurred at home or on a gurney in the emergency room. Hospital staff may have treated the woman in a callous or cavalier way (Ujda & Bendiksen, 2000). Women may have found that their babies were gone by looking at a black ultrasound screen. And they may have had to undergo a surgical procedure, such as a D&C, to make sure that there were no remnants of their pregnancies left behind. These procedures can be frightening and painful, and their invasive nature can reinforce feelings of powerlessness (Ujda & Bendiksen, 2000).

To complicate matters further, when women miscarry, there are few outlets for them to acknowledge their grief. There is no funeral, few condolences, and little compassion. Women often mourn these losses alone, not realizing that many other women around them have probably had similar experiences (Panuthos & Romeo, 1984).

In a study of 174 women whose pregnancies ended before 20 weeks gestation, those most at risk for depression were those women who attributed high personal significance to the miscarriage (e.g., felt like failures because of it), lacked social support, had lower incomes, and did not conceive or give birth after their loss (Swanson, 2000). Partners of women who miscarry are also at risk for depression but were less likely to receive support from others, as was found in a prospective study of women and their partners (Conway & Russell, 2000).

3.2 Infertility

Related to the discussion of miscarriage is another form of childbearing loss: infertility. Infertility is also relatively common. More than six million women in the United States (approximately 10% of women ages 15 to 44) reported impaired fecundity—difficulty in conceiving or carrying a child to term (Fidler & Bernstein, 1999). Miscarriage and infertility are intimately related. Some health care providers will not even start a workup for infertility until a woman has had her second or third miscarriage (Ujda & Bendiksen, 2000).

For women experiencing it, infertility taps into women's deepest feelings of who they are and what they want out of life. Fidler and Bernstein (1999) considered the emotional impact of infertility to be comparable to that of cancer or heart disease. Testing and treatment for infertility can become all consuming. The testing is invasive, expensive, and often painful. It lays bare the most intimate details of women's lives. Sex loses its spontaneity and becomes mechanical. Women may wonder why they are unable to get pregnant when women who do not want children seem to get pregnant with ease. In a study of 19 women in treatment for infertility, the women described infertility as an interruption of life plans. They also described their feelings of guilt, inadequacy, and failure (Ulrich & Weatherall, 2000).

There are also sex differences in response to infertility. In one study, men and women had higher rates of depression and anxiety at baseline and at the 6-month follow-up than men. Women also had lower life satisfaction, higher levels of concerns about sexuality, more self-blame and avoidance of friends, and lower self-esteem than their male partners. The degree of distress for males and females did not change over time. Only a relatively small percentage of patients had clinically significant distress at the various assessment points (Anderson, Sharpe, Rattray, & Irvine, 2003).

It is also important to recognize that not all treatment for infertility ends with the birth of a baby. Approximately half of couples in treatment for infertility never give birth (Bergart, 2000). Couples may endure years of testing, treatment, and miscarriages before coming to the conclusion that they are unable to have a biological child. This can also be experienced as a significant loss. In a longitudinal, qualitative study of 10 women who had unsuccessful infertility treatments, women described how infertility created a developmental crisis for them. It had an impact on their relationships and sense of meaning. These women also described how treatment was often delivered in an impersonal and dehumanizing way (Bergart, 2000).

Even when mothers go on to adopt, they may feel marginalized by other mothers who have biological children. Although adoptive mothers cannot tell birth stories, their path to motherhood is no less heroic. However, some report that even after adopting a baby, the sting of infertility may linger for years (Smith, Surrey, & Watkins, 1998).

3.3 Abortion

According to recent estimates, there are approximately 26 million legal abortions performed each year worldwide (Speckhard & Mufel, 2003). Although it is a relatively common experience, it is arguably the most politically divisive issue of our time. The volatile nature of the topic has influenced how abortion has been studied. Some researchers are anxious to show that it never causes harm to women, because they fear limitation on women's reproductive rights. Others feel that it always or usually causes harm, because they want it to stop. The reality, as is often the case, is somewhere in between.

In their comprehensive review of the literature, Adler and colleagues (Adler et al., 1992) summarized what was known about the emotional impact of abortion. They stated that earlier studies used a psychoanalytic framework to describe psychopathological responses to abortion. More current models used a stress-and-coping model, in that unwanted pregnancy and abortion were seen as potential life stressors that could have positive or negative consequences. Abortion may reduce the stress associated with an unwanted pregnancy, or it could become a stressful event in and of itself. Several characteristics influenced women's reactions to abortion: their feelings about the morality of abortion, the support the women received from their partners or others, and the experience they had in receiving the abortion.

Based on their review, Adler et al. (1992) concluded that first-trimester abortion does not create psychological harm for most women, with a small number of women reporting severe reactions to the procedure. Severe reactions were more likely for women who were ambivalent about their decision, who had lack of partner or parental support, who blamed themselves for the pregnancy, and who were less sure of their decision-making and coping abilities. However, they noted that women's responses are complex, and they may have both positive and negative feelings.

A more recent review (Adler, Ozer, & Tschann, 2003) on abortion in adolescents had similar findings. Adler et al. (2003) noted that rates of depression and PTSD for women who have abortions are low. This was true even when considering whether teens would be more vulnerable to these negative effects than adult women. Adler (2000) noted, however, that there are some methodological issues in studying the question of the emotional impact of abortion. One specific issue is that it is almost impossible to prove the null hypothesis, because there is no way to randomly assign women to abortion and nonabortion groups. Therefore, we can never know what the women's experience would have been like if they had not had an abortion.

Along these same lines, in a review of studies conducted after 1990, Bradshaw and Slade (2003) concluded that after women discovered that they were pregnant, but before their abortions, 40% to 45% experienced significant levels of anxiety, and 20% had significant levels of depression. Women's levels of distress dropped after their abortions, but 30% still had emotional difficulties 1 month later. Abortion did not affect their self-esteem, but it had a negative impact on quality of relationships and sexual functioning for about 20% of women (Bradshaw & Slade, 2003).

Even with these generally positive findings, another study had more negative results. In a sample from the former Soviet Republic of Belarus, Speckhard and Mufel (2003) found that a surprising 82% of women had symptoms of PTSD. This was despite the fact that abortion was used as a primary method of birth control in their country and was therefore a common experience. The authors also found that other emotional and psychiatric symptoms were present in these women, including grief, guilt, dissociation, depression, anxiety, and psychosomatic responses.

Another study of American women (ages 24 to 45 years) found a connection between abortion and substance abuse. In their sample, women who aborted a first pregnancy were four to five times more likely to report substance abuse than women who carried their pregnancies to term or who miscarried (Reardon & Ney, 2000). However, some of this effect could be due to the relatively high percentage of women seeking abortions who have a history of violence (Allanson & Astbury, 2001). In a study of women seeking early abortions in Australia, women with insecure adult attachments were more likely to report high levels of violence, pregnancy, abortion, and emotional problems. Women with secure adult attachments were lower in all these indices (Allanson & Astbury, 2001).

In summary, the results of these studies indicate that many women function well after an abortion, and that their levels of emotional distress are likely to decrease—particularly if they were highly anxious and depressed beforehand. However, for some, the experience can increase the risk of depression, anxiety, and posttraumatic stress. Regardless of your stand on this issue, it is important to acknowledge the experiences of all women.

3.4 Stillbirth/Neonatal Death

Death of a baby at or near term is another form of childbearing loss. Stillbirth occurs in approximately 1 in 80 births and accounts for more than 195,000 deaths per year. It has a variety of causes. Stillbirth could be due to an accident during labor, such as a prolapsed cord, placenta previa, a uterine rupture, or medical negligence. It could be due to an infection, such as group B streptococcus, toxemia in the mother, or physical trauma caused by a car accident or physical assault.

In some cases of stillbirth, the baby dies before labor begins. Mothers may have felt no movement, have started to bleed, or had sudden searing pains. Or there may have been no warning at all. Some women learned of their babies' deaths during a routine examination, when the doctor or midwife could not find a heartbeat.

Sometimes women find themselves in the nightmarish scenario of knowing that their babies are dead but having to continue to be pregnant for days or even weeks, awaiting labor. Unbelievably, they still need to go through labor, knowing that their babies will not be alive at the end. Since the baby has already died, the hospital staff usually gives women strong pain medication for labor. This often exacerbates the surreal feeling of the experience, making it seem like it is happening to someone else.

After a stillbirth, women's bodies may act like they have given birth to a living baby. Their breasts fill with milk, and they have many of the other physical signs of recent birth. Some mothers have described this experience as their whole bodies "weeping" for their lost children (Panuthos & Romeo, 1984).

Not surprisingly, prior infant loss can increase the risk of depression and PTSD. Janssen and colleagues (Janssen, Culsinier, Hoogduin, & deGraauw, 1996) compared 227 women whose babies had died with 213 women who gave birth to live babies. Women whose babies had died had greater depression, anxiety, and somatization 6 months later than the women who had given birth to live babies. One year after their experiences, these women were less depressed and had fewer trauma symptoms than they had at 6 months. However, the authors noted that stillbirth is a stressful life event that can precipitate a marked decline in a women's mental state for several months afterwards.

A prior stillbirth can also influence how women experience a subsequent pregnancy. Hughes, Turton, and Evans (1999) compared women who had a previous stillbirth with a group of matched controls. Not surprisingly, women who had a stillbirth were more depressed and anxious in the third trimesters of their subsequent pregnancies, and they had higher levels of postpartum depression. The results were strongest for women who were most recently bereaved. In the year following delivery, depression was twice as likely for the bereaved compared to the comparison women.

Men and women also have different ways of coping with the loss of a newborn. A phenomenological study compared mothers and fathers whose premature, very LBW babies had died. At the time of the loss, fathers indicated that they felt out of control, and they also expressed a concern for the mothers. They coped by keeping busy. Women indicated they were experiencing intense feelings of loss. They coped by talking to others. They also had more difficulty than the fathers in making sense of the loss and in social situations, such as being around babies. The men and women in the study indicated that males' traditional roles were interfering with their response to their loss (Kavanaugh, 1997).

Death of a baby at term, or shortly after birth, can be highly traumatic. Death can also occur after a baby is safely delivered and appears to be healthy. In the final section, I describe another traumatic form of infant loss—sudden infant death syndrome.

3.5 Sudden Infant Death Syndrome (SIDS)

Sudden infant death syndrome (SIDS) is the unexplained death of a baby less than 1 year of age that remains unexplained even after an autopsy, examination of the death scene, and review of the case history. SIDS is terrifying, because it strikes otherwise healthy infants. Approximately 90% of SIDS deaths occur by 6 months of age. SIDS affects approximately 1 in 700 babies born in the United States, but the rate is lower in other countries (Sears, 1995). According the Centers for Disease Control (CDC, 1999), SIDS is the third most common form of death for babies in the United States.

While researchers have been able to identify some risk factors for SIDS, its cause remains a mystery. Babies exposed to cigarette smoke, who were born prematurely, who sleep on their stomachs, and who were formula fed are at highest risk (CDC, 1999). However, there are many babies who have all these risk factors who do not succumb to SIDS. Conversely, there are babies who have none of these risk factors who do.

In a 30-month prospective study of couples following stillbirth, neonatal death, or SIDS, at each assessment period, couples who had lost a baby reported significantly more distress of one or both partners than couples who had not experienced loss. Interestingly, mothers' distress declined over time, while the distress of fathers rose during the study period. Couples who were most distressed at 2 months reported more marital dissatisfaction at 30 months (Vance, Boyle, Najman, & Thearle, 2002). In another longitudinal study, mothers who had higher educational attainment and more friends showed better adjustment to their infants' deaths. Mothers who coped by seeking social support had less distress at 15 months postloss (Murray & Terry, 1999).

Mothers whose babies die of SIDS are usually overwhelmed by the suddenness of the loss. Babies have died on the day that they had a well-baby check. They have died at their mothers' breasts or while sleeping next to their mothers. In this next section, I share the story of one mother whose babies died of SIDS.

3.5.1 Jonathan's Song: One Mother's Story of SIDS. For Joan, December 8 started like any day. But the events of that day forever changed her life. Joan went to check on her baby after his nap and discovered that he was not breathing. Her neighbor made a frantic 911 call, and the baby was rushed to the hospital. An hour later, the doctor came out to tell Joan and her husband Henk that their son Jonathan had died. He was 3 months old.

All I could think of was that I needed to be with Jonathan. I said: "I want to see him. I've got to be with him." The nurse said "Of course, of course." And they brought us into the room where my little baby lay, wrapped in a white sheet on the gurney.

When I reached the stretcher on which he lay, I pulled the white sheet open, exposing his pale little body. As I sobbed, "Oh, Jonathan, Jonathan, I loved you. I loved you so much." I caressed his naked body with my hand, touching every part, trying to etch into my mind what I soon would no longer be able to see. I looked up at Henk and he was weeping, tears streaming down his face, his head tipped back in disbelief. The nurses scurried to get chairs for both of us. I think they were afraid that one of us would faint. I covered Jonathan back up and picked him up to hold him. As I held him, I stroked his coppery brown hair. I told the nurse that his hair had just started to grow in. Her eyes were red as she wept with us in our grief.

I turned to Henk and said, "What can we do? I can't just walk away and leave him here." The nurses assured us that we could stay as long as we wanted to, and just hold him and be with him. I pulled his little hand out from underneath the sheet and held his fingers and stroked them. I touched his toes and his feet. I looked and looked at his face and hair.

Henk took Jonathan out of my arms and I didn't know what he was going to do. I was afraid that he was taking him away from me. But he just wanted to pray. He committed our son back into the Lord's hands and thanked Him for the time we were able to have with Jonathan. Then he gave him back to me to hold. Before that, I was afraid to let go of Jonathan. After that prayer, I felt that it was time to leave him and go home. The nurse came in and I handed Jonathan to her. I kissed the top of his head, touched him one last time, and stepped out into the corridor.

Everything after that is after. This is about Jonathan, and our story goes on. We said good-bye to him the best way we could and then tried to pick up the pieces. The great pain and emptiness are still quite real, but not as present every day. He was Jonathan—"God's precious gift" as his name means, and as we put on his tombstone. Children are precious. People are precious. Each day is precious. That is what I learned from my son's short life and his death. We miss him so much. That will never fade. I know he is with my Father in heaven and that helps, but there are times when I just want to hold him one more time, nurse him one more time, touch him, hear him just one last time.

But every time I feel that loss, that great void, I also feel grateful for the time we were able to have with one very special little boy, who gave us great joy for an incredibly short time and who we will never forget. No bitter grief could ever poison that, the wonderful sweet time we had with our son Jonathan.

4 CONCLUSION

The birth of a baby is generally a positive event. A new life is beginning. A family is formed. Children become siblings. We now also know that substantial numbers of women are traumatized by perinatal events. Events that take place during the perinatal period can stay with women for the rest of their lives. While some of what happens cannot be avoided, much of it can be, and health care providers can do a better job of caring for childbearing women. There have been two hopeful signs: changes in the treatment of premature babies and how providers handle neonatal death.

The treatment of premature babies has undergone a dramatic change. In the bad old days, parents were routinely excluded from the NICU. They often had little contact with their hospitalized babies and often felt that only "experts" could provide care for them. Research over the past 20 years has demonstrated that keeping parents and babies apart is bad for both. Slowly, but surely, hospital protocols changed. Parents are no longer excluded from caring for their premature babies and are now encouraged to be involved. This can increase mothers' feelings of confidence and minimize their feelings of helplessness.

Hospitals are also better than they used to be in handling stillbirth and neonatal death. Women are allowed to see and hold their babies, whereas before, medical staff often whisked the babies away before mothers could see them. Not being able to see their babies can prolong women's grief. Even something as simple as putting a discreet sign on the door (such as a falling leaf) to let hospital staff know that there has been a death, can keep women from hearing cheery "congratulations" when they are desperately sad.

Many of the changes in hospital protocols originated with women who experienced poor treatment and were determined to improve the situation for others. They lobbied for, and got, changes made to the system. This shows what can be done.

There is still much work to do, however. As I described earlier, women who have been traumatized often do not tell their providers about how their experiences impacted them. Providers remain blithely unaware of the havoc they created. But we know, and we can make their voices heard. We can insist that health care providers not silence women but learn from them about how to do things better. We can also offer women the hope that they can recover from traumatic perinatal events. Women no longer need to suffer in silence. That is good news, indeed.

REFERENCES

Adler, N. E. (2000). Abortion and the null hypothesis. *Archives of General Psychiatry, 57,* 785–786.

Adler, N. E., David, H. P., Major, B. N., Roth, S. H., Russo, N. F., & Wyatt, G. E. (1992). Psychological factors in abortion: A review. *American Psychologist, 47,* 1194–1204.

Adler, N. E., Ozer, E. J., & Tschann, J. (2003). Abortion among adolescents. *American Psychologist, 58,* 211–217.

Allanson, S., & Astbury, J. (2001). Attachment style and broken attachments: Violence, pregnancy, and abortion. *Australian Journal of Psychology, 53,* 146–151.

American Association for Premature Infants. (2000). Overview of prematurity. Retrieved June 1, 2000, from http://www.aapi-online.org

American Medical Association. (1995). *Diagnostic and treatment guidelines on the mental health effects of family violence.* Retrieved from http://www.ama-assn.org

Anderson, G. C. (1991). Current knowledge about skin-to-skin (Kangaroo) care for preterm infants. *Journal of Perinatology, XI,* 216–226.

Anderson, K. M., Sharpe, M., Rattray, A., & Irvine, D. S. (2003). Distress and concerns in couples referred to a specialist infertility clinic. *Journal of Psychosomatic Research, 54,* 353–355.

Astbury, J., Brown, S., Lumley, J., & Small, R. (1994). Birth events, birth experiences, and social differences in postnatal depression. *Australian Journal of Public Health, 18,* 176–184.

Ayers, S., & Pickering, A. D. (2001). Do women get posttraumatic stress disorder as a result of childbirth? A prospective study of incidence. *Birth, 28,* 111–118.

Bergart, A. M. (2000). The experience of women in unsuccessful infertility treatment: What do patients need when medical intervention fails? *Social Work in Health Care, 30,* 45–69.

Blumberg, N. L. (1980). Effects of neonatal risk, maternal attitude, and cognitive style on early postpartum adjustment. *Journal of Abnormal Psychology, 89,* 139–150.

Bradshaw, Z., & Slade, P. (2003). The effects of included abortion on emotional experiences and relationships: A critical review of the literature. *Clinical Psychology Review, 23,* 929–958.

Centers for Disease Control (CDC). (1999). *National vital statistics reports* 47. Retrieved from http://www.cdc.gov

Conway, K., & Russell, G. (2000). Couples' grief and experience of support in the aftermath of miscarriage. *British Journal of Medical Psychology, 73,* 531–545.

Czarnocka, J., & Slade, P. (2000). Prevalence and predictors of posttraumatic stress symptoms following childbirth. *British Journal of Clinical Psychology, 39,* 35–51.

DeYmaz, L. (1996). *Mommy, please don't cry.* Sisters, OR: Multnomah Press.

Diamond, K. (1991). *Motherhood after miscarriage.* Holbrook, MA: Adams Media.

Dombrowski, M. A., Anderson, G. C., Santori, C., & Burkhammer, M. (2001). Kangaroo (skin-to-skin) care with a postpartum woman who felt depressed. *MCN: American Journal of Maternal Child Nursing, 26,* 214–216.

Durik, A. M., Hyde, J. S., & Clark, R. (2000). Sequelae of cesarean and vaginal deliveries: Psychosocial outcomes for mothers and infants. *Developmental psychology, 36,* 251–260.

Feldman, R., Eidelman, A. I., Sirota, L., & Weller, A. (2002). Comparison of skin-to-skin (kangaroo) and traditional care: Parenting outcomes and preterm infant development. *Pediatrics, 110,* 16–26.

Fidler, A. T., & Bernstein, J. (1999). Infertility: From a personal to a public health problem. *Public Health Reports, 114,* 494–511.

Fisher, J., Astbury, J., & Smith, A. (1997). Adverse psychological impact of operative obstetric interventions: A prospective longitudinal study. *Australian and New Zealand Journal of Psychiatry, 31,* 728–738.

Fisher, J. R., Feekery, C. J., Amir, L. H., & Sneddon, M. (2002). Health and social circumstances of women admitted to a private mother–baby unit. A descriptive cohort study. *Australian Family Physician, 31,* 966–970, 973.

Fisher, J. R. W., Feekery, C. J., & Rowe-Murray, H. J. (2002). Nature, severity and correlates of psychological distress in women admitted to a private mother–baby unit. *Journal of Paediatrics and Child Health, 38,* 140–145.

Freda, M. C., Devine, K. S., & Semelsberger, C. (2003). The lived experience of miscarriage after infertility. *American Journal of Maternal/Child Nursing, 28,* 16–23.

Galea, S., Vlahov, D., Resnick, H., Ahern, J., Susser, E., Gold, J., Bucuvalas, M., & Kilpatrick, D. (2003). Trends of probable post-traumatic stress disorder in New York City after the September 11 terrorist attacks. *American Journal of Epidemiology, 158*(6), 514–524.

Genevie, L., & Margolies, E. (1987). *The motherhood report: How women feel about being mothers.* New York: Macmillan.

Golish, T. D., & Powell, K. A. (2003). "Ambiguous loss": Managing the dialectics of grief associated with premature birth. *Journal of Social and Personal Relationships, 20,* 309–334.

Hannah, M. E., Hannah, W. J., Hodnett, E. D., Chalmers, B., Kung, R., Willan, A., Amankwah, K., Cheng, M., Helewa, M., Hewson, S., Saigal, S., Whyte, H., Gafni, A., & the Term Breech Trial 3-Month Follow-up Collaborative Group. (2002). Outcomes at 3 months after planned cesarean vs. planned vaginal delivery for breech presentation at term: The international randomized term breech trial. *Journal of the American Medical Association, 287,* 1822–1831.

Hughes, P., Turton, P., & Evans, C. D. H. (1999). Stillbirth as risk factor for depression and anxiety in the subsequent pregnancy: Cohort study. *British Medical Journal, 318,* 1721–1724.

Janssen, H. J., Cuisinier, M. C., Hoogduin, K. A., & deGraauw, K. P. (1996). Controlled prospective study on the mental health of women following pregnancy loss. *American Journal of Psychiatry, 153,* 226–230.

Kavanaugh, K. (1997). Gender differences among parents who experience the death of an infant weighing less than 500 grams at birth. *Omega: Journal of Death and Dying, 35,* 281–296.

Kendall-Tackett, K. A. (2001). *The hidden feelings of motherhood: Coping with stress, depression and burnout.* Oakland, CA: New Harbinger.

Klier, C. M., Geller, P. A., & Neugebauer, R. (2000). Minor depressive disorder in the context of miscarriage. *Journal of Affective Disorders, 59,* 13–21.

Martius, J. A., Steck, T., Oehler, M. K., & Wulf, K. -H. (1998). Risk factors associated with preterm (<37 + 0 weeks) and early preterm birth (<32 + 0 weeks): Univariate and multivariate analysis of 106,345 singleton births from the 1994 statewide perinatal survey of Bavaria. *European Journal of Obstetrics and Gynecology and Reproductive Biology, 80,* 183–189.

Miles, M. S., Holditch-Davis, D., Burchinal, P., & Nelson, D. (1999). Distress and growth outcomes in mothers of medically fragile infants. *Nursing Research, 48,* 129–140.

Murray, J. A., & Terry, D. J. (1999). Parental reactions to infant death: The effects of resources and coping strategies. *Journal of Social and Clinical Psychology, 18,* 341–369.

Orr, S. T., James, S. A., & Blackmore Prince, C. (2002). Maternal prenatal depressive symptoms and spontaneous preterm births among African-American women in Baltimore, Maryland. *American Journal of Epidemiology, 156,* 797–802.

Panuthos, C., & Romeo, C. (1984). *Ended beginnings: Healing childbearing losses.* Westport, CT: Bergin & Garvey.

Preyde, M., & Ardal, F. (2003). Effectiveness of a parent "buddy" program for mothers of very preterm infants in a neonatal intensive care unit. *Canadian Medical Association Journal, 168,* 969–973.

Reardon, D. C., & Ney, P. G. (2000). Abortion and subsequent substance abuse. *American Journal of Drug and Alcohol Abuse, 26,* 61–75.

Reynolds, J. L. (1997). Posttraumatic stress disorder after childbirth: The phenomenon of traumatic birth. *Canadian Medical Association Journal, 156,* 831–835.

Rothman, B. K. (1982). *Giving birth: Alternatives in childbirth.* New York: Penguin.

Rowe-Murray, H. J., & Fisher, J. R. W. (2001). Operative intervention in delivery is associated with compromised early mother–infant interaction. *British Journal of Obstetrics and Gynaecology, 108,* 1068–1075.

Saisto, T., Salmela-Aro, K., Nurmi, J. E., & Halmesmaki, E. (2001). Psychosocial predictors of disappointment with delivery and puerperal depression: A longitudinal study. *Acta Obstetrica et Gynecologica Scandinavica, 80,* 39–45.

Sears, W. (1995). *SIDS: A parent's guide to understanding and preventing Sudden Infant Death Syndrome.* New York: Little, Brown.

Simkin, P. (1991). Just another day in a woman's life? Women's long-term perceptions of their first birth experience. Part I. *Birth, 18,* 203–210.

Singer, L. T., Fulton, S., Daviller, M., Koshy, D., Salvator, A., & Baley, J. E. (2003). Effects of infant risk status and maternal psychological distress on maternal–infant interactions during the first year of life. *Journal of Developmental and Behavioral Pediatrics, 24,* 233–241.

Smart, L. S. (2003). Old losses: A retrospective study of miscarriage and infant death 1926–1955. *Journal of Women and Aging, 15,* 71–91.

Smith, B., Surrey, J., & Watkins, M. (1998). "Real mothers": Adoptive mothers resisting marginalization and re-creating motherhood. In C. Garcia Coll, J. L. Surrey, & K. Weingarten (Eds.), *Mothering against the odds: Diverse voices of contemporary mothers* (pp. 194–214) New York: Guilford.

Speckhard, A., & Mufel, N. (2003). Universal responses to abortion? Attachment, trauma, and grief responses in women following abortion. *Journal of Prenatal and Perinatal Psychology and Health, 18,* 3–37.

Swanson, K. M. (2000). Predicting depressive symptoms after miscarriage: A path analysis based on the Lazarus paradigm. *Journal of Women's Health and Gender-Based Medicine, 9,* 191–206.

Ujda, R. M., & Bendiksen, R. (2000). Health care provider support and grief after perinatal loss: A qualitative study. *Illness, Crisis and Loss, 8,* 265–285.

Ulrich, M., & Weatherall, A. (2000). Motherhood and infertility: Viewing motherhood through the lens of infertility. *Feminism and Psychology, 10,* 323–336.

Vance, J. C., Boyle, F. M., Najman, J. M., & Thearle, M. J. (2002). Couple distress after sudden infant or perinatal death: A 30-month follow up. *Journal of Paediatrics and Child Health, 38,* 368–382.

Wertz, R. W., & Wertz, D. C. (1989). *Lying in: A history of childbirth in America* (expanded ed.). New Haven, CT: Yale University Press.

4

Stress and Trauma in the Lives of Middle-Aged and Old Women

JANE A. RYSBERG

In the 1980s, a program appeared on the Public Broadcasting System (PBS) entitled *Victory Garden*. The middle-aged host, Jim Wilson, introduced Americans to the joys, tribulations, and many forms of gardening. The television host is also an author, with a recent book entitled *Gardening Through Your Golden Years* (Wilson, 2003). In this book, he makes a variety of suggestions to keep elders gardening. Mr. Wilson has been certified as a Master Gardener, so he can speak about horticulture; he is approaching his eighth decade, so he can speak about aging. In spite of the expertise of the author, why would a publisher want a book on this topic? Gardening is one of the most popular hobbies in America; aging is very popular also. Persons over the age of 65 now comprise approximately 13% of the American population and will make up 20% by the midpoint of this century (Older Americans, 2000).

The message of Wilson's book jibes with popular sentiments, such as "Age is just a number" or "You are only as old as you feel." Does this mean that we live in an age-irrelevant society, where the number of years one has lived on the planet has no relation to our experiences? Generally, age is important for two reasons. First, we know how old we are. Second, society estimates how old we are.

A review of the literature on attitudes toward aging and the elderly (Kite & Johnson, 1988) and a glance at the messages of the advertising media (Lenz, 1993) show evidence of ageism in our nation. Ageism is the prejudice and discrimination against a class of people based on their chronological age (Papalia, Sterns, Feldman, & Camp, 2002). Ageistic thinkers believe that elders are more alike than they are different, and that the similarities are negative. Compared to young adults, older adults must be slower, weaker, lonelier, sicker, and more stupid. Such reasoning could lead to a belief that middle and old age are years that must be filled with stress and trauma, as the march of time never changes course. The lives of older women must be particularly traumatic, as the addition of years has occurred in a sexist society. It is imperative that this conclusion be examined. What are the sources of stress and trauma for middle-aged and elderly women? Can these sources be controlled or modified? Are they inherent in the process of aging, or do they arise from other, external sources?

1 CHANGES OVER TIME

The process of aging encompasses several components. The body changes. The brain and the mind may change. A woman's position in society, her family, and the workforce can change. These changes can be sources of stress and are described below.

1.1 Possible Changes in the Body Over Time

The individual physical experience of aging presents certain challenges. Changes in the appearance and function of the body are so common that jokes about the waist and hairlines of middle-agers are found in most comedians' repertoires. Some changes in the body are inevitable. For example, the incidence of presbyopia (a form of nearsightedness) increases, and visual acuity decreases in individuals between the ages of 40 and 50 (Schieber & Baldwin, 1996).

Other physical changes are common but may be the result of shared environments or behaviors. For many people, diet and exercise patterns change over time. Most adults are strongest and leanest in their 20s, but others can successfully compete in triathlons in their 60s. Regular exercise can increase muscle mass, flexibility, balance, and endurance, even if the program was begun late in life (Fiatrone, O'Neill, & Ryan, 1994). Regular exercise from early in adulthood may prevent age-related declines and increase the life span (Rakowski & Mor, 1992). Finally, there are conditions that are more common in the elderly population. Examples of these are cataracts, glaucoma, arthritis, and hypertension.

These common conditions appear in mild to severe forms. A mild incidence of osteoarthritis might be treated by range-of-motion exercises and aspirin, whereas a severe case of rheumatoid arthritis might be treated with steroids and chemotherapy drugs (e.g., methotrexate) and may lead to hip replacement.

1.2 Possible Behavior Changes Over Time

The combination of probable and possible bodily changes could mean that a woman's experience of living changes markedly and negatively over time. If she has diminished vision and mobility, how can she move efficiently and safely through space? How can she take care of her own needs? For American elders, the answer to both questions is "well" and "poorly." The answer depends upon who and what are measured. Nearly 70% of 80-year-olds in America report that they can complete daily activities such as dressing, shopping, and eating unassisted (U.S. Bureau of the Census, 1995). This may explain why approximately 67% of those over 75 years describe their health as at least "good" (Older Americans, 2000). In certain important areas, age means limitation. Drivers over the age of 65 experience more accidents and die more often in these accidents than do drivers in other age groups (Sterns & Camp, 1998). In a car-oriented society such as our own, a diminished ability to drive can mean loss of independence, social contacts, and self-image.

This is the general experience of aging people. But what about the experience of women as they age? This is an important question, as women make up the majority of the elderly population. Women live, on average, 5 to 6 years longer than men, and women comprise 70% of the population of Americans over the age of 85 (Older Americans, 2000).

Let us look at "Aunt Minnie." In 1950, Aunt Minnie played for the winning Rockford Peaches in the All-American Girls' Professional Baseball League. During her playing career, she suffered several injuries to her back and shoulders. During her early 60s, the aches in her joints were increased by the onset of osteoarthritis. Aunt Minnie gradually gave up her golf clubs, her bowling ball, and her walks in the park. She tried swimming, but the community pool was at the high school, an inconvenient distance from her home. Open swim hours were in the evenings, and Minnie was experiencing difficulty seeing in dim illumination. She disliked driving at night. Aunt Minnie sat more, and while she sat, she watched ESPN and snacked. Soon she discovered an extra 40 pounds on a frame that was becoming diminished due to osteoporosis. At her last physical, the doctor spoke sternly about Minnie's increasing hypertension and issued warnings about the possibility of diabetes in her future. Minnie's response was "What did you expect? I'm old!"

Now that Aunt Minnie identifies herself as old, she is not surprised that she has some social as well as physical difficulties. As television is a solitary activity, Aunt Minnie had not thought to replace her golf, bowling, and walking partners. Some of her past partners, now, like Minnie, in their late 70s, have moved on to low-impact aerobics in their new retirement community, whereas others have passed on. When Minnie calls her niece and talks about the good old days, she really does not assume that her niece will be interested in listening. When her niece suggested logging onto the Web to search for some other alumnae from the Rockford Peaches, Minnie responded that she was too old to learn that computer stuff. For Minnie, small changes in the body had large consequences, behaviorally and physically. Is Minnie representative of older people, or of older women?

According to Smith and Baltes (1998), gender is a significant factor in the experience of aging. Female participants in the Berlin Aging Study were 1.6 times more likely to possess a profile that included undesirable life conditions than were male participants. These life conditions, such as living alone and physical frailty, probably had psychological consequences, as women were found to have a lower subjective well-being than men. Elderly women in America also possess undesirable life conditions, as they are more likely to live in poverty than are males. This is particularly true if they are widowed, members of an ethnic minority, poorly educated, or have a disability (American Association of Retired Persons [AARP], 1994).

Moen (2001) concurred with these general observations. Using the experience of retirement as an example, she described differences in the planning for, expectations of, and transitions in the retirement process for males and females. Her conclusion was that the adult life course is consistently "gendered."

2 THE "GENDERING" OF STRESS?

Stresses for middle-aged and older women can be of two general types. The first type is continuing stressors. These are challenges that continue to exist from an earlier point in life. The second type of stress has to do with factors that are new to this period in their lives. New stressors involve caregiving, loss of loved ones, role changes, and friendships. These are described below.

2.1 Continuing Stress: Stressors From Earlier Developmental Times

A continuing stress is one that started when women were younger. Take, for example, a woman who gave birth to an infant with Down syndrome, had a toddler with Down syndrome, has an adolescent with Down syndrome, and will have an adult child with Down syndrome. As the son or daughter reaches new stages, there will be new responsibilities. The main worry during the child's younger years might have been finding the best educational placement. A decade later, the mother searched for an independent living situation. The elderly mother of a middle-aged adult with Down syndrome may worry about who will be responsible for her child after she has died.

2.1.1 Stress From Previous Trauma. Some continuing stressors have left durable changes. These changes may cause stress. Certain traumas of childhood, youth, or young adulthood have been shown to leave behavioral, psychological, and bodily traces. Kendall-Tackett (2000) reviewed the literature on the long-term physiological consequences of childhood abuse and determined that experience of early traumatic events makes the body more likely to react to subsequent stressors, thus increasing a person's vulnerability to stress. For example, irritable bowel syndrome is two to three times more common in persons reporting abuse in childhood than those who did not. Adult survivors of childhood abuse also reported increased incidence of depression and sleep disorders. Although the trauma of abuse may be in the past, a middle-aged woman who has experienced years of insomnia and gastrointestinal disorders will probably report the somatic events as stressful. She may be fatigued and may eat poorly. She may often feel that she is ill prepared to meet the daily stressful events of her job or in her circle of friends. Her acquaintances may describe her as withdrawn or hypersensitive.

2.2 The Potential for New Stressors

2.2.1 Caregiving. There are also new sources of stress for middle-aged and older women. As we age, those around us also age. The older family members who gave care may now need various kinds of care. This care may be economic, physical, or legal. Although most elders can and wish to live independently, elders may need periodic assistance with certain tasks, such as heavy cleaning or important decisions, or during periods of illness. Other elders need consistent assistance due to worsening physical or mental conditions. According to the National Alliance for Caregiving/AARP (1997), 72% of persons who provide care are female, a finding similar to that for young adult women (see Kendall-Tackett, this volume, chapter 2). The average weekly care contribution is 22 hours per woman (National Alliance of Caregivers, 1998). These caregivers are likely to be related to the elder, typically as wives or daughters. Many of these caregivers regard the provision of assistance as necessary, and some report benefits, such as increased closeness arising from the relationship (Kramer, 1997). Many factors can impact the experience of caregiving, such as the diagnostic category of the individual needing care (Russo, Vitaliano, Brewer, Katon, & Becker, 1995) or the availability of a variety of resources (Robinson & Kaye, 1994). However, being a caregiver to an adult is generally regarded as stressful. A meta-analysis of 84 studies showed that there is a significant difference between caregivers and noncaregivers in perceived stress, depression, self-efficacy, and subjective well-being, with caregivers faring worse in each category (Pinquart & Sorensen, 2003).

In addition to the stress of the moment, caregiving may result in long-term negative effects. In another study, 1,200 caregivers were surveyed. Thirty-one percent of these caregivers had altered their own career path, in ways ranging from turning down promotions to quitting, in order to accommodate the demands of the care situation. The ratio of female to male caregivers was more than two to one. This means that caregiving women may be sacrificing long-term earning potential (National Alliance for Caregiving/AARP, 1997).

Being the recipient of assistance is not without stress. Smith and Goodnow (1999) examined adults' reactions to the receipt of unasked-for support. Older adults reported that the intrusive assistance was more unpleasant than pleasant. The helper and the helpee can increase their own and each other's stress if they do not communicate on an exact definition of needed assistance.

Most caregivers provide the needed care in a competent manner, but not all. According to AARP, the majority of neglect of elders arises from a lack of knowledge (AARP, 1993). Active mistreatment of dependent adults also occurs (see Bergeron, this volume, chapter 7). Pillemer and Finkelhor (1988) estimate that for every one report of elder abuse, 14 others acts of violence or denials of rights are committed that fail to reach public attention. Family members who abuse elders in their care can change their behaviors as a result of treatment and use of supportive services, though in some instances, the tasks of caregiving are too difficult for the provider (Steinmetz, 1993). Family members may determine that unrelated others must care for the elder. Assuming that a suitable care facility can be found, and assuming that the bills can be paid, the elder is moved to a skilled nursing or an assisted-living facility. Perhaps there is no available bed in the only skilled nursing facility in the area, or the price of the care exceeds family resources. The overly stressed caregiver may see "dumping" as the only alternative. The family member abandons the elder; emergency rooms of hospitals are popular sites for dumping confused elders (Lund, 1993).

Consider a middle-aged woman who volunteered to care for her elderly mother. The caregiver has had a loving relationship with her mother and feels much appreciated in her new role. She also receives assistance from her spouse, siblings, and some paid professionals. Although this caregiver might indicate that her responsibilities cause her minimal distress on a daily basis, the situation is not without stress. The middle-aged woman realizes that her present role as a caregiver is very different from her experiences as a mom, although both situations involved preparing favorite foods, monitoring health situations, and seeking suitable entertainments. Her children left home for bright futures. Her mother may leave her care only in death. The middle-aged woman had only two children, but her mother, mother-in-law, father-in-law, and husband may all need care. She raised her children when she was at her physical peak, but she may care for elderly family members as she develops physical limitations. Finally, she may begin to ask the question: "Who will care for me?"

2.2.2 Loss of Loved Ones. No matter how loving is the assistance given to elderly parents, aging spouses, and lifelong friends, care is not cure. Ultimately, friends and family die. The death, whether after a long illness or due to a sudden accident, is a trauma. Various stressors are set in motion by the loss of a loved one. The survivor is faced with the loss of a companion. This means both behavioral and emotional changes. The deceased may be a casual friend who shared a taste for foreign films or may be a college buddy who had shared all of adulthood's adventures. A greater feeling of loss would generally occur with the death of a long-term close friend than with the death of a work colleague known for a short time.

The death of a family member can also mean changes in one's identity. Can one still be a sister when the sibling has died? There is no label for a person who has experienced the death of a sister, but we identify women whose husbands have died as "widows." Widowhood is a common status for middle-aged and older women. According to the U.S. Bureau of the Census (1993), approximately 40% of women over the age of 65 and 80% over the age of 85 are unremarried widows. Only 14% of males over the age of 65 are widowers. An older woman who becomes widowed is likely to remain single. As with the death of friends and other family members, the widow has emotional and behavioral losses. These losses may be more painful as the emotional connection to the spouse was longer and deeper, and their behaviors were more intertwined.

The widow experiences additional losses, including loss of resources. The husband may have provided the bulk of the retirement income and insurance coverage; survivor's benefits may be only half the amount of a pension (Smith & Zick, 1996). In addition, the possession of a husband is a social ticket. Friends and family members may leave widows alone. Some social events are for couples only, whereas bereaved people make social companions feel uncomfortable

(Matthews, 1996). Even if a marriage was less than satisfying, some regret is probably felt at the death of the spouse.

Though the pension ceased with the husband's demise, the house, car, and other property will typically pass to the widow. After a death, a funeral or memorial is often held. This ritual identifies the widow as someone in need of assistance. What if the loss of a spouse is due to a divorce? A woman who experiences a divorce in middle or later life, like a widow, loses companionship and behavioral, social, and emotional support. She also suffers economic losses, which may be more severe than those of a widow. Davies and Denton (2002) compared household income and home ownership of Canadians over the age of 65. The participants were either in intact marriages or had divorced or become separated at age 45 or older. The older single females were the poorest. The authors concluded that the economic implications were so significant that differences in gender and marital statuses should be taken into account by the Canadian legal and retirement systems.

The type of household to which one belongs also impacts health. In an examination of the influence of living arrangements upon health status, "healthy" was defined by a positive self-rating, a low number of depressive symptoms, and few limitations on mobility. In late middle age, both men and women were the healthiest if they lived in an intact marriage. There was no effect of the presence or absence of children in the home. Single women living with children had the most disadvantaged health status (Hughes & Waite, 2002).

2.2.3 Role Changes. According to the *Oxford English Dictionary* (1993), the first definition of stress is "Hardship, adversity, affliction." Most adults would probably accept this meaning of the term, but we might find less agreement on the specifics of hardship or affliction. Certain developmental tasks of middle or older age may be perceived or experienced as more or less stressful depending upon the circumstances surrounding the changes. Examples of these ambivalent developmental tasks are retirement, grandparenthood, and selection of a residence.

2.2.3.1 Grandparenting Due to increases in the life span, a significant number of years can be spent in the role of grandparent. Woman can now expect to live to see at least one of their grandchildren reach adulthood, and many women will bear the title "great grandmother" (Szinovacz, 1998). These family titles are significant. Silverstein and Long (1998) studied the relationship between grandparents and grandchildren over more than two decades. When in their 70s and 80s, grandparents were likely to report greater affection for their grandchildren than they had reported in their 60s. This is in spite of the fact that the grandparents reported less contact with the grandchildren as they became young adults. Declines in the health status of the grandparents tended to predict increases in contact with the adult grandchildren. Silverstein and Long (1998) concluded that grandchildren were real sources of support for their grandparents.

Enjoyment of grandparenthood is tempered by certain factors. One of these is the relationship between the grandparents and their children, the parents of the grandchildren. Positive relationships appear to be circular. If both generations of parents and children have good relationships, then grandparents and grandchildren are more likely to have good relationships (King & Elder, 1995, 1997). Grandparents who believe that the relationship can be positive and important are more likely to be active grandparents, spend more time with grandchildren, and rate their relationships higher (King & Elder, 1998). Conversely, a woman who has had a troubled relationship with her daughter and son-in-law may have infrequent or even conflicted contact with her grandchildren. The grandmother may be distressed as she sees undesirable patterns of family interaction passed down to the next generations.

A growing number of grandparents spend massive amounts of time with their grandchildren. The time is spent in significant caretaking activities, and the relationships are warm and important, yet the relationships cause the grandparents significant stress. A growing number of middle-aged and elderly women are also taking on the roles of parents, as ages for bearing and adopting children increase, particularly for second families. Another scenario is when women become the primary caregivers for their grandchildren. A house that has not held young children for many years suddenly may have to be "baby proofed." Women, who had not thought of what time the school day began or ended for a decade, suddenly find their lives ruled by that schedule. These grandparents are completely responsible for the care of grandchildren who must reside with them due to the incapacitation of the parents due to illness, addiction, incarceration, or absence (Hayslip & Goldberg-Glen, 2000). In addition, the grandchildren may have physical, emotional, or cognitive problems due to neglect or abuse that occurred prior to the separation from the parents (Landers, 1992) or due to trauma associated with the death of their parents.

Grandparents who are potentially suffering from age-related declines must give care to children who may be difficult to raise (Minkler & Roe, 1992). Grandparents may be in reduced economic circumstances due to retirement or may be forced to cut back their commitment to the workforce, experiencing a decline in their standard of living, while the grandchildren continue to need new clothes, medical care, a larger residence, and therapeutic interventions. This means that the households headed by grandparents acting as parents can experience severe economic stress (Casper & Bryson, 1998). This arrangement may be more common for women of color (see Banks, Ackerman, Yee, & West, this volume, chapter 10).

2.2.3.2 Retirement A common joke compares the joy one experiences at being hired with the joy one will feel when one can retire. The event of retirement occurs when someone cleans out their workplace cubicle or receives a gold watch. There is also a process of retirement that involves the change and adjustment in lifestyle and attitudes that a person engages in upon leaving the paid workforce. Many workers might indicate that the changes in attitudes and behaviors are what they are looking forward to most about retirement. Perhaps they intend to put down their competitive persona and pick up neglected relationships and pastimes. In spite of the anticipation (or perhaps because of it), either the event or the process of retirement may be stressful.

What if one's plans for retirement are untenable? The estimate of the income needed to retire did not take into account the decline in the stock market or the size of inflation. Quilting was entirely enjoyable when it was a monthly treat, but it becomes a burden as a daily event. (In addition, are those fabric squares getting smaller? They have to be held at arm's length to be seen.) Mornings spent playing tennis do not materialize, as one's tennis buddies experience significant health problems or move out of state to be near grandchildren. What if retirement was not a planned event? Retirement was expected to occur at 65, but your employer moved the company to Mexico when you were 57. After 3 years of searching for a similar bookkeeping job, you regretfully concluded that you were retired.

What if the planning to exit the world of work occurs not because one wants to retire, but because one needs to retire? Are people who perceive that their health is not good enough to allow them to continue to work stressed by retirement? For women, a significant predictor of retirement is the health of a spouse. Wives who need to care for their husbands are five times more likely to retire than women without this responsibility (Dentinger & Clarkberg, 2002).

Findings such as these suggest that retirement satisfaction cannot be considered as a personal process only, but should also be considered in its social context. This was the conclusion reached by Kim and Moen (2001) when they attempted to answer the question "Is retirement good or bad for subjective well-being?" They noted that researchers had found both subjective distress and well-being in groups of retired persons. Resolution of this tangle may lie in looking separately at the impact of retirement upon males and females and then looking again at retirement as a process experienced by a couple. This was the strategy employed in an investigation of marital satisfaction and retirement. Intact couples were interviewed on a variety of topics, including work, retirement, and marriage. Retirement as an event predicted a decline in marital quality for both spouses. Retirement as a process appeared to promote marital quality, as persons retired more than 24 months showed an improvement in marital quality. Retirement is a process that appears to proceed more smoothly if it is shared. Couples in which one member was retired and one was still active in a career reported the greatest marital conflict (Moen, Kim, & Hofmeister, 2001).

2.2.4 Friendships. There are two ways to experience loneliness. The first is to have limited access to social contacts. The second is due to the absence of important social contacts. In a study of mostly widowed women living in a retirement community, women who were the least depressed had support coming from friends who lived someplace else. This was true even after controlling for the social support available within the retirement community (Potts, 1997). All friends are not created equal. Old friends (friends from past life stages) appeared to be most important. Why? Is it stressful to try to make new friends, or are there some specific benefits to old friends?

From research, we know a great deal about friendships in children and adolescents. However, we know relatively little about friendships in adulthood (Hartup & Stevens, 1997). We know that friends are important to adults, as those who have friends deal with significant situations of stress, such as widowhood, better than those who do not (Dykstra, 1995). There is a cost to relationships with friends, as it is assumed that friendship is equal and reciprocal (Clark, Patarki, & Carver, 1996). If Mary tended to Sally during Sally's recovery from hip replacement surgery, providing companionship and preparing meals and chauffeur service, what will Mary expect during her divorce? Late adulthood may be a time when people are less able to reciprocate but are more in need or are more often in need (Ingersoll-Dayton & Antonucci, 1988). Social support may predict survival, but findings of recent research suggest that the survivors are more likely to be the helpers than the helpees. Even when controlling for variables such as income, alcohol use, mental and physical health, and exercise, persons giving care were almost half as likely to die as were those who were receiving the support. The type of care given did not matter; one could provide a sympathetic ear or help with errands (Brown, Nesse, Vinokur, & Smith, 2003).

Perhaps women live longer because of the support they provide. "Tend and befriend" is the title given to women's stress responses based on the findings of a study of friendship among women (Taylor et al., 2000). Taylor and her colleagues hypothesized that the hormone oxytocin is released when women engage in nurturing activities. Oxytocin is correlated with a feeling of calm and a decline in the perceived stress level. Lee (2003) agreed that women live longer due to the nurturing role and believes that this has evolutionary significance. A comparison of data available from 18th century Sweden and present-day Paraguay supports Lee's hypothesis that natural selection favors longer life spans for those who have important nurturing roles, like grandmothers.

2.2.5 End-of-Life Issues. Adults know that they are not immortal. The issue of dying becomes less abstract and more personal as one moves through life. Middle-aged and older women have observed death from a close perspective. Initially, death might have seemed like something for very elderly grandparents, but then parents also pass away, and now one is attending the funeral of contemporaries. Death anxiety may develop and display itself in many ways. Like any anxiety, death anxiety can change behavior. Some women may deal with it by distancing themselves from death and the process of dying. They may avoid funerals and only speak of death in euphemisms ("taken by the Grim Reaper") (Kastenbaum, 1999). What is it that people fear about death? People fear pain, disfigurement, and loss of bodily control. They also fear the impact on those they will leave behind and their loss of self. Some death anxiety is conscious, and some is unconscious (Fortner & Neimeyer, 1999).

Death anxiety may be vague when we grapple with the belief that we will die of something. What happens when this something becomes a real thing? What happens when a woman is told that she is in the process of dying, from a real disease, in real time? There is a great deal of variation in the experience of dying, contributed by personality, religious beliefs, and types of terminal illness. Kalish (1985) pointed out that there are unique circumstances to dying while old. When presented with this scenario, many older people wish to use the time and control they still have. There may be things that have been left undone, such as writing a will or making peace with a friend or family member.

There are also new decisions to make. The dying individual can be an active participant in making choices about their health care and about rites after death (Kastenbaum, 1999). These types of decisions, collectively called "end-of-life issues," are difficult for the maker and those who assist. This is particularly true in a society such as our own, where death is considered a distasteful subject for discussion. One common anxiety for dying adults is the fear that they will die unattended; they generally wish to die in the presence of family and friends. This wish is least likely to be granted for elderly persons, and the old are most likely to die in isolation (Kastenbaum, 1999).

As the elderly are most likely to die from chronic diseases, such as heart conditions, they have the longest time to be aware of their own trajectory of dying (National Center for Health Statistics, 1999). The dying, elderly woman is aware that although her death will bring sadness to her small circle of survivors, the larger society does not place much value on her passing. The death of a teenager or a young adult is labeled as a tragedy, while the death of an elder is thought of as timely, natural, expected, or even a blessing (Kastenbaum, 1985).

3 VARIATION IN THE AGING EXPERIENCE

It is not an academic exercise to predict the level of stress and trauma a particular elderly female is experiencing. The prediction generally precedes an attempt to suggest remediation or methods of coping. For the suggestion to be appropriate, the prediction must be accurate. It is not enough to know that the older female client has just experienced a traumatic event, such as job loss. The reaction to the loss, and her ability to recover depend on a variety of factors. In order to gain accuracy, more information about variations in the experience of aging is necessary. These variations include sociocultural and biological influences.

3.1 Sociocultural Influences

3.1.1 Lesbian Women. Gabbay and Wahler (2002) reviewed the available literature on lesbian gerontology. There were only 68 articles, including research, personal narratives, and essays on theoretical or professional topics, such as consciousness raising. The main focus of the research was relationships issues. The authors concluded that aging lesbians have been strongly impacted by societal attitudes and have developed unique coping strategies. Additional research is needed and will continue to be needed as the roles of women, lesbian women, and aging women continue to change.

3.1.2 Women of Color. The literature on the impact of culture also needs to grow. A perusal of the available material on ethnic aging demonstrates that what appear to be simple questions do not have simple answers. Elder abuse, for example, would seem to have a universal definition. Moon and Williams (1993) presented scenarios of family life with elders to older women and asked if the described actions constituted abuse. Korean Americans used different standards from those employed by African American or European Americans. Korean Americans identified fewer instances of abuse and would seek help less often than the other sets of respondents. If this difference in definitions is acted upon, elderly Korean American females might be more likely to have experienced harmful events that have not been reported.

A mental health professional might hope that past painful or harmful events would be reported within the caregiving environment. This may be an unrealized hope when interacting with elderly women of color. Family violence may not be reported for fear of losing face, but other types of violence go unreported also. Only 3% of Latin American immigrants who had experienced political violence reported the experience to a clinician. This low incidence of reporting is particularly shocking, as 54% of the traumatized immigrants had symptoms of depression or posttraumatic stress disorder (Eisenman, Gelberg, Liu, & Shapiro, 2003).

Older Latinos may not report important information to care providers, as they have had little experience with health professionals. Almost one third of Latinos report no regular source of health care. Latinas are less likely to receive preventative care such as mammograms and screens for cervical diseases or colon cancer. This means that they are more likely to begin receiving care for diseases, such as cervical cancer, at later stages in the disease (O'Brien et al., 2003).

Some of the gap between a need for care and the receipt of care may be related to economic factors, which include both an inability to pay for care and a lack of access to health insurance. This would be true for most adults who live in poverty. Other factors may be generally true for ethnic minority elders; a lessened proficiency in English will make it difficult to find health care and communicate with many health care providers, whether the original language was Spanish or Mandarin.

Some factors may be true only for specific cultural groups. For example, Latinos may have behaviors and attitudes that predispose them to certain health risks. Sedentary lifestyles and high-fat diets may account for some of the higher incidences of stomach, liver, and gall bladder cancers seen in Latino populations. Recent immigrants from developing nations may have had greater exposure to *Helicobacter pylori*, a bacterium associated with stomach ulcers, which may also have a role in stomach cancer. Finally, the philosophy of fatalism about illness may make Latinos less likely to pursue treatments. An elderly Latina who receives a diagnosis of breast cancer may respond "I'm going to die anyway, why do anything?" (O'Brien et al., 2003).

It is also possible that women of color learn that there is little available care for them. African American women are twice as likely to have heart disease, suffer heart attacks at twice the rate of white women, and are twice as likely to die from heart disease. Some of this disparity in mortality can be attributed to the greater incidence of risk factors, such as high blood pressure and high cholesterol in African American men and women. A recent 4-year nationwide study showed that black women were less likely to receive the standard treatment. Statins (cholesterol-lowering drugs) were 27% less likely to be prescribed for African American women, even in the presence of greater risk factors (Jha et al., 2003).

Do elders in general face a decrease in the probability that appropriate treatments will be delivered? The National Institute of Mental Health convened a 39-person panel to review a decade worth of policy, activity, and research on mood disorders in later life; the panel published its findings in 2003 (Chainey et al., 2003). The panel was composed of experts in mental health, geriatrics, and primary care. Members of the panel concluded that there is a significant gap between the availability of effective treatments for late-life mood disorders and the delivery of these services. The cost of meeting the health care needs of the elderly will be significant, but the present economic and psychic cost of the unmet need is staggering. Elderly women with untreated depression or bipolar disorder suffer from preventable functional and intellectual decline and disability. Their quality of life suffers, as does that of their partners and caregivers. Suicide or death from comorbid conditions can be the ultimate result. What prevents the diagnosis and treatment of mood disorders in the elderly, particularly minority elderly? Factors that affected the probability of receiving appropriate physical care are again important. Significant problems include lack of insurance or lack of mental-health coverage in the available insurance. Elders often lack access to care, and the services that are available are often poorly coordinated (Charney et al., 2003).

3.2 Biological Influences

Reactions to stressful events vary. We can explain some of these differences by examining the social and cultural influences described above. But, this is only half of the story. A panel of physicians and psychologists (Kosslyn et al., 2002) argued that joining psychological findings with biological information would have a dramatic effect on treatment options. Clinical options could be tailor-made for clients. Prevention programs could also be built around an awareness of gene-characteristic links suggesting who might be more likely to be vulnerable to outcome x in environment y.

Interesting research of this type is underway. Results of a recent prospective longitudinal study may suggest an explanation as to why some individuals respond to stressful events with depression, and others do not. Researchers identified two forms of the gene 5-HTT, which assists in the regulation of the neurotransmitter serotonin. People who possessed one or two copies of the short form of this gene were more likely to display depressive symptoms, such as lethargy or feelings of personal worthlessness, diagnosable depression, or thoughts of suicide after experiencing traumatic events such as death in the family or loss of a job. The researchers hypothesized that the short form of the gene is not associated with less serotonin, but in less-effective regulation of the neurotransmitter (Caspi et al., 2003). As traumatic events, such as loss of loved ones, job loss, and changes in one's own health status, may occur more frequently later in life, this discovery may become an important predictor of elders' adaptation to stressful life events.

Important discoveries have already been made about the linkages between genes and characteristics. Zubieta and colleagues (2002) engaged in a series of studies to examine the biological underpinnings of pain perception. In one study (Zubieta et al., 2003), they found that more stoic responses to painful situations were predicted by the possession of two copies of the val-COMT gene. This gene regulates the production of dopamine, a chemical that serves as a messenger between brain cells. Brain scans confirmed that the varying perceptions of participants were not learned responses. Endorphins, which minimize pain, were more active in the brains of participants with two copies of val-COMT.

Zubieta and colleagues (Zubieta et al., 2002) also observed that males and females demonstrated different pain responses in both clinical and experimental settings. One important predictor of a woman's response to painful stimuli is where she is in her menstrual cycle. Pain is generally tolerated better when estrogen is at its highest level. This is relevant to middle-aged and older women, because estrogen levels permanently drop during this phase of life unless women take hormone replacement therapy.

Findings such as these may one day allow physicians to customize pain treatments, not just to fit the cause of the pain, but also to fit the patient. More questions must be answered first. Important among these is the action of age. All of Zubieta's research, thus far, has been conducted on healthy young adults. How does pain perception change with age? How is pain tolerated if strategies that were useful in controlling youthful aches are no longer effective? If pain is best tolerated when the estrogen level is high, what happens to menopausal women?

4 SOME RELIEF FROM DISTRESS

Television talk show hosts, newspaper columnists, and neighbors will tell you that stress can be relieved by long walks, herbal teas, and bubble baths. Any of these might soothe the negative emotions created by the receipt of a parking ticket or a jam in the office copy machine. More significant and durable stressors, such as a fixed income or chronic illness, require more potent relief. The most appropriate remediation would be the elimination of the stressor. Older women may find it difficult or impossible to obtain and keep a job. Medical science has not identified cures for chronic illnesses often found in elders, such as arteriosclerosis or osteoporosis. Providing chemical and behavioral assistance is possible but is not available to all women.

When the source of the stress cannot be removed, the next option is dealing with the stress. A health care professional may make suggestions that sound like those provided by friends: consistent exercise and a balanced diet. Additional alternatives might include biofeedback, anti-anxiety medication, or short-term counseling. In most instances, the focus of treatment is on the body's reaction to the demands placed upon it. People under stress may report feeling fatigue, headaches, stomachaches, or other physical symptoms. They probably do not report feeling a rise in stress hormones, but consistently elevated stress hormones or blood pressure may cause damage over a lifetime of dealing with stress. Bodily changes from long-term stress, such as from a negative family situation or repeated periods of unemployment, may account for the rise in colitis, ulcers, and heart attacks in the later years (Sapolsky, 1992). To determine if an intervention is effective, the health care provider may simply ask "Are you feeling better?" Other times, measurements of blood pressure or cardiac functioning may be taken.

Different remediations will work for different women. An underexplored possibility is the potential contribution of religion or spirituality. The small existing body of research on the role of religious or spiritual practices on health suggests that there are benefits. Seeman, Dubin, and Seeman (2003) critically evaluated the literature on Judeo-Christian and meditation practices, and concluded that well-done studies have found links between these practices and positive health outcomes in the areas of cardiovascular, neuroendocrine, and immune system functions. More research needs to be done, but religious or spiritual practices may have benefits not available in other stress treatments. There is a wide array of possible religious or spiritual practices. Church attendance can occur in the presence of family and friends but may also offer access to new support systems. Whereas health care providers seldom offer transportation or coffee hours, church groups often do.

Successful remediation of stressful feelings may also depend upon the type of stress. Consider death anxiety. Some death anxiety may be appropriate. According to terror-management theory (Pyszcynski, Greenberg, & Solomon, 1999), a fear of dying may ensure that we do the kinds of things that will keep us alive. What if death anxiety is impacting living? A woman would like to offer assistance to a terminally ill friend but cannot bring herself to visit or call the hospital. "Death education" is a multifaceted way of decreasing death anxiety. Information from topics such as medicine, psychology, and philosophy are combined to increase awareness of factual issues in the process of dying as well as sensitivity to the feelings of dying persons and their families. The death anxiety of middle-aged and older adults has been shown to decline after participation in experiential death-education workshops (Abengozar, Bueno, & Vega, 1999).

5 COPING IN LATER LIFE

Given a choice, most women would be unlikely to select "dying young" as a viable option in life. This does not mean that women move through middle and advanced age without experiencing trauma and stress. Some developmental tasks of the later years, such as death of loved ones, or diagnosis of one's own terminal illness, bring pain to all who experience the event. Other developmental tasks, such as retirement, more typically provide a mix of stress and happiness. The presence of these age-specific tasks does not mean that events of earlier times are completed and left behind. Women's coping skills are carried forward, as are their impairments. The stress and trauma of a woman's middle and later years are the result of past and present events, attitudes, and behaviors. A young woman meets challenges, such as job loss and family separation, with greater physical stamina than an elderly woman. The young woman may also have a larger social network upon which to call. The older woman can call upon a larger repertoire of experiences but may be hampered by feelings of regret for failing to meet earlier challenges. The older woman knows that she has less time in which to meet the challenge, but that resolution may occur even in the last moments of life.

Women can prepare themselves to meet some of the typical age-related stressors. They can heed contemporary health guidelines and eat well, exercise, and avoid cigarettes and overindulgence in alcohol. They can seek professional assistance in order to engage in preventive behaviors, such as pap smears and mammograms. They can weigh the advice of practitioners on how to deal with chronic conditions, such as diabetes and hypertension. Women can attempt to maintain positive social and familial relationships, seek out cognitive stimulation, and practice good coping skills. They can avoid or terminate potentially harmful situations, such as being passengers in cars driven by drunken drivers. They can utilize professional resources to protect themselves from some dangers, such as abusive spouses. Women can familiarize themselves with resources to assist in dealing with trauma, such as a diagnosis of breast cancer or increasing dementia in an elderly parent. All of this self-care can occur if social, educational, legal, and medical systems for middle-aged and elderly women are intact and functioning. What happens to women when the safeguards fail, were never in place, or are yet unknown?

5.1 Call for Future Research

It is clear that more research is needed on the process of aging, in general, and aging in women, in particular. It is also clear that these investigations cannot be left as academic exercises. Theory and research must be turned into practical applications. For this to be possible, there must be more resources for services to older women. Ageism and sexism have been powerful roadblocks to the development of the types of agencies, activities, and models of delivery that would maximize the experiences of women in their middle and later years. A decrease in the stress and trauma associated with typical aging events, such as retirement, widowhood, and physical changes, is a just societal goal and an economical goal. It will allow women to provide many more years of valuable services as workers, nurturers, and creative thinkers.

5.2 Women of the Future

This is not a task that can be accomplished once. Research will have to be done and redone. Services will have to be invented and reinvented. Why? Age is a moving target; the term "old woman" is partly defined by the roles women occupy. What will happen to the experience of aging when the seniors of the class of 2004 become the senior citizens of 2052? The young woman of 2004 grew up with the Internet. She played soccer and basketball all through elementary school and was disappointed that she was not good enough for her college varsity basketball team. She was an energetic coach for her children's soccer teams. Thirty years of wear and tear on her knees has caused breakdown in the cartilage.

At age 65, she believes that she is a candidate for knee replacement, having conducted an extensive Web search for information on such surgeries. She has been frustrated in her attempts to enlist her primary care physician's assistance in obtaining a referral for surgery. The 11.5-minute appointment mandated by Medicare leaves time only for a review of basic health information. She cannot afford to pay for the surgery on her own. Her undergraduate degree was in the Management of Information Sciences. She has been steadily employed during her adult life, in a series of interesting positions. However, she had typically been hired as a consultant, so she is not vested in a pension system. She continues to work, mostly telecommuting, which is easy on her knees. She can also choose her work hours, so she can attend the soccer games of her grandchildren and their half- and stepsibs.

She married and divorced twice before her 45th birthday. She received child support from both of her children's fathers but never received spousal support, as she had earned as much, or more, than her spouses. She is not entitled to a portion of her first husband's pension due to the provisions of the divorce settlement. She is glad that she will not have to care for an elderly, ailing husband or in-laws, as her mother did. She spends an hour or so each day on e-mail to family members and in chat rooms with new and old friends, thanks to a large monitor and a super-sized keyboard. She sometimes wishes that there was more direct human contact in her life. She has always availed herself of the plentiful information on how to slow the aging process, but she periodically worries about her 90s. Will she become immobile, demented, or a potential burden to her children? Senior care facilities exist in good number, but the full-service ones are pricey. She really should not have invested the majority of her 401K in that biotech firm. The original animal trials of the experimental fat melting drug had been so promising. But once again, all that the drug produced were very healthy rodents!

If a 65-year-old woman of 2004 and the older woman of 2052 could sit down together, would they feel that they had experienced aging as the same process? Would the woman of 2052 feel that she had greater control over her education, her economics, and her destiny? Would this have diminished the potential for stress and trauma during her middle and later years? Will the woman of the future experience a similar level of death anxiety as a woman in the present? Will the death of a senior citizen ever come to be regarded as great of a loss as that of a young adult?

5.3 Back to the Beginning

Many different older women will read Jim Wilson's new book, *Gardening Through Your Golden Years*. Some will say, "This shows me how I can return to gardening, but I wonder if it will be worth it? Will I have to do things differently, and will I end up with fewer flowers?" Other women will marvel, "Gardening! Who would have thought of it at my age!" While others will scoff "Gardening? Why would I *want* to try it at my age?" Finally, there could be those who say, "Who has time to stop gardening to read the book?" It is to be expected that there will be a tremendous amount of variation in women's experiences of their middle and later years, as there was in their earlier years. It is hoped that at all points on the age continuum, women can be assisted to overcome stress and trauma. It is also to be wished that all women of all ages have a full range of opportunities open to them. It is not necessary that all women take up gardening in their sixth or seventh decade. But it is necessary that they realize that they can find new joys or return to old ones.

REFERENCES

Abengozar, M. C., Bueno, B., & Vega, J. L. (1999). Intervention on attitudes toward death along the life span. *Educational Gerontology, 25*, 435–447.

American Association of Retired Persons (AARP). (1993). *Abused elders or battered women?* Washington, DC: Author.

American Association of Retired Persons (AARP). (1994). *A profile of older Americans*. Washington, DC: Author.

Brown, S. L. Nesse, R. M., Vinokur, A. D., & Smith, D. M. (2003). Providing social support may be more beneficial than receiving it: Results from a prospective study of mortality. *Psychological Science, 14(4)*, 320–327.

Casper, L. M., & Bryson, K. R. (1998). *Co-resident grandparents and their grandchildren: Grandparent maintained families* (Working paper No. 26). Washington, DC: Population Division, U.S. Bureau of the Census.

Caspi, A., Sugden, K., Moffitt, T. E., Taylor, A., Craig, I. W., Harrington, H., McClay, J., Mill, J., Martin, J., Braithwaite, A., & Poulton, R. (2003). Influences of life stress on depression: Moderation by a polymorphism in the 5-HTT gene. *Science, 301*, 386–389.

Charney, D. S., Reynolds, C. F., Lewis, L., Lebowitz, B. D., Sunderland, T. et al. (2003). Depression and bipolar support alliance consensus statement on the unmet needs in diagnosis and treatment of mood disorders in late life. *Archives of General Psychiatry, 60*, 664–672.

Clark, M. S., Patarki, S. P., & Carver, V. H. (1996). Some thoughts and findings on self-presentation of emotions in relationships. In G. J. O. Fletcher & J. Fitness (Eds.), *Knowledge structures in close relationships: A social psychological approach* (pp. 247–274). Mahwah, NJ: Erlbaum.

Davies, S., & Denton, M. (2002). The economic well-being of older women who become divorced or separated in mid- or later life. *Canadian Journal on Aging, 21*, 477–493.

Dentinger, E., & Clarkberg, M. (2002). Informal caregiving and retirement timing among men and women: Gender and caregiving relationships in late midlife. *Journal of Family Issues, 23*, 857–879.

Dykstra, P. A. (1995). Loneliness among the never and formerly married: The importance of supportive friendships and desire for independence. *Journal of Gerontology: Social Sciences, 50*, S321–S329.

Eisenman, D. P., Gelberg, L., Liu, H., & Shapiro, M. F. (2003). Mental health and health-related quality of life among adult Latino primary care patients living in the United States with previous exposure to political violence. *Journal of the American Medical Association, 290*, 627–634.

Fiatrone, M. A., O'Neill, E. F., & Ryan, N. D. (1994). Exercise training and nutritional supplementation for physical fraility in very elderly people. *New England Journal of Medicine, 330*, 1769–1775.

Fortner, B. V., & Neimeyer, R. A. (1999). Death anxiety in older adults: A quantitative review. *Death Studies, 23*, 387–411.

Gabbay, S. G., & Wahler, J. J. (2002). Lesbian aging: Review of a growing literature. *Journal of Gay and Lesbian Social Services: Issues in Practice, Policy and Research, 14*, 1–21.

Hartup W. W., & Stevens, N. (1997). Friendship and adaptation in the life course. *Psychological Bulletin, 121*, 355–370.

Hayslip, B., & Goldberg-Glen, H. R. G. (2000). *Grandparents raising grandchildren: Theoretical, empirical and clinical perspectives*. New York: Spring Publishing Co.

Hughes, M. E., & Waite, L. J. (2002). Health in the household context: Living arrangements and health in late middle age. *Journal of Health and Social Behavior, 43*, 1–21.

Ingersoll-Dayton, B., & Antonucci, T. C. (1988). Reciprocal and non-reciprocal social support: Contrasting sides of intimate relationships. *Journal of Gerontology: Social Sciences, 43*, S65–S73.

Jha, A. K., Varosy, P. D., Kanaya, A. M., Hunninghake, D. B., Hlatky, M. A., Waters, D. D., Furberg, C. D., & Shlipak, M. G. (2003). Differences in medical care and disease outcomes among black and white women with heart disease. *Circulation, 25*, 1089–1094.

Kalish, R. A. (1985). *Death, grief and caring relationships* (2nd ed.). Pacific Grove, CA: Brooks/Cole.

Kastenbaum, R. (1985). Dying and death: A lifespan approach. In J. E. Birren & K. W. Schaie (Eds.), *Handbook of the psychology of aging* (2nd ed.). New York: Van Nostrand Reinhold.

Kastenbaum, R. (1999). Dying and bereavement. In J. C. Cavanaugh & S. K. Whitbourne (Eds.), *Gerontology: An interdisciplinary perspective* (pp. 155–185). New York: Oxford University Press.

Kendall-Tackett, K. A. (2000). Physiological correlates of childhood abuse: Chronic hyper-arousal in PTSD, depression, and irritable bowel syndrome. *Child Abuse and Neglect, 6,* 799–810.

Kim, J., & Moen, P. (2001). Is retirement good or bad for subjective well being? *Current Directions in Psychological Science, 10,* 83–86.

King, V., & Elder, G. H. Jr. (1995). American grandchildren view their grandparents: Linked lives across three rural generations. *Journal of Marriage and the Family, 57,* 165–178.

King, V., & Elder, G. H. Jr. (1997). The legacy of grandparenting: Childhood experiences with grandparents and current involvement with grandchildren. *Journal of Marriage and the Family, 59,* 848–859.

King, V., & Elder, G. H. Jr. (1998). Perceived self-efficacy and grandparenting. *Journal of Gerontology: Social Sciences, 53,* S249–S257.

Kite, M. E., & Johnson, B. T. (1988). Attitudes toward older and younger adults: A meta-analysis. *Psychology and Aging, 3,* 232–244.

Kosslyn, S. M., Cacioppo, J. T., Davidson, R. J., Hugdahl, K., Lovallo, W. R., Spiegel, D., & Rose, R. (2002). Bridging psychology and biology: The analysis of individuals in groups. *American Psychologist, 57,* 341–351.

Kramer, B. J. (1997). Gain in the caregiving experience: Where are we? What next? *Gerontologist, 37,* 218–232.

Landers, S. (1992, March 5). "Second time around families" find aid. *National Association of Social Workers* (p. 5). News.

Lee, R. D. (2003). Rethinking the evolutionary theory of aging: Transfers, not birth, shape senescence in social species. *Proceedings of the National Academy of Sciences, 100,* 9637–9642.

Lenz, E. (1993, August/September). Mirror, mirror .... One woman's reflection on her changing image. *Modern Maturity, 24,* 26–28, 80.

Lund, D. A. (1993). Caregiving. In R. Kastenbaum (Ed.), *Encyclopedia of adult development.* Phoenix, AZ: Oryx.

Matthews, S. H. (1996). Friendships in old age. In N. Vanzsetti & S. Duck (Eds.), *A lifetime of relationships.* (pp. 406–430). Pacific Grove, CA: Brooks/Cole.

Minkler, M., & Roe, K. (1992). *Forgotten caregivers: Grandmothers raising children of the crack cocaine epidemic.* Newbury Park, CA: Sage.

Moen, P. (2001). The gendered life course. In R. H. Binstock (Ed.), *Handbook of aging and social science* (pp. 179–196). San Diego, CA: Academic Press.

Moen, P., Kim, J., & Hofmeister, H. (2001). Couples' work/retirement transitions: Gender and marital quality. *Social Psychology Quarterly, 64,* 57–71.

Moon, A., & Williams, O. (1993). Perceptions of elder abuse and help-seeking patterns among African-American, Caucasian American and Korean-American elderly women. *The Gerontologist, 33,* 386–395.

National Alliance for Caregiving/AARP. (1997). Family caregiving in the U.S.: Findings from a national survey. Washington, DC: Author. Retrieved from http://www.caregiving.org/Finalreport.pdf

National Alliance for Caregiving/National Center on Women and Aging. (1999). The MetLife juggling act study: Balancing caregiving with work and the costs involved. Washington, DC: Author. Retrieved from http://www.caregiving.org/JugglingStudy.pdf

National Center for Health Statistics. (1999). *Deaths: Final data for 1997, 47,* 19.

O'Brien, K., Cokkindes, V., Jemal, A., Cardinez, C. J., Murray, T., Samuels, A., Ward, E., & Thun, M. J. (2003). Cancer statistics for Hispanics, 2003. *CA: A Cancer Journal for Clinicians, 53,* 208–226.

Older Americans. (2000). *Key indicators of well-being. A report by the Federal Interagency Forum on Age Related Statistics.* Washington, DC: Data Dissemination Branch of the National Center on Health Statistics.

Oxford English Dictionary. (1993). Oxford: Oxford University Press.

Papalia, D. E., Sterns, H. L., Feldman, R. D., & Camp, C. J. (2002). *Adult development and aging* (2nd ed., p. 15). Boston, MA: McGraw-Hill.

Pillemer, K., & Finkelhor, D. (1988). The prevalence of elder abuse: A random sample survey. *Gerontologist, 28,* 51–57.

Pinquart, M., & Sorensen, S. (2003). Differences between caregivers and noncaregivers in psychological health and physical health: A meta-analysis. *Psychology and Aging, 18,* 250–267.

Potts, M. K. (1997). Social support and depression among older adults living alone: The importance of friends within and outside of a retirement community. *Social Work, 42,* 348–363.

Pyszcynski, T., Greenberg, J., & Solomon, S. (1999). A dual-process model of defense against conscious and unconscious death-related thoughts: An extension of terror management theory. *Psychological Review, 106,* 835–845.

Rakowski, W., & Mor, V. (1992). The association of physical activity with morality among older adults in the Longitudinal Study of Aging. *Journal of Gerontology: Medical Sciences, 47,* M122–M129.

Robinson, K. M., & Kaye, J. (1994). The relationship between spiritual perspective, social support, and depression in caregiving and noncaregiving wives. *Scholarly Inquiry for Nursing Practice, 8,* 375–389.

Russo, J., Vitaliano, P. P., Brewer, D. D., Katon, W., & Becker, J. (1995). Psychiatric disorders in spouse caregivers of care recipients with Alzheimer's disease and matched controls: A diathesis-stress model of psychopathology. *Journal of Abnormal Psychology, 104,* 197–204.

Sapolsky, R. M. (1992). Stress and neuroendocrine changes during aging. *Generations, 16,* 35–38.

Schieber, F., & Baldwin, C. L. (1996). Vision, audition and aging research. In F. Blanchard-Fields & T. M. Hess (Eds.), *Perspectives on cognitive change in adulthood and aging* (pp. 122–162). New York: McGraw-Hill.

Seeman, T. E., Dubin, L. F., & Seeman, M. (2003). Religiosity/spirituality and health: A critical review of the evidence for biological pathways. *American Psychologist, 58,* 53–63.

Silverstein, M., & Long, J. (1998). Trajectories of grandparents' perceived solidarity with adult grandchildren: A growth curve analysis over 23 years. *Journal of Marriage and the Family, 60,* 912–923.

Smith, J., & Baltes, M. M. (1998). The role of gender in very old age: Profiles of functioning and everyday life patterns. *Psychology and Aging, 13,* 676–695.

Smith, J., & Goodnow, J. J. (1999). Unasked for support and unsolicited advice: Age and the quality of social experience. *Psychology and Aging, 14,* 108–121.

Smith, K. B., & Zick, C. D. (1996). Risk of mortality following widowhood: Age and sex differences by mode of death. *Social Biology, 43,* 59–71.

Steinmetz, S. K. (1993). The abused elderly are dependent. In R. J. Gelles & D. R. Loseke (Eds.), *Current controversies on family violence* (pp. 222–236). Newbury Park, CA: Sage.

Sterns, H. L., & Camp, C. J. (1998). Applied gerontology. *Applied Psychology: An International Review, 47,* 175–198.

Szinovacz, M. E. (1998). Grandparents today: A demographic profile. *The Gerontologist, 38,* 37–52.

Taylor, S. E., Klein, L. C., Lewis, B. P., Gruenewald, T. L., Gurung, A. R., & Updegraff, J. A. (2000). Female responses to stress: Tend and befriend, not fight or flight. *Psychological Review, 107,* 421–429.

U.S. Bureau of the Census. (1993). *Marital status and living arrangements* (Current Population Reports). Washington, DC: U.S. Government Printing Office.

U.S. Bureau of the Census. (1995). *Sixty-five plus in the United States.* Washington, DC: U.S. Government Printing Office.

Wilson, J. W. III. (2003). *Gardening through your golden years.* North Franklin, TN: Cool Springs Press.

Zubieta, J. K., Heitzeg, M. M., Smith, Y. R., Xu, K., Xu, Y., Koeppe, R. A., Stohler, C. S., & Goldman, D. (2003). COMT val158met genotype affects μ-opioid neurotransmitter responses to a pain stressor. *Science, 299,* 1240–1243.

Zubieta, J. K., Smith, Y. R., Bueller, J. A., Xu, Y., Kilbourn, M. R., Jewett, D. M., Meyer, C. R., Koeppe, R. A., & Stohler, C. S. (2002). μ-Opioid receptor-mediated antinociceptive responses differ in men and women. *Journal of Neuroscience, 22,* 5100–5107.

Section II

THE SPECTER OF VIOLENCE AGAINST WOMEN

5

Sexual Violence in the Lives of Girls and Women

KATHLEEN C. BASILE

1 OVERVIEW AND DEFINITION OF THE PROBLEM

Sexual violence is a serious social and public health problem in the United States. Evidence from decades of research has shown that women are at risk for sexual violence throughout their life span. While sexual violence is commonly conceived of as rape, defined as completed or attempted penetration of some sort, sexual violence is much broader and more encompassing than rape. Sexual violence comes in many forms—some that involve physical contact and some that do not. In a recent report, the Centers for Disease Control and Prevention defined sexual violence as completed or attempted penetration of the genital opening or anus by the penis, a hand, a finger, or any other object; penetration of the mouth by the penis or other object; abusive sexual contact without penetration, such as intentional touching of the groin; or noncontact sexual abuse, such as acts of voyeurism (peeping Tom) or sexual harassment (Basile & Saltzman, 2002).

Sexual violence also includes acts such as systematic rape during times of war, sexual trafficking (the buying and selling of girls and women into prostitution and sexual slavery), and female genital mutilation (see Jewkes, Sen, & Garcia-Moreno, 2002, for a review of sexual violence in a global context). Critical to the definition, sexual violence occurs when the survivor does not consent to the sexual activity or when the survivor is unable to consent (e.g., due to age or illness) or unable to refuse (e.g., due to physical violence or threats) (Basile & Saltzman, 2002).

2 PUBLIC HEALTH APPROACH TO SEXUAL VIOLENCE

Public health refers to "what society does to assure that conditions exist in which people can be healthy" (McMahon, 2000, p. 28). Sexual violence should be considered a public health concern for a variety of reasons. First, as will be described in the next section, sexual victimization is a widespread problem that starts early in life and, for many survivors, is repeated over the life span. Second, the consequences of sexual violence are health related. A public health approach treats all forms of violence as health issues, because there are quantifiable physical and psychological injuries that result from them (Mercy, Rosenberg, Powell, Broome, & Roper, 1993). Third, implicit in the public health focus is the idea that public health problems are preventable, and more emphasis should be placed on the front end before a problem begins or becomes widespread. This chapter concludes with more discussion about how the public health approach can be applied to the prevention of sexual violence.

3 MAGNITUDE OF THE PROBLEM

There have been numerous criticisms of official crime statistics, such as the Uniform Crime Reports (UCR) and the National Crime Victimization Survey (NCVS), for their inabilities to capture the true extent of sexual violence victimization (Russell, 1984; Koss, 1992, 1996; Kilpatrick, 2002). The UCR present data on forcible rape and attempted rape reported to and compiled by participating law enforcement agencies and sent to the Federal Bureau of Investigation (FBI) (Kilpatrick, 2002). A major concern of the UCR is that it does not capture people who do not report to the police, and these people include the majority of rape survivors (Kilpatrick, Edmunds, & Seymour, 1992).

The NCVS is a nationwide survey of households in the United States. It is designed to detect both reported and unreported crimes. A weakness of this official survey is that it uses the term "rape" in its questions, which many critics have warned against using due to the stigma associated with this word and the likelihood that respondents would not define their experiences as rape, particularly if the perpetrator was someone they knew (Koss, 1988; Belknap, Fisher, & Cullen, 1999). Further, the NCVS is a crime survey. Critics have pointed out the benefits of including sexual violence items on noncrime surveys, due to the likelihood of obtaining a low response rate in the context of a crime survey if respondents do not consider their experiences with unwanted sex to be crimes

(Koss, 1992). Although the NCVS has recently been revised to address some of the critics' concerns (Bachman & Saltzman, 1995), it still has weaknesses. Many sexual violence researchers argue for the use of self-report noncrime surveys that include several questions about specific behaviors, to facilitate recall and guard against underreporting (Russell, 1984; Koss, 1992, 1993; DeKeseredy, 1995; Belknap et al., 1999). For these reasons, this chapter does not cover the official sources of sexual violence statistics, such as the UCR and the NCVS, but focuses, rather, on self-report surveys that have used behaviorally specific measures.

3.1 Prevalence of Sexual Violence

Most of the prevalence studies of sexual violence use behaviorally specific measures of rape only, as opposed to a broader focus on sexual violence. For these reasons, most of what will be discussed here is rates of rape. According to the National Violence Against Women Survey (NVAWS), an estimated one in six women have experienced an attempted or completed rape at some point in their lifetimes. In 8 out of 10 cases (83%), someone the survivor knew perpetrated the rape (Tjaden & Thoennes, 2000), and 62% of rapists of adult women are intimate partners defined in the NVAWS as current or former spouses, cohabitating partners, boyfriends, or dates, followed by acquaintances (21%), strangers (17%), and other relatives (7%) (Tjaden & Thoennes, 2000).

In the National Women's Study (NWS), intimate partners (current or former spouses or boyfriends) represented 19% of perpetrators; family members represented 27% of perpetrators; strangers represented 22% of perpetrators; and the largest percentage of perpetrators, 29%, included other nonrelatives, such as friends or acquaintances (Kilpatrick et al., 1992). The large majority of survivors of rape and other sexual violence are female, and data show that most perpetrators are male (Tjaden & Thoennes, 2000). Therefore, sexual violence can be characterized as a form of gender-based violence.

3.2 Rape and College-Age Women

Several researchers studied rape experiences among college-age women. Koss and colleagues conducted one of the earliest nationally representative self-report studies of rape and other forms of sexual violence, and they found that approximately one in four college women (27%) had survived rape (15%) or attempted rape (12%) in their lifetimes (Koss, Gidycz, & Wisniewski, 1987). In addition, this study revealed that 14% of women experienced unwanted sexual contact (e.g., fondling, kissing, or petting after continual arguments and pressure, or misuse of authority);

and 12% of women experienced sexual coercion (e.g., penetrative sex after continual arguments and pressure or misuse of authority).

Since this groundbreaking work, more recent studies of college women revealed similar rape rates. In the National College Health Risk Behavior Survey (NCHRBS) by Brener, McMahon, Warren, and Douglas (1999), one in five women (20%) in a nationally representative sample reported that they experienced a completed rape at some point in their lives. Researchers also identified that the college years in particular are vulnerable times for women. In Koss's and colleagues' (1987) study, the authors found that 83 per 1,000 women in their sample experienced attempted or completed rape during a 6-month period while they were in college. More recently, the National College Women Sexual Victimization Study estimated that between one in four and one in five college women are raped during their college years (Fisher, Cullen, & Turner, 2000).

Several U.S. surveys, including the NVAWS, the NWS, and the NCHRBS, revealed that most survivors of rape were young when the first rape occurred. For example, the NCHRBS found that for 71% of survivors, the first rape occurred before the age of 18 (Brener et al., 1999). The NVAWS found that 54% of all first rapes of women occurred before the age of 18, and almost half of these occurred before age 12 (Tjaden & Thoennes, 2000). Similarly, in the NWS, 62% of all rapes occurred before age 18, and 29% occurred before age 12 (Kilpatrick et al., 1992). In light of these findings, rape has been called a problem of youth (Tjaden & Thoennes, 2000; Kilpatrick et al., 1992).

3.3 Child Sexual Abuse

However, child sexual abuse appears to be an even larger problem than rape. Child sexual abuse commonly includes other types of sexual violence, such as fondling, exhibitionism (exposing oneself), and manual stimulation of the perpetrator. It requires different items to assess than are used in rape screening (Koss, Bailey, Yuan, Herrera, & Lichter, 2003). A synthesis of findings from 16 studies on the prevalence of child sexual abuse estimated that 22% of U.S. women were sexually abused in childhood (Gorey & Leslie, 1997).

3.4 Elder Sexual Abuse

Less is known about sexual violence perpetrated against the elderly (usually defined as 60 years or older), but elder abuse has been getting more attention as a serious problem in the United States and all over the world in recent years, as the elderly population has expanded (Wolf,

Daichman, & Bennett, 2002). Findings from the National Elder Abuse Incident Study (NEAIS, 1998) revealed that in 1996, 3% of all nationwide reports of elder (defined here as 50 years or older) abuse were incidents of sexual violence (NEAIS, 1998). This figure is an underestimate, because it does not reflect unreported cases of elder sexual violence. Much of what we know about the characteristics of sexual violence among the elderly comes from studies of nursing homes. In their study of 20 nursing home residents (18 women, 2 men) who experienced sexual violence, Burgess, Dowdell, and Prentky (2000) found that most residents had a preexisting cognitive deficit (e.g., Alzheimer's disease) that made them more vulnerable and made communicating the incident challenging. Muram, Miller, and Cutler (1992), comparing elder rape survivors with younger rape survivors receiving care at a treatment clinic, found that elder survivors were more likely than younger survivors to have been assaulted at home by a stranger. These studies suggest the need for a more comprehensive examination of this vulnerable subgroup of sexual violence survivors.

3.5 Difficulty in Estimating the Problem

   Rape is one of the most underreported crimes, which makes it difficult to count (Bachar & Koss, 2001). The NWS (Kilpatrick et al., 1992) found that 84% of women in their sample did not report their rapes to the police. Reasons for underreporting are numerous. A significant reason appears to be cultural norms that stigmatize and blame women for their assaults. People who survive armed robbery or terrorist attacks are not held responsible for the incident. Rather, they are usually given sympathy. Rape survivors, on the other hand, are often perceived to play some role in their assaults. For instance, women who experience rape still encounter disbelief about the details of the incident by police and physicians (Ullman, 1996a), and they can be blamed for the rape because of what they were wearing at the time of the rape or because they had been drinking alcohol (Campbell et al., 1999). Research has documented several myths about the circumstances of rape that large segments of Americans widely endorse (Lonsway & Fitzgerald, 1994). Some of the most prevalent rape myths are that women lead men on and, therefore, deserve to be raped; women often make false accusations of rape; no woman can be raped against her will; and most rapists are strangers (Brownmiller, 1975; Burt, 1980; Ward, 1995). In such a society, rape survivors often do not disclose experiences of rape and other sexual violence.
   A major contributing factor to nondisclosure of rape is its intimate nature. Because most perpetrators of rape and other sexual violence are known to the survivor (e.g., friends, family members, boyfriends,

coworkers, marital partners), survivors are even more likely to be
perceived as at least partially responsible for the rape (Monson, Byrd, &
Langhinrichsen-Rohling, 1996; Monson, Langhinrichsen-Rohling, &
Binderup, 2000). Women violated by their husbands, in particular, are
given the least amount of sympathy, based in part on cultural beliefs
about marriage and a history of laws that have treated the marriage
license as a "license to rape" (Finkelhor & Yllo, 1985). This intimate context perpetuates an environment in which rape and other sexual violence
are often shameful for survivors and are kept secret.

4 VULNERABILITY FACTORS FOR SEXUAL VIOLENCE

Researchers have examined factors that increase women's vulnerability
to victimization. Vulnerability research seeks to uncover factors that may
increase the likelihood for rape, and it is distinct from victim blaming,
which mistakenly assigns responsibility for victimization to survivors.
One common vulnerability factor for adult rape is a previous history of
child sexual abuse. Child sexual abuse survivors are three to five times
more likely to be raped as adults than respondents who did not experience any type of child abuse (Maker, Kemmelmeier, & Peterson, 2001;
Merrill et al., 1999; West, Williams, & Siegel, 2000).

In addition, poverty and homelessness can increase women's and children's vulnerability to rape and other forms of sexual violence, because
it makes their daily lives more dangerous (e.g., walking alone at night,
less parental supervision of children) (Jewkes et al., 2002). Poverty may
also force women and girls into high-risk occupations, such as sex work
(e.g., prostitution), which has been associated with sexual victimization
(Irwin et al. 1995).

4.1 Substance Abuse and Rape

Researchers have examined the relationships between substance abuse
and victimization. Regarding alcohol use, results are mixed. Greene and
Navarro (1998) found that excessive alcohol use predicted subsequent
sexual victimization among a sample of college women. However, Brecklin and Ullman (2002) found that neither alcohol use by the survivor at
the time of the incident nor alcohol consumption in the last 12 months
was associated with increased risk of rape. Further, in the largest U.S.
longitudinal study to date, recreational drug use, but not alcohol consumption, was found to increase the likelihood of rape (Kilpatrick,
Acierno, Resnick, Saunders, & Best, 1997). Some have pointed out that in
cases of sexual violence, alcohol and other drugs may serve as cues to the

perpetrator. For example, men may perceive women who drink alcohol as "easy," or more interested in sex (Koss et al., 1994; Abbey, Zawacki, Buck, Clinton, & McAuslan, 2001). Drinking alcohol and taking drugs may also put women in settings where encountering a potential perpetrator is more likely (Crowell & Burgess, 1996).

4.1.1 Date Rape Drugs. Although voluntary drug and alcohol use by women has been linked in some of the previous research to victimization, researchers also focused on the use of these substances by men to facilitate the perpetration of sexual violence. This occurs when a perpetrator gives a drug to a potential victim in order to incapacitate and rape her. Alcohol, rohypnol (commonly known as "roofies"), gamma hydroxy butyrate (commonly known as "GHB"), and ketamine (commonly known as "Special K") are some of the most popular drugs used by perpetrators to carry out rape and other forms of sexual violence (California Coalition Against Sexual Assault [CALCASA], 2001). For most of these drugs, the potential victim is not aware she has consumed it (e.g., it is slipped into her drink). Perpetrators choose these kinds of drugs to facilitate rape, because they work quickly to relax muscles and make the intended victim lose her memory for a period of time (usually several hours) after taking the drug (Schwartz, Milteer, & LeBeau, 2000). It is not clear exactly how common drug-facilitated rape is, partly because it is often difficult to determine if drug use was recreational by survivors or used as a weapon by perpetrators to facilitate rape. However, some research exists that suggests it is prevalent. For example, in looking at emergency department records over 6 years, McGregor, Lipowska, Shah, Du Mont, and De Siato (2003) identified 12% of sexual violence cases as suspected to be drug facilitated.

4.1.2 Childhood Victimization. Some researchers have concluded that vulnerability to adult victimization is best understood as an aftereffect of childhood victimization. For example, women who were sexually abused as children may be more likely to use drugs habitually, which, in turn, increases the likelihood of future victimization. Therefore, revictimization can be viewed as both a risk factor for, and a consequence of, sexual violence. For many survivors, rape and other sexual violence are repeated multiple times at different life stages, and evidence suggests that women who experience childhood abuse, followed by revictimization in adolescence, are more vulnerable for future experiences of sexual violence than those who did not experience sexual violence as teens (Siegel & Williams, 2003). Studies indicate that repeat victimization leads to more serious psychological damage than single victimization, possibly because repeated assault reinforces negative central beliefs about the self and others (Follingstad, Brennan, Hause, Polek, & Rutledge, 1991).

With the exception of gender and age, personal characteristics of women are not very useful for predicting who will experience rape and other sexual violence. In sum, most factors associated with rape victimization are ones that women have no control over—being young and female and having a previous history of sexual abuse.

5 CONSEQUENCES OF VICTIMIZATION

The experience of sexual violence has immediate and long-term effects. Although physical wounds can usually heal, the psychological, social, and other health effects of rape and other forms of sexual violence can be longer lasting and debilitating. The following is a discussion of the numerous potential consequences of sexual violence. Because most of the research in this area focuses on consequences in the aftermath of adult rape, child sexual abuse, or both, these are the two types of sexual violence that will be emphasized in the following sections.

5.1 Physical Consequences

There can be both immediate and long-term physical consequences from rape. The immediate consequences can include injuries received during the rape, such as bruises, scrapes, broken bones, and genital trauma. Serious physical injury, particularly genital tearing, is more likely to occur among elderly survivors (Muram et al., 1992). In addition, between 4% and 30% of rape survivors contract sexually transmitted diseases (STDs) as a result of rape (Koss & Heslet, 1992). The number of survivors contracting human immunodeficiency virus (HIV) after rape is unclear, but some cases have been documented (Irwin et al., 1995; Murphy, 1990). In 5% of rapes, pregnancy results (Holmes, Resnick, Kilpatrick, & Best, 1996).

Long-ranging physical symptoms and illnesses associated with rape and child sexual abuse are gastrointestinal disorder, irritable bowel syndrome (Heitkemper et al., 2001), as well as chronic back, neck, head, and facial pain, including lower jaw discomfort (reviewed in Crowell & Burgess, 1996, and Koss et al., 1994). Untreated STDs that result from rape can lead to pelvic inflammatory disease, which is a major cause of infertility (Koss, Heise, & Russo, 1997). Other gynecological problems that can result from rape and child sexual abuse are chronic pelvic pain (Harrop-Griffiths et al., 1988), irregular vaginal bleeding, painful menstrual periods, vaginal discharge (Golding, 1996; Golding, Wilsnack, & Learman, 1998), and premenstrual syndrome (Golding & Taylor, 1996).

5.2 Psychological Consequences

Immediate psychological reactions to rape include shock, disbelief, denial, fear, confusion, anxiety, and withdrawal (Herman, 1992). Serious physical injury or death as a result of rape is rare. But subjective fear of these outcomes during rape is often very high, whether the rapist is known or is a stranger to the survivor (Kilpatrick et al., 1992). Survivors may suffer from intense fear of their rapists after the attack, fearing reattack and feeling anxious about disclosing their assaults to others. Fear of contracting HIV after a rape has also been documented, and this fear is strongest when the perpetrator was a stranger (Resnick et al., 2002). These immediate reactions to rape may continue for several weeks and usually reach peak intensity around the third week (Davidson & Foa, 1991).

Following their initial reactions, women frequently experience low self-esteem, guilt, shame, insomnia, posttraumatic stress disorder (PTSD), and sexual problems. These issues may last for 18 months or longer (Resick, 1987), and for about one quarter of women, psychological problems persist for several years (Hanson, 1990). Avoidance of sex immediately following a rape is common. Other reported sexual problems are lack of desire or interest in sex, fear of sex, and less frequent arousal and orgasms (Becker, Skinner, Abel, & Cichon, 1986). Burgess and Holmstrom (1979) found that of 63 rape survivors in their sample who were sexually active before the rape, 30% (or 19 women) reported that sexual functioning had not returned to normal 4 to 6 years after the rape.

5.2.1 Impact on Beliefs. Rape has a significant impact on how one sees the world. For some women, the experience of rape can lead to conflict between preexisting beliefs and the new set of facts represented by the rape (reviewed in Koss et al., 1994). For example, a survivor who thought the world was fair and just before her assault may begin to question these beliefs postassault. For others, particularly women who have been victimized more than once, negative views of the world as hostile and dangerous are confirmed by rape. Beliefs about safety, power, trust, and intimacy are most vulnerable. Negative changes in belief systems due to rape influence the meaning and interpretation of subsequent experiences. Factors that may influence how a woman perceives and interprets a rape incident include life experiences (particularly previous victimization), family history, beliefs about rape myths and gender roles, race, class, culture, and sexual orientation (Koss, Figueredo, & Prince, 2002). For example, a survivor who believes the rape myth that women provoke rape by the way they dress will perceive her rape differently than a survivor who believes the rapist is solely responsible for the rape. Also, a woman who considers her experience to be "rape" will perceive it differently than a woman who conceptualizes it as "bad sex." However, researchers have learned that similar levels of distress are observed after victimization regardless of how the rape was perceived (Koss, Figueredo, Bell, Tharan, & Tromp, 1996).

5.2.2 Psychiatric Conditions. Several psychiatric diagnoses have been found more frequently among rape survivors, including major depression, obsessive–compulsive disorder, generalized anxiety, and PTSD (Burnam et al., 1988). Generally speaking, depression is more common among women than men. Empirical findings suggest that differences in the levels of sexual violence perpetrated against girls and women by men accounts for a significant portion of the gender gap in depression (reviewed in Koss et al., 2003). Studies have shown that rape-induced depression can last for approximately 3 months, and recurrent major depression over the life course is also more prevalent in rape survivors than in those who did not experience rape (Sorensen & Golding, 1990).

PTSD is the most common diagnosis for trauma victims and has been widely studied among rape survivors. PTSD is a psychological response to an extreme stressor involving threat of death or serious injury (Koss et al., 1994). Examples of PTSD symptoms include feeling numb, not being able to fall asleep or stay asleep, not being able to stop thinking about the traumatic event, and trying to avoid reminders of the traumatic event (Weiss & Marmar, 1996). PTSD was originally developed to describe the reactions of war veterans attempting to reintegrate into society. Later, many of the same symptoms were observed among rape survivors, people exposed to natural disasters, and a range of human-caused traumas. Studies reveal that rape survivors may make up one of the largest groups of PTSD sufferers (Davis & Breslau, 1994). PTSD symptoms are usually present immediately following a rape, and in approximately one third of survivors, PTSD symptoms continue for 3 months or become chronic (Rothbaum, Foa, Riggs, Murdock, & Walsh, 1992).

However, use of PTSD alone to describe the consequences of rape trauma is limiting, as it focuses mainly on fear and anxiety and does not account for all the psychological or health-related symptoms associated with rape (e.g., depression, alcohol and drug abuse, thoughts of suicide, sexual dysfunction, and cognitive changes). In addition, PTSD is better at describing the impact of a single victimization than at describing the trauma associated with repeat victimization (Herman, 1992), such as rape by a husband or partner.

Suicide thoughts and attempts are two psychological consequences that show the largest increase in likelihood for rape survivors compared to women who have never been raped. One study found that 19% of a community sample had attempted suicide after rape, compared to only

2% of nonrape survivors (Kilpatrick et al. 1985). Thoughts of suicide are even more common and have been reported among 33% to 50% of survivors of rape (Ellis, Atkeson, & Calhoun, 1981; Koss, 1988; Resick, Jordan, Girelli, Hutter, & Marhoefer-Dvorak, 1989). Suicide thoughts have been documented among female adolescent survivors of sexual dating violence (Shrier, Pierce, Emans, & DuRant, 1998; Silverman, Raj, Mucci, & Hathaway, 2001) and among college-aged survivors of rape (Brener et al., 1999).

5.3 Social Consequences

Negative consequences on social adjustment after rape are usually short-term. The majority of survivors quickly return to their roles as workers, students, mothers, and partners in a relationship. The quality and amount of social support survivors receive from those who respond to her in the days, weeks, and months following rape play an important role in recovery. However, positive social support does not appear to help survivors as much as negative social reactions hurt them (Davis, Brickman, & Baker, 1991; Ullman, 1996b). Social readjustment to the workplace seems to be a particularly difficult challenge for rape survivors, and one study found productivity to suffer after rape for up to 8 months (Resick, Calhoun, Atkeson, & Ellis, 1981). Rape may be associated with deterioration of intimate relationships (Mackey et al., 1992), which is often related to sexual problems or may stem from damage to beliefs such as those about the trustworthiness of others. Rape can also have a negative effect on the friends, family, and intimate partners of survivors, which further strains relationships (reviewed in Crowell & Burgess, 1996).

5.4 Impact on Health Behaviors

A major consequence of child sexual abuse and adult rape is the negative impact on health and health behaviors. Some of these negative health-related consequences include risky sexual behavior, such as having unprotected sex; having the first consensual sexual experience at an early age; having a relatively large number of sexual partners; trading sex for food, money, shelter, or drugs; and teen pregnancy—all of which may be traumatic after effects of sexual victimization (Allers, Benjack, White, & Rousey, 1993; Boyer & Fine, 1993; Brener et al., 1999). In one study, child sexual abuse survivors reported one or more of the following HIV risk behaviors: using intravenous drugs, receiving treatment for a STD, testing positive for HIV, or having anal sex without a condom (Bensley,

Van Eenwyk, & Simmons, 2000). Adult rape survivors in another study were more likely to be sex workers and to contract a STD than were women who had not been raped (Irwin et al., 1995).

In addition to high-risk sexual behavior, studies have found that survivors of child sexual abuse and rape were more likely than their counterparts to smoke cigarettes, overeat, drink alcohol, not use motor vehicle seat belts (Koss, Koss, & Woodruff, 1991; Walker et al., 1999), smoke crack cocaine, and be homeless (Irwin et al., 1995). A study focusing specifically on high school sexual dating violence in 1997 and 1999 in the state of Massachusetts (Silverman et al., 2001) found similar risks for unhealthy behavior among adolescent girls. In 1997, survivors of sexual dating violence were more likely than nonvictims to be heavy cigarette smokers, drive after drinking alcohol, use cocaine, use diet pills, have consensual sexual intercourse before the age of 15, and use substances before sexual intercourse. In 1999, sexual dating violence was positively associated with binge drinking, anorexia nervosa, not using a condom during sexual intercourse, high numbers of sexual partners, and having been pregnant (Silverman et al., 2001; for data on college students, see Brener et al., 1999). Survivors also have reported self-mutilation, or cutting one's own skin, after rape (Greenspan & Samuel, 1989). Alcohol and drug use may be initiated or increased as a response to rape (Kilpatrick et al., 1997). Child sexual abuse and rape history have been linked to some of the major causes of morbidity and mortality, including extreme obesity and other eating disorders, such as anorexia nervosa and bulimia, among child sexual abuse survivors (Felitti et al., 1998), and hypertension and high cholesterol among rape survivors (Cloutier, Martin, & Poole, 2002).

Many of the long-term behavioral reactions to child sexual abuse and rape, such as alcohol and drug abuse, risky sexual behaviors, and smoking, have been characterized as coping strategies, or behavioral adaptations to trauma. Finkelhor and Browne (1985) proposed the process of traumatic sexualization to explain sex practices that may emerge as a result of child sexual abuse. A child can become traumatically sexualized when the perpetrator repeatedly rewards the child for sexual behavior; when the perpetrator exchanges affection, attention, or gifts for sexual behavior, so that the child learns to use sex as a tool to get what he or she wants; or when a child associates fear and trauma with sexual activities. They argue that child sexual abuse can lead to many of the physical, psychological, and health behavior effects discussed above. These include repeated rape victimization, disinterest in and fear of sex, difficulty having orgasms, or high numbers of sexual partners (Finkelhor & Browne, 1985).

6 RECOVERY

As Herman (1992) documented in her influential book *Trauma and Recovery*, trauma such as sexual violence involves loss of power and disconnection from others, so recovery is based on the empowerment of the survivor and her reconnection to others. Herman (1992) identified three stages in the recovery process after trauma like that experienced by sexual violence survivors.[1] The first is establishing safety. This involves steps taken by the survivor, such as making her environment safe, regaining a sense of control over her body and her life, and managing stress. The second stage is called remembrance and mourning, where the survivor tells about the assault, gives meaning to it, and grieves the experience. The final stage, reconnection, is when the survivor finds new meanings to replace her beliefs that have been challenged by the assault. In this stage, the survivor also develops new relationships and creates a new self and a future. Herman (1992) pointed out that the process of recovery is complex and does not always follow these stages perfectly or in order. In fact, survivors usually go back and forth between the stages during recovery from sexual violence. Some survivors never recover. A critical aspect of recovery is that it cannot happen in isolation. Rather, it must occur in the context of relationships with others (Herman, 1992).

6.1 Resiliency Factors

Researchers have focused on resiliency, or the individual- and community-level factors that help survivors recover after sexual violence. Below is a summary of some of the personal- and community-level factors that have been found in the literature to be associated with recovery from rape and other types of sexual violence. This is by no means an exhaustive review of resiliency factors.

6.1.1 Personal-Level Resiliency Factors. Some individual-level factors have been found to facilitate adjustment after sexual violence. Among survivors of child sexual abuse, several studies have found an association between parental support and better adjustment in terms of lower levels of depression and higher self-esteem (Feiring, Taska, & Lewis, 1998), fewer behavioral difficulties, higher self-worth (Tremblay, Hebert, & Piche, 1999), and better social competence (Spaccarelli & Kim, 1995). In their study of a clinical sample of women who survived child sexual abuse, Hyman, Gold, and Cott (2003) found that social support from

---

[1] See Burgess and Holmstrom (1974), Sutherland and Scherl (1970), and Worell and Remer (1992) for similar recovery models for sexual violence survivors.

others, in the forms of appraisal support (advice or guidance in dealing with problems) and self-esteem support (support that shows that the survivor is valued), is associated with lower levels of PTSD symptoms. These findings suggest that these particular forms of social support might contribute, along with other factors, to the healthy adjustment of child sexual abuse survivors.

Regarding adult rape survivors, recent research has found that beliefs that future assaults were less likely were associated with less distress after rape. Feeling control over the recovery process was most strongly associated with less distress (Frazier, 2003). Campbell, Ahrens, Sefl, Wasco, and Barnes (2001) found that when survivors disclosed information about their rapes, were allowed to talk about their rapes, were believed, and considered the reactions to be positive, they had fewer emotional and physical health problems after the rapes (Campbell et al., 2001). Although negative social reactions to disclosure of rape have been found to hinder recovery (Davis et al., 1991; Ullman, 1996b), the findings of Campbell and colleagues (2001) suggest that in a supportive social environment, sharing the rape experience with others can be a positive experience and may aid in recovery.

6.1.2 Community-Level Resiliency Factors. Harvey (1996) stressed the importance of examining resiliency after sexual violence in an ecological context. An ecological framework is one that combines personal, situational, and sociocultural factors to understand a problem (Heise, 1998). In the context of recovery from trauma, the ecological framework is the interrelationships between individuals and the communities from which they gain identity and meaning (Koss & Harvey, 1991). Trauma, such as that resulting from sexual violence, is seen not only as a threat to individuals, but also to their communities and the abilities of the communities to promote recovery among their affected members (Norris & Thompson, 1995). Harvey (1996) suggested that a survivor's reaction to sexual violence, and recovery from it, are affected by the characteristics of the community in which she lives.

In an ecological model, the community is treated as a potential source of recovery and resiliency after rape and other sexual violence. There are numerous examples of community-level aids to survivor recovery. One example is rape crisis centers (Koss & Harvey, 1991), which exist to help survivors and the community cope with sexual violence through counseling services, community education, and support and advocacy for survivors during the medical and legal processes after sexual violence. Ideally, rape crisis centers exist in a larger coordinated community response to sexual violence. A coordinated community response is a plan to improve communication and integration of survivor advocates, health care providers, law enforcement, and other formal systems in the community (e.g., the legal system, organized religion) in order to strengthen the quality of services to survivors (Heise, Ellsberg, & Gottemoeller, 1999).

Many communities have multidisciplinary groups called sexual assault response teams (SARTs) to oversee collaboration in the immediate response to survivors of sexual violence (Littel, 2001). SART members typically include emergency department medical staff, law enforcement, and survivor advocates, and can include a whole host of others, such as representatives from child and adult protective services, public health departments, and victim witness programs. In some communities, members of a SART work together to interview the survivor at the time of her medical examination. In other communities, the SART members work independently, communicating regularly to discuss a given assault case (West Virginia Foundation for Rape Information and Services, 2003).

Sexual assault nurse examiner (SANE) programs are another important part of the coordinated response to sexual violence. A SANE is a registered nurse who has advanced education in the medical examination of rape survivors for the purpose of evidence collection (Littel, 2001). Most SANE programs began in the 1990s, and they offer specialized medical-evidence-collection training for health care providers to improve the quality of evidence collected and provide a more supportive environment for survivors, with less waiting time in the emergency department, and credible testimony in court (Littel, 2001).

A coordinated community response includes components such as specialized teams and trained examiners. It also offers a survivor-centered approach that brings together services in the community to care for the needs of the survivors and to hold perpetrators accountable for their crimes. For example, Frazier (2003) found that the survivor's process of gaining control over her recovery was strongly associated with less distress after rape. Recovery can be facilitated by the coordinated community response. Many survivors do not disclose or seek services (because of the stigma associated with rape and other reasons detailed earlier in this chapter), and thus are unknown to any formal system. However, those who have access to these services in their community and seek their assistance can benefit from the compassion, efficiency, and speed that a coordinated community response provides.

Unfortunately, coordinated community responses do not exist in every community. In some communities, even resources such as rape crisis centers and other advocacy resources are either not available or are not accessible to all residents, particularly survivors in isolated or rural communities (Lewis, 2003). In other cases, the resources available may not be culturally relevant to all community members. For example, an immigrant survivor who does not speak English will not benefit from English-only advocacy services (Harvey, 1996). Even when a culturally relevant coordinated community response exists, many survivors of sexual violence do not come forward and will, therefore, not benefit from the resources that have been shown to be important for recovery. As Harvey (1996) pointed out, trauma survivors often have complex lives, which may complicate recovery and disconnect them from available resources. For example, a woman who is recovering from rape and who also has a drug addiction receives welfare benefits or is otherwise impoverished, and is a battered wife will have a more challenging recovery process and different needs than others who do not have these life experiences. She may not be in a position to make recovery from rape a top priority in her life.

In an effort to reach as many survivors as possible, it is important for communities to promote their resources and facilitate recovery of survivors in the community. It is also important to link different types of resources in the community (e.g., rape crisis resources with drug dependence resources). Culturally relevant community outreach campaigns are important to make community members aware of the available resources and to facilitate access to them. It is also important to conduct culturally relevant public service and media campaigns to reach out to unidentified rape survivors in the community. In communities lacking the needed resources, "train the trainer" programs are helpful to provide community leaders (e.g., clergy) with skills needed to help sexual violence survivors cope with and adjust to their traumas (Harvey, 1996).

7 CONCLUSION

Girls and women endure rape and other forms of sexual violence at alarming rates across their life spans. This chapter summarized the extent of victimization from rape and child sexual abuse, discussed the known vulnerability factors for victimization, and described the multitude of consequences in the aftermath of rape and child sexual abuse. It also summarized the process of recovery and presented personal and community-level factors that may facilitate recovery for some survivors of sexual violence. In considering solutions, it is important to reemphasize the benefits of using a public health approach as a framework for addressing sexual violence. Public health is a complement to the criminal justice model, because the public health approach emphasizes the importance of changing the social, behavioral, and environmental factors that cause sexual violence, instead of simply reacting to violence after it occurs (Mercy et al., 1993). The public health approach combines a diverse group of scientific disciplines (e.g., sociology, psychology, medicine, education) to create a multidisciplinary approach to prevention (Mercy & Hammond, 1999).

Public health underscores the importance of primary prevention, or preventing sexual violence before it occurs (McMahon & Puett, 1999), by reaching girls and boys early in the life span, before they are victimized or become perpetrators of violence. Although this is an ideal approach to decreasing the rates of sexual violence, it should be used in concert with secondary prevention (focused on those at high risk for either victimization or perpetration) and tertiary prevention (focused on stopping future violence among those who have a history of either victimization or perpetration) (McMahon, 2000). All of the prevention approaches of public health can come together to address sexual violence in an ecological framework. For example, a coordinated community response can attend to survivors after the assault and prevent future victimization (tertiary prevention). It can work on a larger scale to educate at-risk populations (secondary prevention) and the general public (primary prevention) about the prevention of sexual violence. An important avenue of primary prevention that researchers should investigate, from a public health perspective, is identifying factors that protect a particular community and its members from sexual violence. In other words, are certain types of communities less likely to experience victimization, and if so, why? The hope of those working in the field of sexual violence is that while we continue to work as interdisciplinary communities to prevent sexual violence for future generations, all current sexual violence survivors will benefit from resources that are relevant to their personal and cultural needs and recover from the negative impact of their traumas.

REFERENCES

Abbey, A., Zawacki, T., Buck, P. O., Clinton, A. M., & McAuslan, P. (2001). Alcohol and sexual assault. *Alcohol Research and Health: The Journal of the National Institute on Alcohol Abuse and Alcoholism, 25,* 43–51.

Allers, C. T., Benjack, K. J., White, J., & Rousey, J. T. (1993). HIV vulnerability and the adult survivor of child sexual abuse. *Child Abuse and Neglect, 17,* 291–298.

Bachar, K., & Koss, M. P. (2001). From prevalence to prevention: Closing the gap between what we know about rape and what we do. In C. Renzetti, J. Edleson, & R. K. Bergen (Eds.), *Sourcebook on violence against women* (pp. 117–142). Thousand Oaks, CA: Sage.

Bachman, R., & Saltzman, L. E. (1995). *Violence against women: Estimates from the redesigned survey.* Washington, DC: Bureau of Justice Statistics, National Institute of Justice.

Basile, K. C., & Saltzman, L. E. (2002). *Sexual violence surveillance: Uniform definitions and recommended data elements. Version 1.0.* Atlanta, GA: Centers for Disease Control and Prevention, National Center for Injury Prevention and Control.

Becker, J. V., Skinner, L. J., Abel, G. G., & Cichon, J. (1986). Level of postassault sexual functioning in rape and incest victims. *Archives of Sexual Behavior, 15,* 37–49.

Belknap, J., Fisher, B. S., & Cullen, F. T. (1999). The development of a comprehensive measure of sexual victimization of college women. *Violence Against Women, 5,* 185–214.

Bensley, L. S., Van Eenwyk, J., & Simmons, K. W. (2000). Self-reported childhood sexual and physical abuse and adult HIV-risk behaviors and heavy drinking. *American Journal of Preventive Medicine, 18,* 151–158.

Boyer, D., & Fine, D. (1992). Sexual abuse as a factor in adolescent pregnancy and child maltreatment. *Family Planning Perspectives, 23,* 4–10.

Brecklin, L. R., & Ullman, S. E. (2002). The roles of victim and offender alcohol use in sexual assaults: Results from the National Violence Against Women Survey. *Journal of Studies on Alcohol, 63,* 57–63.

Brener, C. D., McMahon, P. M., Warren, C. W., & Douglas, K. A. (1999). Forced sexual intercourse and associated health-risk behaviors among female college students in the United States. *Journal of Consulting and Clinical Psychology, 67,* 252–259.

Brownmiller, S. (1975). *Against our will: Men, women, and rape.* New York: Fawcett Columbine.

Burgess, A. W., & Holmstrom, L. L. (1974). Rape trauma syndrome. *American Journal of Psychiatry, 131,* 981–986.

Burgess, A. W., & Holmstrom, L. L. (1979). Rape: Sexual disruption and recovery. *American Journal of Orthopsychiatry, 49,* 648–657.

Burgess, A. W., Dowdell, E. B., & Prentky, R. A. (2000). Sexual abuse of nursing home residents. *Journal of Psychosocial Nursing, 38,* 10–18.

Burnam, M. A., Stein, J. A., Golding, J. M., Siegel, J. M. et al. (1988). Sexual assault and mental disorders in a community population. *Journal of Consulting and Clinical Psychology, 56,* 843–850.

Burt, M. R. (1980). Cultural myths and supports for rape. *Journal of Personality and Social Psychology, 38,* 217–230.

California Coalition Against Sexual Assault (CALCASA). (2001). *Understanding and preventing drug-facilitated sexual assault* (Vol. 2). Sacramento, CA: Rape Prevention Resource Center, CALCASA.

Campbell, R., Ahrens, C. E., Sefl, T., Wasco, S. M., & Barnes, H. E. (2001). Social reactions to rape victims: Healing and hurtful effects on psychological and physical health outcomes. *Violence and Victims, 16,* 287–302.

Campbell, R., Sefl, T., Barnes, H. E., Ahrens, C. E., Wasco, S. M., & Zaragoza-Diesfeld, Y. (1999). Community services for rape survivors: Enhancing psychological well-being or increasing trauma? *Journal of Consulting and Clinical Psychology, 67,* 847–858.

Cloutier, S., Martin, S. L., & Poole, C. (2002). Sexual assault among North Carolina women: Prevalence and health risk behaviors. *Journal of Epidemiology and Community Health, 56,* 265–271.

Crowell, N. A., & Burgess, A. W. (Eds.). (1996). *Understanding violence against women.* Washington, DC: National Academy Press.

Davidson, J. R., & Foa, E. B. (1991). Diagnostic issues in posttraumatic stress disorder: Considerations for the *DSM-IV. Journal of Abnormal Psychology, 100,* 346–355.

Davis, G. C., & Breslau, N. (1994). Post-traumatic stress disorder in victims of civilian trauma and criminal violence. *Psychiatric Clinics of North America, 17,* 289–299.

Davis, R. C., Brickman, E., & Baker, T. (1991). Supportive and unsupportive responses of others to rape victims: Effects of concurrent victim adjustment. *American Journal of Community Psychology, 19,* 443–451.

DeKeseredy, W. S. (1995). Enhancing the quality of survey data on woman abuse: Examples from a national Canadian study. *Violence Against Women, 1,* 158–173.

Ellis, E. M., Atkeson, B. M., & Calhoun, K. S. (1981). An assessment of long-term reactions to rape. *Journal of Abnormal Psychology, 90,* 263–266.

Feiring, C., Taska, L. S., & Lewis, M. (1998). Social support and children's and adolescent's adaptation to sexual abuse. *Journal of Interpersonal Violence, 13,* 240–260.

Felitti, V. J., Anda, R. F., Nordenberg, D., Williamson, D. F., Spitz, A. M., Edwards, V., Koss, M. P., & Marks, J. S. (1998). Relationship of childhood abuse and household dysfunction to many of the leading causes of death in adults: The Adverse Childhood Experiences Study. *American Journal of Preventive Medicine, 14,* 245–258.

Finkelhor, D., & Browne, A. (1985). The traumatic impact of child sexual abuse: A conceptualization. *American Journal of Orthopsychiatry, 55,* 530–541.

Finkelhor, D., & Yllo, K. (1985). *License to rape: Sexual abuse of wives.* New York: The Free Press.

Fisher, B. S., Cullen, F. T., & Turner, M. G. (2000). *The sexual victimization of college women* (NCJ 182369). Washington, DC: U.S. Department of Justice, National Institute of Justice.

Follingstad, D. R., Brennan, A. F., Hause, E. S., Polek, D. S., & Rutledge, L. L. (1991). Factors moderating physical and psychological symptoms of battered women. *Journal of Family Violence, 6,* 81–95.

Frazier, P. A. (2003). Perceived control and distress following sexual assault: A longitudinal test of a new model. *Journal of Personality and Social Psychology, 84,* 1257–1269.

Golding, J. (1996). Sexual assault history and women's reproductive and sexual health. *Psychology of Women Quarterly, 20,* 101–121.

Golding, J. M., & Taylor, D. L. (1996). Sexual assault history and premenstrual distress in two general population samples. *Journal of Women's Health, 5,* 143–152.

Golding, J. M., Wilsnack, S. C., & Learman, L. A. (1998). Prevalence of sexual assault history among women with common gynecologic symptoms. *American Journal of Obstetrics and Gynecology, 179,* 1013–1019.

Gorey, K. M., & Leslie, D. R. (1997). The prevalence of child sexual abuse: Integrative review adjustment for potential response and measurement biases. *Child Abuse and Neglect, 21,* 391–398.

Greene, D. M., & Navarro, R. L. (1998). Situation-specific assertiveness in the epidemiology of sexual victimization among university women: A prospective path analysis. *Psychology of Women Quarterly, 22,* 589–604.

Greenspan, G. S., & Samuel, S. E. (1989). Self-cutting after rape. *American Journal of Psychiatry, 146,* 789–790.

Hanson, R. K. (1990). The psychological impact of sexual assault on women and children: A review. *Annals of Sex Research, 3,* 187–232.

Harrop-Griffiths, J., Katon, W., Walker, E., Holm, L., Russo, J., & Hickok, L. (1988). The association between chronic pelvic pain, psychiatric diagnoses, and childhood sexual abuse. *Obstetrics and Gynecology, 71,* 589–594.

Harvey, M. R. (1996). An ecological view of psychological trauma and trauma recovery. *Journal of Traumatic Stress, 9,* 3–23.

Heise, L. L. (1998). Violence against women: An integrated, ecological framework. *Violence Against Women, 4,* 262–290.

Heise, L., Ellsberg, M., & Gottemoeller, M. (1999, December). *Ending violence against women.* (Population Reports, Series L, No. 11.) Baltimore: Johns Hopkins University School of Public Health, Population Information Program.

Heitkemper, M., Jarrett, M., Taylor, P., Walker, E., Landenburger, K., & Bond, E. F. (2001). Effect of sexual and physical abuse on symptom experiences in women with irritable bowel syndrome. *Nursing Research, 50,* 15–23.

Herman, J. L. (1992). *Trauma and recovery.* New York: Basic Books.

Holmes, M., Resnick, H., Kilpatrick, D., & Best, C. (1996). Rape related pregnancy: Estimates and descriptive characteristics from a national sample of women. *American Journal of Obstetrics and Gynecology, 175,* 320–325.

Hyman, S. M., Gold, S. N., & Cott, M. A. (2003). Forms of social support that moderate PTSD in childhood sexual abuse survivors. *Journal of Family Violence, 18,* 295–300.

Irwin, K. L., Edlin, B. R., Wong, L., Faruque, S., McCoy, H. V., Word, C., Schilling, R., McCoy, C. B., Evans, P. E., & Holmberg, S. D. (1995). Urban rape survivors: Characteristics and prevalence of human immunodeficiency virus and other sexually transmitted infections. *Obstetrics and Gynecology, 85,* 330–336.

Jewkes, R., Sen, P., & Garcia-Moreno, C. (2002). Sexual violence. In E. G. Krug, L. L. Dahlberg, J. A. Mercy, A. B. Zwi, & R. Lozano (Eds.), *World report on violence and health* (pp. 149–181). Geneva: World Health Organization.

Kilpatrick, D. G. (2002, January). *Making sense of rape in America: Where do the numbers come from and what do they mean?* Symposium conducted at the Centers for Disease Control Rape Prevention and Education Grant Program Regional Meeting, Atlanta, Georgia.

Kilpatrick, D. G., Acierno, R., Resnick, H. S., Saunders, B. E., & Best, C. L. (1997). A 2-year longitudinal analysis of the relationships between violent assault and substance use in women. *Journal of Consulting and Clinical Psychology, 65,* 834–847.

Kilpatrick, D. G., Best, V. L., Veronen, L. J., Amick, A. E., Villeponteaux, L. A., & Ruff, G. A. (1985). Mental health correlates of criminal victimization: A random community survey. *Journal of Consulting and Clinical Psychology, 53,* 866–873.

Kilpatrick, D. G., Edmunds, C. N., & Seymour, A. K. (1992). *Rape in America: A report to the nation.* Arlington, VA: National Victim Center and Medical University of South Carolina.

Koss, M. P. (1988). Hidden rape: Sexual aggression and victimization in a national sample of students in higher education. In A. W. Burgess (Ed.), *Rape and sexual assault* (Vol. 2, pp. 3–25). New York: Garland.

Koss, M. P. (1992). The underdetection of rape: Methodological choices influence incidence estimates. *Journal of Social Issues, 48,* 61–75.

Koss, M. P. (1993). Detecting the scope of rape: A review of prevalence research methods. *Journal of Interpersonal Violence, 8,* 198–222.

Koss, M. P. (1996). The measurement of rape victimization in crime surveys. *Criminal Justice and Behavior, 23,* 55–69.

Koss, M. P., Bailey, J. A., Yuan, N. P., Herrera, V. M., & Lichter, E. L. (2003). Depression and PTSD in survivors of male violence: Research and training initiatives to facilitate recovery. *Psychology of Women Quarterly, 27,* 130–142.

Koss, M. P., Figueredo, A. J., Bell, I., Tharan, M., & Tromp, S. (1996). Traumatic memory characteristics: A cross-validated mediational model of response to rape among employed women. *Journal of Abnormal Psychology, 105,* 421–432.

Koss, M. P., Figueredo, A. J., & Prince, R. J. (2002). Cognitive mediation of rape's mental, physical, and social health impact: Tests of four models in cross-sectional data. *Journal of Consulting and Clinical Psychology, 70,* 1–16.

Koss, M. P., Gidycz, C. A., & Wisniewski, N. (1987). The scope of rape: Incidence and prevalence of sexual aggression and victimization in a national sample of higher education students. *Journal of Consulting and Clinical Psychology, 55,* 162–170.

Koss, M. P., Goodman, L. A., Browne, A., Fitzgerald, L. F., Keita, G. P., & Russo, N. F. (1994). *No safe haven: Male violence against women at home, at work, and in the community.* Washington, DC: American Psychological Association.

Koss, M. P., & Harvey, M. R. (1991). *The rape victim: Clinical and community interventions.* Newbury Park, CA: Sage.

Koss, M. P., Heise, L., & Russo, N. F. (1997). The global health burden of rape. In L. L. O'Toole & J. R. Schiffman (Eds.), *Gender violence: Interdisciplinary perspectives* (pp. 223–241). New York: New York University.

Koss, M. P., & Heslet, L. (1992). Somatic consequences of violence against women. *Archives of Family Medicine, 1,* 53–59.

Koss, M. P, Koss, P. G., & Woodruff, W. (1991). Deleterious effects of criminal victimization on women's health and medical utilization. *Archives of Internal Medicine, 151,* 342–357.

Lewis, S. H. (2003). *Unspoken crimes: Sexual assault in rural America.* Enola, PA: National Sexual Violence Resource Center.

Littel, K. (2001, April). *Sexual assault nurse examiner (SANE) programs: Improving the community response to sexual assault victims* (Office for Victims of Crime Bulletin, NCJ 186366). Washington, DC: U.S. Department of Justice.

Lonsway, K. A., & Fitzgerald, L. F. (1994). Rape myths: In review. *Psychology of Women Quarterly, 18,* 133–164.

Mackey, T., Sereika, S. M., Weissfeld, L. A., Hacker, S. S., Zender, J. F., & Heard, S. L. (1992). Factors associated with long-term depressive symptoms of sexual assault victims. *Archives of Psychiatric Nursing, 6,* 10–25.

Maker, A. H., Kemmelmeier, M., & Peterson, C. (2001). Child sexual abuse, peer sexual abuse, and sexual assault in adulthood: A multi-risk model of revictimization. *Journal of Traumatic Stress, 14,* 351–368.

McGregor, M. J., Lipowska, M., Shah, S., Du Mont, J., & De Siato, C. (2003). An exploratory analysis of suspected drug-facilitated sexual assault seen in a hospital emergency department. *Women and Health, 37,* 71–80.

McMahon, P. M. (2000). The public health approach to the prevention of sexual violence. *Sexual Abuse: A Journal of Research and Treatment, 12,* 27–36.

McMahon, P. M., & Puett, R. C. (1999). Child sexual abuse as a public health issue: Recommendations of an expert panel. *Sexual Abuse: A Journal of Research and Treatment, 11,* 257–266.

Mercy, J. A., & Hammond, W. R. (1999). Preventing homicide: A public heath perspective. In M. D. Smith & M. A. Zahn (Eds.), *Studying and preventing homicide: Issues and challenges* (pp. 274–294). Thousand Oaks, CA: Sage.

Mercy, J. A., Rosenberg, M. L., Powell, K. E., Broome, C. V., & Roper, W. L. (1993). Public health policy for preventing violence. *Health Affairs, 12,* 7–29.

Merrill, L. L., Newell, C. E., Thomsen, C. J., Gold, S. R., Milner, J. S., Koss, M. P., & Rosswork, S. G. (1999). Childhood abuse and sexual revictimization in a female Navy recruit sample. *Journal of Traumatic Stress, 12,* 211–225.

Monson, C. M., Byrd, G. R., & Langhinrichsen-Rohling, J. (1996). To have and to hold: Perceptions of marital rape. *Journal of Interpersonal Violence, 11,* 410–424.

Monson, C. M., Langhinrichsen-Rohling, J., & Binderup, T. (2000). Does "no" really mean "no" after you say "yes?" Attributions about date and marital rape. *Journal of Interpersonal Violence, 15,* 1156–1174.

Muram, D., Miller, K., & Cutler, A. (1992). Sexual assault of the elderly victim. *Journal of Interpersonal Violence, 7,* 70–76.

Murphy, S. M. (1990). Rape, sexually transmitted diseases, and human immunodeficiency virus infection. *International Journal of STD and AIDS, 1,* 79–82.

National Elder Abuse Incident Study (NEAIS). (1998, September). *The National Elder Abuse Incident Study: Final report.* Washington, DC: National Center on Elder Abuse.

Norris, F. H., & Thompson, M. P. (1995). Applying community psychology to the prevention of trauma and traumatic life events. In J. Freedy & S. Hobfoll (Eds.), *Traumatic stress: From theory to practice* (pp. 49–71). New York: Plenum.

Resick, P. A. (1987). Psychological effects of victimization: Implications for the criminal justice system. *Crime and Delinquency, 33,* 468–478.

Resick, P. A., Calhoun, K. S., Atkeson, B. M., & Ellis, E. M. (1981). Social adjustment in victims of sexual assault. *Journal of Consulting and Clinical Psychology, 49,* 705–712.

Resick, P. A., Jordon, C. G., Girelli, S. A., Hutter, C. K., & Marhoefer-Dvorak, S. (1989). A comparative outcome study of behavioral group therapy for sexual assault victims. *Behavior Therapy, 19,* 385–401.

Resnick, H., Monnier, J., Seals, B., Holmes, M., Nayak, M., Walsh, J., Weaver, T. L., Acierno, R., & Kilpatrick, D. G. (2002). Rape-related HIV risk concerns among recent rape victims. *Journal of Interpersonal Violence, 17,* 746–759.

Rothbaum, B. O., Foa, E. B., Riggs, D. S., Murdock, T., & Walsh, W. (1992). A prospective examination of posttraumatic stress disorder in rape victims. *Journal of Traumatic Stress, 5,* 455–475.

Russell, D. E. H. (1984). *Sexual exploitations: Rape, child sexual abuse and workplace harassment.* Newbury Park, CA: Sage.

Schwartz, R. H., Milteer, R., & LeBeau, M. A. (2000). Drug-facilitated sexual assault ("date rape") [Comment]. *Southern Medical Journal, 93,* 558–561.

Shrier, L. S., Pierce, J. D., Emans, S. J., & DuRant, R. H. (1998). Gender differences in risk behaviors associated with forced or pressured sex. *Archives of Pediatrics and Adolescent Medicine, 152,* 57–63.

Siegel, J. A., & Williams, L. M. (2003). Risk factors for sexual victimization of women: Results from a prospective study. *Violence Against Women, 9,* 902–930.

Silverman, J. G., Raj, A., Mucci, L. A., & Hathaway, J. E. (2001). Dating violence against adolescent girls and associated substance use, unhealthy weight control, sexual risk behavior, pregnancy, and suicidality. *Journal of the American Medical Association, 286,* 572–579.

Sorensen, S. B., & Golding, J. M. (1990). Depressive sequelae of recent criminal victimization. *Journal of Traumatic Stress, 3,* 337–350.

Spaccarelli, S., & Kim, S. (1995). Resilience criteria and factors associated with resilience in sexually abused girls. *Child Abuse and Neglect, 9,* 1171–1182.

Sutherland, S., & Scherl, D. J. (1970). Patterns of response among victims of rape. *American Journal of Orthopsychiatry, 40,* 503–511.

Tjaden, P., & Thoennes, N. (2000). *Full report of prevalence, incidence, and consequences of violence against women: Findings from the national violence against women survey* (NCJ 183781). Washington, DC: U.S. Department of Justice, National Institute of Justice.

Tremblay, C., Hebert, M., & Piche, C. (1999). Coping strategies and social support as mediators of consequences in child sexual abuse victims. *Child Abuse and Neglect, 23,* 929–945.

Ullman, S. E. (1996a). Do social reactions to sexual assault victims vary by support provider? *Violence and Victims, 11,* 143–157.

Ullman, S. E. (1996b). Social reactions, coping strategies, and self-blame attributions in adjustment to sexual assault. *Psychology of Women Quarterly, 20,* 505–526.

Walker, E. A., Gelfand, A., Katon, W. J., Koss, M. P., von Korff, M., Bernstein, D., & Russo, J. (1999). Adult health status of women with histories of childhood abuse and neglect. *American Journal of Medicine, 107,* 332–339.

Ward, C. A. (1995). *Attitudes toward rape: Feminist and social psychological perspectives.* Newbury Park, CA: Sage.

Weiss, D. S., & Marmar, C. R. (1996). The impact of event scale—revised. In J. P. Wilson & T. Keane (Eds.), *Assessing psychological trauma and PTSD* (pp. 493–511). New York: Guilford.

West, C. M., Williams, L. M., & Siegel, J. A. (2000). Adult sexual revictimization among black women sexually abused in childhood: A prospective examination of serious consequences of abuse. *Child Maltreatment, 5,* 49–57.

West Virginia Foundation for Rape Information and Services. (2003). *Sexual assault response team.* Fairmont, WV: WV FRIS, Inc. Retrieved from http://www.fris.org/sart.html

Wolf, R., Daichman, L., & Bennett, G. (2002). Abuse of the elderly. In E. G. Krug, L. L. Dahlberg, J. A. Mercy, A. B. Zwi, & R. Lozano (Eds.), *World report on violence and health* (pp. 125–145). Geneva: World Health Organization.

Worell, J., & Remer, P. (1992). *Feminist perspectives in therapy: An empowerment model for women.* Chichester, England: John Wiley & Sons.

6

Intimate Partner Violence: Implications for Women's Physical and Mental Health

JACQUELYN C. CAMPBELL AND KATHLEEN A. KENDALL- TACKETT

In 1998, approximately 900,000 women in the United States were beaten or raped by their intimate partners. Although violence by intimates has decreased in the past decade—down from a high of 1.1 million women in 1993—the numbers are still staggering (Rennison, 2001). In this chapter, we review the literature on intimate partner violence: how often it occurs, the devastating physical and mental health effects, and how women learn to leave abusive relationships.

Intimate partner violence (IPV) disproportionately affects women. Between 1993 and 1998, IPV accounted for 22% of violent crimes against women, whereas it accounted for only 3% of violent crimes against men (Rennison, 2001). Women are significantly more likely to be physically or sexually assaulted by a current or former intimate partner than an acquaintance, family member, friend, or stranger (Tjaden & Thoennes, 2000). Over the course of women's lives, approximately 25% to 35% have experienced IPV (Tjaden & Thoennes, 2000). As high as these figures are, they most likely underestimate the true incidence and prevalence of IPV. Poor women and young women are particularly at risk (Tjaden & Thoennes, 2000). Women who are separated and divorced are also at increased risk, but because these are cross-sectional surveys, it is not clear if the marital dissolution occurred before or after the violence. There is also some evidence that women from ethnic minority backgrounds, especially Native American and African American women, are at increased risk (Tjaden & Thoennes, 2000), although the support for this conclusion is less consistent.

According to the Centers for Disease Control and Prevention, IPV can occur in all kinds of intimate relationships, including between married couples and nonmarried couples whose partners are either living together or dating or who share a child in common or who have been intimate in the past, regardless of marital status (Saltzman, Fanslow, McMahon, & Shelley, 1999). Thus, IPV encompasses the full range of intimate relationships of adolescents and adults.

Intimate partner violence is not restricted to heterosexual relationships; it also occurs in same-sex relationships (Renzetti, 1992; West, 1998). One population-based study found that the prevalence of IPV among same-sex male couples was significantly higher than the level among same-sex female couples (Tjaden, Thoennes, & Allison, 1999); however, the number of same-sex couples in that study was relatively small. The fundamental dynamic of abuse in same-sex couples appears to be similar to that of heterosexual couples (Greenwood et al., 2002). However, we cannot assume that studies conducted with heterosexual couples can be directly translated to the experiences of same-sex couples, and more research is needed in this area (Relf, 2001).

One topic that has been studied extensively is the immediate and long-term consequences of IPV. In the next section, we describe the impact of IPV on women.

1 CONSEQUENCES OF INTIMATE PARTNER VIOLENCE

Intimate partner violence has severe, and sometimes lethal, effects on women. These consequences include physical injury, stress-related health effects, mental health effects, abuse during pregnancy, and the physical effects of forced sexual intercourse. Homicide—the most serious consequence of IPV—is discussed in a subsequent section.

1.1 Physical Injury

Physical injury is the most obvious effect of IPV, and IPV is one of the most common causes of injury for women (Rand, 1997). In a review of studies from American emergency departments (EDs), 11% to 30% of injured women had been beaten by their partners (Rand, 1997). Battered women were more likely to be injured in the head, face, neck, thorax, breasts, and abdomen than women who had been injured in other circumstances (Grisso et al., 1999). Although the majority of battered women state that they have been injured as a result of the abuse they received, less than half say that they sought health care specifically for those injuries (Bachman & Saltzman, 1995). Women are more likely to delay seeking treatment for their injuries. Only a small percentage of abused women who seek care in EDs do so for injuries that they just received (Dearwater et al., 1998). These findings suggest the need for universal, rather than incident-based, screening in urgent and emergency care settings.

Whether women are injured depends on the characteristics of their male partners, rather than characteristics of the women who were beaten. Two recent studies conducted in EDs identified several risk factors for female IPV injury. These characteristics included male partner histories of arrest, substance abuse, low education, lack of employment, and ex-partner status (Grisso et al., 1999; Kyriacou et al., 1999).

1.2 Stress-Related Health Effects

In addition to injury, there is mounting evidence that IPV has long-term negative health consequences for survivors, even after the abuse has ended (Campbell & Lewandowski, 1997; Koss, Koss, & Woodruff, 1991). This can translate into lower health status, lower quality of life, and higher rates of health care use (McCauley et al., 1995; Tollestrup et al., 1999; Wisner, Gilmer, Saltzman, & Zink, 1999). Intimate partner violence can directly and indirectly raise the risk for a variety of physical health problems, such as chronic pain (e.g., headaches and back pain) or recurring central nervous system symptoms, such as fainting or seizures (Diaz-Olavarrieta, Campbell, Garcia de la Cadena, Paz, & Villa, 1999; Coker, Smith, Bethea, King, & McKeown, 2000; Leserman, Li, Drossman, & Hu, 1998; Plichta, 1996; Ratner, 1993; Tollestrup et al., 1999; Wisner et al., 1999). Some of these physical problems may be related to trauma-related alterations in their neurophysiology (e.g., a lower pain threshold), whereas others may be more directly due to the abuse. For instance, 10% to 44% of abused women report being choked or receiving blows to the head that result in loss of consciousness (McCauley et al., 1995; Sharps, Campbell, Campbell, Gary, & Webster, 2001). Loss of consciousness can lead to serious medical problems, including neurological sequelae.

Battered women also exhibit significantly more self-reported gastrointestinal symptoms (e.g., loss of appetite or eating disorders) and diagnosed functional gastrointestinal disorders (e.g., irritable bowel syndrome) associated with chronic stress (Campbell et al., 2002; Coker et al., 2000; Diaz-Olavarrieta et al., 1999; Leserman et al., 1998).

These disorders may begin during an acutely violent relationship, with its attendant stress. Or these disorders may have begun because of women's histories of childhood abuse, only to be exacerbated by partner abuse (Leserman et al., 1998). Regardless, it is important to recognize that gastrointestinal symptoms can last far beyond the violent relationship. Similarly, self-reported cardiac symptoms, such as hypertension and chest pain, have been associated with IPV (Plichta, 1996; Tollestrup et al., 1999). It is plausible to hypothesize interactions among genetic tendencies for hypertension, lifestyle risk behaviors, such as smoking (Letourneau, Holmes, & Chasendunn-Roark, 1999), personality characteristics, such as hostility (Smith & Ruiz, 2002), and stress from the violent relationships increasing cardiovascular risk. Yet these mechanisms have not been thoroughly investigated. Stress and depression can also suppress the immune system via elevated levels of the stress hormone cortisol (Kendall-Tackett, 2003). This can also increase the likelihood of many types of diseases.

1.3 Physical Effects Related to Forced Sex

Intimate partner violence can also include partner sexual abuse. Approximately 40% to 45% of battered women are also sexually assaulted, which can compound their health problems (Coker et al., 2000; Campbell & Soeken, 1999). Not surprisingly, women who are also sexually assaulted experience higher rates of gynecological problems. Differential symptoms and conditions include sexually transmitted diseases, vaginal bleeding or infection, fibroids, decreased sexual desire, genital irritation, pain on intercourse, chronic pelvic pain, and urinary tract infections (Campbell & Soeken, 1999; Coker et al., 2000; Koss et al., 1991; Leserman et al., 1998; Letourneau et al., 1999; McCauley et al., 1995; Plichta, 1996; Schei & Bakketeig, 1989; Tollestrup et al., 1999). In one large study, the odds of having a gynecological problem were three times greater for victims of IPV (McCauley et al., 1995).

Battered women have also described sexually abusive and controlling acts, such as male partners' refusal to use condoms or contraception and verbal sexual degradation (Campbell & Soeken, 1999). These issues may partially explain why battered women have higher rates of sexually transmitted diseases, including HIV, and unintended pregnancies than their nonabused counterparts (Coker & Richter, 1998; Maman, Campbell, Sweat, & Gielen, 2000; McCauley et al., 1995; Wingood & DiClemente, 1997; Wood & Jewkes, 1997). Qualitative data from in-depth interviews demonstrate how abuse interacts with women's social, psychological, and cultural contexts to influence their decisions and actions to prevent pregnancies and sexually transmitted diseases. These studies highlight the difficulty of true condom or contraception negotiation in violent relationships, especially in countries and cultures where norms do not accord women equal say in such decisions (Coker & Richter, 1998; Heise, Ellsberg, & Gottemoeller, 1999; Lempert, 1996; Maman et al., 2000; Maman et al., 2002; Wood & Jewkes, 1997).

1.4 Abuse During Pregnancy

Unfortunately, pregnancy does not necessarily offer protection from abuse and may, for some women, increase its occurrence. In a major review, Gazmararian and colleagues (1996) found that approximately 4% to 8% of women were beaten while pregnant (with a range of 1% to 20%). Abuse during pregnancy increases the risk of death for both mother and child (Jejeebhoy, 1998; Parsons & Harper, 1999). Another cause of fetal death, elective pregnancy termination, has also been related to IPV in large, but uncontrolled, studies in the United States (e.g., Glander, Moore, Michielutte, & Parsons, 1998). Physical abuse during pregnancy is associated with health problems during pregnancy, such as sexually transmitted diseases, including HIV, urinary tract infections, substance abuse, depression, and other mental health symptoms (Martin, Kilgallen, Dee, Dawson, & Campbell, 1998). In-depth interviews of women (Campbell, Oliver, & Bullock, 1993) suggest that abuse during pregnancy may be an important link between the overlap of IPV and child abuse seen in U.S. research (Straus & Gelles, 1990).

1.4.1 Low Birth Weight Babies. Although many U.S. studies have noted apparent associations of abuse during pregnancy with such deleterious infant outcomes as preterm delivery, fetal distress, antepartum hemorrhage, and preeclampsia, the evidence is inconsistent across studies (Gazmararian, Petersen, Spitz, Goodwin, Saltzman, & Marks, 2000). Much of the focus has been on IPV as a risk factor for having babies of low birth weight (LBW). Although prior evidence from single studies was mixed, a recent meta-analysis of 14 published studies from North America and Europe showed a weak, but significant, association between abuse during pregnancy and LBW (OR 1.4, 95% confidence interval 1.1 to 1.8; Murphy, Schei, Myhr, & DuMont, 2001). Variations among samples, subsamples, and potential causal pathways may explain some of the differences in individual studies. One study suggested a stronger relationship between abuse and birth weight among middle-class rather than low-income women (Bullock & McFarlane, 1989). One possible explanation for this finding is that there are fewer competing causes of LBW in middle-class samples. For these women, the contribution of IPV to LBW may be more obvious.

LBW may occur because of premature delivery caused by trauma, or it may occur in term infants as a result of complex causal pathways (Murphy et al., 2001). For example, low maternal weight gain and smoking have been found to be mediators of the abuse–LBW connection in several studies (Campbell et al., 1999; McFarlane, Parker, & Soeken, 1996). Abusing partners may pressure their wives or girlfriends not to gain weight, or abuse may cause stress that has, in turn, been associated with smoking, low weight gain, and consequent LBW (Campbell et al., 1999; McFarlane et al., 1996). Maternal ethnicity may also interact with abuse to cause LBW, but that connection needs to be further explored (Heise et al., 1999). Torres and colleagues (2000) found that acculturation was negatively associated with prevalence of abuse during pregnancy, whereas partners' attitudes that IPV was acceptable and that women's primary roles should be wife and mother were positively associated with abuse during pregnancy.

1.5 Mental Health Consequences

Depression and posttraumatic stress disorder (PTSD) are the most prevalent mental health sequelae of IPV, with women often experiencing both (Campbell & Soeken, 1999; Campbell, Sullivan, & Davidson, 1995; Cascardi, O'Leary, & Schlee, 1999; Golding, 1999; McCauley et al., 1995; Ratner, 1993; Silva, McFarlane, Soeken, Parker, & Reel, 1997). In her meta-analysis, Golding (1999) demonstrated an increased risk for depression and PTSD associated with IPV, even above that resulting from childhood sexual assault. Depression in battered women has also been associated with other life stressors that often accompany IPV, such as childhood abuse, daily hassles, a large number of children, changes in residence, forced sex, marital separations, negative life events, and child behavior problems (Campbell, Kub, Belknap, & Templin, 1997; Campbell & Soeken, 1999; Cascardi et al., 1999). Some battered women may be chronically depressed, and their depression is exacerbated by the stress of a violent relationship. Violence can also trigger a woman's first episode of depression, and women's depression has been shown to decrease with decreasing IPV (Campbell & Soeken, 1999; Silva et al., 1997). Even so, the trajectory of the interrelationship of violence experiences and mental health problems needs further study. Women are more vulnerable to depression than men in the general population. Some of that vulnerability may be due to IPV, although that premise has never been specifically tested.

The risk for PTSD among battered women is almost as great as that for depression (Golding, 1999; Silva et al., 1997; Woods & Isenberg, 2001). Women are especially vulnerable to PTSD if their abuse was severe or if they have experienced prior trauma (Campbell et al., 1995; Silva et al.,

1997). Suicidality, although less often studied, has also been associated with IPV in the United States, Scandinavia, and Papua New Guinea (Bergman & Brismar, 1991; Counts, 1987; Golding, 1999; Thompson et al., 1999).

Abused women also had significantly more anxiety, insomnia, and social dysfunction than their nonabused counterparts. In one study, physical abuse had a stronger effect than psychological abuse on all the symptoms (Ratner, 1993). Sleep disturbances appear to be related to a complex interaction of physical, psychological, and environmental mechanisms, although there is only one known study of IPV and sleep (Humphreys, Lee, Neylan, & Marmar, 1999). Women in developing countries, such as Nicaragua and Pakistan, also report depression and anxiety from IPV (Ellsberg, Caldera, Herrera, Winkvist, & Kullgren, 1999; Fikree & Bhatt, 1999).

Finally, abused women are also more likely to abuse substances than their nonabused counterparts (Golding, 1999; McCauley et al., 1995; Ratner, 1993; Sharps, Campbell et al., 2001; Martin et al., 1998). In at least two studies, when researchers controlled for demographic variables and partner substance use, the apparent increased risk of alcohol abuse among female victims disappeared (Kyriacou et al., 1999; Plichta, 1996; Sharps, Campbell et al., 2001). However, in another population-based study, the association persisted (Brookoff, O'Brien, Cook, Thompson, & Williams, 1997). Although causal pathways between IPV and substance abuse are difficult to determine, one ED study suggested that in most cases, women were abused before they started abusing substances (Stark & Flitcraft, 1996).

One hypothesis about the relationship between substance use and IPV is that it is mediated through PTSD. This hypothesis is plausible and has been substantiated by research in other populations (Kulka et al., 1990). Women with PTSD might use drugs or alcohol to calm themselves down or to cope with the three PTSD-specific sets of symptoms: intrusion, avoidance, and hyperarousal. A population-based study found substance use both a risk factor for and sequelae of PTSD. This is especially true when women have experienced multiple types of trauma and violence (Kilpatrick, Acierno, Resnick, Saunders, & Best, 1997). Women may also abuse substances because they are in relationships with substance-abusing men, or because they want to escape from the reality of IPV. In any case, it is important for providers to understand the complex interplay between IPV, substance abuse, and mental health if they want to offer effective interventions.

1.6 Medical Care Usage

As the above-cited studies revealed, women who are abused have poorer overall mental and physical health and have more injuries than their nonabused counterparts. Not surprisingly, they also use more medical care of all types, including prescriptions, hospitalizations, and visits to the ED (Koss et al., 1991; Leserman et al., 1998; Tollestrup et al., 1999; Wisner et al., 1999). In a Canadian population-based study, battered women sought health care approximately three times more often than nonbattered women (Ratner, 1993). Medical care use is also related to the severity of physical assault. Women who are more severely abused use more medical care in the year following their assault than women whose abuse was less severe (Koss et al., 1991). This increased medical care comes at a price. In a well-designed health plan comparison, battered women generated approximately 92% more costs per year, with mental health services accounting for the majority of the excess costs (Wisner et al., 1999).

1.7 Summary

Women clearly have serious health problems as a result of IPV. It is well documented that they are in the health care system frequently. However, they generally do not present with obvious trauma, even in EDs (Dearwater et al., 1998). Abuse is a risk factor for many physical illnesses. Some have an obvious cause. Others are more subtle. It may be years before we can determine the exact mechanism by which problems, such as chronic pain or neurological symptoms, occur. If abuse contributes to conditions such as smoking, unhealthy nutrition, substance abuse, and stress, interventions aimed at these problems, without addressing IPV, will not succeed. In the next section, we describe one of the most serious health consequences of IPV—homicide.

2 ABUSE OF FEMALE PARTNERS AND HOMICIDE

Partner abuse is most frightening when it leads to murder. Each year, 1,200 to 2,000 American women are killed by their intimate partners (Greenfield et al., 1998). The U.S. Crime Report indicates that one third of all female homicide victims were murdered by a husband, ex-husband, or boyfriend (Greenfield et al., 1998). The percentages are even higher (40% to 50%) when ex-boyfriends are included among perpetrators. As much as 80% of the time, women were beaten, sometimes for years, before they were killed (Campbell, 1992; Campbell, Sharps, & Glass, 2000). In one recent study, 70% of female homicide victims in the total sample, and 79% of the women killed between the ages of 18 and 50, were physically abused by their partners before they were killed (Campbell et al., 2003).

Adolescents are also at risk for intimate partner homicide. This form of "youth violence" is not often recognized. Homicide is the third leading cause of death for girls and young women ages 15 to 24 (National Center for Injury Prevention and Control, 2001). From 1993 to 1999, boyfriends committed 10% of the homicides of girls ages 12 to 15. For young women (ages 16 to 19), the proportion was 22%. And for women in the 20 to 24 age group, 32% of homicides were committed by intimate partners. These percentages do not include homicides by ex-boyfriends, which would have increased the numbers. In contrast, 1% to 2% of the homicides of young men were perpetrated by girlfriends in the same age groups (Wisner et al., 1999).

Battered women are often acutely aware that they are in serious danger, but almost half underestimate their risk (Campbell et al., 2003). They may be most at risk when they sever their dangerously abusive relationships (Campbell et al., 2002; Wilson & Daly, 1993). Women frequently remain in their relationships because they fear that they will be killed if they leave. The public has not always treated their fears as valid (Langford, 1996). Battering men feel the ultimate loss of control when their intimate partners leave. Many have been heard to say something like: "If I can't have you, no one can." Approximately one third of intimate partner homicides are followed by suicide of the male partner.

The risk factors for intimate partner homicide have been identified in several studies (Browne, Williams, & Dutton, 1998). A recent 12-city study identified the following risk factors for lethal abuse: perpetrator unemployment, prior arrest for domestic violence, access to a gun, stepchild in the home, never living together, estrangement, forced sex, threats to kill, and threats with a weapon (Campbell et al., 2003). Of these, the strongest risk factor was perpetrator access to a gun, increasing the risk by more than five times (Bailey et al., 1997). Estrangement, especially when the partner is highly controlling, was the next most powerful risk factor (Wilson & Daly, 1993). Stalking a partner after she has left can also indicate controlling behavior. Stepchildren in the home also increased risk significantly (Campbell et al., 2003; Daly, Wiseman, & Wilson, 1997), as did forced sex, abuse during pregnancy, and prior attempts to strangle the victim (Campbell & Soeken, 1999; McClane, Strack, & Hawley, 2001; McFarlane, Campbell, & Sharps, 2002; McFarlane, Parker, & Soeken, 1995; Taliaferro, Mills, & Walker, 2001). Finally, if women feel they are in grave danger, this should be taken seriously, no matter the rest of the situation (Campbell et al., 2003; Weisz, Tolman, & Saunders, 2000).

In one study, only 4% of the women who were killed had ever used domestic violence shelter services. But, 56% had seen a health care provider at least once in the year before they were killed. A quarter of these women had been seen in EDs. Most visits were to their primary providers, or they were seen for prenatal care (Sharps et al., 2001).

These encounters are missed opportunities for health care providers to prevent a death. Another tragedy is that children either witnessed the murders of their mothers or found their mothers' bodies in almost half of the intimate partner homicides (Campbell et al., 2003). If several of the risk factors are present, it is important that women and their care providers appreciate the levels of danger in these women's lives and take steps necessary to ensure their safety.

As bleak as this picture we have presented is, there is good news. Women can, and do, leave abusive relationships. In the final section, we describe common patterns in abusive relationships, how women go about leaving, and how they recover from them.

3 PATTERNS OF WOMEN'S RESPONSES TO INTIMATE PARTNER VIOLENCE

Recent studies have examined the process of women leaving abusive relationships. These studies have illuminated the complexity of women's experiences with, and responses to, intimate partner violence. Women's responses to abuse reflect a dynamic process that evolves according to the nature of the abuse, their interpretations of the abuse, and their relationships overall. This body of research demonstrates the strengths and creative resistance strategies that women draw upon in the face of intimate partner violence. Abused women also weigh the pragmatic consequences of remaining in or severing the relationships.

3.1 Process of Experiencing and Recovering From Abusive Relationships

Landenburger (1998, 1989) described factors that were related to women's choices about their relationships over time. These included factors that assisted or hindered women in leaving their abusive relationships. Based on qualitative analysis of in-depth interviews, Landenburger identified four phases of abusive relationships: binding, enduring, disengaging, and recovering. Women went through the four phases, but not necessarily in order. The meanings they ascribed to the abuse, their interactions with their abusive partners, and their perceptions of themselves influenced their leaving and healing processes.

3.1.1 The Phases of Abusive Relationships. Landenburger called the first phase of an abusive relationship the binding stage. This phase occurs when the relationship is new and promising. Women respond to abuse with increased efforts to make the relationship work and to prevent future abuse. They try many logical and creative strategies to appease their abusers. In the second phase, enduring, women tolerate the abuse, because they value the positive aspects of the relationship, and because they feel at least partially responsible for the abuse. During this phase, women experience a "shrinking of self," in which women's personal needs, desires, and goals are put aside in order to fully attend to the needs, desires, and goals of the abusive partner. All this activity is in an effort to prevent or reduce further abuse (Landenburger, 1998). Women may sometimes seek help at this time. But, they do not openly disclose the abuse to others, because they fear for their safety and worry about damage to their partners' social status. In the health care setting, they might seek help for symptoms related to the abuse but continue to mask the violence.

The disengaging phase involves women labeling their situations as abusive and recognizing that they do not deserve abuse. Women may come to this point when they become aware of the danger that they and their children are in or see their children being affected by witnessing the violence. They might get to that point when they realize that they are becoming violent in response to their partners' violence, or they may even try to kill their abuser. They may find themselves ready to leave when they achieve financial independence (Campbell, Rose, Kub, & Nedd, 1998). The final break may take several attempts, as women struggle with independent living and safety concerns. Once they have dealt with the many barriers that could trap them in abusive relationships, women enter a recovery phase. During this time, they remain separated from the abuser. At this point, women may still be acknowledging some good aspects of their relationships. They want the abuse to stop, but they may want to maintain the positive aspects of the relationship.

Landenburger's phases have been supported by the findings of other researchers. For example, Mills (1985) found that women's success in leaving abusive relationships was influenced by whether they considered themselves "victims" or "survivors." Women who thought of themselves as survivors were more likely to be successful in leaving. Ulrich (1991) found that some women leave once they realize that they could never achieve their self-potential while in their abusive relationships. Belknap (1999, 2000) discovered that women's sense of self was related to women's silence. When women believed that they were responsible for the abuse, they were more likely to keep the abuse secret. Self-blame, combined with the fear that no one would believe their stories, kept women silent (Belknap, 1999, 2000).

"Reclaiming self" is another construct that describes women's responses to intimate partner violence (Merritt-Gray & Wuest, 1995; Wuest & Merritt-Gray, 1999). Wuest and Merritt-Gray used feminist grounded-theory method with narrative data from 13 rural women. These women described the process of living in, and eventually leaving, abusive relationships. They used three strategies in reclaiming self: counteracting abuse, breaking free, and not going back to the relationship.

The strategies these women used in resisting the abuse contradict the view of battered women as passive victims. Early in their relationships, women described how they "relinquished parts of self" when their partners first became abusive. They tended to minimize the abuse. They also began "fortifying defenses," which referred to participating in activities that promoted self-reflection, enhanced their capabilities for independence, and improved their knowledge of ways to achieve freedom from abuse.

The final phase involves sustaining the separation from the abusive partner, or "not going back" (Wuest & Merritt-Gray, 1999). The process of leaving an abusive relationship can be long and drawn-out. It can be so intense that once women finally leave, they are physically and emotionally exhausted. For women to stay free, they need to find and maintain a safe place to live. They must navigate through the maze of social systems, search for employment, apply for financial assistance, and enlist the assistance of law enforcement. They may be involved in custody disputes or have ongoing problems with stalking or harassment from abusive partners. Abused women are also resourceful in their approaches to violent relationships.

Campbell and colleagues (Campbell et al., 1998) conducted a 3-year longitudinal study. At the beginning of the study, the majority of the sample was still in the abusive relationship, so the results do not reflect women's experiences of abusive relationships in the distant past. The overall goal of women in this study was to achieve nonviolence, rather than leave the intimate relationship. Women's stories revealed that the notion of "staying" or "leaving" is a gross oversimplification of women's status in the relationship. For example, an "in/out" category was developed to describe women who were ambivalent about maintaining or leaving their relationships. These women may have left, or had their partners thrown out, more than once. However, they continued to have positive feelings for their partners, and though certain that they wanted the abuse to end, they were not convinced that the entire relationship had to be sacrificed to achieve nonviolence.

Another important insight gained from the study was that leaving the intimate relationship and ending the violence were often independent outcomes. For some women, violence continues, and may even escalate, after they leave their abusive partners. The sad reality is that women are easily stalked by their ex-partners. Their partners can also harass them for years via legal proceedings, child custody and visitation rules, and other reasons for continued contact. Professionals must understand that ending an abusive relationship does not necessarily end the violence for women and their children. Any efforts made to assist and support women must be made with full recognition of this dangerous reality. In addition, professionals need to eliminate flip responses, such as "why don't you just leave?," from their vocabularies and their thinking (Campbell et al., 1998).

In summary, the theoretical frameworks of women's responses to intimate partner violence have become more complex and sophisticated over the past 30 years. Recent research directly contradicts the image of women as passive victims in abusive relationships. Rather, women actively respond to the abusive behaviors with creative and intelligent strategies, their goal being to be free of violence (Lempert, 1996). Sometimes, they want to maintain the relationship. But more often, the relationship ends. Though this is a complicated process, a pattern of normative stages or phases have been described in qualitative research. Women have highlighted the reality of ongoing danger and harassment from the perpetrator in their narrative accounts. These insights also come via review of homicide data. Professionals who wish to intervene must be aware that simply leaving an abusive relationship does not necessarily ensure the safety of women and their children. Rather, the level of danger may increase for some time after leaving. Evaluation of danger and review of safety plans must be an integral component of work with women, even after they have left abusive partners.

4 CONCLUSIONS

Intimate partner violence is clearly a large public health problem in North America and around the world. Whereas we recognize the impact of IPV on women's physical and mental health, we must also recognize battered women's many strengths and their resourcefulness in addressing both their health problems and the abuse (Campbell et al., 1998; Lempert, 1996). Those assessing and intervening with abused women need to have respect for their autonomy, and offer assessment and intervention in a spirit of advocacy and collaboration, as well as express concern for their health and safety. Worldwide research, prevention, and intervention agendas in injury, maternal/child health, mental health, and HIV/AIDS must not go forward without appropriate recognition of the role of IPV in women's health.

REFERENCES

Bachman, R., & Saltzman, L. E. (1995). *Violence against women: Estimates from the redesigned survey.* Washington, DC: Bureau of Justice Statistics, National Institute of Justice.

Bailey, J. E., Kellermann, A. L., Somes, G. W., Banton, J. G., Rivara, F. P., & Rushforth, N. P. (1997). Risk factors for violent death of women in the home. *Archives of Internal Medicine, 157,* 777–782.

Belknap, R. A. (1999). Why did she do that? Issues of moral conflict in battered women's decision making. *Issues in Mental Health Nursing, 20,* 387–404.

Belknap, R. A. (2000). Eva's story: One woman's life viewed through the interpretive lens of Gilligan's theory. *Violence Against Women, 6,* 586–605.

Bergman, B., & Brismar, B. (1991). Suicide attempts by battered wives. *Acta Psychiatrica Scandanavia, 83,* 380–384.

Brookoff, D., O'Brien, K. K., Cook, C. S., Thompson, T. D., & Williams, C. (1997). Characteristics of participants in domestic violence. *Journal of the American Medical Association, 277*(17), 1369–1373.

Browne, A., Williams, K. R., & Dutton, D. C. (1998). Homicide between intimate partners. In M. D. Smith & M. Zahn (Eds.), *Homicide: A sourcebook of social research* (pp. 149–164). Thousand Oaks, CA: Sage.

Bullock, L. F., & McFarlane, J. (1989). Higher prevalence of low birth weight infants born to battered women. *American Journal of Nursing, 89,* 1153–1155.

Campbell, J. C. (1992). "If I can't have you, no one can": Power and control in homicide of female partners. In J. Radford & D. Russell (Eds.), *Femicide: The politics of women killing* (pp. 99–112). New York: Twayane Publishers.

Campbell, J. C., Dienemann, J., Jones, A. S., Schollenberger, J., Gielen, A., O'Campo, P., & Wynne, C. (2002). Intimate partner violence and physical health consequences in a sample of female HMO enrollees. *Archives of Internal Medicine, 162,* 1157–1163.

Campbell, J. C., Kub, J., Belknap, R. A., & Templin, T. (1997). Predictors of depression in battered women. *Violence Against Women, 3*(3), 271–293.

Campbell, J. C., & Lewandowski, L. (1997). Mental and physical health effects of intimate partner violence on women and children. *Psychiatric Clinics of North America, 20,* 353–374.

Campbell, J. C., Oliver, C., & Bullock, L. (1993). Why battering during pregnancy? *AWHONN'S Clinical Issues, 4*(3), 343–349.

Campbell, J. C., Rose, L., Kub, J., & Nedd, D. (1998). Voices of strength and resistance: A contextual and longitudinal analysis of women's responses to battering. *Journal of Interpersonal Violence, 13,* 743–761.

Campbell, J. C., Ryan, J., Campbell, D. W., Torres, S., King, C., Stallings, R., & Fuchs, S. (1999). Physical and nonphysical abuse and other risk factors for low birthweight among term and preterm babies: A multiethnic case control study. *American Journal of Epidemiology, 150*(7), 714–726.

Campbell, J. C., Sharps, P. W., & Glass, N. E. (2000). Risk assessment for intimate partner homicide. In G. F. Pinard & L. Pagani (Eds.), *Clinical assessment of dangerousness: Empirical contributions* (pp. 136–157). New York: Cambridge University Press.

Campbell, J. C., & Soeken, K. (1999). Forced sex and intimate partner violence: Effects on women's health. *Violence Against Women, 5,* 1017–1035.

Campbell, J. C., Webster, D., Koziol-McLain, J., Block, C. R., Campbell, D. W., Curry, M. A., Gary, F., McFarlane, J., Sachs, C., Sharps, P., Ulrich, Y. Wilt, S. A., Manganello, J., Xu, X., Schollenberger, J., Frye, V. A., & Laughon, K. (2003). Risk factors for intimate partner femicide. *American Journal of Public Health, 93,* 1089–1097.

Campbell, R., Sullivan, C. M., & Davidson, W. S. (1995). Women who use domestic violence shelters: Changes in depression over time. *Psychology of Women Quarterly, 19,* 237–255.

Cascardi, M., O'Leary, K. D., & Schlee, K. A. (1999). Co-occurrence and correlates of posttraumatic stress disorder and major depression in physically abused women. *Journal of Family Violence, 14,* 227–250.

Coker, A. L., & Richter, D. L. (1998). Violence against women in Sierra Leone: Frequency and correlates of intimate partner violence and forced sexual intercourse. *African Journal of Reproductive Health, 2*(1), 61–72.

Coker, A. L., Smith, P. H., Bethea, L., King, M. R., & McKeown, R. E. (2000). Physical health consequences of physical and psychological intimate partner violence. *Archives of Family Medicine, 9,* 451–457.

Counts, D. A. (1987). Female suicide and wife abuse in cross cultural perspective. *Suicide and Life-Threatening Behavior, 17*, 194–204.

Daly, M., Wiseman, K. Z., & Wilson, M. (1997). Women and children sired by previous partners incur excess risk of uxoricide. *Homicide Studies, 1*, 61–71.

Dearwater, S. R., Coben, J. H., Nah, G., Campbell, J. C., McLoughlin, E., Glass, N., & Bekemeier, B. (1998). Prevalence of domestic violence in women treated at community hospital emergency department. *Journal of the American Medical Association, 480*(5), 433–438.

Diaz-Olavarrieta, C., Campbell, J. C., Garcia de la Cadena, C., Paz, F., & Villa, A. (1999). Domestic violence against patients with chronic neurologic disorders. *Archives of Neurology, 56*, 681–685.

Ellsberg, M., Caldera, T., Herrera, A., Winkvist, A., & Kullgren, G. (1999). Domestic violence and emotional distress among Nicaraguan women: Results from a population-based study. *American Psychologist, 54*(1), 30–36.

Fikree, F. F., & Bhatt, L. I. (1999). Domestic violence and health of Pakistani women. *International Journal of Gynecology & Obstetrics, 65*(2), 195–201.

Gazmararian, J. A., Lazorick, S., Spitz, A., Ballard, T. J., Saltzman, L. E., & Marks, J. S. (1996). Prevalence of violence against pregnant women: A review of the literature. *Journal of the American Medical Association, 275*(24), 1915–1920.

Gazmararian, J. A., Petersen, R., Spitz, A. M., Goodwin, M. M., Saltzman, L. E., & Marks, J. S. (2000). Violence and reproductive health: Current knowledge and future research directions. *Maternal and Child Health, 4*(2), 79–84.

Glander, S. S., Moore, M. L., Michielutte, R., & Parsons, L. H. (1998). The prevalence of domestic violence among women seeking abortion. *Obstetrics &.Gynecology, 91*(6), 1002–1006.

Golding, J. M. (1999). Intimate partner violence as a risk factor for mental disorders: A meta-analysis. *Journal of Family Violence, 14*(2), 99–132.

Greenfield, L. A., Rand, M. R., Craven, D., Klaus, P. A., Perkins, C. A., Ringel, C. et al. (1998). *Violence by intimates: Analysis of data on crimes by current or former spouses, boyfriends and girlfriends.* Washington, DC: U.S. Department of Justice.

Greenwood, G. L., Relf, M. V., Huang, B., Pollack, L. M., Canchola, J., & Catania, J. A. (2002). Battering victimization among a probability-based sample of men who have sex with men (MSM). *American Journal of Public Health, 92*, 1964–1969.

Grisso, J. A., Schwarz, D. F., Hirschinger, N., Sammel, M., Brensinger, C., Santanna, J., Lowe, R. A., Anderson, E., Shaw, L. M., Bethel, C. A., & Teeple, L. (1999). Violent injuries among women in an urban area. *The New England Journal of Medicine, 341*(25), 1899–1905.

Heise, L. L., Ellsberg, M. C., & Gottemoeller, M. (1999). Ending violence against women. *Population Reports, 27*(4), 1–43.

Humphreys, J. C., Lee, K. A., Neylan, T. C., & Marmar, C. R. (1999). Sleep patterns of sheltered battered women. *Image: Journal of Nursing Scholarship, 31*, 139–143.

Jejeebhoy, S. J. (1998). Associations between wife-beating and fetal and infant death: Impressions from a survey in rural India. *Studies in Family Planning, 29*(3), 300–308.

Kendall-Tackett, K. A. (2003). *Treating the lifetime health effects of childhood victimization.* New York: Civic Research Institute.

Kilpatrick, D. G., Acierno, R., Resnick, H. S., Saunders, B. E., & Best, C. L. (1997). A two-year longitudinal analysis of the relationships between violent assault and substance use in women. *Journal of Consulting and Clinical Psychology, 65*(5), 834–847.

Koss, M. P., Koss, P. G., & Woodruff, W. J. (1991). Deleterious effects of criminal victimization on women's health and medical utilization. *Archives of Internal Medicine, 151*, 342–347.

Kulka, R. A., Schlenger, W. E., Fairbank, J. A., Hough, R. L., Jordan, B. K., Marmar, C. R., & Weiss, D. S. (1990). *Trauma and the Vietnam war generation: Report of findings from the national Vietnam veterans readjustment study.* New York: Bruner-Mazel.

Kyriacou, D. N., Anglin, D., Taliaferro, E., Stone, S., Tubb, T., Linden, J. A., Muelleman, R., Barton, E., & Kraus, J. F. (1999). Risk factors for injury to women from domestic violence against women. *The New England Journal of Medicine, 341*(25), 1892–1898.

Landenburger, K. (1989). A process of entrapment in and recovery from an abusive relationship. *Issues in Mental Health Nursing, 3,* 209–227.

Landenburger, K. M. (1998). Exploration of women's identity: Clinical approaches with abused women. In J. C. Campbell (Ed.), *Empowering survivors of abuse: Health care for battered women and their children* (pp. 61–69). Thousand Oaks, CA: Sage.

Langford, D. R. (1996). Policy issues for improving institutional response to domestic violence. *Journal of Nursing Administration, 26,* 39–45.

Lempert, L. B. (1996). Women's strategies for survival: Developing agency in abusive relationships. *Journal of Family Violence, 11,* 269–290.

Leserman, J., Li, D., Drossman, D. A., & Hu, Y. J. B. (1998). Selected symptoms associated with sexual and physical abuse among female patients with gastrointestinal disorders: The impact on subsequent health care visits. *Psychological Medicine, 28,* 417–425.

Letourneau, E. J., Holmes, M., & Chasendunn-Roark, J. (1999). Gynecologic health consequences to victims of interpersonal violence. *Women's Health Issues, 9*(2), 115–120.

Maman, S., Campbell, J. C., Sweat, M., & Gielen, A. C. (2000). The intersection of HIV and violence: Directions for future research and interventions. *Social Science & Medicine, 50,* 459–478.

Maman, S., Mbwambo, J., Hogan, N. M., & Campbell, J. C. (2002). HIV-positive women report more lifetime partner violence: Findings from a voluntary counseling and testing clinic in Dar es Salaam, Tanzania. *American Journal of Public Health, 92*(8), 1331–1337.

Martin, S. L., Kilgallen, B., Dee, D. L., Dawson, S., & Campbell, J. C. (1998). Women in a prenatal care/substance abuse treatment program: Links between domestic violence and mental health. *Maternal and Child Health Journal, 2*(2), 85–94.

McCauley, J., Kern, D. E., Kolodner, K., Dill, L., Schroeder, A. F., DeChant, H. K., Ryden, J., Bass, E., & Derogatis, L. (1995). The "battering syndrome": Prevalence and clinical characteristics of domestic violence in primary care internal medicine practices. *Annals of Internal Medicine, 123*(10), 737–746.

McClane, G., Strack, G. B., & Hawley, D. (2001). Violence: Recognition, management, and prevention—A review of 300 attempted strangulation cases, Part III: Injuries in fatal cases. *Journal of Emergency Medicine, 21,* 311–315.

McFarlane, J., Campbell, J. C., & Sharps, P. W. (2002). Abuse during pregnancy and femicide: Urgent implications for women's health. *Obstetrics & Gynecology, 100,* 27–36.

McFarlane, J., Parker, B., & Soeken, K. J. (1995). Abuse during pregnancy: Frequency, severity, perpetrator, and risk factors of homicide. *Public Health Nursing, 12,* 284–289.

McFarlane, J., Parker, B., & Soeken, K. (1996). Abuse during pregnancy: Associations with maternal health and infant birth weight. *Nursing Research, 45*(1), 37–42.

Merritt-Gray, M., & Wuest, J. (1995). Counteracting abuse and breaking free: The process of leaving revealed through women's voices. *Health Care for Women International, 16,* 399–412.

Mills, T. (1985). The assault on the self: Stages in coping with abusive husbands. *Qualitative Sociology, 8,* 103–123.

Murphy, C. C., Schei, B., Myhr, T. L., & DuMont, J. (2001). A meta-analysis of infant birthweight and abuse during pregnancy. *Canadian Medical Association Journal, 164,* 1567–1572.

National Center for Injury Prevention and Control. (2001). *Injury Fact Book 2001–2002.* Atlanta, GA: Centers for Disease Control and Prevention.

Parsons, L. H., & Harper, M. A. (1999). Violent maternal deaths in North Carolina. *Obstetrics &.Gynecology, 94*(6), 990–993.

Plichta, S. B. (1996). Violence and abuse: Implications for women's health. In M. K. Falik & K. S. Collins (Eds.), *Women's health: The Commonwealth Fund Survey.* Baltimore: Johns Hopkins University Press.

Rand, M. R. (1997). *Violence-related injuries treated in hospital emergency departments*. (Bureau of Justice Statistics Special Report). Washington, DC: U.S. Department of Justice.

Ratner, P. A. (1993). The incidence of wife abuse and mental health status in abused wives in Edmonton, Alberta. *Canadian Journal of Public Health, 84*(4), 246–249.

Relf, M. V. (2001). Battering and HIV in men who have sex with men: A critique and synthesis of the literature. *Journal of the Association of Nurses in AIDS Care, 12*(3), 41–48.

Rennison, C. (2001). *Violent victimization and race, 1993–98*. Washington, DC: Bureau of Justice Statistics, U.S. Department of Justice.

Renzetti, C. M. (1992). *Violent betrayal: Partner abuse in lesbian relationships*. Thousand Oaks, CA: Sage.

Saltzman, L. E., Fanslow, J. L., McMahon, P. M., & Shelley, G. A. (1999). *Intimate partner violence surveillance: Uniform definitions and recommended data elements, Version 1.0*. Atlanta, GA: National Center for Injury Prevention and Control, Centers for Disease Prevention.

Schei, B., & Bakketeig, L. S. (1989). Gynaecological impact of sexual and physical abuse by spouse: A study of a random sample of Norwegian women. *British Journal of Obstetrics & Gynecology, 96*, 1379–1383.

Sharps, P. W., Campbell, J. C., Campbell, D. W., Gary, F. A., & Webster, D. W. (2001). The role of alcohol use in intimate partner femicide. *American Journal on Addictions, 10*, 122–135.

Sharps, P. W., Koziol-McLain, J., Campbell, J., McFarlane, J., Sachs, C., & Xu, X. (2001). Health care providers' missed opportunities for preventing femicide. *Preventive Medicine, 33*(5), 373–380.

Silva, C., McFarlane, J., Soeken, K., Parker, B., & Reel, S. (1997). Symptoms of post-traumatic stress disorder in abused women in a primary care setting. *Journal of Women's Health, 6*(5), 543–552.

Smith, T. W., & Ruiz, J. M. (2002). Psychosocial influences on the development and course of coronary heart disease: Current status and implications for research and practice. *Journal of Consulting & Clinical Psychology, 70*(3), 548–568.

Stark, E., & Flitcraft, A. H. (1996). *Women at risk: Domestic violence and women's health*. Thousand Oaks, CA: Sage.

Straus, M. A., & Gelles, R. J. (1990). *Physical violence in American families: Risk factors and adaptations to family violence in 8,145 families*. New Brunswick, NJ: Transaction Publishers.

Taliaferro, E., Mills, T., & Walker, S. (2001). Walking and talking victims of strangulation. Is there a new epidemic? A commentary. *Journal of Emergency Medicine, 21*, 3.

Thompson, M. P., Kaslow, N. J., Kingree, J. B., Puett, R., Thompson, N. J., & Meadows, L. (1999). Partner abuse and posttraumatic stress disorder as risk factors for suicide attempts in a sample of low-income, inner-city women. *Journal of Traumatic Stress, 12*, 59–72.

Tjaden, P., & Thoennes, N. (2000). *Full report of the prevalence, incidence, and consequences of violence against women* (NCJ-183781). Washington, DC: National Institute of Justice.

Tjaden, P., Thoennes, N., & Allison, C. J. (1999). Comparing violence over the life span in samples of same-sex and opposite-sex cohabitants. *Violence & Victims, 14*(4), 413–426.

Tollestrup, K., Sklar, D., Frost, F. J., Olson, L., Weybright, J. E., Sandvig, J., & Larson, M. (1999). Health indicators and intimate partner violence among women who are members of a managed care organization. *Preventive Medicine, 29*, 431–440.

Torres, S., Campbell, J. C., Campbell, D. W., Ryan, J., King, C., Price, P. J., Stallings, R., Fuchs, S., & Laude, M. (2000). Abuse during and before pregnancy: Prevalence and cultural correlates. *Violence and Victims, 15*(3), 303–322.

Ulrich, Y. C. (1991). Women's reasons for leaving abusive spouses. *Health Care for Women International, 12*, 465–473.

Weisz, A., Tolman, R. M., & Saunders, D. G. (2000). Assessing the risk of severe domestic violence: The importance of survivors' predictions. *Journal of Interpersonal Violence, 15*, 75–90.

West, C. M. (1998). Leaving a second closet: Outing partner violence in same-sex couples. In J. L. Jasinski & L. M. Williams (Eds.), *Partner violence: A comprehensive review of 20 years of research* (pp. 163–183). Thousand Oaks, CA: Sage.

Wilson, M. W., & Daly, M. (1993). Spousal homicide risk and estrangement. *Violence & Victims, 8,* 3–15.

Wingood, G., & DiClemente, R. (1997). The effects of an abusive primary partner on the condom use and sexual negotiation practices of African-American women. *American Journal of Public Health, 87,* 1016–1018.

Wisner, C. L., Gilmer, T. P., Saltzman, L. E., & Zink, T. M. (1999). Intimate partner violence against women. Do victims cost health plans more? *Journal of Family Practice, 48,* 439–443.

Wood, K., & Jewkes, R. (1997). Violence, rape, and sexual coercion: Everyday love in a South African township. *Gender & Development, 5*(2), 41–46.

Woods, S. J., & Isenberg, M. A. (2001). Adaptation as a mediator of intimate abuse and traumatic stress in battered women. *Nursing Science Quarterly, 14*(3), 215–221.

Wuest, J., & Merritt-Gray, M. (1999). Not going back: Sustaining the separation in the process of leaving abusive relationships. *Violence Against Women, 5,* 110–133.

7

Abuse of Elderly Women in Family Relationships: Another Form of Violence Against Women

L. RENE BERGERON

Each year, between 450,000 and 2 million older people are abused by family members (Jordan, 2001; *National Elder Abuse Incidence Study* [NEAIS], 1998). Although researchers do not agree on the actual number of abused elders, they agree that elder abuse is grossly underreported (called "the iceberg theory") (NEAIS, 1998). As the population ages, so too will the numbers of victims. Elder abuse is another form of violence that disproportionately affects women. Older women in the United States are more likely to be neglected, physically and sexually abused, and financially exploited than their male counterparts. Approximately two thirds of elder abuse victims are women (Tatara, 1993). Only abandonment is more common in elderly males (NEAIS, 1998; Phillips, 2000).

In the 1990s, the American Association of Retired Persons (AARP) organized a national forum to determine whether domestic abuse of older women was of national concern. Affiliating with the Wisconsin Coalition Against Domestic Violence, AARP surveyed all 50 states and concluded that older battered women were an underserved population (Wilke & Vinton, 2003). Teaster (2003) reported that women 60 years and older accounted for 56% of reported abuse, men accounted for 39%, and 5% of reports did not distinguish gender.

Researchers also recognize that abuse of elderly men may be highly underreported, and that men may not seek assistance, because they do not view themselves as victims. This chapter will not focus on the plight of male victims. Nonetheless, as is evident above, I fully recognize that male victims exist and are in need of protection and services as much as their female counterparts.

1 ELDER ABUSE WITHIN THE FAMILY

All types of elder abuse occur in various settings, including, but not exclusive to, health institutions, retirement centers, elders' homes, or within homes of caregivers. However, most reports of elder abuse involve community-dwelling elders and not those within institutional settings (NEAIS, 1998). Studies on elder abuse consistently show that family members, in most cases, are those who abuse elders living in the community (NEAIS, 1998). This chapter will discuss only that abuse occurring outside of institutions and within the family.

1.1 Definitions of Abuse

Elder abuse of older women within family systems is beginning to be referred to in the literature as another form of domestic violence, or as family violence in later life (Brandl & Horan, 2002). Such abuse is established by the age of the victim (which, depending on the state's reporting laws, may be defined as 50, 60, or 65 years or older) and who perpetrates the abuse (there needs to be a relationship involving trust, such as between a family member or caregiver) (Wilke & Vinton, 2003). The category of abuse also influences whether the term "domestic violence" is applied.

Universal definitions of elder abuse do not exist; however; all states have the same, general, five basic categories of defining abuse (Wolf, 2000a). Category 1 is neglect that may either be inflicted by the older person him or herself (self-neglect) or inflicted by a caregiver who does not meet the basic physical, emotional, or general living needs of the elder. Any form of neglect can be traumatic to an older person, but self-neglect, because it does not involve a perpetrator, is not considered to be a form of domestic elder abuse. However, neglect involving a perpetrator may happen because of the perpetrator's need to control the victim for self-gain. Current forensic work and research document that some cases of severe neglect can lead to the death of the elder. This is extremely upsetting when such deaths are a result of intentional neglect inflicted by a caregiver. Such acts have recently led to the passage of criminal neglect laws in several states. The other four categories of abuse always involve a perpetrator and, like neglect, may range from mild to severe abuse.

Category 2 is physical abuse. Physical abuse is any nonaccidental physical contact resulting in injury to the elder, including bruising, lacerations, shoving leading to injury, and torture, such as cigarette burns and so forth. Some state laws and researchers consider sexual abuse as one form of physical abuse, and others separate these two forms of violence into distinct categories. Therefore, it is typical to consider sexual abuse as a Category 3. Sexual abuse is the involvement of an elder in any undesired sexual contact. This includes the wide range of sexually assaultive acts ranging from requesting the elder to observe pornography or live sexual acts, to fondling of the elder and requesting the elder fondle the perpetrator, to acts of rape.

Category 4 refers to psychological or emotional abuse. For elderly people, this form of abuse can inflict great trauma, lead to isolation, and promote fear and compliance without leaving any observable evidence as may be found in neglect and physical and sexual abuse. It is usually used as a form of control by a perpetrator and is usually coupled with other forms of abuse.

Category 5 refers to financial exploitation of an elder by strangers, con artists and scam artists, providers of services, and family members. Financial exploitation also includes random one-time acts or a series of victimization acts (e.g., contractors, taxi services, selling of goods). It also includes improper use of legal devices, such as power of attorneys and guardianship. This category is complex in that skillful perpetrators may convince the elder to "give" them money, thereby making it difficult to prove that a crime has been committed and difficult for the elder to see the occurrence of victimization. Domestic abuse of an older person involves financial exploitation at the hands of intimate partners or family members. They may seek access to the elder's money through fear and intimidation, or deception, or they may solicit money with no intention of paying it back, or in exchange for equivalent services (e.g., bartering). Many times, this group of perpetrators uses other forms of abusive acts (e.g., physical or emotional abuse) to ensure continued financial control. Legal entities are focusing more attention than before on financial exploitation. More effort is being put into criminally prosecuting cases of financial exploitation involving both intimate perpetrators of ongoing financial abuse and stranger-perpetrated financial abuse, which may or may not be a one-time defrauding of the elder.

1.2 The Role of Isolation

Abuse of older women is difficult to detect because of two forms of isolation that occur as one ages: society promotes one type, and the perpetrator of abuse promotes the other type. Often, it is the combination of the two that makes it so difficult to detect elder abuse.

Society tends to disengage from the older person as a result of ageism. In U.S. culture, older people are no longer valued as a contributing part of society, thereby becoming an "invisible" population. Women in the U.S. culture are subject to discrimination because of ageism and also because of sexism. Thus, they are in double jeopardy of being "invisible" as compared to men. So, even as an older person remains engaged with society by shopping in stores, riding public transportation, or eating out at restaurants, those that serve them or sit next to them may not even notice them.

Perpetrators of abuse also isolate women to lessen the detection of abuse and ensure the perpetrator's control over the victims. Therefore, the very people needing to be "discovered" by an outsider often remain alone or with limited contacts behind closed doors. This makes detecting elder abuse more difficult than detecting child abuse and more difficult than detecting some cases of intimate partner violence, even though elder victims share many of the same attributes found in both groups. Consequently, health care professionals must be knowledgeable about and screen for elder abuse when they work with older women (Ahmad & Lachs, 2002; Bergeron, 2004; Brandl & Horan, 2002).

2 TYPES OF FAMILIAL ELDER ABUSE

Research on abused older women is said to be about 30 years behind that of child abuse and intimate partner violence research. In addition, early research on elder abuse was compromised by the promotion of the caregiver-stress model as the primary reason elderly women are abused (Bergeron, 2001, 2004; Brandl & Horan, 2002; Phillips, 2000; Wolf, 2000). The caregiver-stress model states that abuse of an older person happens because she is frail and dependent upon the care provider, thereby creating a burden of care that leads to frustration and a lashing out by the care provider. Other studies do not find this to be an overarching model but reflective of only a small percentage of cases (Brandl & Raymond, 1997; Phillips, 2000; Wolf, 2000a, 2000b). Better explanations for this type of abuse are contained in theories of intimate partner violence (IPV). However, an IPV framework is also limited, because it does not explain why adult children may abuse their parents. An ecological model may be an appropriate way of viewing abuse and neglect of elder women, because it views violence as a result of complex individual, interpersonal, and societal factors (Wolf, 2000a). The following case examples demonstrate the complexities of abuse by family members.

2.1 Abuse by Adult Children

Older women's relationships with their adult children are complicated by the dynamics of family systems, the duty of care mothers feel toward their children, regardless of their ages, and the history of the family. Adult children become abusive for a variety of reasons. Although some abuse is due to caregivers being overburdened, research on caregiver stress does not support the notion that the majority of abuse occurs because of it (Wolf, 2000a). Instead, personality problems or current needs of the adult or child, or mental health or developmental issues may be determining factors (Wolf, 2000a). The best way to demonstrate complexities is through case examples.

2.1.1 Case 1: Mary and Allen. Mary, 75 years old, is alert but does not drive a car and is physically frail. She lives in a two-bedroom trailer that she owns. Her son, Allen, 42 years of age, lives with her. Allen works odd jobs and is an alcoholic. She and Allen often fight about his drinking, his friends, and his lack of full-time work. He complains that she requires a lot of care and he cannot handle the pressure, as he does all the shopping, some of the cooking and housework, and various household maintenance tasks. In addition, Mary has a dog that urinates and defecates in the trailer when Allen is not home to let it out. This has caused the homemaker service to disengage as a provider of service. The visiting nurses association (VNA) has also disengaged, because Allen was intoxicated and belligerent once when a nurse went to visit Mary. Subsequently, the VNA labeled her as "noncompliant" because of her refusal to restrict Allen from the trailer. Neighbors have called the police when they have heard the breakage of household items and yelling. Although he has never hit her, he has placed ads in the newspaper that her trailer is up for sale. He has also removed items from the trailer to sell.

It is false to assume that Allen lives with his mother in order to provide her with care. And, it is dangerous to make this assumption when assessing this case. Although he may be viewed as the primary caregiver, Allen does not live with his mother primarily to perform caregiving tasks. Instead, his motivation for caregiving is rooted in his need for housing due to his lack of financial security and complications from his alcoholism. In this case, Allen's needs supersede those of his mother's. In an effort to ensure they are met, he controls her through intimidation (yelling, being belligerent), psychological abuse (threatening behaviors, belittling her), and instrumental aggression (throwing and breaking her things)—all of which are Category 4 types of abuse. These behaviors allow him to exploit her financially, a Category 5 type of abuse. Neglect (Category 1) of Mary is questioned here. The potential for physical abuse (Category 2) is high because of Allen's alcoholism and the volatile nature of their relationship.

Mary is bound to Allen through motherhood. Members of the current generation of older women have their identities secured in marriage and family, with a strong sense of commitment to husbands and children. Therefore, her reasons for not asking him to leave are complex. First, she feels responsible for him because of his inability to secure full-time employment. Second, she feels that if she had been a "better" mother, perhaps he would not have developed a drinking problem and be so "disrespectful." Furthermore, community services are often unable to meet the needs of elders in the community, because funding is subject to political approvals, private grants, and individual clients' ability to pay. Particularly for elders living in rural communities, consistent daily care through agency contact may be impossible to secure. Thus, her third reason for not asking him to leave is her worry about her ability to care for herself without Allen, as she has no other formal or informal systems to assist her on a daily basis. Although helpful, the homemakers and visiting nurses were only with her for a collective 4 hours per week. In actuality, although she did not want to lose their services, what she missed most was their company, because she needed much more assistance than they were providing. Allen is consistent, even though he is not reliable. He drives her places she needs to go, he is security for her when the furnace does not work in the winter, he takes care of the yard, and, when he is sober, he helps her to bed, tends to some meal preparation, and does some general household chores.

Fourth, although her dog has created work for her and contributes greatly to an unsanitary household, she will not have the dog removed. Her dog provides her with the emotional support that her son does not (see Boat & Knight, 2000, for a review of how to assist clients with pets). Hence, she feels somewhat violated by this request from the home care providers, and her independent nature will not allow her to be dictated to by these providers. In fact, one could argue that Mary is victimized by her son and again by the health care agencies assigned to provide her with care.

The withdrawal of services by the home care providers, in this case, begs professionals to reevaluate the provision of home care when servicing elderly abused women. Traditional elder home services were developed for frail elders, not abused elders. Consequently, elder abuse raises many ethical concerns for in-home providers. For example, agencies are responsible for the safety and health of their workers in the field and may need to limit services to homes that pose a threat because of unsanitary conditions or a possible threat of violence focused on the worker. On the other hand, agencies also have an ethical duty to clients, particularly those who are in compromising situations, to provide care that will enhance their lives and minimize abuse. But, home care workers are rarely trained in how to handle elder abuse. They usually go out as single workers to homes and rarely have cell phones. Additionally, their pay is not reflective of the level of expertise needed to provide services in such homes, or of the deplorable home conditions they may enter. Also, many home care workers are not educated in the dynamics of family relationships. For example, in this case, until this mother knows her son will have some security, and that she will not have to surrender her dog to maintain home care services, she will choose to sustain herself without help in this volatile and dysfunctional relationship with her son. Professionals should not misconstrue this to mean that she does not want to be helped.

2.1.2 Case 2 Mila and Kim. Mila is 80 years old and lives with her only daughter, Kim. Mila divorced her husband 15 years ago due to long-standing domestic violence. She moved in with her daughter, Kim, a single mother of two children, while she waited for an opening (a minimum of a 2-year wait) in public housing. This created a workable relationship, because Mila was able to contribute to the household expenses and provide after-school childcare for her grandchildren. When her name came up for an apartment unit, Kim discouraged her from moving. Also, Kim has remained close to her father, in spite of the history of violence against her mother. Thus, Mila still endures outings, holidays, and visits with him. In the last 5 years, Mila has developed macular degenerative disease and is considered legally blind. She is also compromised physically due to a heart condition. Mila has stated she would like to move into public housing, or even a nursing home, because she feels vulnerable around her ex-husband. Kim, however, continues to discourage her from moving, saying she is receiving good care where she is and is greatly loved by her family.

This case presents some of the same factors found in the case of Mary and Allen, but it is greatly complicated by the involvement of Mila's ex-husband and the culture of the family to be the primary care providers. Members of this family may also have the cultural values "that emphasize hiding family shame, avoiding conflicts in the family, and promoting tolerance" (Ahmad & Lachs, 2002, p. 803). Mila moved into her daughter's home by mutual agreement. That agreement was that Mila would contribute to household expenses by paying rent and by providing care to her grandchildren. Kim would ensure that her daily living needs of housing, clothing, and medical care were met. In the beginning, both considered Mila's stay temporary. As with many cases of parents moving in with their children, there was little discussion beforehand about possible impediments to the arrangement; in this case, namely, Kim's relationship with her father and her tendency to downplay the violence her mother suffered by him. Kim does not understand, or else is denying, the courage it took her mother to divorce her father in her later years. The divorce, coupled with Mila's expectation of having some distance from her ex-husband, needed intense discussion before the move. If both had been honest with each other during this discussion, they may have eliminated Kim's home as an appropriate temporary housing option.

After a year, Kim became comfortable with, and dependent upon, her mother's supplemental financial assistance and childcare, which has greatly assisted Kim's ability to maintain employment. Even with her mother's blindness, the grandchildren come home from school to a family member and thoroughly enjoy their grandmother's company. The use of a family member as a childcare provider greatly reduces Kim's sense of guilt and maintains the family value of caregiving by family members. Kim's behavior, although cushioned in family values, is exploiting her mother financially (Category 5) by restricting her right to self-determine where she wants to live. Mila's funds are being used to supplement Kim's household. In addition, her daughter's denial of the history of family violence and her demand on her mother to maintain "civil" contact with her father is emotionally abusive (Category 4) and is placing her mother in physical risk (Category 2) by being in situations where she is alone with her ex-husband.

The subtle coercion by Kim in linking Mila's desire to move out as being in opposition to the family values makes it hard for Mila, now physically compromised, to assert herself. Mila does not want to alienate her daughter, whom she deeply loves. Moreover, she fears being denied access to her grandchildren should she anger Kim. Currently, most states do not automatically recognize a grandparent's right to access grandchildren, and formal petitions to family court are required should parents deny access. Her daughter also makes her feel guilty for divorcing her father, who had always financially provided for the family, never drank, attended church regularly, and loves his family. Kim continually reminds her mother that her father stopped hitting her years before the divorce, and although he can still be insulting and belittling to her, he does not pose a physical threat as he once did. Kim has not restricted her father from visiting her home when she is not there, so it is not uncommon for him to "stop by" when Mila is alone during the day. Kim does not see the danger in his visits and has even expressed relief to know someone checks in on her mother before the children come home. The peace from her ex-husband that she sought in her later years is being denied to her by this family system, and, thus, the domestic violence continues.

The family's desire to care for one another keeps Mila isolated from home care providers, with whom she might confide about wanting to move out. No one but this family is aware of Mila's entrapment. It may be that Mila's physician will be her only source of assessment for abuse.

Yet, only 2% of reported elder abuse cases come from physicians (Ahmad & Lachs, 2002). And unless the right questions are asked, the physician may miss the needs of this older woman.

2.2 Abuse by Spouses

Spouses represent the second largest category of perpetrators of elder abuse (Cyphers, 1999). Spousal abuse may result from early onset in a long-term relationship (e.g., a long history of abuse throughout the marriage); or late onset in a long-term relationship (e.g., a result of health changes, alcoholism, dementia); or early onset in a new relationship (e.g., cohabitation or remarriage after divorce or widowhood) (Brandl & Raymond, 1997). Harris (1996) reported that although older women suffering from spouse abuse may be fewer in numbers than their younger counterparts, many of the risk factors are the same. Unfortunately, older abused women are not screened adequately by health care professionals for elder abuse (Bergeron, 2004).

2.2.1 Case 3: Marilyn, Charles, and Steven. Marilyn, 74 years of age, remarried a year after her husband died. The man she married was also widowed, lived several towns away, and previously had been a casual acquaintance of Marilyn and her husband. Marilyn gave up her home to move in with Charles. She disposed of most of her belongings as well. They consolidated some funds, but each kept their own personal savings account. Because her children lived out of state, she gave Charles durable power of attorney (DPOA) over her finances and medical care. She was also Charles' DPOA. Charles held all the DPOA documents, and she paid little attention to their finances, entrusting Charles with financial decisions as she had done with her first husband, Steven. After about 6 months of marriage, Charles began to become verbally abusive, saying things like she was nothing like his first wife and that he could not understand how Steven could stand being married to her for 20 years. His verbal abuse escalated after their 1st-year anniversary to slapping her periodically. Because she was ashamed of her predicament and did not want to worry her children or friends who had cautioned her against marrying so soon, she did not tell anyone. After 2 years of abuse, she sought mental health services for depression. Because she did not want Charles to know she was seeing a private counselor, she went to her savings account to withdraw money to pay privately. It was then that she discovered that her personal savings account had been reduced from $350,000 over the course of the 2 years to $10,000.

In many ways, Marilyn is a typical older woman to be abused physically, emotionally, and financially (Categories 2, 4, and 5). Like many older women, she grew comfortable in marriage and in a traditional division of duties. She had a good first marriage. She had cared for the home, shared yard work with her husband, relied on him as the primary family provider, and deferred all financial decisions to him. This arrangement worked well in her first marriage. She did not allow herself adequate grieving and adjustment time after Steven's death. She developed a false sense of security in her new relationship because of her and Steven's casual acquaintance with Charles. She also assumed Charles would be like Steven and, therefore, transferred the trust she felt for Steven to Charles, instead of employing some strong legal protective devices. She was also too willing to "give up" her old life. In short, she was vulnerable through widowhood and the previously trustworthy relationship of her first marriage (Quinn, 2000).

Depression is a typical victim reaction that may go undetected by far-away family and friends who see the victim only occasionally. Clearly, Marilyn's shame complicated detection, because she would attempt to cover up her situation with those who cared about her. Her decision to receive mental health services was a strength in this case, but it also placed the burden of discovery on the mental health clinician's ability to sensitively ask the right questions and engage Marilyn in treatment, as Marilyn may be slow to disclose the abuse. Her age may also be an impediment to discovery and receipt of services. Typically, health professionals do not adequately screen for elder abuse when they do depression screening. When they screen, their approach may be to secure "caregiving" for the victim instead of employing and nurturing her strengths to live independently (Seaver, 1996). Therefore, Marilyn is at risk for not receiving appropriate support, even if she receives mental health services and discloses abuse.

This case does not present any information on Charles' first marriage. One might guess that he was probably equally as controlling and abusive of his first wife. Securing a history of a person's past abusive actions is the best predictor that he will abuse in the future (Dunlop, Rothman, Condon, Hebert, & Martinez, 2000). Charles had "groomed" Marilyn for becoming a victim. Their courtship was short, she married him when she was most vulnerable, and her children lived out of state. He capitalized on her aversion to money matters by not insisting she become involved in their financial decisions. Instead, he encouraged her tendencies to "leave it up to him." He employed a legal device that allowed him access to her accounts in a town where she is not well known, but he is. He also manipulated her into selling her primary asset, her home. Ownership of one's home is a substantial "bargaining" chip in preventing and escaping domestic violence (Seaver, 1996). He gave her a false sense of security by initiating a DPOA with her as his agent, yet he held the document. He also carefully escalated the abuse slowly, giving her a chance to become comfortable, employing verbal abuse first, coupling it later with physical assaults.

Given time, his slapping may also move to more abusive acts. Based on the evidence of emotional, physical, and financial abuse, if sexual intimacy occurred with this couple after the other forms of abuse began, it was probably coercive and abusive, adding sexual abuse (Category 3) to the list of abuse suffered by Marilyn. Perpetrators of partner abuse effectively use any means of power to control their victims, seeking to humiliate their victims and gradually isolate them from people who care about them (Brandl, 2000).

Although researchers and service providers are now taking an interest in older abused women, older victims of domestic violence have been left out of the paradigm of domestic violence research and service provisions. Older women are different from younger victims. They are less likely to go to a shelter they have not visited beforehand. If physically impaired or in need of medical monitoring, traditional shelters may not be able to accommodate them. They are more likely to need financial advocacy to protect assets acquired over the years. They may present with health issues assumed by health professionals to be the result of old age. For example, a fall could be attributed to unsteadiness, bruising could be attributed to thinning skin and less fat tissue, and a broken bone could be attributed to osteoporosis. Older women deciding to remain living with their spouses may be misconstrued by professionals as their having grown accustomed to abuse and not wanting help, thereby eliminating creative approaches that may preserve the union but reduce the abuse and empower the victim through different responses to the perpetrators (Brandl & Horan, 2002).

2.2.2 Case 4: Carol. Carol provides care to her husband, who has lost the use of his right side due to a stroke. She bathes him, helps him transfer from bed to wheelchair, feeds him when necessary, and provides for his physical well-being. Early in their marriage, he had been physically abusive. But over the years, the physical abuse stopped, although he remained verbally abusive. Since his stroke, he has become frustrated with his limitations and has begun to physically abuse her again. He has spit on her when she attempted transfers. He has driven his wheelchair into her legs, urinated on her, and squeezed her arm with his good hand until she cried. She reported some of his behaviors to his in-home physical therapist without disclosing the past abusive relationship. The physical therapist spoke to him about his "acting out" behaviors but did not report this case to authorities because of viewing him as a vulnerable older adult due to his physical incapacities.

This case demonstrates the reverse of what is often reported in the literature—a caregiver being abused by the care recipient (Bergeron, 2001; Phillips, de Ardon, & Briones, 2000). Even without knowledge of the past history of domestic violence, Carol should be protected from her husband's current actions, and this case should be reported. Because her husband is still competent, he is responsible for his behaviors, which cannot and should not be excused because of impaired health. However, the past history of abuse solidifies that this is a dangerous situation for Carol. Because of previous abuse, an imbalance of power already exists in this relationship. Therefore, although her husband is impaired and dependent upon her for care, he is able to control her through aggressive, degrading acts (Category 4) and physical abuse (Category 2). Carol, who as caregiver can level some strong consequences on him for his actions, e.g., nursing home placement, does not consider doing so due to her subservient role rooted in their past. Phillips, de Ardon, and Briones (2000) found a positive (although not strong) correlation that increasing frustration felt by the care recipient due to impairment leads to greater acts of violence against the caregiver.

Carol's acceptance of this behavior places her in a vulnerable position. Caregivers who do not receive help are prone to depression and poor health (Rodriguez, Bauer, McLoughlin, & Grumbach, 1999). If violence must also be endured as part of the caregiving duties, not only will Carol's mental and physical health be greatly compromised, but she will also become prone to injury. When health care providers "excuse" violent actions because of ill health of the perpetrator, they devalue the safety needs of the caregiver and reinforce that the abuse should be excused (Brandl, 2000). This couple's marital history needs to be explored, consequences need to be identified, and counseling should be implemented to determine if it is reasonable for this couple to remain together with Carol as the primary caregiver.

Unfortunately, elder abuse reporting laws do not always allow for protection of the well elders because of the language in many laws that allows only for the protection of vulnerable elders (see below). Caregivers who were victims of past domestic violence and are physically well are not usually viewed by elder protective workers as more, or at least as equally, vulnerable as are their physically impaired care receivers (Bergeron, 2001). Even with this flaw, health care personnel can encourage caregivers to meet their own health care needs above that of the care recipient and be sensitive to the impact of family histories on the provision of care. Health care and mental health professionals can also reinforce that abuse by the care recipient should not be tolerated by the caregiver, and they can suggest alternate care arrangements.

3 INTERVENTION WITH ABUSED OLDER WOMEN

As the above cases illustrate, abusive families are often dealing with alcoholism or drug abuse, mental illness, dysfunctional family relationships, complex family histories, dementia of the victim or the perpetrator, ignorance about aging, poverty, and lack of services to replace the caregiving role of the perpetrator should he or she be removed. It is also often difficult to prosecute cases of elder abuse, particularly cases involving family members as perpetrators. The victim may be a poor witness due to dementia or other health issues or may become hostile and uncooperative if required to testify against a family member. Brandl and Raymond (2001) put it this way: "A victim with an ongoing relationship with an abuser often wants the abuse to end but the relationship to continue" (p. 63). Younger women in violent intimate partner relationships often express a similar sentiment (see Campbell & Kendall-Tackett, this volume, chapter 6).

In cases of financial exploitation, it is often difficult to decide what the true intention of the older person was, unless the victim clearly states that personal property or finances were stolen outright. Older people often do not want outside intrusion. And, today's older women do not have the same philosophy about personal rights as do their younger counterparts; they tend to view marriage for life and obligation to family above personal satisfaction, or maybe even personal safety (Phillips, 2000). Last, family systems are complex, bound by ethnic traditions and values, and have unique histories and family secrets.

3.1 Reporting Elder Abuse

One way professionals can intervene is by reporting elder abuse to the proper agency. Every state has abuse reporting laws, although they lack the standardization found in child abuse and intimate partner violence laws. Moreover, many laws are designed to protect "vulnerable" elders, leaving competent and physically well elders without protection from state adult and elderly protetive services (Bergeron, 2001a; Wolf, 2000). These reporting laws may be divided into two major groups: mandatory reporting (any suspicion of abuse must be reported) or voluntary reporting (the potential reporter may determine if and when to file suspicion of abuse). The agency with which to file a report also varies depending on the state, so, accordingly, it is important to know what agency has been given the authority to accept reports, investigate, substantiate, and service suspected victims. The Elder Abuse Center's Web site (http://www.elderabusecenter.org/) provides a directory of state reporting agencies, found by clicking on their "Links & Directories" sidebar and then clicking on "State Adult Protective Services Web Sites." The individual Web sites provide the necessary information on where to report suspected elder abuse. All laws protect the reporter from civil lawsuits, providing there is no malicious intent, and strive to protect the anonymity of the reporter.

Elder abuse laws are social service based, and only recently have individual state legislatures considered criminalizing some aspects of elder abuse. Thus, once a report is filed, the authorized agent approaches the situation as both an investigator and a problem solver. This is different than in child abuse investigations and domestic violence cases, where victims of abuse tend to be viewed as victims of crime. Because family members usually perpetrate elder abuse, social workers investigate and decide which cases should be reported to criminal authorities. The reasons for this remain valid (Callahan, 2000). Older people, unless deemed incompetent, have the civil right to decide how and with whom they want to live.

3.2 Other Interventions

For elderly abused wives, the approach is similar to their younger counterparts. They are first helped by being listened to and supported by not allowing them to remain in isolation (Brandl, 2000). Support groups for abused women may be wonderful sources of strength and mutual aid (Seaver, 1996). Helping women reconnect with friends and family, offering education about what constitutes abuse, providing respite away from care recipients, and slowly empowering victims by giving hope are useful techniques. Above all, professionals must become educated about stress and trauma in the later years. Joining task forces, reading journal articles, attending conferences on older abused victims, and learning from the experts in the field can assist more professionals in becoming competent in this area (Brandl, 2000; Wolf, 2000a).

In cases of spouse abuse, communities need to offer preventative services. Encouraging adult education to offer day and evening classes on financial management or encouraging widow support groups would have been useful for Marilyn in Case 3. Educating women about the importance of personal finances can be accomplished by forming coalitions with real estate agencies, investment firms, and banks. Teaching clients the usefulness and dangers of certain legal devices is a must for any agency or professional group that offers information about power of attorneys, conservatorships, and guardianships. It should also never be assumed that marriage constitutes an absolute obligation to provide in-home care. As in Case 4, careful discharge planning and intense monitoring after discharge may have helped Carol disclose the previous abuse and seek other solutions for her husband's care, thereby decreasing the abuse.

Additionally, teaching victims safety techniques within the home, helping women learn who their neighbors are, encouraging the securing of important papers, and advising on how to de-escalate an argument may be some useful strategies for victims (Brandl, 2000). Teaching safety techniques to professionals who enter such homes, holding agencies accountable for appropriate tools and training, and forming appropriate teams so a worker does not enter a home alone are also critical steps in "protecting the protectors." Such approaches may have kept services in Mary's (Case 1) home.

Becoming familiar with the history, culture, and dynamic of each family system is vital in understanding how both the caregiver and care receiver view their roles within the family. Case 2 could have a successful resolution if the primary physician obtained a social history and carefully screened Mila for abuse.

Professionals must become aware of resources that can help educate them about abuse in later life. The December 2003 issue (Volume 9, Number 12) of the journal *Violence Against Women*, is devoted to domestic violence in later life. (To learn more about this issue or order a copy, go to http://www.sagepub.com.) The National Elder Abuse Center (NEAC) offers an important Web site (http://www.elderabusecenter.org) with helpful links to state laws, current research, and overviews of elder abuse victim and perpetrator typologies. And, the *Journal of Elder Abuse and Neglect* (Haworth Press, Inc.) is a multidisciplinary journal devoted to elder abuse issues.

Practitioners in the field of family violence and elder abuse, mental health professionals, and home care services must develop creative ways for assisting older women. Women may not want to abdicate what they perceive as their duty to provide care. That does not mean they wish to be abused. Monitoring homes of abused older people can lessen the abuse. This means that health care providers must be trained in intervention techniques for elder abuse and have resources to meet their own safety needs.

4 CONCLUSION

The cases described earlier demonstrate the complexities of working with older women in abusive family situations. Although there is still much we do not know, these are exciting times for practitioners interested in abuse of older women. Practitioners must become aware that every older woman deserves to be screened as a potential victim of abuse (see Bergeron, 2004, and Fisher & Dryer, 2003, for in-depth approaches at screening techniques). Treatments must be offered that build on her strengths, regardless of her decision to live with or without the perpetrator. In cases of abuse that occur because of perpetrator needs (as in Case 1), if the perpetrator can be helped and his or her needs can be met, the abuse may be greatly modified or stopped.

In cases where abusive patterns are reinforced because of cultural norms and family denial (as in Case 2), assistance begins with care providers privately meeting with the woman, away from her caregivers, and sensitively asking her who is involved in her care, and does she approve of those involved. Physicians, including all specialties and dentists, must become better equipped to screen for abuse. Agency policies that require some time alone with the patient and with the caregiver are critical in screening for abuse of older women. In Case 1 and Case 2, assuming that caregiver stress was the reason for the abuse would impair a good assessment of the situations and reinforce that the victim was somehow responsible for the abuse. Therefore, an ecological model that forces professionals to look at multiple factors is required.

Abuse of older women will continue to grow as the population of older people grows. Older women deserve as much protection and innovation of services as any other group of women suffering from trauma and stress. Professionals need to learn ways of screening for suspected abuse and understand their duty to report it to the proper agency. Then, they need to become partners in the prevention and intervention processes.

REFERENCES

Ahmad, M., & Lachs, M. (2002). Elder abuse and neglect: What physicians can and should do. *Cleveland Clinic Journal of Medicine, 69*(10), 801–808.

Bergeron, L. R. (2001). An elder abuse case study: Caregiver stress or domestic violence? You decide. *Journal of Gerontological Social Work, 34*(4), 47–63.

Bergeron, L. R. (2004). Elder abuse: Clinical assessment and obligation to report. In K. Kendall-Tackett (Ed.), *Health consequences of abuse in the family: A clinical guide for evidence-based practice* (pp. 109–128). Washington, DC: American Psychological Association.

Boat, B., & Knight, J. (2000). Experiences and needs of adult protective services case managers when assisting clients who have companion animals. *Journal of Elder Abuse and Neglect, 12*(3/4), 145–155.

Brandl, B. (2000). Power and control: Understanding domestic abuse in later life. *Generations, 24*(2), 39–45.

Brandl, B., & Horan, D. (2002). Domestic violence in later life: An overview for health care providers. *Women and Health, 35*(2/3), 41–54.

Brandl, B., & Raymond, J. (1997). Unrecognized elder abuse victims. *Journal of Case Management, 6*(2), 62–68.

Callahan, J. (2000). Elder abuse revisited. *Journal of Elder Abuse and Neglect, 12*(1), 33–36.

Cyphers, G. (1999). Elder abuse and neglect. *Policy and Practice, 57*(3), 25–28.

Dunlop, B., Rothman, M., Condon, K., Hebert, K., & Martinez, I. (2000). Elder abuse: Risk factors and use of case data to improve policy and practice. *Journal of Elder Abuse and Neglect, 12*(3/4), 95–122.

Fisher, J. W., & Dyer, C. B. (2003, April). The hidden health menace of elder abuse: Physicians can help patients surmount intimate partner violence. *Postgraduate Medicine online, 113*(4). Retrieved from http://www.postgradmed.com/issues/2003/04_03/apr03.htm

Harris, S. (1996). For better or for worse: Spouse abuse grown old. *Journal of Elder Abuse and Neglect, 8*(1), 1–33.

Jordan, L. C. (2001). Elder and domestic violence: Overlapping issues and legal remedies. *American Journal of Family Law, 15*(2), 147–156.

National Elder Abuse Incidence Study (NEAIS). (1998). *The Final Report.* Washington, DC: The National Center on Elder Abuse, The American Public Human Services Association.

Phillips, L. (2000). Domestic violence and aging women. *Geriatric Nursing, 21*(4), 188–193.

Phillips, L., de Ardon, E., & Briones, G. (2000). Abuse of female caregivers by care recipients another form of elder abuse. *Journal of Elder Abuse and Neglect, 12*(3/4), 123–143.

Quinn, M. J. (2000). Undoing undue influence. *Journal of Elder Abuse and Neglect, 12*(2), 9–17.

Rodriguez, M., Bauer, H., McLoughlin, E., & Grumbach, K. (1999). Screening and intervention for intimate partner abuse. *Journal of the American Medical Association, 282*(5), 468–474.

Seaver, C. (1996). Muted lives: Old battered women. *Journal of Elder Abuse and Neglect, 8*(2), 3–21.

Tatara, T. (1993). Understanding the nature and scope of domestic elder abuse with the use of state aggregate data: Summaries of the key findings of a national survey of state APS and aging agencies. *Journal of Elder Abuse and Neglect, 5*(4), 35–57.

Teaster, P. (2003). *A response to the abuse of vulnerable adults: The 2000 survey of state adult protection services.* (National Committee for the Prevention of Elder Abuse, The National Association of Adult Protective Services Administrators, The National Center of Elder Abuse). Washington, DC: The National Center on Elder Abuse.

Wilke, D., & Vinton, L. (2003). Domestic violence and aging: Teaching abuse their intersection [Special section]. *Domestic Violence and Social Work Education, 39*(2), 225–235.

Wolf, R. (2000a). Elder abuse and family violence: Testimony presented before the U.S. Senate Special Committee on Aging. *Journal of Elder Abuse and Neglect, 8*(1), 81–96.

Wolf, R. (2000b). The nature and scope of elder abuse. *Generations, 24*(2), 6–13.

8

Health Issues Associated with Violence Against Women

STEPHANIE J. DALLAM

As described in previous chapters, each year, countless girls and women are exposed to violence. Violence against women occurs across all social groups, age groups, and religious and political persuasions. Even in countries sympathetic to women's equality, such violence is widespread—often beginning during childhood. For instance, in a nationally representative survey of 8,000 U.S. women, more than half the surveyed women reported that they were physically assaulted as a child by an adult caretaker or as an adult by another adult. In addition, nearly one fifth reported having been raped at some time in their lives. Of those who reported being raped, 54% were under the age of 18 when they were first assaulted (Tjaden & Thoennes, 1998).

Similar rates of violence and violation can be found in Canada. During in-depth, face-to-face interviews with a random sample of 420 women living in Toronto, Canada, over 97% of the women interviewed reported personally experiencing some form of sexual violation. One fourth of the women reported that they were physically assaulted by a male intimate, one half reported that they were raped or almost raped, and nearly half of the respondents reported that they experienced some kind of sexual abuse before reaching age 16 (Randall & Haskell, 1995).

Experiencing interpersonal violence is extremely stressful. Most traumatic are those events that induce terror, shame, and humiliation by reducing the individual to an object, thereby challenging deeply held assumptions of safety, fairness, ability to control events, and predictability (Cardena, Butler, & Spiegel, 2003). As such, personal human cruelty has far more devastating effects on the individual than natural disaster or accident (Foa, 1997). Accordingly, the psychological trauma associated with violence against women is intensified by the fact that the vast majority of victims are attacked by an acquaintance, family member, or intimate partner (National Victim Center, 1992). In a prospective study of female assault victims, Foa and colleagues found that at within 1 to 2 weeks of the crime, 90% of rape victims met symptom (though not duration) criteria for posttraumatic stress disorder (PTSD). At the 12-week assessment, 51% of the rape victims were diagnosed with PTSD (Foa, Rothbaum, Riggs, & Murdock, 1991). High rates of depression can also be found in survivors of sexual assault. For instance, two community surveys found the incidence of depression to be 100% in women who suffered sexual abuse involving penetration during childhood (Bifulco, Brown, & Adler, 1991; Cheasty, Clare, & Collins, 1998).

In addition to the well-documented adverse effects of trauma on mental health, a growing body of literature has presented findings that violence has a significant impact on physical health as well (see, e.g., Dallam, 2001; Felitti et al., 1998; Kendall-Tackett, 2003). This chapter will summarize the effects of early trauma on the developing brain and provide an overview of the complex interaction between the neurobiological effects of violence and subsequent health-related outcomes in women.

1 THE END IS IN THE BEGINNING: NEUROBIOLOGICAL EFFECTS OF EARLY MALTREATMENT

1.1 Effects of Chronic Maltreatment on Brain Growth and Function

Increasingly sophisticated neurobiological studies show that early trauma may adversely influence brain development and permanently alter the functioning of biological stress response systems in the brain (Bremner, this volume, chapter 9; De Bellis, 2002; Penza, Heim, & Nemeroff, 2003; Teicher, 2002). Prenatal life, infancy, childhood, and adolescence are critical periods characterized by increased vulnerability to stressors. During early childhood, the developing brain undergoes rapid growth characterized by high turnover of neuronal connections (Charmandari, Kino, Souvatzoglou, & Chrousos, 2003). During this period of plasticity, brain development is shaped by external signals (Perry, Pollard, Blakely, Baker, & Vigilante, 1995), with trauma exerting a particularly deleterious effect. Brain scans using magnetic resonance imaging (MRI) have demonstrated that maltreated children and adolescents with PTSD have significantly smaller intracranial and cerebral volumes than matched controls with no history of maltreatment. This lower brain volume is correlated with age of onset and duration of the abusive experiences and severity of dissociative and PTSD symptoms in the children studied (De Bellis et al., 1999).

Compared to their nonabused peers, abused children exhibit evidence of deficient development of the left-brain hemisphere (Ito, Teicher, Glod, & Ackerman, 1998) and a smaller corpus callosum—a brain structure that bridges the left and right hemispheres (Teicher, 2002). Other brain abnormalities reported in abused children include evidence of increased irritability in limbic structures, abnormal frontotemporal electrical activity, reduced functional activity of the cerebellar vermis, and altered anterior cingulate neuronal metabolism (De Bellis, Keshavan, Spencer, & Hall, 2000; Teicher, Andersen, Polcari, Anderson, & Navalta, 2002; Teicher et al., 2003).

These brain changes appear to affect cognitive functioning. For instance, compared to matched controls, children with PTSD secondary to maltreatment have been reported to perform poorly on measures of attention, abstract reasoning, and memory (Beers & De Bellis, 2002; Moradi, Doost, Taghavi, Yule, & Dalgleish, 1999). Studies in adult women with PTSD secondary to childhood abuse have found deficits in hippocampal-based declarative verbal memory and smaller hippocampal volume, as measured with MRI (Bremner et al., 1995; Bremner et al., 2003). The degree of decreased hippocampal volume correlates with the severity of dissociative symptoms and PTSD found in the abused women (Stein, Koverola, Hanna, Torchia, & McClarty, 1997).

1.2 Effect of Early Trauma on Neuroendocrine Function

As part of their normal functioning, the nervous and endocrine systems engage in a back and forth dance through which they control the body's physiology by continuously increasing or decreasing the activity of various neurotransmitters and hormones. The brain orchestrates this dance with the goal of maintaining a state of homeostasis or equilibrium. Stressful events disrupt the brain's delicate balance, and the brain responds by activating the sympathetic nervous system and the hypothalamic–pituitary–adrenal (HPA) axis and by releasing endogenous opioids. During acute stress, the brain and the various neuroendocrine systems work together with the goal of ensuring the short-term survival of the individual. Prolonged stress, on the other hand, can lead to sensitization of stress–response systems, resulting in enduring disruptions in neuroendocrine function.

1.2.1 Reactions to Acute Stress. The "fight-or-flight" response is generally regarded as the prototypic human response to stress (Taylor et al., 2000).

When the brain detects a stressful situation, the sympathetic nervous system is stimulated. The adrenal medulla responds to sympathetic stimulation by secreting into the bloodstream two catecholamines: epinephrine (also known as adrenaline) and norepinephrine (or noradrenaline). The onset of action is immediate. Within seconds, increased catecholamine levels result in hyperarousal, along with increased heart rate, respiration, blood pressure, and muscle tone. Simultaneous changes in the brain cause a state of hypervigilance in which the individual tunes out all noncritical information. This is called the fight-or-flight response, as the body prepares itself to fight with, or run away from, the potential threat.

Although the biobehavioral fight-or-flight theory has dominated stress research for the past 50 years, it has been disproportionately based on studies of adult males (Taylor et al., 2000). Further research suggests that this response is most related to traumas that are surmountable—in other words, situations where fighting back or getting away may be possible. A different reaction to severe trauma has been described in young children—particularly young girls. Perry has shown that when fighting or physically fleeing is not feasible, trauma may elicit a "freeze" or surrender response, in which the individual detaches from the events and withdraws inwardly (Perry et al., 1995; Perry, 2000). This dissociative reaction appears to be mediated by activation of the endogenous opiate and dopaminergic systems in the brain (Perry et al., 1995; Bohus et al., 1999).

Perry's research has shown that children often experience a combination of hyperarousal and dissociation during stressful events. When confronted with a traumatic event, the child will feel threatened, and the arousal systems will activate. With increasing threat, the child moves along the arousal continuum. At some point along this continuum, the child becomes so overwhelmed that endogenous opioids are released (Perry et al., 1995). Endogenous opioids bind to receptors on nearby brain cells and, thereby, reduce or block the spread of pain messages from the body through the brain (Zubieta et al., 2001). The result is a marked decrease in arousal, decreased awareness of pain, and a decrease in heart rate and blood pressure despite increases in circulating epinephrine.

Stressful events also activate the HPA. The hypothalamus is a structure in the middle part of the brain that controls a variety of autonomic functions aimed at maintaining homeostasis. When stressed, the hypothalamus releases corticotropin-releasing factor (CRF), a hormone associated with feelings of anxiety and fear. The CRF travels to the pituitary, where it stimulates the release of adrenocorticotropic hormone (ACTH) (Gutman & Nemeroff, 2003). The ACTH, in turn, stimulates the adrenal cortex—the outer layer of the adrenal gland that sits on top of the kidney—to release glucocorticoids, mainly in the form of cortisol. Cortisol has wide-ranging physiologic effects throughout the body. These include suppressing the immune response (thereby decreasing pain and inflammation), increasing the level of circulating glucose (increasing energy), and dampening fear responses to the stressor.

At the onset of a traumatic event, there is a dose-dependent increase in both catecholamines and cortisol, with the levels of each hormone increasing relative to the severity of the stressor (Yehuda, 2001). During the stress response, the body continues to strive for balance. Thus, whereas catecholamines stimulate hyperarousal, cortisol functions as an "antistress" hormone, helping to suppress and contain the neural defense reactions that if left unchecked might overwhelm the body (Munck, Guyre, & Holbrook, 1984; Yehuda, 2001). When the trauma has ended, negative feedback mechanisms are activated to counteract the stress hormones and return the heart rate, blood pressure, and other physiological adaptations to normal.

1.2.2 Reactions to Chronic Stress: Sensitization. During acute stress, the stress response is terminated with the end of the trauma. However, when trauma is severe and ongoing, compensatory mechanisms can become overactivated and incapable of restoring the brain's previous state of equilibrium. The physiological system is then forced to reorganize its basal patterns. The more intense and prolonged the traumatic event, the more likely there will be reorganization of these neural systems. This physiological reorganization may predispose trauma victims for the development of psychopathology after exposure to additional stress.

Perry's research has shown that chronically traumatized children will often, at baseline, be in a state of low-level fear, which is reflected in their body's physiology (e.g., increased heart rate, muscle tone, rate of respiration) (Perry et al., 1995). Overactivation of the fight or flight response can lead to chronically elevated levels of catecholamines, resulting in abnormalities in cardiovascular regulation, along with an increased startle response, profound sleep disturbances, regulation problems, and generalized anxiety (Perry, 1994, 2000; Perry et al., 1995). The endogenous opioid system can also become overreactive, resulting in the secretion of large amounts of endogenous opioids when exposed to a stimulus resembling the initial traumatic stressor (Van der Kolk, 1994). In turn, peritraumatic dissociations, especially numbing, have been found to be strong predictors of later PTSD and greater severity of PTSD symptoms (Birmes et al., 2003; Griffin, Resick, & Mechanic, 1997).

The predominant adaptive style of the child in the acute traumatic situation will determine which posttraumatic symptoms will develop—hyperarousal or dissociative (Perry, 2000). As the developing brain organizes around this internalization of the fear response, in time, equivalent neural activation can be elicited by decreasingly intense stimuli. As a result, full-blown hyperarousal or dissociation can be elicited by apparently minor stressors (Perry et al., 1995). This process, whereby the brain adapts to adverse events by becoming increasingly sensitive to stress-related cues, is known as "sensitization" (Plotsky, Owens, & Nemeroff, 1998). Chronic stress from early abuse is also associated with sensitization of the HPA axis, which increases further if additional traumas are experienced in adulthood (Heim et al., 2002). For example, adults with PTSD have been shown to have a highly sensitized HPA axis characterized by increased negative-feedback regulation, resulting in decreased basal cortisol levels and increased vulnerability to subsequent stress (Golier & Yehuda, 1998). Evidence of HPA axis activation can also be found in adults with affective disorders, substance abuse disorders, somatization, and chronic pain syndromes (Contoreggi et al., 2003; Crofford, 1996; Gutman & Nemeroff, 2003; Heim, Ehlert, Hanker, & Hellhammer, 1998).

Overall, early-life traumatic events, occurring during a period of neuronal plasticity, appear to permanently render neuroendocrine stress response systems supersensitive, resulting in a brain that is more irritable, impulsive, suspicious, and reactive to stress (Teicher, 2002). These changes may manifest in a number of psychiatric conditions. For instance, chronically traumatized children may display signs of PTSD, attention deficit/ hyperactivity disorder (ADHD), major depression, various dissociative disorders, oppositional–defiant disorder, conduct disorder, separation anxiety, or specific phobia (Perry & Azad, 1999; Perry et al., 1995).

1.3 Effect of Chronic Maltreatment on Immune Function

The immune system is composed of many interdependent tissues and cells that collectively protect the body from bacterial, parasitic, fungal, and viral infections and from the growth of tumor cells. Research with animals suggests that short bursts of stress may enhance immune function (Dhabhar, 2000). Chronic stress, on the other hand, has been associated with immune dysregulation and altered or amplified cytokine production, which may be expressed as either immunosuppression or inappropriate immune activation (Miller, Cohen, & Ritchey, 2002).

Evidence for immunosuppression is provided by studies finding that acute stress is accompanied by impaired wound healing, blunted humoral responses to immunization, reduced control of latent herpes viruses, and increased risk for upper respiratory infection (Cohen, Miller, & Rabin, 2001; Cohen, Tyrrell, & Smith, 1991; Herbert & Cohen, 1993; Kiecolt-Glaser, Glaser, Gravenstein, Malarkey, & Sheridan, 1996; Kiecolt-Glaser, Marucha, Malarkey, Mercado, & Glaser, 1995; Sheridan, Dobbs, Brown, & Zwilling, 1994). In addition, one of the primary organs of the immune system, the thymus gland, has been found to be significantly smaller in abused and neglected children when compared to those of nonabused children, with the size correlating with the severity and length of maltreatment (Fukunaga et al., 1992).

Evidence for inappropriate immune activation comes from preclinical and clinical studies showing that chronic psychological stress may increase production of the proinflammatory cytokine, interleukin-6 (IL-6), while simultaneously diminishing the immune system's sensitivity to cortisol—the hormone that normally terminates the inflammatory response (Kiecolt-Glaser et al., 2003; Stark et al., 2001). The IL-6 normally triggers inflammation to help fight infections and has been found to increase with aging (Kiecolt-Glaser et al., 2003). The effect of prolonged stress on IL-6 levels was examined in a longitudinal community study of persons caring for a spouse with dementia. Long-term caregiving was associated with IL-6 levels that were four times higher than those measured in a comparison group of noncaregivers. Three years after some of the caregivers' spouses died, their IL-6 levels remained elevated, suggesting that the caregiver's immune systems had been prematurely aged (Kiecolt-Glaser et al., 2003).

High levels of IL-6 are associated with cardiovascular disease, depression, osteoporosis, arthritis, Type 2 diabetes, and some cancers (Kiecolt-Glaser et al., 2003). In addition, inflammation has been found to play an important role in the pathogenesis of numerous allergic, autoimmune, rheumatologic, and cardiovascular diseases—illnesses that are worsened by stress (Nisipeanu & Korczyn, 1993; Rozanski, Blumenthal, & Kaplan, 1999; Whitacre, Cummings, & Griffin, 1995; Wright, Rodriquez, & Cohen, 1998; Zautra, Burleson, Matt, & Roth, 1994). Because prolonged stress appears to promote inflammatory processes, it is theorized that stressful events may set the stage for poor health by creating a situation in which inflammatory processes are allowed to flourish unchecked (Kiecolt-Glaser et al., 2003).

2 EFFECTS OF MALTREATMENT ON PHYSICAL HEALTH

Numerous aspects of physical health appear to be adversely affected by childhood maltreatment. The effects of maltreatment on physical health can be divided into four general, overlapping categories: subjective health perceptions, medical utilization, unexplained physical symptoms, and occurrence of serious illness and chronic disease.

2.1 Health Perceptions

Experiencing violence has been found to negatively impact how women view their overall physical health. For example, a meta-analysis by Golding, Cooper, and George (1997) examined health perceptions in victims of sexual assault by combining data on over 10,000 men and women from seven population surveys. The data revealed that a history of sexual assault, either in childhood or adulthood, was associated with poorer subjective health, with individuals with histories of multiple assaults reporting the worst health. Similar findings were reported in a survey of 1,225 women randomly selected from the membership of a large health maintenance organization (HMO). A history of childhood maltreatment was significantly associated with lower ratings of overall health, increased numbers of distressing physical symptoms, and greater functional disability. Women reporting multiple types of maltreatment demonstrated the greatest health decrements for both self-reported symptoms and physician-coded diagnoses (Walker et al., 1999).

2.2 Health Care Utilization

A history of physical or sexual assault during either childhood or adulthood is a powerful predictor of subsequent increased health care utilization (Bergman & Brismar, 1991; Felitti, 1991; Koss, Woodruff, & Koss, 1990). For example, research has shown that abused women use a disproportionate amount of health care services, including prescriptions and visits to primary care providers, emergency departments, and community mental health centers (Farley & Patsalides, 2001; Plichta, 1992). Abused women also tend to be admitted to the hospital more frequently and undergo more surgical procedures than their nonabused peers (Moeller, Bachmann, & Moeller, 1993; Salmon & Calderbank, 1996).

A partial quantification of the health care costs attributable to a history of childhood maltreatment was provided by a large-scale study of 1,225 randomly selected female members of an HMO. Women with histories of childhood maltreatment were found to have significantly higher primary care and outpatient costs, along with more frequent emergency department visits, than women without such a history. Moreover, a linear relationship was found between the amount and type of maltreatment experienced and increased costs. Patients who reported no childhood maltreatment had the lowest health care costs; women who reported any abuse or neglect had median annual health care costs that were $97 greater; women who reported sexual abuse had health care costs that were $245 greater; and those who reported the most types of maltreatment had the highest costs, an average of $439 more annually. These differences persisted after controlling for demographic and chronic disease variables (Walker et al., 1999).

The health care costs are similarly increased after victimization during adulthood. For example, Koss, Koss, and Woodruff (1991) examined the long-term consequences of criminal victimization on physical health among 390 adult women. Severely victimized women, compared with nonvictims, reported more distress and less well-being, made physician visits twice as frequently in the index year, and had outpatient costs that were 2.5 times greater. Criminal victimization severity was the most powerful predictor of physician visits and outpatient costs. Another large survey of health plan members showed that victims of intimate partner violence had health care costs that were approximately 92% higher than general female enrollees (Wisner, Gilmer, Saltzman, & Zink, 1999). Moreover, it is not only traumatic injuries that cause victimized women to seek medical care. Years after being assaulted, women continued to seek help for a variety of medical, gynecological, and psychiatric disorders, including suicide attempts (Bergman & Brismar, 1991).

2.3 Physical Complaints and Functional Disorders

A strong, graded relationship has been found between severity of past victimization and physical complaints in adulthood (Golding et al., 1997; Moeller et al., 1993). Leserman, Li, Hu, and Drossman (1998) sought to quantify the strength of the relationship between stress and health in 239 female patients from a referral-based gastroenterology clinic. Four factors (abuse history, lifetime traumas, turmoil in childhood family, and recent stressful life events) were found to be related to poorer health status (e.g., more pain symptoms, bed disability days, physician visits, functional disability, and psychological distress); together these stressors accounted for 32% of the variance in the women's overall current health (Leserman et al., 1998). A similar study of 668 middle-class females in a gynecological practice found that the number of different types of abuse experienced during childhood was the only variable that contributed significantly to the prediction of adult health and well-being (Moeller et al., 1993). Childhood maltreatment is also strongly associated with unexplained medical complaints, with abused women reporting problems in twice as many body systems as nonabused women (Lechner, Vogel, Garcia-Shelton, Leichter, & Steibel, 1993).

When no organic cause can be found to explain a patient's somatic complaints, the symptoms are considered "functional." Common functional disorders include fibromyalgia, a chronic condition characterized by fatigue and widespread muscle pain; irritable bowel syndrome, a gastrointestinal disorder characterized by frequent episodes of constipation, diarrhea, abdominal pain, and bloating in the absence of demonstrable organic pathology; and chronic pelvic pain. Functional disorders disproportionately affect women and are often linked to histories of traumatic stress. For instance, reports of unexplained symptoms are ubiquitous in the trauma literature (e.g., Saxe et al., 1994; Waitzkin & Magana, 1997; Van der Kolk et al., 1996). Likewise, an increased prevalence of childhood physical or sexual abuse has been associated with a number of functional health problems (see Table 8.1). These include chronic pelvic pain (Drossman et al., 1990; Harrop-Griffiths et al., 1988; Heim et al., 1998; Reiter, Shakerin, Gambone, & Milburn, 1991; Springs & Friedrich, 1992; Walker et al., 1992), irritable bowel syndrome (Drossman et al., 1990), fibromyalgia (Boisset-Pioro, Esdaile, & Fitzcharles, 1995; Imbierowicz & Egle, 2003), musculoskeletal pain (Drossman et al., 1990; Leserman et al., 1998; Linton, 1997), premenstrual dysphoric disorder (Girdler et al., 1998; Girdler et al., 2003), and chronic headaches (Domino & Haber, 1987; Drossman et al., 1990; Felitti, 1991; Romans, Belaise, Martin, Morris, & Raffi, 2002).

A history of abuse is also frequently reported in patients with chronic fatigue (Drossman et al., 1990; Romans et al., 2002). In addition, there is overlap between these disorders. For instance, about half of women with chronic pelvic pain also have irritable bowel syndrome (Whitehead, Palsson, & Jones, 2002); and women with fibromyalgia frequently suffer from numerous other unexplained disorders, including chronic fatigue syndrome, irritable bowel syndrome, temporomandibular disorder, and chronic headaches (Aaron & Buchwald, 2001).

For many years, women's unexplained somatic complaints were dismissed as manifestations of psychiatric illness or attention-seeking behavior (e.g., Bishop, 1980; Ford, 1997). Recent studies, however, challenge this assumption. Current research shows that mental illness may coexist with, but does not account for, the occurrence of unexplained physical complaints in women (Dickinson, deGruy, Dickinson, & Candib, 1999; Golding et al., 1997; Henningsen, Zimmermann, & Sattel, 2003). Although the etiology of functional disorders remains poorly understood, there is increasing evidence that disorders considered

TABLE 8.1
Functional Health Problems That Are Found More Frequently in
Women With a History of Victimization

Chronic fatigue

Chronic musculoskeletal pain

Chronic pelvic pain

Chronic headaches

Fibromyalgia

Irritable bowel syndrome

Premenstrual dysphoric disorder

Somatization

"functional" in the past may, in fact, result from HPA axis dysfunction similar to that found in PTSD and depression (Dallam, 2001; Heim et al., 1998; Kendall-Tackett, 2003). For example, alterations in HPA axis functioning have been reported in patients with fibromyalgia (Crofford, 1996), somatization (Heim et al., 1998; Gracely, Petzke, Wolf, & Clauw, 2002), irritable bowel syndrome (Milla, 2001), and chronic pelvic pain (Heim et al., 1998). Also, central hyperexcitability of pain-processing pathways, along with a decreased pain threshold, has been described in both fibromyalgia (Straud et al., 2003) and irritable bowel syndrome (Verne & Price, 2002). Although we have much to learn about functional disorders, current evidence suggests that they may ultimately be found to be a manifestation of the lasting neurobiological effects of prolonged stress on the brain.

2.4 Serious Illness and Chronic Disease

In addition to increased physical symptoms and greater medical utilization, victimization is also associated with increased rates of serious illness and chronic disease. For instance, a survey of a random community sample found that a number of illnesses were reported more often in women who had experienced sexual and physical abuse, both in childhood and in adult life. These included chronic fatigue, bladder problems, headaches, asthma, diabetes, and heart problems (Romans et al., 2002). Associations have also been found between early sexual abuse and several health conditions in the elderly. Stein and Barrett-Connor (2000) analyzed health data on more than 1,300 elderly white, middle-class men and women from a Southern California community. In women, early sexual assault appeared to increase the risk of arthritis and breast cancer, with multiple abuse episodes increasing disease risk by two- to threefold compared with a single episode. In men, early sexual assault appeared to increase the risk of thyroid disease.

The most comprehensive study of the effects of childhood maltreatment on adult health is the Adverse Childhood Experiences (ACE) study. The ACE study is a large-scale, ongoing epidemiological study that assesses the impact of numerous adverse childhood experiences on a variety of health behaviors and outcomes in adulthood. The investigators surveyed over 9,000 adults on adverse childhood experiences soon after they had a standardized medical evaluation at a large HMO. The participants were questioned about the presence of eight adverse experiences during childhood, including psychological, physical, or sexual abuse; violence against the mother; or living with household members who were substance abusers, mentally ill, suicidal, or ever imprisoned. The results revealed a strong, consistent, graded relationship between the number of adverse experiences and the presence of serious adult diseases, including ischemic heart disease, cancer, chronic lung disease, skeletal fractures, and liver disease. For example, those who experienced four or more types of adverse childhood experiences were 60% more likely to have diabetes and twice as likely to suffer cancer, stroke, or heart disease (Felitti et al., 1998). Taken together, these findings suggest that childhood maltreatment and household dysfunction may be related to the development of chronic diseases that are among the most common causes of death and disability in the United States (see Table 8.2).

3 THE MEDIATING EFFECT OF HEALTH- RISK BEHAVIORS

The relationship between childhood maltreatment and serious illnesses in adulthood appears to be partially mediated through participation in health-risk behaviors. The Centers for Disease Control (2003) identified a number of hazardous behaviors that contribute dramatically to leading causes of morbidity and mortality in adults, including cardiovascular disease, diabetes, and cancer. These behaviors include the following:

- Tobacco use
- Alcohol and other drug use
- Unhealthy dietary behaviors
- Inadequate physical activity
- Sexual behaviors that may result in HIV infection, other sexually transmitted diseases, and unintended pregnancies
- Behaviors that may result in violence or unintentional injuries (for example, injuries from motor vehicle crashes)

TABLE 8.2
Serious Health Problems That Are Found More Frequently in Women
With a History of Victimization

Arthritis

Asthma

Breast cancer

Cancer

Chronic lung disease

Diabetes

Heart disease

Liver disease

Skeletal fractures

Stroke

Each year, approximately 40 million illnesses and injuries and about a quarter of all deaths in the United States are caused by addictive substances (McGinnis & Foege, 1999). Substantial morbidity and social problems also result from indiscriminate sexual activities, including unintended pregnancies and HIV infection (Grunbaum et al., 2001). In addition, participation in one health-risk behavior has been found to significantly increase the likelihood of participating in others (Grunbaum et al., 2001; Zakarian, Hovell, Conway, Hofstetter, & Slymen, 2000). In fact, one nationally representative study of over 10,000 youth in the United States found that cigarette smoking, marijuana use, binge drinking, fighting, and having sex with multiple sexual partners clustered to form a "risk-behavior syndrome" (Escobedo, Reddy, & DuRant, 1997).

A childhood history of victimization or adversity has been found to be a strong risk factor for subsequent participation in a variety of unhealthy behaviors during adolescence and adulthood (Diaz, Simatov, & Rickert, 2000; Felitti et al., 1998; Fergusson, Horwood, & Lynskey, 1997; Raj, Silverman, & Amaro, 2000). The Commonwealth Fund Adolescent Health Survey, based on a nationally representative cross-sectional sample of 6,730 children in grades 5 through 12, found that adolescent girls were more likely than adolescent boys to experience physical abuse and were twice as likely to report having been sexually abused (Sarigiani, Ryan, & Petersen, 1999). After controlling for demographic characteristics (grade level, ethnicity, family structure, and socioeconomic status), girls who experienced either physical or sexual abuse were at increased risk of engaging in a variety of health-risk behaviors, including binging and purging behavior, regular smoking, regular drinking, and recent illicit drug use. The risk was strongest for those who reported both physical and sexual abuse (Diaz et al., 2000).

The relationship between sexual abuse and sexual risk taking among high school students was examined using data from the 1997 Massachusetts Youth Risk Behavior Survey, a self-report questionnaire administered to a representative sample of over 4,000 high school students. Only sexually experienced adolescents (n = 1,610) were included in the study. Almost one third of sexually experienced adolescent girls (n = 779) and one tenth of adolescent boys (n = 831) reported a history of sexual abuse. Adolescent girls and boys with histories of sexual abuse reported greater sexual risk taking than those without such a history. After controlling for related demographics and risk behaviors, sexually abused girls were significantly more likely than those without such a history to have had earlier first coitus, to have had three or more sex partners, and to have been pregnant (Raj et al., 2000).

Similar results were reported in a prospective study that followed a birth cohort of 510 girls into adulthood. At age 18, women who reported child sexual abuse, especially those reporting severe abuse involving intercourse, had significantly higher rates of early-onset consensual sexual activity, multiple sexual partners, unprotected intercourse, sexually transmitted disease, and sexual assault after the age of 16. Analyses revealed a multifactoral causal relationship in which various factors, such as family instability, impaired parent–child relationships, and childhood sexual abuse resulted in the early-onset sexual activity that, in turn, led to heightened risks of other adverse outcomes in adolescence (Fergusson et al., 1997).

Childhood victimization or adversity has also been found to be a strong risk factor for subsequent participation in a variety of unhealthy behaviors during adulthood. In fact, the ACE study, a survey of mostly middle-aged adult HMO members, found a strong graded relationship between the numbers of different adversities experienced in childhood and every health-risk behavior they studied, including cigarette smoking, obesity, physical inactivity, alcoholism, drug abuse, depression, suicide attempts, sexual promiscuity, and sexually transmitted diseases. Many of these relationships were strong. For example, those participants who experienced four or more types of adverse childhood experiences were more than seven times more likely to consider themselves alcoholics, almost five times more likely to have used illicit drugs, and more than 10 times more likely to have injected illicit drugs (Felitti et al., 1998). Further analysis revealed that adverse events during childhood may account for one half to two thirds of serious problems with drug use (Dube et al., 2003).

4 BIOLOGICAL INFLUENCES IN HEALTH- RISK BEHAVIOR

Participation in various health-risk behaviors may, for many women, reflect the lasting adverse neurobiological and emotional effects of violence. The evidence for such a relationship is especially strong for substance abuse. For example, posttraumatic stress symptoms are significantly associated with problematic drug and alcohol use in girls (Lipschitz, Grilo, Fehon, McGlashan, & Southwick, 2000), and emerging research has found that polysubstance abusers with no past or current psychiatric diagnosis show sensitization of the HPA axis similar to that found in PTSD (Contoreggi et al., 2003). Moreover, a longitudinal study of a national probability sample of 3,006 women found that after a new sexual assault, odds of both alcohol abuse and drug usage were significantly increased, even among women with no previous substance use or assault history (Kilpatrick, Acierno, Resnick, Saunders, & Best, 1997). Further support for a causal relationship is provided by numerous clinical studies in which addicted women have reported using substances expressly for the purpose of coping with the adverse effects of victimization (Ballon,

TABLE 8.3
Health- Risk Behaviors That Are Found More Frequently in Women
With a History of Victimization

Alcoholism
Binging and purging behavior
Cigarette smoking
Earlier first coitus
Illicit drug use
Physical inactivity
Sexual promiscuity
Unprotected sexual behaviors

Courbasson, & Smith, 2001; Harrison, Hoffmann, & Edwall, 1989). A list of health-risk behaviors that are found more frequently in women with a history of victimization than in their nonabused peers can be found in Table 8.3.

5 CONCLUSION

Millions of women in our society are the victims of violence at some point in their lives. Typically concealed and unacknowledged, violence against women nonetheless leaves lasting scars. These consequences include acute injuries and stress as well as long-term physical and mental health problems. In fact, childhood victimization is related to the development of serious diseases that are among the most common causes of death and disability in the United States. These include ischemic heart disease, chronic lung disease, skeletal fractures, liver disease, stroke, diabetes, and cancer.

Although we have yet to understand the specific pathways through which maltreatment exerts its influence on adult health, research showing enduring neurobiological effects of child abuse on the developing brain provides a plausible explanation for the consistency and dose-response relationships found between adverse childhood experiences and adult health problems. For instance, an emerging body of research reveals that the developing brain is exquisitely sensitive to, and can be permanently altered by, adverse experiences during childhood. Prolonged stress also leads to sensitization of stress–response systems, resulting in long-term disruptions in neuroendocrine and immune function. These physiological maladaptations likely represent long-term risk factors for the development of both mental and physical health problems after exposure to additional stress in later life.

The relationship between victimization and health is further mediated by engaging in high-risk behaviors, such as cigarette smoking, substance abuse, and risky sexual practices. These health-risk behaviors may reflect an attempt to cope with alterations in brain function and to escape painful emotional states. At the same time, they represent potent risk factors for many of the leading causes of morbidity and mortality in women, including cardiovascular disease, diabetes, and cancer. The interaction of these various neurobiological and behavioral responses to the stress of victimization may provide the framework through which early abuse is transformed from psychosocial experience into both mental illness and organic disease (Felitti, 2002).

The extensive health consequences that flow from violence have serious consequences, not only for individuals but also for society. The large increases in medical utilization associated with victimization represent an enormous economical burden for society. In addition, the violence that occurs behind closed doors is mirrored in various forms of community violence. In the end, the emotional and physical health of all citizens is affected by the climate of fear and insecurity that lingers in violence's wake. As such, the health costs associated with interpersonal violence are truly beyond measure.

REFERENCES

Aaron, L. A., & Buchwald, D. (2001). Fibromyalgia and other unexplained clinical conditions. *Current Rheumatology Reports, 3,* 116–122.

Ballon, B. C., Courbasson, C. M., & Smith, P. D. (2001). Physical and sexual abuse issues among youths with substance use problems. *Canadian Journal of Psychiatry, 46,* 617–621.

Beers, S. R., & De Bellis, M. D. (2002). Neuropsychological function in children with maltreatment-related posttraumatic stress disorder. *American Journal of Psychiatry, 159,* 483–486.

Bergman, B., & Brismar, B. (1991). A 5-year follow-up study of 117 battered women. *American Journal of Public Health, 81,* 1486–1489.

Bifulco, A., Brown, G. W., & Adler, Z. (1991). Early sexual abuse and clinical depression in adult life. *British Journal of Psychiatry, 159,* 115–122.

Birmes, P., Brunet, A., Carreras, D., Ducasse, J. L., Charlet, J. P., Lauque, D., Sztulman, H., & Schmitt, L. (2003). The predictive power of peritraumatic dissociation and acute stress symptoms for posttraumatic stress symptoms: A three-month prospective study. *American Journal of Psychiatry, 160,* 1337–1339.

Bishop, E. R., Jr. (1980). Diagnosis and management of hysteria. *Southern Medical Journal, 73,* 775–779.

Bohus, M. J., Landwehrmeyer, G. B., Stiglmayr, C. E., Limberger, M. F., Bohme, R., & Schmahl, C. G. (1999). Naltrexone in the treatment of dissociative symptoms in patients with borderline personality disorder: An open-label trial. *Journal of Clinical Psychiatry, 60,* 598–603.

Boisset-Pioro, M. H., Esdaile, J. M., & Fitzcharles, M. A. (1995). Sexual and physical abuse in women with fibromyalgia syndrome. *Arthritis and Rheumatism, 38,* 235–241.

Bremner, J. D., Randall, P., Scott, T. M., Capelli, S., Delaney, R., McCarthy, G., & Charney, D. S. (1995). Deficits in short-term memory in adult survivors of childhood abuse. *Psychiatry Research, 59,* 97–107.

Bremner, J. D., Vythilingam, M., Vermetten, E., Southwick, S. M., McGlashan, T., Nazeer, A., Khan, S., Vaccarino, L. V., Soufer, R., Garg, P. K., Ng, C. K., Staib, L. H., Duncan, J. S., & Charney, D. S. (2003). MRI and PET study of deficits in hippocampal structure and function in women with childhood sexual abuse and posttraumatic stress disorder. *American Journal of Psychiatry, 160,* 924–932.

Cardena, E., Butler, L. D., & Spiegel, D. (2003). Stress disorders. In G. Stricker, T. A. Widiger, & I. B. Weine (Eds.), *Handbook of psychology* (Vol. 8, pp. 229–249). New York: John Wiley.

Centers for Disease Control. (2003). *Assessing health risk behaviors among young people: Youth Risk Behavior Surveillance System* [Electronic version]. Atlanta, GA: Author. Retrieved from http://www.cdc.gov/nccdphp/aag/aag_yrbss.htm

Charmandari, E., Kino, T., Souvatzoglou, E., & Chrousos, G. P. (2003). Pediatric stress: Hormonal mediators and human development. *Hormone Research, 59,* 161–179.

Cheasty, M., Clare, A. W., & Collins, C. (1998). Relation between sexual abuse in childhood and adult depression: Case-control study. *British Medical Journal, 316*(7126), 198–201.

Cohen, S., Miller, G. E., & Rabin, B. S. (2001). Psychological stress and antibody response to immunization: A critical review of the human literature. *Psychosomatic Medicine, 63,* 7–18.

Cohen, S., Tyrrell, D. A., & Smith, A. P. (1991). Psychological stress and susceptibility to the common cold. *New England Journal of Medicine, 325*(9), 606–612.

Contoreggi, C., Herning, R. I., Na, P., Gold, R. W., Chrousos, G., Negro, T. J., Better, W., & Cadet, J. L. (2003). Stress hormone responses to corticotropin-releasing hormone in substance abusers without severe comorbid psychiatric disease. *Biological Psychiatry, 54,* 873–878.

Crofford, L. (1996). The hypothalamic–pituitary–adrenal axis in the fibromyalgia syndrome. *Journal of Musculoskeletal Pain, 4,* 181–200.

Dallam, S. J. (2001). The long-term medical consequences of childhood trauma. In K. Franey, R. Geffner, & R. Falconer (Eds.), *The cost of child maltreatment: Who pays? We all do* (pp. 1–14). San Diego, CA: Family Violence & Sexual Assault Institute (FVSAI).

De Bellis, M. D. (2002). Developmental traumatology: A contributory mechanism for alcohol and substance use disorders. *Psychoneuroendocrinology, 27,* 155–170.

De Bellis, M. D., Keshavan, M. S., Clark, D. B., Casey, B. J., Giedd, J. N., Boring, A. M., Frustaci, K., & Ryan, N. D. (1999). A. E. Bennett Research Award. Developmental traumatology. Part II: Brain development. *Biological Psychiatry, 45,* 1271–1284.

De Bellis, M. D., Keshavan, M. S., Spencer, S., & Hall, J. (2000). N-Acetylaspartate concentration in the anterior cingulate of maltreated children and adolescents with PTSD. *American Journal of Psychiatry, 157*(7), 1175–1177.

Dhabhar, F. S. (2000). Acute stress enhances while chronic stress suppresses skin immunity. The role of stress hormones and leukocyte trafficking. *Annals of the New York Academy of Sciences, 917,* 876–893.

Diaz, A., Simatov, E., & Rickert, V. I. (2000). The independent and combined effects of physical and sexual abuse on health. Results of a national survey. *Journal of Pediatric and Adolescent Gynecology, 13,* 89.

Dickinson, L. M., deGruy, F. V., III, Dickinson, W. P., & Candib, L. M. (1999). Health-related quality of life and symptom profiles of female survivors of sexual abuse. *Archives of Family Medicine, 8,* 35–43.

Domino, J. V., & Haber, J. D. (1987). Prior physical and sexual abuse in women with chronic headache: Clinical correlates. *Headache, 27,* 310–314.

Drossman, D. A., Leserman, J., Nachman, G., Li, Z. M., Gluck, H., Toomey, T. C., & Mitchell, C. M. (1990). Sexual and physical abuse in women with functional or organic gastrointestinal disorders. *Annals of Internal Medicine, 113,* 828–833.

Dube, S. R., Felitti, V. J., Dong, M., Chapman, D. P., Giles, W. H., & Anda, R. F. (2003). Childhood abuse, neglect, and household dysfunction and the risk of illicit drug use: The Adverse Childhood Experiences study. *Pediatrics, 111,* 564–572.

Escobedo, L. G., Reddy, M., & DuRant, R. H. (1997). Relationship between cigarette smoking and health risk and problem behaviors among U.S. adolescents. *Archives Pediatric Adolescent Medicine, 151,* 66–71.

Farley, M., & Patsalides, B. M. (2001). Physical symptoms, posttraumatic stress disorder, and healthcare utilization of women with and without childhood physical and sexual abuse. *Psychological Reports, 89,* 595–606.

Felitti, V. J. (1991). Long-term medical consequences of incest, rape, and molestation. *Southern Medical Journal, 84,* 328–331.

Felitti, V. J. (2002). The relationship between adverse childhood experiences and adult health: Turning gold into lead. *The Permanente Journal, 6*(1), 44–47.

Felitti, V. J., Anda, R. F., Nordenberg, D., Williamson, D. F., Spitz, A. M., Edwards, V., Koss, M. P., & Marks, J. S. (1998). Relationship of childhood abuse and household dysfunction to many of the leading causes of death in adults. The Adverse Childhood Experiences (ACE) Study. *American Journal of Preventive Medicine, 14,* 245–258.

Fergusson, D. M., Horwood, L. J., & Lynskey, M. T. (1997). Childhood sexual abuse, adolescent sexual behaviors and sexual revictimization. *Child Abuse and Neglect, 21,* 789–803.

Foa, E. B. (1997). Trauma and women: Course, predictors, and treatment. *Clinical Psychiatry, 5*(Suppl. 9), 25–28.

Foa, E. B., Rothbaum, B. O., Riggs, D. S., & Murdock, T. B. (1991). Treatment of posttraumatic stress disorder in rape victims: A comparison between cognitive-behavioral procedures and counseling. *Journal of Consulting and Clinical Psychology, 59,* 715–723.

Ford, C. V. (1997). Somatization and fashionable diagnoses: Illness as a way of life. *Scandinavian Journal of Work, Environment and Health, 23*(Suppl. 3), 7–16.

Fukunaga, T., Mizoi, Y., Yamashita, A., Yamada, M., Yamamoto, Y., Tatsuno, Y., & Nishi, K. (1992). Thymus of abused/neglected children. *Forensic Science International, 53,* 69–79.

Girdler, S. S., Pedersen, C. A., Straneva, P. A., Leserman, J., Stanwyck, C. L., Benjamin, S., & Light, K. C. (1998). Dysregulation of cardiovascular and neuroendocrine responses to stress in premenstrual dysphoric disorder. *Psychiatry Research, 81,* 163–178.

Girdler, S. S., Sherwood, A., Hinderliter, A. L., Leserman, J., Costello, N. L., Straneva, P. A., Pedersen, C. A., & Light, K. C. (2003). Biological correlates of abuse in women with premenstrual dysphoric disorder and healthy controls. *Psychosomatic Medicine, 65,* 849–856.

Golding, J. M., Cooper, M. L., & George, L. K. (1997). Sexual assault history and health perceptions: Seven general population studies. *Health Psychology, 16,* 417–425.

Golier, J., & Yehuda, R. (1998). Neuroendocrine activity and memory-related impairments in posttraumatic stress disorder. *Development and Psychopathology, 10,* 857–869.

Gracely, R. H., Petzke, F., Wolf, J. M., & Clauw, D. J. (2002). Functional magnetic resonance imaging evidence of augmented pain processing in fibromyalgia. *Arthritis and Rheumatism, 46*(5), 1333–1343.

Griffin, M. G., Resick, P. A., & Mechanic, M. B. (1997). Objective assessment of peritraumatic dissociation: Psychophysiological indicators. *American Journal of Psychiatry, 154,* 1081–1088.

Grunbaum, J. A., Kann, L., Kinchen, S. A., Williams, B., Ross, J. G., Lowry, R., & Kolbe, L. (2001, June 28). Youth risk behavior surveillance—United States, 2001 [Electronic version]. *Morbidity and Mortality Weekly Report (MMWR) Surveillance Summaries, 51*(SS04), 1–64. Retrieved from http://www.cdc.gov/mmwr/preview/mmwrhtml/ss5104a1.htm

Gutman, D. A., & Nemeroff, C. B. (2003). Persistent central nervous system effects of an adverse early environment: Clinical and preclinical studies. *Physiology and Behavior, 79,* 471–478.

Harrison, P. A., Hoffmann, N. G., & Edwall, G. E. (1989). Differential drug use patterns among sexually abused adolescent girls in treatment for chemical dependency. *International Journal of Addictions, 24,* 499–514.

Harrop-Griffiths, J., Katon, W., Walker, E., Holm, L., Russo, J., & Hickok, L. (1988). The association between chronic pelvic pain, psychiatric diagnoses, and childhood sexual abuse. *Obstetrics and Gynecology, 71,* 589–594.

Heim, C., Ehlert, U., Hanker, J. P., & Hellhammer, D. H. (1998). Abuse-related posttraumatic stress disorder and alterations of the hypothalamic–pituitary–adrenal axis in women with chronic pelvic pain. *Psychosomatic Medicine, 60,* 309–318.

Heim, C., Newport, D. J., Wagner, D., Wilcox, M. M., Miller, A. H., & Nemeroff, C. B. (2002). The role of early adverse experience and adulthood stress in the prediction of neuroendocrine stress reactivity in women: A multiple regression analysis. *Depression and Anxiety, 15,* 117–125.

Henningsen, P., Zimmermann, T., & Sattel, H. (2003). Medically unexplained physical symptoms, anxiety, and depression: A meta-analytic review. *Psychosomatic Medicine, 65,* 528–533.

Herbert, T. B., & Cohen, S. (1993). Stress and immunity in humans: A meta-analytic review. *Psychosomatic Medicine, 55,* 364–379.

Imbierowicz, K., & Egle, U. T. (2003). Childhood adversities in patients with fibromyalgia and somatoform pain disorder. *European Journal of Pain, 7,* 113–119.

Ito, Y., Teicher, M. H., Glod, C. A., & Ackerman, E. (1998). Preliminary evidence for aberrant cortical development in abused children: A quantitative EEG study. *Journal of Neuropsychiatry and Clinical Neurosciences, 10,* 298–307.

Kendall-Tackett, K. (2003). *Treating the lifetime health effects of childhood victimization.* Kingston, NJ: Civic Research Institute.

Kiecolt-Glaser, J. K., Glaser, R., Gravenstein, S., Malarkey, W. B., & Sheridan, J. F. (1996). Chronic stress alters the immune response to influenza virus vaccine in older adults. *Proceedings of the National Academy of Sciences, USA, 93,* 3043–3047.

Kiecolt-Glaser, J. K., Marucha, P. T., Malarkey, W. B., Mercado, A. M., & Glaser, R. (1995). Slowing of wound healing by psychological stress. *Lancet, 346,* 1194–1196.

Kiecolt-Glaser, J. K., Preacher, K. J., MacCallum, R. C., Atkinson, C., Malarkey, W. B., & Glaser, R. (2003). Chronic stress and age-related increases in the proinflammatory cytokine IL-6. *Proceedings of the National Academy of Sciences, USA, 100,* 9090–9095.

Kilpatrick, D. G., Acierno, R., Resnick, H. S., Saunders, B. E., & Best, C. L. (1997). A 2-year longitudinal analysis of the relationships between violent assault and substance use in women. *Journal of Consulting and Clinical Psychology, 65,* 834–847.

Koss, M. P., Koss, P. G., & Woodruff, W. J. (1991). Deleterious effects of criminal victimization on women's health and medical utilization. *Archives of Internal Medicine, 151,* 342–347.

Koss, M. P., Woodruff, W. J., & Koss, P. G. (1990). Relation of criminal victimization to health perceptions among women medical patients. *Journal of Consulting and Clinical Psychology, 58,* 147–152.

Lechner, M. E., Vogel, M. E., Garcia-Shelton, L. M., Leichter, J. L., & Steibel, K. R. (1993). Self-reported medical problems of adult female survivors of childhood sexual abuse. *Journal of Family Practice, 36,* 633–638.

Leserman, J., Li, Z., Hu, Y. J., & Drossman, D. A. (1998). How multiple types of stressors impact on health. *Psychosomatic Medicine, 60,* 175–181.

Linton, S. J. (1997). A population-based study of the relationship between sexual abuse and back pain: Establishing a link. *Pain, 73,* 47–53.

Lipschitz, D. S., Grilo, C. M., Fehon, D., McGlashan, T. M., & Southwick, S. M. (2000). Gender differences in the associations between posttraumatic stress symptoms and problematic substance use in psychiatric inpatient adolescents. *Journal of Nervous and Mental Disease, 188,* 349–356.

McGinnis, J. M., & Foege, W. H. (1999). Mortality and morbidity attributable to use of addictive substances in the United States. *Proceedings of the Association of American Physicians, 111,* 109–118.

Milla, P. J. (2001). Irritable bowel syndrome in childhood. *Gastroenterology, 120,* 287–290.

Miller, G. E., Cohen, S., & Ritchey, A. K. (2002). Chronic psychological stress and the regulation of pro-inflammatory cytokines: A glucocorticoid-resistance model. *Health Psychology, 21,* 531–541.

Moeller, T. P., Bachmann, G. A., & Moeller, J. R. (1993). The combined effects of physical, sexual, and emotional abuse during childhood: Long-term health consequences for women. *Child Abuse and Neglect, 17,* 623–640.

Moradi, A. R., Doost, H. T., Taghavi, M. R., Yule, W., & Dalgleish, T. (1999). Everyday memory deficits in children and adolescents with PTSD: Performance on the Rivermead Behavioural Memory Test. *Journal of Child Psychology and Psychiatry, 40,* 357–361.

Munck, A., Guyre, P. M., & Holbrook, N. J. (1984). Physiological functions of glucocorticoids in stress and their relation to pharmacological actions. *Endocrine Reviews, 5,* 25–44.

National Victim Center. (1992). *Rape in America. A report to the nation.* Arlington, VA: Author.

Nisipeanu, P., & Korczyn, A. D. (1993). Psychological stress as a risk factor for exacerbations in multiple sclerosis. *Neurology, 43,* 1311–1322.

Penza, K. M., Heim, C., & Nemeroff, C. B. (2003). Neurobiological effects of childhood abuse: Implications for the pathophysiology of depression and anxiety. *Archives of Women's Mental Health, 6,* 15–22.

Perry, B. D. (1994). Neurobiological sequelae of childhood trauma: Post-traumatic stress disorders in children. In M. Murberg (Ed.), *Catecholamines in post-traumatic stress disorder: Emerging concepts* (pp. 253–276). Washington, DC: American Psychiatric Press.

Perry, B. D. (2000). Trauma and terror in childhood: The neuropsychiatric impact of childhood trauma. Retrieved October 1, 2004 from http://www.childtrauma.org/CTAMATERIALS/trauma_and_terror.asp.

Perry, B. D., & Azad, I. (1999). Post-traumatic stress disorders in children and adolescents. *Current Opinion in Pediatrics, 11,* 121–132.

Perry, B. D., Pollard, R., Blakely, T., Baker, W., & Vigilante, D. (1995). Childhood trauma, the neurobiology of adaptation and "use-dependent" development of the brain: How "states" become "traits." *Infant Mental Health Journal, 16,* 271–291.

Plichta, S. (1992). The effects of woman abuse on health care utilization and health status: A literature review. *Women's Health Issues, 2,* 154–163.

Plotsky, P. M., Owens, M. J., & Nemeroff, C. B. (1998). Psychoneuroendocrinology of depression: Hypothalamic–pituitary–adrenal axis. *Psychiatric Clinics of North America, 21,* 293–307.

Raj, A., Silverman, J. G., & Amaro, H. (2000). The relationship between sexual abuse and sexual risk among high school students: Findings from the 1997 Massachusetts Youth Risk Behavior Survey. *Maternal and Child Health Journal, 4,* 125–134.

Randall, M., & Haskell, L. (1995). Sexual violence in women's lives. Findings from the Women's Safety Project, a community-based survey. *Violence Against Women, 1,* 6–31.

Reiter, R. C., Shakerin, L. R., Gambone, J. C., & Milburn, A. K. (1991). Correlation between sexual abuse and somatization in women with somatic and nonsomatic chronic pelvic pain. *American Journal of Obstetrics and Gynecology, 165,* 104–109.

Romans, S., Belaise, C., Martin, J., Morris, E., & Raffi, A. (2002). Childhood abuse and later medical disorders in women. An epidemiological study. *Psychotherapy and Psychosomatics, 71,* 141–150.

Rozanski, A., Blumenthal, J. A., & Kaplan, J. R. (1999). Impact of psychological factors on the pathogenesis of cardiovascular disease and implications for therapy. *Circulation, 99,* 2192–2217.

Salmon, P., & Calderbank, S. (1996). The relationship of childhood physical and sexual abuse to adult illness behavior. *Journal of Psychosomatic Research, 40,* 329–336.

Sarigiani, P. A., Ryan, L., & Petersen, A. C. (1999). Prevention of high-risk behaviors in adolescent women. *Journal of Adolescent Health, 25,* 109–119.

Saxe, G. N., Chinman, G., Berkowitz, R., Hall, K., Lieberg, G., Schwartz, J., & van der Kolk, B. A. (1994). Somatization in patients with dissociative disorders. *American Journal of Psychiatry, 151,* 1329–1334.

Sheridan, J. F., Dobbs, C., Brown, D., & Zwilling, B. (1994). Psychoneuroimmunology: Stress effects on pathogenesis and immunity during infection. *Clinical Microbiology Reviews, 7,* 200–212.

Springs, F. E., & Friedrich, W. N. (1992). Health risk behaviors and medical sequelae of childhood sexual abuse. *Mayo Clinic Proceedings, 67,* 527–532.

Stark, J. L., Avitsur, R., Padgett, D. A., Campbell, K. A., Beck, F. M., & Sheridan, J. F. (2001). Social stress induces glucocorticoid resistance in macrophages. *American Journal of Physiology. Regulatory, Integrative and Comparative Physiology, 28,* 1799–1805.

Stein, M. B., & Barrett-Connor, E. (2000). Sexual assault and physical health: Findings from a population-based study of older adults. *Psychosomatic Medicine, 62,* 838–843.

Stein, M. B., Koverola, C., Hanna, C., Torchia, M. G., & McClarty, B. (1997). Hippocampal volume in women victimized by childhood sexual abuse. *Psychological Medicine, 27,* 951–959.

Straud, R., Cannon, R. C., Mauderli, A. P., Robinson, M. E., Price, D. D., & Vierck, C. J., Jr. (2003). Temporal summation of pain from mechanical stimulation of muscle tissue in normal controls and subjects with fibromyalgia syndrome. *Pain, 102,* 87–95.

Taylor, S. E., Cousino-Klein, L., Lewis, B. P., Gruenewald, T. L., Gurung, R. A. R., & Updegraff, J. A. (2000). Biobehavioral responses to stress in females: Tend-and-befriend, not fight-or-flight. *Psychological Review, 107,* 411–429.

Teicher, M. H. (2002). Scars that won't heal: The neurobiology of child abuse. *Scientific American, 286,* 68–75.

Teicher, M. H., Andersen, S. L., Polcari, A., Anderson, C. M., & Navalta, C. P. (2002). Developmental neurobiology of childhood stress and trauma. *Psychiatric Clinics of North America, 25,* 397–426.

Teicher, M. H., Andersen, S. L., Polcari, A., Anderson, C. M., Navalta, C. P., & Kim, D. M. (2003). The neurobiological consequences of early stress and childhood maltreatment. *Neuroscience and Biobehavioral Reviews, 27*(1–2), 33–44.

Tjaden, P., & Thoennes, N. (1998). *Prevalence, incidence, and consequences of violence against women: Findings from the National Violence Against Women Survey* (No. NCJ183781). Washington, DC: U.S. Department of Justice.

Van der Kolk, B. A. (1994). The body keeps the score: Memory and the emerging psychobiology of posttraumatic stress. *Harvard Review of Psychiatry, 1,* 253–265.

Van der Kolk, B. A., Pelcovitz, D., Roth, S., Mandel, F. S., McFarlane, A., & Herman, J. L. (1996). Dissociation, somatization, and affect dysregulation: The complexity of adaptation of trauma. *American Journal of Psychiatry, 153*(Suppl. 7), 83–93.

Verne, G. N., & Price, D. D. (2002). Irritable bowel syndrome as a common precipitant of central sensitization. *Current Rheumatology Reports, 4,* 322–328.

Waitzkin, H., & Magana, H. (1997). The black box in somatization: Unexplained physical symptoms, culture, and narratives of trauma. *Social Science and Medicine, 45,* 811–825.

Walker, E. A., Gelfand, A., Katon, W. J., Koss, M. P., Von Korff, M., Bernstein, D., & Russo, J. (1999). Adult health status of women with histories of childhood abuse and neglect. *American Journal of Medicine, 107,* 332–339.

Walker, E. A., Katon, W. J., Hansom, J., Harrop-Griffiths, J., Holm, L., Jones, M. L., Hickok, L., & Jemelka, R. P. (1992). Medical and psychiatric symptoms in women with childhood sexual abuse. *Psychosomatic Medicine, 54,* 658–664.

Walker, E. A., Unutzer, J., Rutter, C., Gelfand, A., Saunders, K., VonKorff, M., Koss, M. P., & Katon, W. (1999). Costs of health care use by women HMO members with a history of childhood abuse and neglect. *Archives of General Psychiatry, 56,* 609–613.

Whitacre, C. C., Cummings, S. D., & Griffin, A. C. (1995). The effects of stress on autoimmune disease. In R. Glaser & J. K. Kiecolt-Glaser (Eds.), *Handbook of human stress and immunity* (pp. 77–100). New York: Academic Press.

Whitehead, W. E., Palsson, O., & Jones, K. R. (2002). Systematic review of the comorbidity of irritable bowel syndrome with other disorders: What are the causes and implications? *Gastroenterology, 122,* 1140–1156.

Wisner, C. L., Gilmer, T. P., Saltzman, L. E., & Zink, T. M. (1999). Intimate partner violence against women: Do victims cost health plans more? *Journal of Family Practice, 48,* 439–443.

Wright, R. J., Rodriquez, M. S., & Cohen, S. (1998). Review of psychosocial stress and asthma: An integrated biopsychosocial approach. *Thorax, 53,* 1066–1074.

Yehuda, R. (2001). Biology of posttraumatic stress disorder. *Journal of Clinical Psychiatry, 62*(Suppl. 17), 41–46.

Zakarian, J. M., Hovell, M. F., Conway, T. L., Hofstetter, C. R., & Slymen, D. J. (2000). Tobacco use and other risk behaviors: Cross-sectional and predictive relationships for adolescent orthodontic patients. *Nicotine and Tobacco Research, 2,* 179–186.

Zautra, A. J., Burleson, M. H., Matt, K. S., & Roth, S. A. (1994). Interpersonal stress, depression, and disease activity in rheumatoid arthritis and osteoarthritis patients. *Health Psychology, 13,* 139–148.

Zubieta, J. K., Smith, Y. R., Bueller, J. A., Xu, Y., Kilbourn, M. R., Jewett, D. M., Meyer, C. R., Koeppe, R. A., & Stohler, C. S. (2001). Regional μ-opioid receptor regulation of sensory and affective dimensions of pain. *Science, 13,* 293(5528), 311–315.

9

The Neurobiology of Childhood Sexual Abuse in Women with Posttraumatic Stress Disorder

J. DOUGLAS BREMNER

1 THE INVISIBLE EPIDEMIC OF CHILDHOOD ABUSE IN WOMEN

As described in previous chapters, the "invisible epidemic" of childhood sexual abuse is a major public health problem that is twice as common in women as in men (MacMillan et al., 1997; McCauley et al., 1997). Sexual abuse is also the most common cause of posttraumatic stress disorder (PTSD) in women, affecting 10%, or about 13 million, of women in the country at some time in their lives (Kessler, Sonnega, Bromet, Hughes, & Nelson, 1995). In about one out of three women with a history of abuse, PTSD becomes a lifelong problem (Saigh & Bremner, 1999).

Childhood trauma is also associated with increased rates of depression, substance abuse, dissociation, and borderline personality disorder (Bremner, 2002a). Research funding for HIV/AIDS is $1,800 per affected person per year in the United States, whereas funding for depression is only $18 and is much lower for abuse-related PTSD. This is in spite of the fact that, for example, we lose $31 billion per year in lost productivity in the United States because of depression, which is related to workers coming to work but not being productive (Stewart, Ricci, Chee, Hahn, & Morganstein, 2003). Lack of functioning has resulted in a situation in which essentially nothing is known about the long-term effects of childhood abuse on the brain.

2 NORMAL BRAIN DEVELOPMENT

The normal human brain undergoes changes in structure and function across the life span from early childhood to late in life. Understanding these normal developmental changes is critical for determining the difference between normal development and pathology, and how normal development and pathology interact. Although the bulk of brain development occurs in utero, the brain continues to develop after birth. In the first 5 years of life, there is an overall expansion of brain volume related to development of both gray matter and white matter structures. However, from 7 to 17 years of age, there is a progressive increase in white matter (felt to be related to ongoing myelination) and decrease in gray matter (felt to be related to neuronal pruning), whereas overall brain size stays the same (Casey, Giedd, & Thomas, 2000; Durston et al., 2001; Giedd et al., 1999b; Paus et al., 1999). Gray matter areas that undergo the greatest increases throughout this latter developmental epoch include the frontal cortex and parietal cortex (Rapoport et al., 1999; Sowell et al., 1999). Basal ganglia decrease in size, whereas corpus callosum (Giedd, Blumenthal, & Jeffries, 1999a; Thompson et al., 2000), hippocampus, and amygdala (Giedd, Castellanos, Rajapakse, Vaituzis, & Rapoport, 1997; Giedd et al., 1996b; Pfefferbaum et al., 1994) appear to increase in size during childhood, although there may be developmental-sex-laterality effects for some of these structures (Giedd et al., 1996a). Overall brain size is 10% larger in boys than girls during childhood (Giedd et al., 1996a).

2.1 Developmental Aspects of the Effects of Stress on Brain Stress-Responsive Systems

Stress has lasting effects on brain circuits and systems, with differing effects based on the stage of development at which the stressors occur. Brain regions in a network are involved in the stress response, including the hippocampus, amygdala, cingulate, and prefrontal cortex. Neurohormonal systems that play critical roles in stress include the hypothalamic–pituitary–adrenal (HPA) axis and noradrenergic systems.

2.1.1 Activation of the HPA Axis. Stress is associated with activation of the HPA axis (see also Dallam, this volume, chapter 8). Corticotropin-releasing factor (CRF) is released from the hypothalamus, with stimulation of adrenocorticotropic hormone (ACTH) release from the pituitary. This results in glucocorticoid (cortisol) release from the adrenal, which, in turn, has a negative-feedback effect on the axis at the level of the pituitary, as well as central brain sites, including hypothalamus and hippocampus. In addition to its role in triggering the HPA axis, CRF acts centrally to mediate fear-related behaviors (Arborelius, Owens, Plotsky, & Nemeroff, 1999), and it triggers other neurochemical responses to stress, such as the noradrenergic system via the brain stem locus coeruleus (Melia & Duman, 1991).

2.1.1.1 Animal Studies Studies in animals showed that early stress has lasting effects on the HPA axis. During infancy, animals do not demonstrate HPA axis responses to stress. However, infant animals exposed to stressors demonstrate increases in immediate early genes (e.g., c-*fos* and nerve growth factor inducible gene), in the paraventricular nucleus of the hypothalamus (Smith, Kim, Van Oers, & Levine, 1997). These studies demonstrate that a stress-responsive system is present, even though it does not invoke the HPA axis at that stage of development. A variety of early stressors, including maternal deprivation, resulted in increased glucocorticoid response to subsequent stressors (Levine, Weiner, & Coe, 1993; Stanton, Gutierrez, & Levine, 1988). Maternally deprived rats had decreased numbers of glucocorticoid receptors, as measured by dexamethasone binding, in the hippocampus, hypothalamus, and frontal cortex (Ladd, Owens, & Nemeroff, 1996). Early postnatal adverse experiences increased hypothalamic CRF mRNA, median eminence CRF content, and stress-induced glucocorticoid (Plotsky & Meaney, 1993) and ACTH release (Ladd et al., 1996). These effects could be mediated by an increase in synthesis of CRH mRNA following stress (Makino, Smith, & Gold, 1995).

In nonhuman primates, adverse early experiences resulted in long-term effects on behaviors, as well as elevated levels of corticotropin-releasing factor (CRF) in the cerebrospinal fluid (Coplan et al., 1996). The CRF is expressed in hippocampus, amygdala, prefrontal cortex, and other limbic brain areas, and it plays a critical role in regulation of the stress response (Arborelius et al., 1999). The CRF and glucocorticoid receptors develop at varying rates in early life (Avishai-Eliner, Yi, & Baram, 1996; Eghbal-Ahmadi et al., 1998), and increased CRF, with early stress acting in the amygdala, leads to potentiated behavioral and neurohormonal responses that persist throughout life (Avishai-Eliner, Hatalski, Tabachnik, Eghbal-Ahmadi, & Baram, 1999; Brunson, Avishai-Eliner, Hatalski, & Baram, 2001; Brunson, Grigoriadis, Lorang, & Baram, 2002; Hatalski, Guirguis, & Baram, 1998). These observations suggest early adverse experience permanently affects the HPA axis.

2.1.2 Noradrenergic Brain Systems. Early stressors also result in long-term alterations in noradrenergic brain systems. The majority of noradrenergic cell bodies are located in the locus coeruleus, a nucleus in the dorsal pons region of the brain stem, with a dense network made up of axons that extend throughout the cerebral cortex and to multiple cortical and subcortical areas. These areas include the hippocampus, amygdala, thalamus and hypothalamus, bed nucleus of stria terminalis, nucleus accumbens, as well as descending projections that synapse at the level of the thoracic spinal cord (Foote, Bloom, & Aston-Jones, 1983). Exposure to stressors results in activation of the locus coeruleus, with release of norepinephrine throughout the brain (Abercrombie & Jacobs, 1987). Acute stressors, such as a cat seeing a dog or another aggressive cat, result in an acute increase in the firing of neurons in the locus coeruleus (Levine, Litto, & Jacobs, 1990), with increased release of norepinephrine in the hippocampus and medial prefrontal cortex (Finlay, Zigmond, & Abercrombie, 1995). Chronic stress is associated with potentiated release of norepinephrine in the hippocampus, with exposure to subsequent stressors (Bremner, Krystal, Southwick, & Charney, 1996; Nisenbaum, Zigmond, Sved, & Abercrombie, 1991).

Early stress is associated with lifelong increases in sensitivity of the noradrenergic system (Sanchez, Ladd, & Plotsky, 2001). Noradrenergic input stimulates release of CRF from the paraventricular nucleus of the hypothalamus. Maternal separation resulted in an increased release of norepinephrine in the paraventricular nucleus of the hypothalamus. Maternal separation also resulted in a decrease in the -2 autoreceptor of the locus coeruleus (Francis, Caldji, Champagne, Plotsky, & Meaney, 1999). Because the -2 receptor is inhibitory, this would be expected to result in an increase in locus coeruleus activity, with increased noradrenergic reactivity. In summary, early stress is associated with lasting increases in noradrenergic responsivity.

2.1.3 Effect of Early Stressors on Brain Structure and Function. Early stressors result in alterations in hippocampal structure, with associated deficits in memory function, an effect related to elevated levels of glucocorticoids (McEwen et al., 1992; Sapolsky, 1996; Uno, Tarara, Else, Suleman, & Sapolsky, 1989; Woolley, Gould, & McEwen, 1990), inhibition of neurogenesis (Gould, Tanapat, McEwen, Flugge, & Fuchs, 1998; Malberg, Eisch, Nestler, & Duman, 2000), increased glutamate (Moghaddam, Adams, Verma, & Daly, 1997) or CRF (Brunson, Eghbal-Ahmadi, Bender, Chen, & Baram, 2001), and decreased levels of brain-derived nerve growth factor (NGF) (Duman, Heninger, & Nestler, 1997; Nibuya, Morinobu, & Duman, 1995; Smith, Makino, Kvetnansky, & Post, 1995). Changes in the environment (e.g., social enrichment or learning) can also enhance neurogenesis and slow the normal age-related decline in neurogenesis (Gould, Beylin, Tanapat, Reeves, & Shors, 1999; Kempermann, Kuhn, & Gage, 1998). Treatment with serotonin reuptake inhibitors (SSRIs) promotes neurogenesis (Malberg et al., 2000).

Rat pups that are handled frequently within the first few weeks of life (picking up rat pups and then returning them to their mother) had increased Type II glucocorticoid receptor binding, which persisted throughout life, with increased feedback sensitivity to glucocorticoids and reduced glucocorticoid-mediated hippocampal damage in later life (Meaney, Aitken, van Berkel, Bhatnager, & Sapolsky, 1988). These effects appear to be due to a type of "stress inoculation" from the mother's repeated licking of the handled pups (Liu, Diorio, Day, Francis, & Meaney, 2000). Considered together, these findings suggest that early in the postnatal period, there is naturally occurring brain plasticity in key neural systems that may "program" an organism's biological response to stressful stimuli. These findings may have implications for victims of childhood abuse.

2.1.3.1 The Stress Circuit Brain areas involved in the stress circuit (amygdala, prefrontal cortex, and hippocampus) have in common that they mediate different aspects of memory and visuospatial processing. The medial prefrontal cortex consists of several related areas, including orbitofrontal cortex, anterior cingulate (area 25-subcallosal gyrus, and Area 32), and anterior prefrontal cortex (Area 9) (Devinsky, Morrell, & Vogt, 1995; Vogt, Finch, & Olson, 1992). The medial prefrontal dopaminergic system is one of the most sensitive areas in the brain to even mild stressors (Roth, Tam, Ida, Yang, & Deutch, 1988). Lesions in this area result in a failure to mount the peripheral cortisol and sympathetic response to stress (Devinsky et al., 1995; Vogt et al., 1992). This area also has important inhibitory inputs to the amygdala that mediate extinction to fear responding. Animals with lesions of the medial prefrontal cortex are unable to extinguish fear responses after trials of fear conditioning (Morgan & LeDoux, 1995; Morgan, Romanski, & LeDoux, 1993). Human subjects with lesions of the prefrontal cortex show dysfunction of normal emotions and an inability to relate in social situations that require correct interpretation of the emotional expressions of others. These findings suggest that dysfunction of the medial prefrontal cortex may play a role in pathological emotions that sometimes follow exposure to extreme stressors, such as childhood sexual abuse.

Other brain areas that are interconnected with the medial prefrontal cortex play important roles in the stress response. The amygdala plays a central role in conditioned fear responses (Davis, 1992; LeDoux, 1993). The declarative memory functions of the hippocampus are important in accurately identifying the signal of potential threat during stress situations. The hippocampus is also involved in fear responses to the context of a stressful situation, in addition to its role in declarative memory. Posterior cingulate, parietal and motor cortex, and cerebellum are functionally related to the anterolateral prefrontal cortex (superior and middle frontal gyri) (Selemon & Goldman-Rakic, 1988), mediating visuospatial processing that is critical to survival in life-threatening situations (Devinsky et al., 1995; Vogt et al., 1992). The excessive vigilance seen in abuse-related PTSD may be associated with increased demands on brain areas involved in visuospatial aspects of memory function and planning of response to potentially threatening stimuli.

3 NEUROBIOLOGICAL STUDIES IN TRAUMATIZED CHILDREN

Few studies have been conducted in traumatized children. Research on traumatized children has been complicated by issues related to psychiatric diagnosis and assessment of trauma (Cicchetti & Walker, 2001). Some studies have not specifically examined psychiatric diagnosis, while others have focused on children with trauma and depression, and others on children with trauma and PTSD. No studies have specifically looked at sexually abused girls with PTSD. Sexually abused girls (in which effects of a specific psychiatric diagnosis were not examined) had normal baseline cortisol and blunted ACTH response to CRF (De Bellis et al., 1994a).

Another study of traumatized boys and girls, in which the diagnosis of PTSD was established, showed increased levels of cortisol measured in 24-hour urine (De Bellis et al., 1999a). Emotionally neglected boys and girls, in whom diagnosis was not assessed from a Romanian orphanage, had elevated cortisol levels over a diurnal period compared to controls (Gunnar, Morison, Chisolm, & Schuder, 2001). Maltreated school-aged boys and girls with clinical-level internalizing problems, without specific diagnoses, had elevated cortisol levels compared to controls (Cicchetti & Rogosch, 2001).

In a study of ACTH response to CRF challenge in boys and girls with depression, with and without a history of childhood abuse, children with depression and abuse had an increased ACTH response to CRF challenge compared to nonabused children with depression. These children were in a chaotic environment at the time of the study, indicating that the ongoing stressor may have played a role in the potentiation of the ACTH response to CRF (Kaufman et al., 1997). Although issues of diagnosis and subject population have introduced variability in these results, preliminary findings suggest increased cortisol levels early in the trauma response in children.

4 LONG- TERM EFFECTS OF EARLY ABUSE ON HPA AXIS AND NORADRENERGIC FUNCTION IN WOMEN WITH PTSD

Studies have also looked at the long-term neurobiological effects of early abuse in women. One early study showed that women with childhood abuse-related PTSD had increased cortisol levels at baseline in 24-hour urine samples (Lemieux & Coe, 1995). Adult women with a history of childhood abuse showed increased suppression of cortisol with low-dose (0.5 mg) dexamethasone (Stein, Yehuda, Koverola, & Hanna, 1997).

We performed a comprehensive assessment of the HPA axis in 52 women with diagnoses of PTSD, with and without histories of childhood abuse, including measurement of cortisol in plasma every 15 minutes over a 24-hour period. Subjects included women with a history of early childhood (premenarchal), penetrative sexual abuse by self-report with ($n = 21$) and without ($n = 15$) current abuse-related PTSD, and women without abuse or current PTSD ($n = 16$). Subjects were admitted to a General Clinical Research Center inpatient unit for measurement of plasma cortisol over a 24-hour period. All patients were medication free for 4 weeks or more before the study. Of the women with a history of abuse without PTSD, 40% had a history of depression. All subjects were studied during the early follicular phase of their menstrual cycles. Abused women with PTSD ($n = 19$) had lower levels of cortisol in the afternoon (12 to 5 p.m.) compared to the other groups ($p < 0.05$). Abused women with PTSD had a blunted ACTH response to CRF compared to non-PTSD nonabused women. There were no significant differences between the groups in cortisol response to CRF or ACTH, although PTSD women had a tendency to have lower cortisol relative to the other groups (Bremner et al., 2003a).

We also developed methods for assessment of neuroendocrine responses to stress in stress-related neuropsychiatric disorders. In an initial study, we looked at male and female patients with PTSD with a range of primary traumas, using a cognitive-stress challenge with problem solving under time pressure and with negative feedback. PTSD patients had increased cortisol levels at baseline in the pre-stress period, consistent with anticipatory anxiety, although their 24-hour cortisol during a resting period was low relative to controls.

During the challenge, both groups had an increase in cortisol, with patients continuing to be higher than controls but returning to control levels in the poststress phase (Bremner et al., 2002). We assessed cortisol response to traumatic reminders in women with abuse-related PTSD using personalized scripts of their childhood trauma. Women with PTSD had fourfold higher increases in cortisol with the traumatic scripts compared to abused non-PTSD women (Figure 9.1). Stress-induced elevations in cortisol were correlated with baseline PTSD symptom levels, measured with the Clinician Administered PTSD Scale (CAPS) (Elzinga, Schmahl, Vermetten, van Dyck, & Bremner, 2002). Adult women with depression and a history of early childhood abuse had an increased cortisol response to a stressful cognitive challenge relative to

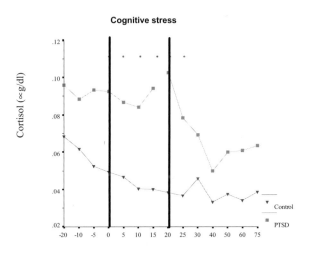

Time (minutes)

FIGURE 9.1. **Cortisol response to traumatic remembrance.** Women with abuse and PTSD had a fourfold higher increase in cortisol following exposure to a traumatic script of their own childhood sexual abuse relative to abused women without PTSD.

controls (Heim et al., 2000), and they showed a blunted ACTH response to CRF challenge (Heim, Newport, Bonsall, Miller, & Nemeroff, 2001).

These studies suggest that early abuse is associated with long-term changes in the HPA axis. One possible formulation is increased central CRF release (Baker et al., 1999; Bremner et al., 1997a), with blunted ACTH response to CRF due to down regulation of pituitary CRF receptors. Cortisol may be normal or low at baseline, depending on avoidance of reminders and other psychological parameters. However, with traumatic reminders or daily stressors, there is an exaggerated release of cortisol.

There is also some evidence for alterations in noradrenergic function in women with abuse-related PTSD. Studies in children with abuse, in which diagnosis of PTSD was not established, found increased catecholamines in 24-hour urine (including norepinephrine, epinephrine, and dopamine) (De Bellis, Lefter, Trickett, & Putnam, 1994b). Studies of boys and girls with the diagnosis of PTSD are consistent with elevations in catecholamines (De Bellis et al., 1999a). One study of women with sexual-assault-related PTSD did not find an overall increase in startle response, although there were greater asymmetries of startle response in the PTSD women (Morgan, Grillon, Lubin, & Southwick, 1997). Women with childhood sexual-abuse-related PTSD, compared to women with abuse without PTSD, had increased electromyogram (EMG) readings, heart rates, and skin conductance responses during exposure to traumatic scripts (Orr et al., 1998). These findings are consistent with increased sympathetic nervous system activity in abuse-related PTSD.

5 BRAIN IMAGING OF TRAUMATIZED CHILDREN

Few brain-imaging studies have been performed in children with PTSD. An early study showed alterations in electroencephalogram (EEG) measures of brain activity in boys and girls with a variety of traumas who were not selected for diagnosis compared to healthy children. About half of the children in these studies had a psychiatric diagnosis. Abnormalities were located in the anterior frontal cortex and temporal lobe and were localized to the left hemisphere (Ito et al., 1993; Schiffer, Teicher, & Papanicolaou, 1995). Two studies have found reductions in brain volume in children with trauma and PTSD symptoms (Carrion et al., 2001; De Bellis et al., 1999b), although studies have not found reductions in hippocampal volume in boys and girls with PTSD, either at baseline or over a longitudinal period (Carrion et al., 2001; De Bellis, Hall, Boring, Frustaci, & Moritz, 2001; De Bellis et al., 1999b). One study used single voxel proton magnetic resonance spectroscopy (proton MRS) to measure relative concentration of N-acetylaspartate and creatinine (a marker of neuronal viability) in the anterior cingulate of 11 children with maltreatment-related PTSD and 11 controls. The authors found a reduction in the ratio of N-acetylaspartate to creatinine in PTSD, relative to controls (De Bellis, Keshavan, Spencer, & Hall, 2000).

Studies have also found the size of the corpus callosum to be smaller in children with abuse and PTSD, relative to controls (De Bellis et al., 1999b). They also found that the superior temporal gyrus had a larger volume, relative to controls (De Bellis et al., 2002). In a study of abused children in whom diagnosis was not specified, there was an increase in T2 relaxation time in the cerebellar vermis, suggesting dysfunction in this brain region (Anderson, Teicher, Polcari, & Renshaw, 2002).

6 HIPPOCAMPAL VOLUME IN WOMEN WITH CHILDHOOD ABUSE- RELATED PTSD

The studies reviewed above introduced the possibility that stress may lead to damage to the hippocampus in human subjects (Bremner, 1998; Bremner, 2002a; Pitman, 2001). Early abuse is associated with deficits in hippocampal-based memory, as tested by paragraph recall and word learning tasks, with the severity of abuse correlating with degree of impairment (Bremner et al., 1995). Several studies from our group and others found a reduction in magnetic resonance imaging (MRI)-based hippocampus volume in men with combat-related PTSD (Bremner et al., 1995; Gilbertson et al., 2002; Gurvits et al., 1996; Villarreal et al., 2002). Studies have also found smaller hippocampal volume in men and women with early abuse-related PTSD (Bremner et al., 1997b) and in women with early abuse-related PTSD (Stein, Koverola, Hanna, Torchia, & McClarty, 1997).

A study in women with PTSD related to domestic violence in adulthood did not show smaller hippocampal volume (Notestine, Stein, Kennedy, Archibald, & Jernigan, 2002). We found smaller hippocampal volume in women with abuse and PTSD compared to women with abuse without PTSD and to nonabused non-PTSD women (Bremner et al., 2003c). There were no differences in whole brain volumes in adult women with abuse-related PTSD (Bremner et al., 2003b). Studies of hippocampal volume in depression, a common outcome of early abuse in women, have been conflicting (Bremner, 2002b). In a recent study, we found that smaller hippocampal volume in women was specific to depression, with a history of early childhood sexual abuse. There were no changes in women with depression without a history of early abuse (Vythilingam et al., 2002).

In summary, there are several studies in women with abuse-related PTSD showing a smaller volume of the hippocampus, at least in patients with chronic and severe illnesses. A recent study in PTSD patients, primarily related to early abuse, found a 5% increase in hippocampal volume measured with MRI and a 20% increase in memory function after a year of treatment with the SSRI paroxetine (Vermetten, Vythilingam, Southwick, Charney, & Bremner, 2003).

7 MAPPING THE NEURAL CIRCUITRY OF PTSD IN WOMEN WITH CHILDHOOD SEXUAL ABUSE HISTORIES

Functional neuroimaging studies have been performed in adult women with childhood abuse-related PTSD to map out the neural circuitry of abuse-related PTSD (Bremner, 2003; Bremner & Vermetten, 2001). These studies are consistent with dysfunction in a network of related brain areas, including the medial prefrontal cortex and hippocampus. We measured brain blood flow with PET and $[^{15}O]H_2O$ during exposure to personalized scripts of childhood sexual abuse. Twenty-two women with a history of childhood sexual abuse underwent injection of $H_2[^{15}O]$, followed by positron emission tomography (PET) imaging of the brain while listening to neutral and traumatic (personalized childhood sexual abuse events) scripts. Brain blood flow during exposure to traumatic versus neutral scripts was compared between sexually abused women, with and without PTSD.

Memories of childhood sexual abuse were associated with greater increases in blood flow in portions of anterior prefrontal cortex (superior and middle frontal gyri—Areas 6 and 9), posterior cingulate (Area 31), and motor cortex in sexually abused women with PTSD compared to sexually abused women without PTSD. Abuse memories were associated with alterations in blood flow in the medial prefrontal cortex, with decreased blood flow in subcallosal gyrus—Area 25, and a failure of activation in anterior cingulate—Area 32 (Figure 9.2). There was also decreased blood flow in the right hippocampus, fusiform/inferior temporal gyrus, supramarginal gyrus, and visual association cortex in PTSD relative to non-PTSD women (Bremner et al., 1999a). This study replicated findings of decreased function in medial prefrontal cortex and increased function in posterior cingulate in combat-related PTSD during exposure to combat-related slides and sounds (Bremner et al., 1999b).

In another study, eight women with childhood sexual abuse and PTSD were compared to eight women with abuse but without PTSD using PET during exposure to script-driven imagery of childhood abuse. The authors found increases in orbitofrontal cortex and anterior temporal pole in both groups of subjects, with greater increases in these areas in the PTSD group. The patients with PTSD showed a relative failure of anterior cingulate/medial prefrontal cortex activation compared to

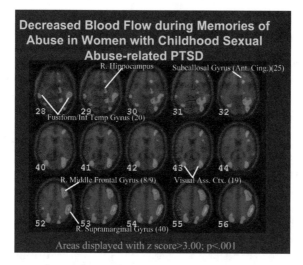

FIGURE 9.2. **Neural correlates of traumatic remembrance.** Women with PTSD relative to abused women without PTSD had decreased blood flow in the anterior cingulate/medial prefrontal cortex and hippocampus during exposure to traumatic scripts of their childhood sexual abuse.

controls. The patients with PTSD (but not the controls) showed decreased blood flow in anteromedial portions of prefrontal cortex and left inferior frontal gyrus (Shin et al., 1999).

These studies have relied on specific traumatic cues to activate personalized traumatic memories of childhood abuse and PTSD symptoms in patients with PTSD. Another method with which to probe neural circuits in PTSD is to assess neural correlates of retrieval of emotionally valenced declarative memory. In this type of paradigm, instead of using a traditional declarative memory task, such as retrieval of word pairs, like "gold–west," which has been the standard of memory research for several decades, words with emotional valence, such as "stench–fear" are utilized (Bremner et al., 2001). Although there has been relatively little research on retrieval of emotionally valenced words, it is of interest from the standpoint of PTSD as a method for activating neural pathways relevant to trauma and memory. If PTSD patients demonstrate a pattern of brain activation during retrieval of emotionally valenced declarative memory that is similar to that seen during exposure to other tasks that stimulate brain networks mediating PTSD symptoms, such as exposure to personalized scripts of childhood trauma or exposure to trauma-related pictures and sounds, then that would provide convergent evidence for dysfunction of a specific neural circuit in the processing of emotional memory in PTSD.

We recently used PET in the examination of neural correlates of retrieval of emotionally valenced declarative memory in 10 women with a history of childhood sexual abuse and the diagnosis of PTSD and 11 women without abuse or PTSD. We hypothesized that retrieval of emotionally valenced words would result in an altered pattern of brain activation in patients with PTSD similar to that seen in prior studies of exposure to cues of personalized traumatic memories. Specifically, we hypothesized that retrieval of emotionally valenced words in patients with PTSD, relative to those without PTSD, would result in decreased blood flow in medial prefrontal cortex (subcallosal gyrus and other parts of anterior cingulate), hippocampus, and fusiform gyrus/inferior temporal cortex (Figure 9.3), with increased blood flow in posterior cingulate, motor and parietal cortex, and dorsolateral prefrontal cortex.

Patients with PTSD, during retrieval of emotionally valenced word pairs, showed greater decreases in blood flow in an extensive area, which included orbitofrontal cortex, anterior cingulate, and medial prefrontal cortex (Brodmann's Areas 25, 32, 9), left hippocampus, and fusiform gyrus/inferior temporal gyrus, with increased activation in posterior cingulate, left inferior parietal cortex, left middle frontal gyrus, and visual association and motor cortex. There were no differences in patterns of brain activation during retrieval of neutral word pairs between patients and controls. These findings were similar to

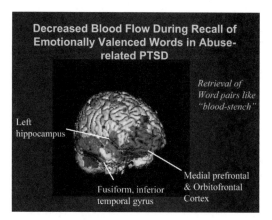

FIGURE 9.3. **Neural correlates of remembrance of emotional words.** Women with PTSD relative to women without PTSD had decreased blood flow in the medial prefrontal cortex/anterior cingulate and hippocampus during remembrance of emotional word pairs (e.g., "rape–mutilate").

prior imaging studies in PTSD from our group using trauma-specific stimuli for symptom provocation. This adds further supportive evidence for a dysfunctional network of brain areas involved in memory, including the hippocampus, medial prefrontal cortex, and cingulate, in PTSD (Bremner et al., 2003c).

Another study examined neural correlates of the Stroop task in sexually abused women with PTSD. The Stroop task involves color naming semantically incongruent words (e.g., name the color of the word green printed in the color red). The Stroop task has been consistently found to be associated with activation of the anterior cingulate in normal subjects, an effect attributed to the divided attention or inhibition of responses involved in the task.

Emotional Stroop tasks (e.g., name the color of a trauma-specific word like rape) in abused women with PTSD have also been shown to be associated with a delay in color naming in PTSD (Foa, Feske, Murdock, Kozak, & McCarthy, 1991). Women with early childhood sexual-abuse-related PTSD (*n* = 12) and women with abuse but without PTSD (*n* = 9) underwent PET measurement of cerebral blood flow during exposure to control, color-Stroop, and emotional-Stroop conditions. Women with abuse with PTSD (but not abused women without PTSD) had a relative decrease in anterior cingulate blood flow during exposure to the emotional (but not color) classic Stroop task. During the color-Stroop, there were also relatively greater increases in blood flow in non-PTSD compared with PTSD women in right visual association cortex, cuneus, and right inferior parietal lobule. These findings were consistent with dysfunction of the anterior cingulate/medial prefrontal cortex in women with early abuse-related PTSD (Bremner et al., 2004).

Other studies have found deficits in anterior cingulate and medial prefrontal cortex in childhood trauma populations. One study used single voxel proton MRS to measure relative concentrations of N-acetylaspartate and creatinine (a marker of neuronal viability) in the anterior cingulate of 11 children with maltreatment-related PTSD and 11 controls. The authors found a reduction in the ratio of N-acetylaspartate to creatinine in PTSD relative to controls (De Bellis et al., 2000).

We compared hippocampal function and structure in 33 women with and without early childhood sexual abuse and PTSD. Women with abuse with and without PTSD were studied during encoding of a verbal memory paragraph, compared to a control conjunction, in conjunction with measurement of brain blood flow with PET. Subjects underwent four PET scans using methods described by us previously in detail (Bremner et al., 1999a; Bremner et al., 1999b) in conjunction with encoding of a control task and an active paragraph encoding. There were no differences in blood flow during the control task between groups. However, there were significantly greater increases in blood flow during verbal memory encoding in the hippocampus in abused women without PTSD relative to those with PTSD ($F = 14.93$; df 1,20; $p < 0.001$). Abused women with PTSD also had smaller left hippocampal volume on MRI volumetrics compared to those without PTSD and nonabused non-PTSD women. Differences in hippocampal activation were statistically significant after covarying for left hippocampal volume, suggesting that failure of activation was not secondary to smaller hippocampal volume in patients with PTSD. There was a significant relationship between increased dissociative states as measured with the CADSS and smaller left hippocampal volume as measured with MRI in abused women as measured with logistic regression (R Squared = 0.30, $F = 3.90$; df = 1; $p < 0.05$) (Bremner et al., 2003b).

8 WOMEN WITH EARLY ABUSE AND BORDERLINE PERSONALITY DISORDER

We also studied women sexually abused in childhood with the primary diagnosis of borderline personality disorder (BPD). About 50% of these women had comorbid PTSD (Schmahl, McGlashan, & Bremner, 2002). Our group (Schmahl, Vermetten, Elzinga, & Bremner, 2003), and others (Driessen et al., 2000), found smaller hippocampal and amygdala volume in women with abuse and BPD. We developed a paradigm involving exposure to scripts of an abandonment situation, which is specific to the psychopathology of BPD, and which differentially affects women with BPD compared to PTSD as measured by psychophysiological responding

(Schmahl, Elzinga, & Bremner, 2002). We assessed cerebral blood flow with PET in 20 abused women with and without BPD while they listened to scripts describing neutral and personal abandonment events. Memories of abandonment were associated with greater increases in blood flow in bilateral dorsolateral prefrontal cortex and right cuneus, and greater decreases in anterior cingulate in women with BPD compared to women without BPD. These findings show some overlap between abused women with BPD and PTSD, specifically in the area of decreased anterior cingulate/medial prefrontal cortical function.

9 SUMMARY AND CONCLUSIONS

In a series of studies, our group and others have outlined circuits and systems underlying early abuse-related PTSD in women. These studies are consistent with increased HPA and noradrenergic function in women with abuse-related PTSD. Although baseline cortisol in adult women with abuse-related PTSD appears to be low, traumatic reminders and other stressors result in exaggerated release of cortisol. There is also evidence for increased catecholaminergic function in women with abuse-related PTSD. Studies in women with chronic long-standing PTSD have found smaller hippocampal volume, memory deficits, and failure of hippocampal activation during memory tasks. These findings are consistent with animal studies showing that early stress is associated with hippocampal damage and associated memory deficits. Brain imaging studies have consistently found decreased anterior cingulate/medial prefrontal cortical function in women with abuse-related PTSD during recall of traumatic memories. Other less well-replicated findings include increased dorsolateral prefrontal cortex and posterior cingulate function, and decreased hippocampal function.

Studies to date suggest that the developmental epoch during which trauma occurs and other factors, such as chronicity of trauma exposure and illness, are important factors to consider in trauma research. For instance, the brain continues to develop in early childhood and adolescence, with increasing volume of the amygdala and hippocampus and decreasing frontal cortex volume. Studies have found that a history of trauma in childhood can increase the risk of PTSD following exposure to a trauma in adulthood, such as combat trauma in Vietnam, by as much as fourfold. This is true even in individuals without any history of psychiatric disorder before entering the military (Bremner, Southwick, Johnson, Yehuda, & Charney, 1993).

Patients with long-standing and chronic PTSD do not respond as well to treatment as do patients with more acute-onset PTSD (Meadows & Foa, 1999). These findings are convergent with research in animal studies

(Bouton & Swartzentruber, 1991), suggesting that once traumatic memories have become established as indelible memories in the brain, they are resistant to subsequent modification and alteration. Patients with early-onset PTSD differ from patients with adult-onset PTSD, showing increased depression, substance abuse, and character pathology. Conversely, adult-onset PTSD is characterized by a greater degree of classical PTSD symptoms, including increased anxiety and hyperarousal (Prigerson, Maciejewski, & Rosenheck, 2001). One might speculate that these differences are related to effects on different brain structures (e.g., depression is linked to prefrontal dysfunction). However, we have little evidence on which to base these speculations.

Animal studies showed that environmental influences early in development can have effects on the brain and neurohormonal systems that persist throughout life. For example, as noted above, animals exposed to stressors early in life show heightened response (e.g., increased glucocorticoid responses) to subsequent stressors that persists throughout the life span. Although it was previously thought that humans do not have the capacity to grow new neurons in adulthood (neurogenesis), recently, the capacity for neurogenesis in the human hippocampus was discovered. It is thought that the creation of new neurons is related to the processes of new learning and memory. Deprived versus enriched and learning-enhanced environments early in life can affect hippocampal neurogenesis for the rest of the life span (Gould et al., 1999; Kempermann, Kuhn, & Gage, 1997). The implications of these findings are that early abuse may inhibit neurogenesis and result in lifelong problems in learning, as well as may promote some of the PTSD symptoms that may be mediated by the hippocampus.

REFERENCES

Abercrombie, E. D., & Jacobs, B. L. (1987). Single-unit response of noradrenergic neurons in the locus coeruleus of freely moving cats. II. Adaptation to chronically presented stressful stimuli. *Journal of Neuroscience, 7,* 2844–2848.

Anderson, C. M., Teicher, M. H., Polcari, A., & Renshaw, P. F. (2002). Abnormal T2 relaxation time in the cerebellar vermis of adults sexually abused in childhood: Potential role of the vermis in stress-enhanced risk for drug abuse. *Psychoneuroendocrinology, 27,* 231–244.

Arborelius, L., Owens, M. J., Plotsky, P. M., & Nemeroff, C. B. (1999). The role of corticotropin-releasing factor in depression and anxiety disorders. *Journal of Endocrinology, 160,* 1–12.

Avishai-Eliner, S., Hatalski, C. G., Tabachnik, E., Eghbal-Ahmadi, M., & Baram, T. Z. (1999). Differential regulation of glucocorticoid receptor messenger RNA (GR-mRNA) by maternal deprivation in immature rat hypothalamus and limbic regions. *Brain Research, 114,* 265–268.

Avishai-Eliner, S., Yi, S. -J., & Baram, T. Z. (1996). Developmental profile of messenger RNA for the corticotropin-releasing hormone receptor in the rat limbic system. *Developmental Brain Research, 91,* 159–163.

Baker, D. B., West, S. A., Nicholson, W. E., Ekhator, N. N., Kasckow, J. W., Hill, K. K., Bruce, A. B., Orth, D. N., & Geracioti, T. D. (1999). Serial CSF corticotropin-releasing hormone levels and adrenocortical activity in combat veterans with posttraumatic stress disorder. *American Journal of Psychiatry, 156,* 585–588.

Bouton, M. E., & Swartzentruber, D. (1991). Sources of relapse after extinction in Pavlovian and instrumental learning. *Clinical Psychology Reviews, 11,* 123–140.

Bremner, J. D. (1998). Neuroimaging in posttraumatic stress disorder. *Psychiatric Annals, 28,* 445–450.

Bremner, J. D. (2002a). *Does stress damage the brain? Understanding trauma-related disorders from a mind-body perspective.* New York: W.W. Norton.

Bremner, J. D. (2002b). Structural changes in the brain in depression and relationship to symptom recurrence. *CNS Spectrums, 7,* 129–139.

Bremner, J. D. (2003). Long-term effects of childhood abuse on brain and neurobiology. *Child and Adolescent Psychiatric Clinics of North America, 12,* 271–292.

Bremner, J. D., Krystal, J. H., Southwick, S. M., & Charney, D. S. (1996). Noradrenergic mechanisms in stress and anxiety: I. Preclinical studies. *Synapse, 23,* 28–38.

Bremner, J. D., Licinio, J., Darnell, A., Krystal, J. H., Owens, M., Southwick, S. M., Nemeroff, C. B., & Charney, D. S. (1997a). Elevated CSF corticotropin-releasing factor concentrations in posttraumatic stress disorder. *American Journal of Psychiatry, 154,* 624–629.

Bremner, J. D., Narayan, M., Staib, L. H., Southwick, S. M., McGlashan, T., & Charney, D. S. (1999a). Neural correlates of memories of childhood sexual abuse in women with and without posttraumatic stress disorder. *American Journal of Psychiatry, 156,* 1787–1795.

Bremner, J. D., Randall, P. R., Capelli, S., Scott, T. M., McCarthy, G., & Charney, D. S. (1995). Deficits in short-term memory in adult survivors of childhood abuse. *Psychiatry Research, 59,* 97–107.

Bremner, J. D., Randall, P. R., Vermetten, E., Staib, L., Bronen, R. A., Mazure, C. M., Capelli, S., McCarthy, G., Innis, R. B., & Charney, D. S. (1997b). MRI-based measurement of hippocampal volume in posttraumatic stress disorder related to childhood physical and sexual abuse: A preliminary report. *Biological Psychiatry, 41,* 23–32.

Bremner, J. D., Soufer, R., McCarthy, G., Delaney, R. C., Staib, L. H., Duncan, J. S., & Charney, D. S. (2001). Gender differences in cognitive and neural correlates of remembrance of emotional words. *Psychopharmacology Bulletin, 35,* 55–87.

Bremner, J. D., Southwick, S. M., Johnson, D. R., Yehuda, R., & Charney, D. S. (1993). Childhood physical abuse in combat-related posttraumatic stress disorder. *American Journal of Psychiatry, 150,* 235–239.

Bremner, J. D., Staib, L., Kaloupek, D., Southwick, S. M., Soufer, R., & Charney, D. S. (1999b). Neural correlates of exposure to traumatic pictures and sound in Vietnam combat veterans with and without posttraumatic stress disorder: A positron emission tomography study. *Biological Psychiatry, 45,* 806–816.

Bremner, J. D., & Vermetten, E. (2001). Stress and development: Behavioral and biological consequences. *Development and Psychopathology, 13,* 473–489.

Bremner, J. D., Vermetten, E., Vythilingam, M., Afzal, N., Schmahl, C., Elzinga, B. E., & Charney, D. S. (2004). Neural correlates of the classical neutral and emotional Stroop in women with abuse-related posttraumatic stress disorder. *Biological Psychiatry, 55,* 612–620.

Bremner, J. D., Vythilingam, M., Anderson, G., Vermetten, E., McGlashan, T., Heninger, G., Rasmusson, A., Southwick, S. M., & Charney, D. S. (2003a). Assessment of the hypothalamic–pituitary–adrenal (HPA) axis over a 24-hour diurnal period and in response to neuroendocrine challenges in women with and without early childhood sexual abuse and posttraumatic stress disorder (PTSD). *Biological Psychiatry, 54,* 710–718.

Bremner, J.D., Vythilingam, M., Vermetten, E., Adil, J., Khan, S., Nazeer, A., Afzal, N., McGlashan, T., Anderson, G., Heninger, G. R., Southwick, S. M., & Charney, D. S. (2002). Cortisol response to a cognitive stress challenge in posttraumatic stress disorder (PTSD) related to childhood abuse. *Psychoneuroendocrinology, 28,* 733–750.

Bremner, J. D., Vythilingam, M., Vermetten, E., Southwick, S. M., McGlashan, T., Nazeer, A., Khan, S., Vaccarino, L. V., Soufer, R., Garg, P., Ng, C. K., Staib, L. H., Duncan, J. S., & Charney, D. S. (2003b). MRI and PET study of deficits in hippocampal structure and function in women with childhood sexual abuse and posttraumatic stress disorder (PTSD). *American Journal of Psychiatry, 160,* 924–932.

Bremner, J. D., Vythilingam, M., Vermetten, E., Southwick, S. M., McGlashan, T., Staib, L., Soufer, R., & Charney, D. S. (2003c). Neural correlates of declarative memory for emotionally valenced words in women with posttraumatic stress disorder (PTSD) related to early childhood sexual abuse. *Biological Psychiatry, 53,* 289–299.

Brunson, K. L., Avishai-Eliner, S., Hatalski, C. G., & Baram, T. Z. (2001). Neurobiology of the stress response early in life: Evolution of a concept and the role of corticotropin releasing hormone. *Molecular Psychiatry, 6,* 647–656.

Brunson, K. L., Eghbal-Ahmadi, M., Bender, R., Chen, Y., & Baram, T. Z. (2001). Long-term, progressive hippocampal cell loss and dysfunction induced by early-life administration of corticotropin-releasing hormone reproduce the effects of early-life stress. *Proceedings of the National Academy of Sciences USA, 98,* 8856–8861.

Brunson, K. L., Grigoriadis, D. E., Lorang, M. T., & Baram, T. Z. (2002). Corticotropin-releasing hormone (CRH) downregulates the function of its receptor (CRF-1) and induces CRF-1 expression in hippocampal and cortical regions of the immature rat brain. *Experimental Neurology, 176,* 75–86.

Carrion, V. G., Weems, C. F., Eliez, S., Patwardhan, A., Brown, W., Ray, R. D., & Reiss, A. L. (2001). Attenuation of frontal asymmetry in pediatric posttraumatic stress disorder. *Biological Psychiatry, 50,* 943–951.

Casey, B. J., Giedd, J. N., & Thomas, K. M. (2000). Structural and functional brain development and its relation to cognitive development. *Biological Psychiatry, 54,* 241–257.

Cicchetti, D., & Rogosch, F. A. (2001). The impact of child maltreatment and psychopathology on neuroendocrine functioning. *Development and Psychopathology, 13,* 783–804.

Cicchetti, D., & Walker, E. F. (2001). Stress and development: Biological and psychological consequences. *Development and Psychopathology, 13,* 413–418.

Coplan, J. D., Andrews, M. W., Rosenblum, L. A., Owens, M. J., Friedman, S., Gorman, J. M., & Nemeroff, C. B. (1996). Persistent elevations of cerebrospinal fluid concentrations of corticotropin-releasing factor in adult nonhuman primates exposed to early-life stressors: Implications for the pathophysiology of mood and anxiety disorders. *Proceedings of the National Academy of Sciences USA, 93,* 1619–1623.

Davis, M. (1992). The role of the amygdala in fear and anxiety. *Annual Review of Neuroscience, 15,* 353–375.

De Bellis, M. D., Baum, A. S., Keshavan, M. S., Eccard, C. H., Boring, A. M., Jenkins, F. J., & Ryan, N. D. (1999a). A. E. Bennett Research Award: Developmental traumatology: Part I: Biological stress systems. *Biological Psychiatry, 45,* 1259–1270.

De Bellis, M. D., Chrousos, G. P., Dorn, L. D., Burke, L., Helmers, K., Kling, M. A., Trickett, P. K., & Putnam, F. W. (1994a). Hypothalamic pituitary adrenal dysregulation in sexually abused girls. *Journal of Clinical Endocrinology and Metabolism, 78,* 249–255.

De Bellis, M. D., Hall, J., Boring, A. M., Frustaci, K., & Moritz, G. (2001). A pilot longitudinal study of hippocampal volumes in pediatric maltreatment-related posttraumatic stress disorder. *Biological Psychiatry, 50,* 305–309.

De Bellis, M. D., Keshavan, M. S., Clark, D. B., Casey, B. J., Giedd, J. N., Boring, A. M., Frustaci, K., & Ryan, N. D. (1999b). A. E. Bennett Research Award: Developmental traumatology: Part II. Brain development. *Biological Psychiatry, 45,* 1271–1284.

De Bellis, M. D., Keshavan, M. S., Frustaci, K., Shifflett, H., Iyengar, S., Beers, S. R., & Hall, J. (2002). Superior temporal gyrus volumes in maltreated children and adolescents with PTSD. *Biological Psychiatry, 51*, 544–552.

De Bellis, M. D., Keshavan, M. S., Spencer, S., & Hall, J. (2000). *N*-acetylaspartate concentration in the anterior cingulate of maltreated children and adolescents with PTSD. *American Journal of Psychiatry, 157*, 1175–1177.

De Bellis, M. D., Lefter, L., Trickett, P. K., & Putnam, F. W. (1994b). Urinary catecholamine excretion in sexually abused girls. *Journal of the American Academy of Child and Adolescent Psychiatry, 33*, 320–327.

Devinsky, O., Morrell, M. J., & Vogt, B. A. (1995). Contributions of anterior cingulate to behavior. *Brain, 118*, 279–306.

Driessen, M., Herrmann, J., Stahl, K., Zwaan, M., Meier, S., Hill, A., Osterheider, M., & Petersen, D. (2000). Magnetic resonance imaging volumes of the hippocampus and the amygdala in women with borderline personality disorder and early traumatization. *Archives of General Psychiatry, 57*, 1115–1122.

Duman, R. S., Heninger, G. R., & Nestler, E. J. (1997). A molecular and cellular theory of depression. *Archives of General Psychiatry, 54*, 597–606.

Durston, S., Hulshoff, P., Hilleke, E., Casey, B. J., Giedd, J. N., Buitelaar, J. K., & Van Engeland, H. (2001). Anatomical MRI of the developing human brain: What have we learned? *Journal of the American Academy of Child and Adolescent Psychiatry, 40*, 1012–1020.

Eghbal-Ahmadi, M., Hatalski, C. G., Lovenberg, T. W., Avishai-Eliner, S., Chalmers, D. T., & Baram, T. Z. (1998). The developmental profile of the corticotropin releasing factor receptor (CRF-2) in rat brain predicts distinct age-specific functions. *Developmental Brain Research, 107*, 81–90.

Elzinga, B. M., Schmahl, C. S., Vermetten, E., van Dyck, R., & Bremner, J. D. (2003). Increased cortisol responses to the stress of traumatic reminders in abuse-related PTSD. *Neuropsychopharmacology, 28*, 1656–1665.

Finlay, J. M., Zigmond, M. J., & Abercrombie, E. D. (1995). Increased dopamine and norepinephrine release in medial prefrontal cortex induced by acute and chronic stress: Effects of diazepam. *Neuroscience, 64*, 619–628.

Foa, E. B., Feske, U., Murdock, T. B., Kozak, M. J., & McCarthy, P. R. (1991). Processing of threat related information in rape victims. *Journal of Abnormal Psychology, 100*, 156–162.

Foote, S. L., Bloom, F. E., & Aston-Jones, G. (1983). Nucleus locus coeruleus: New evidence of anatomical and physiological specificity. *Physiology and Behavior, 63*, 844–914.

Francis, D. D., Caldji, C., Champagne, F., Plotsky, P. M., & Meaney, M. J. (1999). The role of corticotropin-releasing factor-norepinephrine systems in mediating the effects of early experience on the development of behavioral and endocrine responses to stress. *Biological Psychiatry, 46*, 1153–1166.

Giedd, J. N., Blumenthal, J., & Jeffries, N. O. (1999a). Development of the normal human corpus callosum during childhood and adolescence: A longitudinal MRI study. *Progress in Neuropsychopharmacology and Biological Psychiatry, 23*, 571–588.

Giedd, J. N., Blumenthal, J., Jeffries, N. O., Castellanos, F. X., Liu, H., Zijdenbos, A., Paus, T., Evans, A. C., & Rapoport, J. L. (1999b). Brain development during childhood and adolescence: A longitudinal MRI study. *Nature Neuroscience, 2*, 861–863.

Giedd, J. N., Castellanos, F. X., Rajapakse, J. C., Vaituzis, A. C., & Rapoport, J. L. (1997). Sexual dimorphism of the developing human brain. *Progress in Neuropsychopharmacology and Biological Psychiatry, 21*, 1185–1201.

Giedd, J. N., Snell, J. W., Lange, N., Rajapakse, J. C., Casey, B. J., Kozuch, P. L., Vaituzis, A. C., Vauss, Y. C., Hamburger, S. D., Kaysen, D., & Rapoport, J. L. (1996a). Quantitative magnetic resonance imaging of human brain development: Ages 14–18. *Cerebral Cortex, 6*, 551–560.

Giedd, J. N., Vaituzis, A. C., Hamburger, S. D., Lange, N., Rajapakse, J. C., Kaysen, D., Vauss, Y. C., & Rapoport, J. L. (1996b). Quantitative MRI of the temporal lobe, amygdala, and hippocampus in normal human development: Ages 4–18 years. *Journal of Comparative Neurology, 366,* 223–230.

Gilbertson, M. W., Shenton, M. E., Ciszewski, A., Kasai, K., Lasko, N. B., Orr, S. P., & Pitman, R. K. (2002). Smaller hippocampal volume predicts pathologic vulnerability to psychological trauma. *Nature Neuroscience, 5,* 1242–1247.

Gould, E., Beylin, A., Tanapat, P., Reeves, A., & Shors, T. J. (1999). Learning enhances adult neurogenesis in the hippocampal formation. *Nature Neuroscience, 2,* 260–265.

Gould, E., Tanapat, P., McEwen, B. S., Flugge, G., & Fuchs, E. (1998). Proliferation of granule cell precursors in the dentate gyrus of adult monkeys is diminished by stress. *Proceedings of the National Academy of Sciences USA, 95,* 3168–3171.

Gunnar, M. R., Morison, S. J., Chisolm, K., & Schuder, M. (2001). Salivary cortisol levels in children adopted from Romanian orphanages. *Development and Psychopathology, 13,* 611–628.

Gurvits, T. G., Shenton, M. R., Hokama, H., Ohta, H., Lasko, N. B., Gilbertson, M. B., Orr, S. P., Kikinis, R., & Lolesz, F. A. (1996). Magnetic resonance imaging study of hippocampal volume in chronic combat-related posttraumatic stress disorder. *Biological Psychiatry, 40,* 192–199.

Hatalski, C. G., Guirguis, C., & Baram, T. Z. (1998). Corticotropin releasing factor mRNA expression in the hypothalamic paraventricular nucleus and the central nucleus of the amygdala is modulated by repeated acute stress in the immature rat. *Journal of Neuroendocrinology, 10,* 663–669.

Heim, C., Newport, D. J., Bonsall, R., Miller, A. H., & Nemeroff, C. B. (2001). Altered pituitary–adrenal axis responses to provocative challenge tests in adult survivors of childhood abuse. *American Journal of Psychiatry, 158,* 575–581.

Heim, C., Newport, D. J., Heit, S., Graham, Y. P., Wilcox, M., Bonsall, R., Miller, A. H., & Nemeroff, C. B. (2000). Pituitary–adrenal and autonomic responses to stress in women after sexual and physical abuse in childhood. *Journal of the American Medical Association, 284,* 592–597.

Ito, Y., Teicher, M. H., Glod, C. A., Harper, D., Magnus, E., & Gelbard, H. A. (1993). Increased prevalence of electrophysiological abnormalities in children with psychological, physical and sexual abuse. *Journal of Neuropsychiatry and Clinical Neuroscience, 5,* 401–408.

Kaufman, J., Birmaher, B., Perel, J., Dahl, R. E., Moreci, P., Nelson, B., Wells, W., & Ryan, N. D. (1997). The corticotropin-releasing hormone challenge in depressed abused, depressed nonabused, and normal control children. *Biological Psychiatry, 42,* 669–679.

Kempermann, G., Kuhn, H. G., & Gage, F. H. (1997). More hippocampal neurons in adult mice living in an enriched environment. *Nature, 386,* 493–495.

Kempermann, G., Kuhn, H. G., & Gage, F. H. (1998). Experience-induced neurogenesis in the senescent dentate gyrus. *Journal of Neuroscience, 18,* 3206–3212.

Kessler, R. C., Sonnega, A., Bromet, E., Hughes, M., & Nelson, C. B. (1995). Posttraumatic stress disorder in the national comorbidity survey. *Archives of General Psychiatry, 52,* 1048–1060.

Ladd, C. O., Owens, M. J., & Nemeroff, C. B. (1996). Persistent changes in CRF neuronal systems produced by maternal separation. *Endocrinology, 137,* 1212–1218.

LeDoux, J. L. (1993). In search of systems and synapses. *Annals of the New York Academy of Sciences, 72,* 149–157.

Lemieux, A. M., & Coe, C. L. (1995). Abuse-related posttraumatic stress disorder: Evidence for chronic neuroendocrine activation in women. *Psychosomatic Medicine, 57,* 105–115.

Levine, E. S., Litto, W. J., & Jacobs, B. L. (1990). Activity of cat locus coeruleus noradrenergic neurons during the defense reaction. *Brain Research, 531,* 189–195.

Levine, S., Weiner, S. G., & Coe, C. L. (1993). Temporal and social factors influencing behavioral and hormonal responses to separation in mother and infant squirrel monkeys. *Psychoneuroendocrinology, 4,* 297–306.

Liu, D., Diorio, J., Day, J. C., Francis, D. D., & Meaney, M. J. (2000). Maternal care, hippocampal synaptogenesis and cognitive development in rats. *Nature Neuroscience, 8,* 799–806.

MacMillan, H. L., Fleming, J. E., Trocme, N., Boyle, M. H., Wong, M., Racine, Y. A., Beardslee, W. R., & Offord, D. R. (1997). Prevalence of child physical and sexual abuse in the community: Results from the Ontario Health Supplement. *Journal of the American Medical Association, 278,* 131–135.

Makino, S., Smith, M. A., & Gold, P. W. (1995). Increased expression of corticotropin-releasing hormone and vasopressin messenger-ribonucleic acid (messenger RNA) in the hypothalamic paraventricular nucleus during repeated stress-association with reduction in glucocorticoid messenger-RNA levels. *Endocrinology, 136,* 3299–3309.

Malberg, J. E., Eisch, A. J., Nestler, E. J., & Duman, R. S. (2000). Chronic antidepressant treatment increases neurogenesis in adult rat hippocampus. *Journal of Neuroscience, 20,* 9104–9110.

McCauley, J., Kern, D. E., Kolodner, K., Dill, L., Schroeder, A. F., DeChant, H. K., Ryden, J., Derogatis, L. R., & Bass, E. G., (1997). Clinical characteristics of women with a history of childhood abuse: Unhealed wounds. *Journal of the American Medical Association, 277,* 1362–1368.

McEwen, B. S., Angulo, J., Cameron, H., Chao, H. M., Daniels, D., Gannon, M. N., Gould, E., Mendelson, S., Sakai, R., Spencer, R., & Woolley, C. S. (1992). Paradoxical effects of adrenal steroids on the brain: Protection versus degeneration. *Biological Psychiatry, 31,* 177–199.

Meadows, E. A., & Foa, E. B. (1999). Cognitive-behavioral treatment of traumatized adults. In P. A. Saigh & J. D. Bremner (Eds.), *Posttraumatic stress disorder: A comprehensive text* (pp. 376–390). Needham Heights, MA: Allyn & Bacon.

Meaney, M. J., Aitken, D., van Berkel, C., Bhatnager, S., & Sapolsky, R. M. (1988). Effect of neonatal handling on age-related impairments associated with the hippocampus. *Science, 239,* 766–769.

Melia, K. R., & Duman, R. S. (1991). Involvement of corticotropin-releasing factor in chronic stress regulation of the brain noradrenergic system. *Proceedings of the National Academy of Sciences USA, 88,* 8382–8386.

Moghaddam, B., Adams, B., Verma, A., & Daly, D. (1997). Activation of glutamatergic neurotransmission by ketamine: A novel step in the pathway from NMDA receptor blockade to dopaminergic and cognitive disruptions associated with the prefrontal cortex. *Journal of Neuroscience, 17,* 2921–2927.

Morgan, C. A., Grillon, C., Lubin, H., & Southwick, S. M. (1997). Startle reflex abnormalities in women with sexual assault-related posttraumatic stress disorder. *American Journal of Psychiatry, 154,* 1076–1080.

Morgan, C. A., & LeDoux, J. E. (1995). Differential contribution of dorsal and ventral medial prefrontal cortex to the acquisition and extinction of conditioned fear in rats. *Behavioral Neuroscience, 109,* 681–688.

Morgan, C. A., Romanski, L. M., & LeDoux, J. E. (1993). Extinction of emotional learning: Contribution of medial prefrontal cortex. *Neuroscience Letters, 163,* 109–113.

Nibuya, M., Morinobu, S., & Duman, R. S. (1995). Regulation of BDNF and trkB mRNA in rat brain by chronic electroconvulsive seizure and antidepressant drug treatments. *Journal of Neuroscience, 15,* 7539–7547.

Nisenbaum, L. K., Zigmond, M. J., Sved, A. F., & Abercrombie, E. D. (1991). Prior exposure to chronic stress results in enhanced synthesis and release of hippocampal norepinephrine in response to a novel stressor. *Journal of Neuroscience, 11,* 1478–1484.

Notestine, C. F., Stein, M. B., Kennedy, C. M., Archibald, S. L., & Jernigan, T. L. (2002). Brain morphometry in female victims of intimate partner violence with and without posttraumatic stress disorder. *Biological Psychiatry, 51,* 1089–1101.

Orr, S. P., Lasko, N. B., Metzger, L. J., Ahern, C. E., Berry, N. J., & Pitman, R. K. (1998). Psychophysiological assessment of women with posttraumatic stress disorder resulting from childhood sexual abuse. *Journal of Consulting and Clinical Psychology, 66,* 906–913.

Paus, T., Zijdenbos, A., Worsley, K., Collins, D. L., Blumenthal, J., Giedd, J. N., Rapoport, J. L., & Evans, A. C. (1999). Structural maturation of neural pathways in children and adolescents: In vivo study. *Science, 283,* 1908–1911.

Pfefferbaum, A., Mathalon, D. H., Sullivan, E. V., Rawles, J. M., Zipursky, R. B., & Lim, K. O. (1994). A quantitative magnetic resonance imaging study of changes in brain morphology from infancy to late adulthood. *Archives of Neurology, 34,* 71–75.

Pitman, R. K. (2001). Investigating the pathogenesis of posttraumatic stress disorder with neuroimaging. *Journal of Clinical Psychiatry, 62,* 47–54.

Plotsky, P. M., & Meaney, M. J. (1993). Early postnatal stress and the hypothalamic–pituitary–adrenal axis. *Molecular Brain Research, 18,* 195–200.

Prigerson, H. G., Maciejewski, P. K., & Rosenheck, R. A. (2001). Combat trauma: Trauma with highest risk of delayed onset and unresolved posttraumatic stress disorder symptoms, unemployment, and abuse among men. *Journal of Nervous and Mental Disease, 189,* 99–108.

Rapoport, J. L., Giedd, J. N., Blumenthal, J., Hamburger, S. D., Jeffries, N. O., Fernandez, T., Nicolson, R., Bedwell, J., Lenane, M., Zijdenbos, A., Paus, T., & Evans, A. (1999). Progressive cortical change during adolescence in childhood-onset schizophrenia: A longitudinal magnetic resonance imaging study. *Archives of General Psychiatry, 56,* 649–654.

Roth, R. H., Tam, S. Y., Ida, Y., Yang, J. X., & Deutch, A. Y. (1988). Stress and the mesocorticolimbic dopamine systems. *Annals of the New York Academy of Sciences, 537,* 149–157.

Saigh, P. A., & Bremner, J. D. (Eds.). (1999). *Posttraumatic stress disorder: A comprehensive text.* Needham Heights, MA: Allyn & Bacon.

Sanchez, M. M., Ladd, C. O., & Plotsky, P. M. (2001). Early adverse experience as a developmental risk factor for later psychopathology: Evidence from rodent and primate models. *Development and Psychopathology, 13,* 419–449.

Sapolsky, R. M. (1996). Why stress is bad for your brain. *Science, 273,* 749–750.

Schiffer, F., Teicher, M. H., & Papanicolaou, A. C. (1995). Evoked potential evidence for right brain activity during the recall of traumatic memories. *Journal of Neuropsychiatry and Clinical Neuroscience, 7,* 169–175.

Schmahl, C. G., Elzinga, B. M., & Bremner, J. D. (2002). Individual differences in psychophysiological reactivity in adults with childhood abuse. *Clinical Psychology and Psychotherapy, 9,* 271–276.

Schmahl, C. G., McGlashan, T., & Bremner, J. D. (2002). Neurobiological correlates of borderline personality disorder. *Psychopharmacology Bulletin, 36,* 69–87.

Schmahl, C. G., Vermetten, E., Elzinga, B. M., & Bremner, J. D. (2003). Magnetic resonance imaging of hippocampal and amygdala volume in women with childhood abuse and borderline personality disorder. *Psychiatry Research: Neuroimaging, 122,* 193–198.

Selemon, L. D., & Goldman-Rakic, P. S. (1988). Common cortical and subcortical targets of the dorsolateral prefrontal and posterior parietal cortices in the rhesus monkey: Evidence for a distributed neural network subserving spatially guided behavior. *Journal of Neuroscience, 8,* 4049–4068.

Shin, L. H., McNally, R. J., Kosslyn, S. M., Thompson, W. L., Rauch, S. L., Alpert, N. M., Metzger, L. J., Lasko, N. B., Orr, S. P., & Pitman, R. K. (1999). Regional cerebral blood flow during script-driven imagery in childhood sexual abuse-related PTSD: A PET investigation. *American Journal of Psychiatry, 156,* 575–584.

Smith, M. A., Kim, S. Y., Van Oers, H. J. J., & Levine, S. (1997). Maternal deprivation and stress induce immediate early genes in the infant rat brain. *Endocrinology, 138,* 4622–4628.

Smith, M. A., Makino, S., Kvetnansky, R., & Post, R. M. (1995). Stress and glucocorticoids affect the expression of brain-derived neurotrophic factor and neurotrophin-3 mRNA in the hippocampus. *Journal of Neuroscience, 15,* 1768–1777.

Sowell, E. R., Thompson, P. M., Holmes, C. J., Batth, R., Jernigan, T. L., & Toga, A. W. (1999). Localizing age-related changes in brain structure between childhood and adolescence using statistical parametric mapping. *NeuroImage, 9,* 587–597.

Stanton, M. E., Gutierrez, Y. R., & Levine, S. (1988). Maternal deprivation potentiates pituitary–adrenal stress responses in infant rats. *Behavioral Neuroscience, 102,* 692–700.

Stein, M. B., Koverola, C., Hanna, C., Torchia, M. G., & McClarty, B. (1997). Hippocampal volume in women victimized by childhood sexual abuse. *Psychological Medicine, 27,* 951–959.

Stein, M. B., Yehuda, R., Koverola, C., & Hanna, C. (1997). Enhanced dexamethasone suppression of plasma cortisol in adult women traumatized by childhood sexual abuse. *Biological Psychiatry, 42,* 680–686.

Stewart, W. F., Ricci, J. A., Chee, E., Hahn, S. R., & Morganstein, D. (2003). Cost of lost productive work time among U.S. workers with depression. *Journal of the American Medical Association, 289,* 3135–3144.

Thompson, P. M., Giedd, J. N., Woods, R. P., MacDonald, D., Evans, A. C., & Toga, A. W. (2000). Growth patterns in the developing brain detected by using continuum mechanical tensor maps. *Nature, 404,* 190–193.

Uno, H., Tarara, R., Else, J. G., Suleman, M. A., & Sapolsky, R. M. (1989). Hippocampal damage associated with prolonged and fatal stress in primates. *Journal of Neuroscience, 9,* 1705–1711.

Vermetten, E., Vythilingam, M., Southwick, S. M., Charney, D. S., & Bremner, J. D. (2003). Long-term treatment with paroxetine increases verbal declarative memory and hippocampal volume in posttraumatic stress disorder. *Biological Psychiatry, 54,* 693–702.

Villarreal, G., Hamilton, D. A., Petropoulos, H., Driscoll, I., Rowland, L. M., Griego, J. A., Kodituwakku, P. W., Hart, B. L., Escalona, R., & Brooks, W. M. (2002). Reduced hippocampal volume and total white matter in posttraumatic stress disorder. *Biological Psychiatry, 52,* 119–125.

Vogt, B. A., Finch, D. M., & Olson, C. R. (1992). Functional heterogeneity in cingulate cortex: The anterior executive and posterior evaluative regions. *Cerebral Cortex, 2,* 435–443.

Vythilingam, M., Heim, C., Newport, C. D., Miller, A. H., Vermetten, E., Anderson, E., Bronen, R., Staib, L., Charney, D. S., Nemeroff, C. B., & Bremner, J. D. (2002). Reduced hippocampal volume in adult major depression: The role of childhood trauma. *American Journal of Psychiatry, 159,* 2072–2080.

Woolley, C. S., Gould, E., & McEwen, B. S. (1990). Exposure to excess glucocorticoids alters dendritic morphology of adult hippocampal pyramidal neurons. *Brain Research, 531,* 225–231.

Section III

STRESS AND TRAUMA IN THE LIVES OF WOMEN OF COLOR, WOMEN WITH DISABILITIES, AND LESBIAN WOMEN

10

Stress and Trauma in the Lives of Women of Color

MARTHA E. BANKS, ROSALIE J. ACKERMAN, BARBARA W. K. YEE, AND CAROLYN M. WEST

Women of Color experience the traumas described throughout this volume. In addition, they experience acute and chronic individual and institutionalized racism, resulting in different stress responses. The focus of this chapter is on the responses of Women of Color, with an emphasis on the nature of individual and community stressors, cultural changes experienced by Women of Color, and acute and chronic health differences among women of various ethnicities.

Women from all ethnic and racial backgrounds can experience trauma and stress. However, much of the previous literature has neglected the experiences of Women of Color (Nader, Dubrow, & Stamm, 1999). These women are particularly vulnerable to trauma in every aspect of their lives, including their homes, communities, and places of employment. Despite social and economic advances, these traumatic events are common, repeated, and ongoing, rather than a single past traumatic event. For example, racism can be subtle or more overt, such as racial slurs or physical attacks. Regardless of the form, racial oppression can contribute to psychological trauma, including posttraumatic stress disorder (PTSD), among targeted individuals (Sanchez-Hucles, 1998). Furthermore, many of our trauma theories are ahistorical. This is an oversight, because the legacy of trauma can be multigenerational. For example, although they never experienced lynchings, forced relocation to reservations, and imprisonment in internment camps, these atrocities may cause "insidious trauma" among second- and third-generation family members (Root, 1992).

Below, we describe the four largest racial groups in the United States: African Americans, Hispanics, Asian Americans, and American Indians. In addition, we address issues unique to immigrant women representing a wide range of racial and ethnic groups.

1 DESCRIPTION OF ETHNIC GROUPS

Who are Women of Color? The goal of this section is to place trauma and stress in a larger historical and cultural context. By reviewing the demographic characteristics of the four largest ethnic groups, highlighting significant historical trauma, and emphasizing cultural strengths that may act as protective factors, we will accomplish this objective.

1.1 African American and Caribbean-Americans

Approximately 12% of the U.S. population, or 34 million people, identify themselves as African American. The Black population is increasing in diversity, as greater numbers of immigrants arrive from Africa and Caribbean countries. Many African Americans trace their ancestry to the African slave trade. Their enslavement was characterized by forced separations of families, beatings, sexual assaults, and losses of language and culture. Although African Americans now span all socioeconomic classes and professions, the legacy of slavery and discrimination continues to influence their social and economic standing. In 1999, for example, almost 25% of Black families had incomes below the poverty line. Many of these impoverished families reside in urban areas, which are plagued with high rates of community violence (U.S. Department of Health and Human Services, 2001). Despite these challenges, African Americans have developed adaptive beliefs, traditions, and practices. For instance, religious commitment and prayer are common among this group. The family, both immediate and extended, has been and remains a source of comfort and strength (Oates, 1998).

1.2 Hispanic Americans

According to Census 2000, 35 million people, or approximately 13% of the U.S. population, are categorized as Hispanic Americans. Almost two thirds are persons of Mexican origin, followed by Puerto Ricans, Cubans, and Central Americans. Although the majority of Hispanics (64%) were born in the United States, it is important to consider the historical events that brought Latinos to the United States. Mexicans have been U.S. residents longer than any other Hispanic ethnic group. For example, economic hardships in Mexico and the need for laborers have increased the flow of Mexicans to the United States. Central Americans, the newest Hispanic ethnic group, arrived in the United States between 1980 and 1990. Many immigrants were fleeing political terror and atrocities in El Salvador, Guatemala, and Nicaragua (U.S. Department of Health and Human Services, 2001).

Different migration histories contribute to demographic variations among Hispanic ethnic groups. For example, Cuban Americans tend to be older, more educated, and economically advantaged, followed by Puerto Ricans, and Mexican Americans. Furthermore, Hispanic groups vary in their levels of acculturation. Some are fourth or fifth generation and very acculturated, whereas others are newly arrived immigrants who continue to embrace their culture and customs (U.S. Department of Health and Human Services, 2001). Despite their diversity, many Hispanics value familism or family unity, respect, and loyalty. In addition, religion plays an important role in the lives of Hispanics (Oates, 1998).

1.3 Asian Americans

Asian Americans are a diverse group that originates from three major geographic locations: (a) East Asia, which includes China, Japan, and Korea; (b) Southeast Asia, which includes Cambodia, Laos, and Vietnam; and (c) South Asia, which includes India, Pakistan, and Sri Lanka (Oates, 1998). Between 1990 and 2000, the number of people identifying themselves as Asian American reached 10 million people, or 3.6% of the U.S. population (U.S. Census Bureau, 2001).

The Chinese were among the first Asian group to come to the United States. Between 1848 and 1882, the discovery of gold in California and the growing railroad industry drew large numbers of Chinese immigrants. However, the government passed laws, such as the Chinese Exclusion Act of 1882, that limited Asian immigration. Migration to the United States grew following the 1965 Immigration Act that supported family reunification and discouraged discrimination against Asians. During the late 1970s and 1980s, the U.S. government, for political and humanitarian reasons, accepted large numbers of Southeast Asian refugees from Vietnam, Cambodia, and Laos (U.S. Department of Health and Human Services, 2001).

Asian Americans reflect diversity in terms of ethnicity, culture, and religion (Buddhism, Confucianism, Hinduism, Christianity, and Islam). This group is also linguistically diverse, with more than 100 languages and dialects spoken. On average, Asian Americans have completed more formal education than other ethnic groups. However, there are ethnic group differences. Descendents from the Indian subcontinent (India, Pakistan, Bangladesh) tend to be more educated than Cambodians, Hmong, and Laotians. The rates of poverty also vary across ethnic groups. Japanese Americans (7%) were least impoverished, followed by Chinese, Korean, and Thai Americans, who reported poverty rates of 14%. Southeast Asians, such as Cambodians (43%) and Hmong (64%), reported the highest poverty rates (U.S. Department of Health and Human Services, 2001). Despite their diversity, Asians value family relationships, respect for authority, and elders. In addition, they value responsibility, self-control, discipline, and educational achievement (Oates, 1998).

1.4 American Indians

According to the U.S. Census Bureau, 4.1 million people, or 1.5% of the U.S. population, identify themselves as American Indians and Alaska Natives (Eskimos and Aleuts). Despite increased willingness to acknowledge Indian ancestry and increased birth rates, this ethnic group remains small. American Indians and Alaska Natives were self-governing people who thrived in North America. This began to change when Europeans "discovered" and colonized North America. In the 17th century, European contact exposed native people to infectious diseases. Over time, almost every tribe was subjected to forced removal from their ancestral homelands, brutal colonization, and confinement to reservations. As a result, the population began to decline. During the 1970s, American Indians and Alaska Natives began to demand greater authority in their communities, which led to the reemergence of tribal courts and councils (U.S. Department of Health and Human Services, 2001).

There are hundreds of different native peoples and languages across North America. Limited educational opportunities and high unemployment rates are common community problems. As a result, approximately 25% of American Indians live in poverty. Alcohol-related problems, diabetes, and inadequate health care contribute to premature death. Consequently, this is a relatively young population, with an average age of 28 (U.S. Department of Health and Human Services, 2001). In spite of these social and economic challenges, many American Indian families value respect for elders, cooperation, group cohesion, and respect for religion (Oates, 1998).

1.5 Immigrant Women

The experiences of immigrant women differ from those of Women of Color born in the United States. For some, the stress involves new language, different customs, changes in diet, and changes in socioeconomic status. Immigrant women often experience racism for the first time in North America; Turrittin, Hagey, Guruge, Collins, and Mitchell (2002) described that experience for nurses immigrating to Canada. Some people immigrate to the United States to avoid war and terrorism in their countries but then encounter terrorism in the United States (Pantin, Schwartz, Prado, Feaster, & Szapocznik, 2003; Trautman et al., 2002).

In conclusion, despite economic and social advances, ethnic women are disproportionately more likely to be young, impoverished, and less educated (U.S. Department of Health and Human Services, 2001). All these demographic factors are associated with increased levels of trauma. For example, in a sample of inner-city, low-income Latinas and Black women, more interpersonal violence and trauma were reported above estimates of women nationwide, including witnessing murder, seeing violence between their parents, and homelessness. Not surprisingly, almost one quarter of these women met diagnostic criteria for lifetime posttraumatic stress disorder (Hien & Bukszpan, 1999). However, it is also important to remember that each ethnic group has developed cultural strengths, which enable them to deal with violence in their families (Oates, 1998).

2 VIOLENCE AS AN INDIVIDUAL AND COMMUNITY STRESSOR

As we have seen from previous chapters, violence is a common occurrence in the lives of all women. This is also true for Women of Color. Millions of these women are victims of female genital mutilation (Adeyemo, 2003), trafficking in women for the purpose of prostitution (Farley, 2003), wife burning (Singh & Unnithan, 1999), and "honor" killings (e.g., acid being thrown on women as punishment for being raped or refusing arranged marriages; Kulwicki, 2002). Community violence is a common source of trauma, especially for Black women in the United States (Jenkins, 2002). In some studies, it was reported that as many as 30% of Black women have witnessed violence in their communities, such as shootings and stabbings. More prevalent than witnessing assault is the loss of an intimate because of violence (Jenkins, 2002). In 2002, 1,184 African American women were murdered. These victims leave behind children, mothers and fathers, sisters and brothers, and friends who suffer elevated rates of psychological distress, loss, and grief.

3 WOMEN, STRESS, AND TRAUMA: IMPACT OF CULTURE AND IMMIGRATION

Immigrant women and Women of Color experience stress and trauma through cultural and life experiential lenses (Yee, 1999a). Although the research has not ascertained whether immigrant woman are at higher risk, or have higher prevalence rates in an epidemiological framework, smaller-scale studies indicate that they are at high risk and are an under-served group of women. Future research must systematically examine how culture, stigma, and acculturation influence stress and trauma experiences among immigrant women and Women of Color.

Culture and the acculturative processes influence stress and trauma experiences of immigrant women and Women of Color. Culture may exact direct and indirect effects on health, stress, and trauma (Yee, forth-coming, 2004). Cultural factors influence access via language capabilities, learning processes, cognitive information processing, and motivational strategies. Culture shapes perceptions of health and illness and the vari-ety of coping and help-seeking strategies. Cultures have a variety of belief/emotional/behavioral prescriptions and culturally patterned scripts to deal with life's problems. The efficacy of cultural prescriptions and scripts are dependent upon the social–cultural context in which these cultural solutions are used. Culture influences everything from help-seeking behaviors to health decision-making processes. Culture influences the definition of life problems, determines who helps to solve the issues, when and under what circumstances the problems will be resolved, where the issues will be dealt with, and how the issues will be addressed. Acculturation will temper the strength and form of culture's influence upon health, stress, and trauma.

Stressors may come from everyday living, during immigration, and the transitions that occur with acculturation across generations (Yee, Huang, & Lew, 1998). For instance, dramatic changes in gender and fam-ily roles may shift with acculturation to American lifestyles. According to Tran and Des Jardins (2000), culture may shape beliefs, attitudes, and behaviors in stress reactions and trauma experiences. Collectivist cultures (e.g., cultures that adhere to the tenets of Confucianism) shape social and family norms and support high interdependence and close family bonds (Louie, 2000). Any breach of this family interdependence and close family bonds may create a "loss of face" and produce shame that reflects on all members of the family (Yee et al., 1998). Traditional gender roles, such as patriarchal cultural norms, may lead to oppression of women and disempower women to support maintenance of an abusive relationship. Traditional values that encourage staying in a marriage at all costs because of strong obligations to the family unit, make it almost impossi-ble to exit an abusive relationship.

Cultural differences in the stigmatization of stress and trauma have yet to be empirically tested for ethnic minority groups in general, and for ethnic minority women in particular. Some studies suggest that cul-tural differences in stigmatization of stress, trauma, and mental health conditions exact significant influence over outcomes for minority women. For instance, in a special issue of the *Journal of Mental Health* on stigma, editors Penn and Wykes (Penn & Wykes, 2003) suggested that stigma, discrimination, and mental illness are strongly related in our society, and that stigma and discrimination are significant barriers that decrease access to mental health services. As important as the relationship is between stigma, discrimination, and mental illness, it is significantly larger for ethnic minorities than for Caucasians due to a lifetime of discrimination and perceived alienation among ethnic minorities. With the added dimension of female gender and older ages, these minority women are at double or triple jeopardy. Key strategies have been identified to overcome the effects of stigmatization and discrimination. According to Couture and Penn (2003), protest strategy (deliberately suppressing stigmatizing attitudes by asking individuals not to consider or think about using negative stereotypes), education, and promotion of contact with the stigmatized group are effective. Apparently, the latter shows the greatest promise as an intervention to dispel negative stereotypes. It appears that the greater the amount (and quality of exposure) of previous exposure to the stigmatized group, the greater the perceived variability among this group. In other words, greater exposure and quality of that exposure produce lessening of stereotypical beliefs of that stigmatized group.

Another fascinating area of research examines the intergenerational transmission of relationship violence among Vancouver families (Kwong, Bartholomew, Henderson, & Trinke, 2003). These investigators found that physical and psychological abuse predicted all forms of relationship abuse in a consistent manner, as explained by the general social-learning theory. Whereas 18% of this sample was Asian, the article does not describe ethnic group comparisons. The Chinese sample was underrepresented by 10% in comparison to the population in Vancouver, despite translation of the survey into Cantonese and Mandarin. Factors related to Chinese underrepresentation in sampling include the stigmatizing effects of conducting a survey on a taboo topic, such as relationship violence; a poor understanding of research by immigrant women; and many other barriers to conducting research with Asian and immigrant populations (see Yee, 1999b, for a review).

3.1 Research Gaps

A significant research issue that has major implications for closing the health disparities in stress and trauma among immigrant women and Women of Color is the change in collection of federal data outlined in the Office of Management and Budget Statistical Policy Directive No. 15: Race and Ethnic Standards for Federal Statistics and Administrative Reporting (*Federal Register*, July 9, 1997; Office of Management and Budget, 1997). This OMB Policy Directive 15 mandates federal collection of race and ethnic data by important timetables, such as the 2000 Census.

An important change is the separation of Asian and Pacific Islanders, due to a bimodal distribution on a variety of health and socioeconomic indicators, into their two respective groups.

The collection and reporting of federal data will enhance our knowledge of the stress and trauma among racial and ethnic groups. However, complexities, such as inclusion of multiple race assessments and their outcomes, have yet to be delineated (Mays, Ponce, Washington, & Cochran, 2003). In a publication entitled *Unequal Burden, Unequal Data: Registries Helping Close the Gap* (National Cancer Registrars Association, 1999), the authors argued that good racial and ethnic or subethnic cancer data can help to close disparities in cancer, because prevention and intervention can be targeted and designed for high-risk ethnic groups. Missing racial and ethnic data from databases, such as the sexually transmitted disease case registry or mortality/morbidity, can hinder our efforts to close disparities (Chen, Etkind, Coman, Tang, & Whelan, 2003). These authors suggested that surname or ethnic marketing lists, birth records, and matching case address with census block data to infer race or ethnicity could be used as proxy for missing data. The same racial and ethnic data arguments can be made about closing the gap in stress and trauma for immigrant women and Women of Color.

Other research gaps investigating stress and trauma among immigrant women and Women of Color come from reports entitled *Advancing the Federal Research Agenda on Violence against Women* (Kruttschnitt, McLaughlin, & Petrie, forthcoming 2004) and *Violence Against Women: The Health Sector Responds* (Velzeboer, Ellsberg, Arcas, & Garcia-Moreno, 2003). These reports may or may not focus specifically on immigrants or Women of Color, but implications can be drawn for what research must be conducted on these high-risk populations of women. These reports suggest that gender-based violence is complex, with multiple risk factors that contribute to incidence and severity of violence against women, such as alcohol and drug abuse, poverty, and childhood witnessing of or experiencing violence. However, it is a multicausal problem that has serious physical and mental health outcomes for women. The scant empirical research on the stress and trauma experienced by immigrants and Women of Color only creates more questions to be answered, and much research has yet to be done to fully understand this area.

Much of the research focuses upon intimate-partner violence. However, two thirds of homicides occur outside this social context. Key questions to be answered are as follows:

- Does cultural and social stereotyping of immigrant women and Women of Color increase the risk for violence, or could they be protective factors?

- Do cultural norms for intimate-partner and social roles/relationships put immigrant women at greater risk for abuse?
- Do the epidemiological pattern and findings hold for immigrant women and Women of Color across the life span?

The steering committee for the Workshop on Issues in Research on Violence Against Women (Kruttschnitt et al., forthcoming, 2004) suggest that data are inadequate on the incidence and prevalence rates of female victimization. This type of data is woefully inadequate for the population of immigrant women and Women of Color. If these studies are funded, it would be far less expensive to ensure that immigrant women and Women of Color are oversampled at the inception of such studies, rather than taken as an afterthought. Longitudinal studies must also be funded in order to examine the long-term family, mental, and physical health consequences of stress and trauma among these underserved, high-risk groups of women. Closer attention should be paid to how the immediate social and neighborhood context impinges upon the lives of immigrant women and Women of Color. Inner-city neighborhoods put women in these neighborhoods at higher risk for stress, trauma, and victimization. Clear investigation into the risk and protective aspects of a community's social capital is required, and a closer examination of the influence of culture, acculturation, and stigma may help us better understand the experiences of these women.

Sexual assault by strangers must take into account the community/neighbor characteristics of social capital, as well as the interaction between social and cultural group norms. For instance, do certain immigrant or racial/ethnic group stereotypes create the perception that women from these groups would be passive victims and, therefore, more likely to be easier victims of predatory acts?

The last area of research that needs much exploration is in the area of stress-and-trauma service utilization by immigrant women and Women of Color. Key questions to be answered are as follows:

- Does culture influence the likelihood of reporting victimization and utilization of mental health services?
- Under what conditions would immigrant women and Women of Color report and seek health and mental health services?
- Do educational interventions that seek to do primary, secondary, and tertiary prevention work equally well for immigrant women and Women of Color?

4 ETHNIC DIFFERENCES IN STRESS RESPONSES

A variety of stress responses have been examined to determine differences among ethnic groups. One concern about the research in this area is that the majority of the studies compare African Americans and European Americans; other ethnic groups are relatively ignored. In addition, little of the research is disaggregated by gender, so there is an inadequate base of knowledge about the stress responses of Women of Color. Below are examples of recent research that addresses issues of stress faced by Girls and Adolescents of Color and Women of Color, such as being in caregiving roles, having traumatic childbearing experiences, facing aging issues, suffering violence, and facing disability. The overview of the stress responses will be followed by a look at the buffers and coping strategies that allow Women of Color to survive ongoing stress.

4.1 Stress-Related Illnesses

"African Americans are twice as likely as white people to have chronic diseases" (Cummings, Neff, & Husaini, 2003, p. 24). Cardiovascular diseases, including hypertension, have been recognized as physiological reactions to stress (Guyll, Matthews, & Bromberger, 2001; Jones, Beach, Forehand, & Family Health Project Research Group, 2003; Jones, Beach, Forehand, & Foster, 2003; Kotchen et al., 1998; Musante et al., 2000; Troxel, Matthews, Bromberger, & Sutton-Tyrrell, 2003; U.S. Department of Health and Human Services, Office on Women's Health, 2003). "African Americans, compared with whites, have a greater prevalence of hypertension, develop high BP at an earlier age, and have more frequent occurrences of hypertension-related diseases" (Steffen, Hinderliter, Blumenthal, & Sherwood, 2001, p. 523).

There are many mental health problems noted that differ among ethnic groups. Zhang and Snowden (1999) found significant ethnic differences in the prevalence rates of disorders among African Americans, Asian Americans, European Americans, and Latinas and Latinos.

Turner and Lloyd (2003) explored the extent of adverse life experiences (e.g., witnessing violence, traumatic news, death events) and resulting substance abuse among African Americans, European Americans, Cubans, and other Latinas and Latinos. They found that African Americans, on average, experienced half again as many adverse life events as members of other ethnic groups. Yet, among these ethnic groups, African Americans were least likely to develop substance abuse problems. African American women, in particular, are unlikely to use illicit substances (Beatty, 2003).

4.2 Girls and Adolescents

Two major stressors for adolescent Women of Color are concerns about unwanted early sexual activity that can result in pregnancy or transmission of diseases, including HIV/AIDS. As Scott and Eliav (this volume, chapter 1) noted, "children and adolescents' coping resources are more easily overwhelmed by traumatic experiences than those of adults" (p. 26). Therefore, young Women of Color are easily overwhelmed by those concerns. This is further compounded by Elders' and Albert's (1998) observation that most of the unwanted early sexual activity involves men 10 to 15 years older than the vulnerable adolescent women. As stated in Elders and Albert (1998), "Women with histories of sexual abuse are significantly more likely to experience suicidal ideation during pregnancy than nonabused counterparts" (p. 649).

4.3 Caregiving

Kendall-Tackett (this volume, chapter 2) addressed the gender expectation that women take care of others through "tending and befriending." For African American women, the history of slavery and the ensuing limitations to household service have placed an additional burden on them (Jones & Shorter-Gooden, 2003). Women of Color often care for aging parents and parents-in-law (Adams, Aranda, Kemp, & Takagi, 2002). A major stress of parenting for African American mothers is trying to protect their children from life-threatening racism (Boyd-Franklin & Franklin, 2000; Wyatt, 1997).

Because many Women of Color have limited financial resources (Adler & Coriell, 1997; Brewer, 1995; McCallum, Arnold, & Bolland, 2002; McLoyd, 1998; Smith, 1995), they have minimal support in the provision of such care. If, in addition, they have disabilities, their limited resources must be shared among themselves, their children, their parents, and other relatives (Corbett, 2003; Feldman & Tegart, 2003).

4.4 Birth Experience, Infertility, Childbearing Loss

Women of Color have a significantly higher prevalence of birth difficulties than women of other ethnic groups. The maternal mortality rate for African American women is three times that of European American women and twice that of Latinas. Similarly, infant mortality rates for African Americans are nearly three times those for European Americans. Asian Americans have the lowest rates of infant mortality. For African Americans, the high incidence of infant mortality appears to be correlated with parallel disparities in low birth weight (U.S. Department of Health & Human Services, Office on Women's Health, 2003).

As Campbell and Kendall-Tackett (this volume, chapter 6) noted, social class masks the effects of intimate partner violence on birth weight.

Because Women of Color are predominantly members of lower socioeconomic classes, intimate partner violence during pregnancy is seldom considered in research on health status of newborns. Another stressor that leads to low birth weight is the youth of adolescent mothers (Elders & Albert, 1998).

There is considerable social pressure for African American women to become mothers. This is particularly stressful for African American women who experience fibroid tumors at a higher rate than European American women (Marshall et al., 1997). Hysterectomy is often the treatment African American women receive; the result of hysterectomy is, of course, infertility.

4.5 Middle and Old Age

There are several issues of stress and aging for Women of Color that need to be considered:

- What are the implications of aging for older Women of Color?
- Is ageism perceived after a lifetime of sexism and racism?
- How does age affect stress, and how is this related to (declining) health?

Rysberg (this volume, chapter 4) noted, "Elderly women in America also possess undesirable life conditions as they are more likely to live in poverty than are males. This is particularly true if they are widowed, members of an ethnic minority, poorly educated and/or disabled." Lott (2002) observed that "Social class affects health status through differences in access to health-promoting resources, differences in access to high-quality treatment, and differences in attitudes and beliefs held by health care workers" (p. 106). According to Cummings, Neff, and Husaini (2003), "Lifelong exposure to health hazards, economic disadvantage, and limited access to health care place African American elderly people at greater risk of functional impairment and chronic illness" (p. 24).

Many older Women of Color need to continue working during old age to try to make ends meet (Banks & Ackerman, 2003). There is considerable stress to continue to work despite declining physical stamina and other health concerns (Feldman & Tegart, 2003; Nabors & Pettee, 2003). The literature on adjustment to retirement does not apply to them.

Due to the prevalence of violence and illness in many Communities of Color, older Women of Color are actively involved in grandparenting relationships. For example, some are raising bereaved grandchildren after their daughters have become victims of intimate partner homicide

(Banks & Ackerman, 1999). Others are actively parenting ill daughters, as well as grandchildren. This adds considerable stress to the lives of older Women of Color (Smith, 1995).

4.6 Violence Against Women

More than half of all groups of Women of Color experience physical violence in their lifetimes:

- Fifty-two percent of African American women are subject to physical assault at some point in their lifetimes, compared to 53% of Hispanic/Latino women, and 51% of White women.
- Among American Indians/Alaska Native women of all ages, 61% stated they had been victims of a physical assault. This group of women had the highest percentage of rapes—34%. This rate was almost twice that found among White (18%) and African American women (19%).
- Among all women, Hispanic women are the least likely group to be victims of rape. Hispanic women (53%) were more likely than non-Hispanic women (52%) to be victims of physical assault.
- Asian American/Pacific Islander women are the least likely group to be victims of physical assault during their lifetimes (50%) among all women. They are the least likely to be victims of stalking (5%) or rape (7%) (U.S. Department of Health and Human Services, Office on Women's Health, 2003, p. 25).

Dallam (this volume, chapter 8) described the life-changing effects of violence upon health status (see also Axelrod et al., 1999; Dearwater et al., 1998; Golding, 1999; Manetta, 1999; Wolkenstein & Sterman, 1998). Much of the violence is described is a direct effect of sexism. It is not clear how violence due to racism impacts on the health of Women of Color. Gendered violence is specifically acknowledged with terminology such as sexual assault (Basile, this volume, chapter 5), but there is typically no parallel terminology for "racial assault." Similar to sexual assault, however, victims of racial assault are confronted with disbelief and silencing (West, 2002). Campbell and Kendall-Tackett (this volume, chapter 6) describe several situations in which intimate partner violence occurs. One situation, which disproportionately affects Women of Color, in which intimate partner violence occurs, is in prostitution (Farley, 2003). This is part of the legacy of slavery, in which African American women were treated as property and were stereotyped as promiscuous (Wyatt, 1997).

For African American women, silencing takes the form of disacknowledgment of gendered violence in order to counter the negative stereotypes of African American men. Nichols (2002) described the silencing that prevents African American women from publicly acknowledging intimate partner violence (see also Jones & Shorter-Gooden, 2003). Such silence allows the violence to escalate to homicide. Bell and Mattis (2000) wrote, "African American women whose partners hold powerful social positions—for example, police officers, pastors, or lawyers—sometimes find themselves being intimidated by their partners, their partner's friends and coworkers, or by members of the community. These women may find that expected modes of support and protection, for example, congregational support or police protection, are unavailable to them" (p. 525).

Brice-Baker (1994) wrote about the difficulties African-Caribbean women encounter when they try to leave abusive relationships. Problems include lack of citizenship (and ineligibility for public assistance), lack of shelters in the community, language barriers, reluctance to deal with the police, and fear of deportation (of either the victim or the perpetrator). As a result, many African-Caribbean women stay in abusive relationships, because they believe that the consequences of leaving outweigh those of staying.

One of the serious health consequences for victims of interpersonal violence, and particularly for women who are victims of intimate partner violence, is traumatic brain injury (Ackerman & Banks, 2002, 2003; Ackerman, Banks, & Corbett, 1998; Banks & Ackerman, 2002; Banks, Ackerman, & Corbett, 1995; Valera & Berenbaum, 2003). In order to silence victims and prevent them from communicating with others, perpetrators target the victim's head as a means of disabling them; this includes choking, shaking, and hitting. Some of the neuropsychological consequences are experienced by the victims for the rest of their lives (Abbott, 1997; Manetta, 1999). There is impact on the ability to think clearly, work, manage household duties, and relate normally to others, in addition to the posttraumatic stress documented for many victims of violence (Valera & Berenbaum, 2003). The chronic and repetitive nature of intimate partner violence leads to multiple injuries without adequate time for recovery, such as is provided for athletes sustaining similar injuries (Lovell et al., 2003).

4.7 Women With Disabilities

Women of Color, especially African American and Native American women, are more likely than European American women to experience disability (Banks, 2003a, 2003b). As stated in Cummings, Neff, and Husaini (2003), "Black men have 60 percent more restricted-activity days than white men, and Black women experience 33 percent more days of restriction than white women. African Americans sustain higher levels of functional disability and become impaired at earlier ages than their white counterparts" (p. 24).

Some of the traumatic experiences of Women of Color with disabilities have been documented with attention to the combination of gender and ethnic issues involved in the stress following or in conjunction with those traumas. The stresses include adjustment after homicidal violence (Mukherjee, Reis, & Heller, 2003); HIV infection (Baesler, Derlega, Winstead, & Barbee, 2003; Feist-Price & Wright, 2003); eating disorders (Bagley, Character, & Shelton, 2003); chronic metabolic, joint, and circulatory diseases (Feldman & Tegart, 2003; Nabors & Pettee, 2003; Yee, Nguyen, & Ha, 2003); obtaining accommodation for education and employment (Neal-Barnett & Mendelson, 2003; Vande Kemp, Chen, Erickson, & Friesen, 2003); sexuality (Dotson, Stinson, & Christian, 2003); substance abuse (Beatty, 2003); deafness (Corbett, 2003); and interstitial cystitis (Ackerman & Banks, 2003).

5 BUFFERS OR MYTHS: RESILIENCE AND EFFECTIVE COPING STRATEGIES

Much research on People of Color has included two major assumptions about buffers that enhance survival despite racism. Those assumptions refer to extended family (Tatum, 1999) and religious communities as support networks (Musgrave, Allen, & Allen, 2002).

For example, some assume that all Women of Color have large family networks. This reflects a common assumption but ignores the reality that many Women of Color who are single mothers do not have supportive familial or other support networks and are subject to the stressors faced by European American women, as well as to the stressor of racism (Brewer, 1995; see also George & Dickerson, 1995, for a discussion of the impact of poverty on traditional African American grandparenting and parenting roles). The lack of support results in a variety of long-term and short-term health problems, such as depression, anxiety, substance abuse, hypertension, and eating disorders (Jones & Shorter-Gooden, 2003).

In addition, participating in churches or other faith-based organizations can come with some hidden costs. Among them are expected financial contributions (offerings, tithes, donations) and time in support of religious institution activities. Moreover, in many traditional religions, the roles for women are limited, resulting in additional sexist stress in an environment that many assume to be supportive. For Women of Color, this is further compounded by racism if the religious images are of Europeans and European Americans. Religious institutions also provide perspectives on health status. Women with disabilities are unlikely to find religious doctrine that provides them directly with examples and supportive suggestions for management of their disabilities; in some instances, people with disabilities are portrayed as bad and are excluded from most important aspects of worship (World Council of Churches, 2003).

Strong ethnic identity is another significant buffer that assists members of nondominant ethnic groups in coping with the stress of racism (Utsey, Chae, Brown, & Kelly, 2002). It has also been shown to be beneficial for overall health (Bowen-Reid & Harrell, 2002).

Women of Color are at considerable disadvantage for the receipt of good health care. Many are uninsured and unable to afford care for themselves and their families. In addition, information about health care options and advice for healthy living are not available in forms, including in different languages, that are accessible (Yee et al., 2003). Ackerman and Banks (2003) and Banks (2003b) noted that certain disorders are underdiagnosed in women, especially Women of Color, and that they are not referred for available treatments, such as cognitive rehabilitation and biofeedback.

6 SUMMARY

Women and girls from all ethnic and racial backgrounds can experience trauma and stress. Previous research literature has neglected the experiences of Women of Color. These women are vulnerable to trauma in every aspect of their lives, including their homes, communities, and places of employment. Despite social and economic advances, these traumatic events are common, repeated, and ongoing. This cycle of violence leads to a variety of injuries, including brain injury, that contribute to multiple health and disease complications, mental health problems, and complex symptoms across the life span.

Women of Color are repeatedly stressed by both racism and sexism. Racism and sexism can be subtle or overt, such as job discrimination, slurs, or physical attacks. Racial and sexual oppression can contribute to psychological trauma, including PTSD, yet many of our trauma theories are ahistorical. This is an oversight, because the legacy of trauma of oppressed people can be multigenerational. European American women never experienced lynching, forced relocation to reservations, or imprisonment in internment camps. These atrocities may cause "insidious trauma" among second- and third-generation family members.

Future research must systematically examine how culture, stigma, and acculturation influence stress and trauma experiences among immigrant women and Women of Color. Acculturation will temper the strength and form of culture's influence upon health, stress, and trauma. Databases, such as those used to track sexually transmitted diseases and mortality and morbidity should be disaggregated by gender and ethnicity in order to document the disparate impact of stress and trauma on Women of Color. Researchers need disaggregated data concerning the following:

- Accurate incidence and prevalence rates of female victimization
- Long-term family, mental, and physical health consequences of stress and trauma among these underserved, high-risk groups of women
- Cultural factors that impinge on health, quality of health care, attitudes of health care providers, cleanness of water and environments, and employment
- Brain injuries
- Resilience and effective coping strategies

REFERENCES

Abbott, J. (1997). Injuries and illnesses of domestic violence. *Annals of Emergency Medicine, 29,* 781–785.

Ackerman, R. J., & Banks, M. E. (2002). Epilogue: Looking for the threads: Commonalities and differences. In F. R. Ferraro (Ed.), *Minority and cross-cultural aspects of neuropsychological assessment* (pp. 387–415). Heereweg, Lisse, The Netherlands: Swets & Zeitlinger.

Ackerman, R. J., & Banks, M. E. (2003). Assessment, treatment, and rehabilitation for interpersonal violence victims: Women sustaining head injuries. In M. E. Banks & E. Kaschak (Eds.), *Women with visible and invisible disabilities: Multiple intersections, multiple issues, multiple therapies* (pp. 343–363). Binghamton, NY: Haworth.

Ackerman, R. J., Banks, M. E., & Corbett, C. A. (1998). When women deal with head injuries. In O. Nnaemeka (Ed.), *Women in Africa and the African Diaspora: Building bridges of knowledge and power. Volume II: Health, human rights, and the environment* (pp. 5–22). Indianapolis, IL: Association of African Women Scholars.

Adams, B., Aranda, M. P., Kemp, B., & Takagi, K. (2002). Ethnic and gender differences in distress among Anglo American, African American, Japanese American, and Mexican American spousal caregivers of persons with dementia. *Journal of Clinical Geropsychology, 8,* 279–301.

Adeyemo, S. A. (2003). The cultural and socio-psychological implications of female circumcision. *Psychology and Education: An Interdisciplinary Journal, 40,* 50–54.

Adler, N. E., & Coriell, M. (1997). Socioeconomic status and women's health. In S. J. Gallant, G. P. Keita, & R. Royak-Schaler (Eds.), *Healthcare for women: Psychological, social, and behavioral influences.* Washington, DC: American Psychological Association.

Axelrod, J., Myers, H. F., Durvasula, R. S., Wyatt, G. E., & Cheng, M. (1999). The impact of relationship violence, HIV, and ethnicity on adjustment in women. *Cultural Diversity and Ethnic Minority Psychology, 5,* 263–275.

Baesler, E. J., Derlega, V. J., Winstead, B. A., & Barbee, A. (2003). Prayer as interpersonal coping in the lives of mothers with HIV. In M. E. Banks & E. Kaschak (Eds.), *Women with visible and invisible disabilities: Multiple intersections, multiple issues, multiple therapies* (pp. 283–295). Binghamton, NY: Haworth.

Bagley, C., Character, C. A., & Shelton, L. (2003). Eating disorders among urban and rural African American and European American women. In M. E. Banks & E. Kaschak (Eds.), *Women with visible and invisible disabilities: Multiple intersections, multiple issues, multiple therapies* (pp. 57–79). Binghamton, NY: Haworth.

Banks, M. E. (2003a). Disability in the family: A life-span perspective. *Cultural Diversity and Ethnic Minority Psychology, 9,* 367–384.

Banks, M. E. (2003b). Preface [Women with visible and invisible disabilities: Multiple intersections, multiple issues, multiple therapies]. In M. E. Banks & E. Kaschak (Eds.), *Women with visible and invisible disabilities: Multiple intersections, multiple issues, multiple therapies* (pp. xxiii–xli). Binghamton, NY: Haworth.

Banks, M. E., & Ackerman, R. J. (1999). *Intimate/domestic violence resources: Breaking the cycle.* Retrieved December 22, 2003, from http://abackans.com/dvresour.html

Banks, M. E., & Ackerman, R. J. (2002). Physical (especially head) injuries experienced by African American women victims of intimate partner violence. In C. West (Ed.), *Battered, black, and blue: Violence in the lives of black women* (pp. 134–143). Binghamton, NY: Haworth.

Banks, M. E., & Ackerman, R. J. (2003). All things being unequal: Culturally relevant roads to employment. In F. E. Menz & D. F. Thomas (Eds.), *Bridging gaps: Refining the disability research agenda for rehabilitation and the social sciences—Conference proceedings* (pp. 35–64). Menomonie: University of Wisconsin–Stout, Stout Vocational Rehabilitation Institute, Research and Training Centers.

Banks, M. E., Ackerman, R. J., & Corbett, C. A. (1995). Feminist neuropsychology: Issues for physically challenged women. In J. Chrisler & A. Hemstreet (Eds.), *Variations on a theme: Diversity and the psychology of women* (pp. 29–49). Albany: State University of New York.

Beatty, L. (2003). Substance abuse, disabilities, and Black women: An issue worth exploring. In M. E. Banks & E. Kaschak (Eds.), *Women with visible and invisible disabilities: Multiple intersections, multiple issues, multiple therapies* (pp. 223–236). Binghamton, NY: Haworth.

Bell, C. C., & Mattis, J. (2000). The importance of cultural competence in ministering to African American victims of domestic violence. *Violence Against Women, 6,* 515–532.

Bowen-Reid, T. L., & Harrell, J. P. (2002). Racist experiences and health outcome: An examination of spirituality as a buffer. *Journal of Black Psychology, 28,* 18–36.

Boyd-Franklin, N., & Franklin, A. J. (2000). *Boys into men: Raising our African American teenage sons.* New York: Plume.

Brewer, R. M. (1995). Gender, poverty, culture, and economy: Theorizing female-led families. In B. J. Dickerson (Ed.), *African American single mothers: Understanding their lives and families* (pp. 164–178). Thousand Oaks, CA: Sage.

Brice-Baker, J. R. (1994). Domestic violence in African-American and African-Caribbean families. *Journal of Social Distress and the Homeless, 3,* 23–38.

Campbell, J. C., & Kendall-Tackett, K. A. (2005). Intimate partner violence: Implications for women's physical and mental health. In K. A. Kendall-Tackett (Ed.), *The handbook of women, stress, and trauma* (pp. 123–140). New York: Taylor & Francis.

Chen, J., Etkind, P., Coman, G., Tang, Y., & Whelan, M. (2003). Eliminating missing race/ethnicity data from a sexually transmitted disease case registry. *Journal of Community Health, 28,* 257–265.

Corbett, C. A. (2003). Special issues in psychotherapy for minority deaf women. In M. E. Banks & E. Kaschak (Eds.), *Women with visible and invisible disabilities: Multiple intersections, multiple issues, multiple therapies* (pp. 311–329). Binghamton, NY: Haworth.

Couture, S. M., & Penn, D. L. (2003). Interpersonal contact and the stigma of mental illness: A review of the literature. *Journal of Mental Health, 12,* 291–305.

Cummings, S. M., Neff, J. A., & Husaini, B. A. (2003). Functional impairment as a predictor of depressive symptomatology: The role of race, religiosity, and social support. *Health and Social Work, 28,* 23–32.

Dearwater, S. R., Coben, J. H., Campbell, J. C., Nah, G., Glass, N., McLoughlin, E., & Bekemeir, B. (1998). Prevalence of intimate partner abuse in women treated at community hospital emergency departments. *Journal of the American Medical Association, 280*, 433–438.

Dotson, L. A., Stinson, J., & Christian, L. (2003). "People tell me I can't have sex": Women with disabilities share their personal perspectives on health care, sexuality, and reproductive rights. In M. E. Banks & E. Kaschak (Eds.), *Women with visible and invisible disabilities: Multiple intersections, multiple issues, multiple therapies* (pp. 195–209). Binghamton, NY: Haworth.

Elders, M. J., & Albert, A. E. (1998). Adolescent pregnancy and sexual abuse. *Journal of the American Medical Association, 280*, 648–649.

Farley, M. (2003). Prostitution and the invisibility of harm. In M. E. Banks & E. Kaschak (Eds.), *Women with visible and invisible disabilities: Multiple intersections, multiple issues, multiple therapies* (pp. 247–280). Binghamton, NY: Haworth.

Feist-Price, S., & Wright, L. B. (2003). African American women living with HIV/AIDS: Mental health issues. In M. E. Banks & E. Kaschak (Eds.), *Women with visible and invisible disabilities: Multiple intersections, multiple issues, multiple therapies* (pp. 27–44). Binghamton, NY: Haworth.

Feldman, S. I., & Tegart, G. (2003). Keep moving: Conceptions of illness and disability of middle-aged African-American women with arthritis. In M. E. Banks & E. Kaschak (Eds.), *Women with visible and invisible disabilities: Multiple intersections, multiple issues, multiple therapies* (pp. 127–143). Binghamton, NY: Haworth.

George, S. M., & Dickerson, B. J. (1995). The role of the grandmother in poor single-mother families and households. In B. J. Dickerson (Ed.), *African American single mothers: Understanding their lives and families* (pp. 146–163). Thousand Oaks, CA: Sage.

Golding, J. M. (1999). Intimate partner violence as a risk factor for mental disorders: A meta-analysis. *Journal of Family Violence, 14*(2), 99–132.

Guyll, M., Matthews, K. A., & Bromberger, J. T. (2001). Discrimination and unfair treatment: Relationship to cardiovascular reactivity among African American and European American women. *Health Psychology, 20*, 315–325.

Hien, D., & Bukszpan, C. (1999). Interpersonal violence in a "normal" low-income control group. *Women and Health, 29*, 1–16.

Jenkins, E. J. (2002). Black women and community violence: Trauma, grief, and coping. In C. M. West (Ed.), *Violence in the lives of Black women: Battered, Black, and blue* (pp. 29–44). Binghamton, NY: Haworth.

Jones, C., & Shorter-Gooden, K. (2003). *Shifting: The double lives of Black Women in America.* New York: HarperCollins.

Jones, D. J., Beach, S. R. H., Forehand, R., & Family Health Project Research Group. (2003). Partner abuse and HIV infection: Implications for psychosocial adjustment in African American women. *Journal of Family Violence, 18*, 257–268.

Jones, D. J., Beach, S. R. H., Forehand, R., & Foster, S. E. (2003). Self-reported health in HIV-positive African American women: The role of family stress and depressive symptoms. *Journal of Behavioral Medicine, 26*, 577–599.

Kendall-Tackett, K. A. (2005). Caught in the middle: Stress in the lives of young adult women. In K. A. Kendall-Tackett (Ed.), *The handbook of women, stress, and trauma* (pp. 33–51). New York: Taylor & Francis.

Kotchen, J. M., Shakoor-Abdullah, B., Walker, W. E., Chelius, T. H., Hoffmann, R. G., & Kotchen, T. A. (1998). Hypertension control and access to medical care in the inner city. *American Journal of Public Health, 88*, 1696–1699.

Kruttschnitt, C., McLaughlin, B. L., & Petrie, C. V. (Eds.). (forthcoming, 2004). *Advancing the federal research agenda on violence against women.* Steering committee for the Workshop on Issues in Research on Violence Against Women, National Research Council, The National Academies Press. Retrieved December 22, 2003, from http://nap.edu/books/0309091098/html/

Kulwicki, A. D. (2002). The practice of honor crimes: A glimpse of domestic violence in the Arab world. *Issues in Mental Health Nursing, 23,* 77–87.

Kwong, M. J., Bartholomew, K., Henderson A. J. Z., & Trinke, S. J. (2003). The intergenerational transmission of relationship violence. *Journal of Family Psychology, 17,* 288–301.

Lott, B. (2002). Cognitive and behavioral distancing from the poor. *American Psychologist, 57,* 100–110.

Louie, S. C. (2000). Interpersonal relationships: Independence versus interdependence. In J. L. Chin (Ed.), *Relationships among Asian American women* (pp. 211–230). Washington, DC: American Psychological Association.

Lovell, M. R., Collins, M. W., Iverson, G. L., Field. M., Maroon, J. C., Cantu, R., Podell, K., Powell, J. W., Belza, M., & Fu, F. H. (2003). Recovery from mild concussion in high-school athletes. *Journal of Neurosurgery, 98,* 296–301.

Manetta, A. A. (1999). Interpersonal violence and suicidal behavior in midlife African American women. *Journal of Black Studies, 29,* 510–522.

Marshall, L. M., Spiegelman, D., Barbieri, R. L., Goldman, M. B., Manson, J. E., Colditz, G. A., Willett, W. C., & Hunter, D. J. (1997). Variation in the incidence of uterine leiomyoma among premenopausal women by age and race. *Obstetrics and Gynecology, 90,* 967–973.

Mays, V. M., Ponce, N. A., Washington, D. L., & Cochran, S. D. (2003). Classification of race and ethnicity: Implications for public health. *Annual Review of Public Health, 24,* 83–110.

McCallum, D. M., Arnold, S. E., & Bolland, J. M. (2002). Low-income African-American women talk about stress. *Journal of Social Distress and the Homeless, 11*(3), 249–263.

McLoyd, V. C. (1998). Socioeconomic disadvantage and child development. *American Psychologist, 53,* 185–204.

Mukherjee, D., Reis, J. P., & Heller, W. (2003). Women living with traumatic brain injury: Social isolation, emotional functioning and implications for psychotherapy. In M. E. Banks & E. Kaschak (Eds.), *Women with visible and invisible disabilities: Multiple intersections, multiple issues, multiple therapies* (pp. 1–26). Binghamton, NY: Haworth.

Musante, L., Treiber, F. A., Kapuku, G., Moore, D., Davis, H., & Strong, W. B. (2000). The effects of life events on cardiovascular reactivity to behavioral stressors as a function of socioeconomic status, ethnicity, and sex. *Psychosomatic Medicine, 62,* 760–767.

Musgrave, C. A., Allen, C. E., & Allen, G. J. (2002). Spirituality and health for Women of Color. *American Journal of Public Health, 92,* 557–560.

Nabors, N. A., & Pettee, M. F. (2003). Womanist therapy with African American women with disabilities. In M. E. Banks & E. Kaschak (Eds.), *Women with visible and invisible disabilities: Multiple intersections, multiple issues, multiple therapies* (pp. 331–341). Binghamton, NY: Haworth.

Nader, K., Dubrow, N., & Stamm, B. H. (1999). *Honoring differences: Cultural issues in treatment of trauma and loss.* Philadelphia, PA: Brunner/Mazel.

National Cancer Registrars Association. (1999). Unequal burden, unequal data: Registries helping close the gap. *Journal of Registry Management, 26,* 117–168.

Neal-Barnett, A. M., & Mendelson, L. L. (2003). Obsessive compulsive disorder in the workplace: An invisible disability. In M. E. Banks & E. Kaschak (Eds.), *Women with visible and invisible disabilities: Multiple intersections, multiple issues, multiple therapies* (pp. 169–178). Binghamton, NY: Haworth.

Nichols, R. R. (2002). Striving for a more excellent way. In C. M. West (Ed.), *Violence in the lives of Black women: Battered, Black, and blue* (pp. 187–192). Binghamton, NY: Haworth.

Oates, G. C. (1998). Cultural perspectives on intimate violence. In N. A. Jackson & G. C. Oates (Eds.), *Violence in intimate relationships: Examining sociological and psychological issues* (pp. 225–243). Woburn, MA: Butterworth-Heinemann.

Office of Management and Budget. (1997, July 9). Office of Management and Budget Statistical policy directive No. 15: Race and ethnic standards for Federal statistics and administrative reporting. *Federal Register, 62*(131), 36873–36946.

Pantin, H. M., Schwartz, S. J., Prado, G., Feaster, D. J., & Szapocznik, J. (2003). Posttraumatic stress disorder symptoms in Hispanic immigrants after the September 11th attacks: Severity and relationship to previous traumatic exposure. *Hispanic Journal of Behavioral Sciences, 25,* 56–72.

Penn, D. L., & Wykes, T. (2003). Editorial: Stigma, discrimination and mental illness. *Journal of Mental Health, 12,* 203–208.

Root, M. P. P. (1992). Reconstructing the impact of trauma on personality. In L. S. Brown & M. Ballon (Eds.), Personality and psychopathology (pp. 229–265). New York: Guilford.

Rysberg, J. (2005). Stress and trauma in the lives of middle-aged and old women. In K. A. Kendall-Tackett (Ed.), *The handbook of women, stress, and trauma* (pp. 75–97). New York: Taylor & Francis.

Sanchez-Hucles, J. V. (1998). Racism: Emotional abusiveness and psychological trauma for ethnic minorities. *Journal of Emotional Abuse, 1,* 69–87.

Scott, K., & Eliav, J. (2005). Relational stress and trauma in the lives of girls and teens. In K. A. Kendall-Tackett (Ed.), *The handbook of women, stress, and trauma* (pp. 9–32). New York: Taylor & Francis.

Singh, R. N., & Unnithan, N. P. (1999). Wife burning: Cultural cues for lethal violence against women among Asian Indians in the United States. *Violence Against Women, 5,* 641–653.

Smith, A. A. (1995). Sisterhood among African-American mothers of daughters addicted to crack cocaine. In K. M. Vaz (Ed.), *Black women in America* (pp. 357–368). Thousand Oaks, CA: Sage.

Steffen, P. R., Hinderliter, A. L., Blumenthal, J. A., & Sherwood, A. (2001). Religious coping, ethnicity, and ambulatory blood pressure. *Psychosomatic Medicine, 63,* 523–530.

Tatum, B. D. (1999). *Assimilation blues: Black families in White communities: Who succeeds and why?* New York: Basic Books.

Tran, C. G., & Des Jardins, K. (2000). Domestic violence in Vietnamese refugee and Korean immigrant communities. In J. L. Chin (Ed.), *Relationships among Asian American Women* (pp. 71–96). Washington, DC: American Psychological Association.

Trautman, R., Tucker, P., Pfefferbaum, B., Lensgraf, S. J., Doughty, D. E., Buksh, A., & Miller, P. D. (2002). Effects of prior trauma and age on posttraumatic stress symptoms in Asian and Middle Eastern immigrants after terrorism in the community. *Community Mental Health Journal, 38,* 459–474.

Troxel, W. M., Matthews, K. A., Bromberger, J. T., & Sutton-Tyrrell, K. (2003). Chronic stress burden, discrimination, and subclinical carotid artery disease in African American and Caucasian women. *Health Psychology, 22,* 300–309.

Turner, R. J., & Lloyd, D. A. (2003). Cumulative adversity and drug dependence in young adults: Racial/ethnic contrasts. *Addiction, 98,* 305–315.

Turrittin, J., Hagey, R., Guruge, S., Collins, E., & Mitchell, M. (2002). The experiences of professional nurses who have migrated to Canada: Cosmopolitan citizenship or democratic racism? *International Journal of Nursing Studies, 39,* 655–667.

U.S. Census Bureau. (2001). *Overview of race and Hispanic origin: Census 2000 brief.* Retrieved February 9, 2002, from http://www.census.gov/population/www/socdemo/race.html

U.S. Department of Health and Human Services. (2001). *Mental health: Culture, race, and ethnicity—A supplement to mental health: A report to the Surgeon General.* Rockville, MD: U.S. Department of Health and Human Services, Substance Abuse and Mental Health Services Administration, Center for Mental Health Services.

U.S. Department of Health and Human Services, Office on Women's Health. (2003, July). The health of minority women. Retrieved January 19, 2004 from http://www.4woman.gov/owh/pub/minority/minority.pdf

Utsey, S. O., Chae, M. H., Brown, C. F., & Kelly, D. (2002). Effect of ethnic group membership on ethnic identity, race-related stress and quality of life. *Cultural Diversity and Ethnic Minority Psychology, 8,* 366–377.

Valera, E. M., & Berenbaum, H. (2003). Brain injury in battered women. *Journal of Consulting and Clinical Psychology, 71,* 797–804.

Vande Kemp, H., Chen, J. S., Erickson, G. N., & Friesen, N. L. (2003). ADA accommodation of therapists with disabilities in clinical training. In M. E. Banks & E. Kaschak (Eds.), *Women with visible and invisible disabilities: Multiple intersections, multiple issues, multiple therapies* (pp. 155–168). Binghamton, NY: Haworth.

Velzeboer, M., Ellsberg, M., Arcas, C. C., & Garcia-Moreno, C. (2003). *Violence against women: The health sector responds.* Washington, DC: Pan American Health Organization and World Health Organization.

West, C. M. (2002). Battered, Black, and blue: An overview of violence in the lives of Black women. In C. M. West (Ed.), *Violence in the lives of Black women: Battered, Black, and blue* (pp. 5–27). Binghamton, NY: Haworth.

Wolkenstein, B. H., & Sterman, L. (1998). Unmet needs of older women in a clinic population: The discovery of possible long-term sequelae of domestic violence. *Professional Psychology: Research and Practice, 29,* 341–348.

World Council of Churches. (2003, August 26–September 2). A church of all and for all—An interim statement. Retrieved September 10, 2003, from http://www2.wcc-coe.org/ccdocuments2003.nsf/index/plen-1.1-en.html

Wyatt, G. E. (1997). *Stolen women: Reclaiming our sexuality, taking back our lives.* New York: John Wiley & Sons.

Yee, B. W. K. (1999a). Life-span development of Asian and Pacific Islanders: Impact of gender and age roles. In B. W. K. Yee, N. Mokuau, & S. Kim (Eds.), *Developing cultural competence in Asian American and Pacific Islander communities: Opportunities in primary health care and substance abuse prevention* (pp. 91–142). Cultural Competence Series, Volume V (DHHS Pub. No. [SMA] 98-3193) [Special Collaborative Edition]. Washington, DC: Center for Substance Abuse Prevention (SAMHSA), Bureau of Primary Health Care (HRSA) and Office of Minority Health (DHHS).

Yee, B. W. K. (1999b). Influence of traditional and cultural health practices among Asian women. In *Agenda for research on women's health for the 21st century* (pp. 150–165). Report of the Task Force on the NIH Women's Health Research Agenda for the 21st Century, Volume 6: Differences among Populations of Women (NIH Publications No. 99-4390), Santa Fe, NM, July 1997 Office of Research on Women's Health, National Institutes of Health.

Yee, B. W. K. (forthcoming 2004). Cultural factors and health. In N. Anderson (Ed.), *Encyclopedia of health and behavior.* Thousand Oaks, CA: Sage.

Yee, B. W. K., Huang, L. N., & Lew, A. (1998). Families: Life-span socialization in a cultural context. In L. C. Lee & N. W. S. Zane (Eds.), *Handbook of Asian American psychology* (pp. 83–135). Thousand Oaks, CA: Sage.

Yee, B. W. K., Nguyen, H. T., & Ha, M. (2003). Chronic disease health beliefs and lifestyle practices among Vietnamese adults: Influences of gender and age. In M. E. Banks & E. Kaschak (Eds.), *Women with visible and invisible disabilities: Multiple intersections, multiple issues, multiple therapies* (pp. 111–125). Binghamton, NY: Haworth.

Zhang, A. Y., & Snowden, L. R. (1999). Ethnic characteristics of mental disorders in five U.S. communities. *Cultural Diversity and Ethnic Minority Psychology, 5,* 134–146.

11

Stress and Trauma in the Lives of Women with Disabilities[1]

LINDA R. MONA, REBECCA P. CAMERON, AND
DANETTE CRAWFORD

Social and behavioral sciences have explored the life experiences of
people with disabilities for over 40 years (Hamilton, 1950; Hohmann,
1975; Nagi, 1965; Siller, 1963). Much of this work focused on the effects of
impairment and functionality on the larger life experiences of the disability community. However, some early scholars began to explore the
effects of the environmental, social, and political experiences of disability
on the lives and well-being of this community (DeJong, 1984; Hohenshil
& Humes, 1979). With increased knowledge about the ways in which the
interaction between impairment and environment can affect the individual and social lives of people with disabilities (Pledger, 2003), a heightened awareness has resulted in the incidence of trauma and stress among
individuals within the disability community. Specifically, issues pertain-
ing to stress and trauma among women with disabilities have begun to

---

[1] This chapter is dedicated to our coauthor, Danette Crawford, who recently
passed away. Most of Danette's young career was focused on issues around
trauma and women with disabilities. From advocacy work to academic writings,
her energy to educate others about this underdiscussed topic was never ending.
We are honored that we had the opportunity to collaborate with her on one of her
last contributions to the literature.

be revealed (Nosek & Howland, 1997; Nosek, Howland, & Hughes, 2001; Waxman Fiduccia & Wolfe, 1999).

About one fifth of U.S. citizens have some type of disability, with the percentage somewhat higher for women and girls (21.3%) than among men and boys (19.8%) (Banks, 2003). Research suggests an incidence of sexual and physical violence among women with disabilities that is higher than in the general population (Sobsey & Doe, 1991; Nosek & Howland, 1997). Furthermore, women with disabilities are at high risk for a longer duration of abuse than their able-bodied counterparts (Nosek, Howland, & Young, 1997). Based upon this information, how disability has been defined and the ways in which trauma in the lives of women with disabilities is characterized becomes of great interest.

This chapter will address stress and trauma in the lives of women with disabilities by exploring the ways in which disability is defined and conceptualized, describing what we know about women with disabilities, and outlining the types and levels of trauma they experience. Barriers to services and treatment will be addressed, and factors contributing to resiliency among women with disabilities will be offered. By reviewing the stated issues, we are striving to inform readers about the complexity of the issues and charge future researchers and academicians with the importance of examining this topic more broadly.

1 DEFINITIONS AND MODELS OF DISABILITY

1.1 Definitions of Disability

Disability has traditionally been defined exclusively by either physical or mental impairment and limitations on functioning (Nagi, 1969; Americans with Disabilities Act, 1990). More recently, Olkin (1999) explored the definition of disability according to three main questions:

What conditions—physical, cognitive, psychoemotional, sensory—
    would be included in a definition of disability?
How do relevant laws define disability?
Under what conditions do people consider themselves a person with a
    disability?

By answering these questions, a much broader view is taken of the disability experience by including notions of impairment, legislative and political components, and identity within a particular group. If we were to classify based upon impairment status alone, a vast amount of information characterizing persons with disabilities would be lost. When we redirect attention away from impairment alone and incorporate it with social, individual, and environmental factors, disability can begin to be seen in a more holistic manner. In fact, many barriers confronted when living with a disability can disappear with societal (e.g., policies and legislation that protect the rights of people with disabilities) and environmental (e.g., architectural access) supports. The ways in which disability has been conceptualized throughout the years also assists with being better able to clearly describe this population.

1.2 Models of Disability

Historically, four theoretical frameworks have shaped disability-related cultural discourse: the moral model, the medical model, the social/minority model, and the New Paradigm of Disability. These four models are described below.

1.2.1 Moral Model. The oldest of these paradigms is the moral model of disability. As articulated by Olkin (1999), this view is based on the assertion that disability is a physical manifestation of sin or moral lapse. Under this model, disability may also be constructed as a test of faith or divine opportunity for spiritual growth and increased enlightenment. The moral model was often used as a cultural justification for the social ostracism and isolation of persons with disabilities, because their physical difficulties were constructed as an outward reflection of their moral character. Aspects of this model still resonate in our conceptualization of disability. For example, individuals with disabilities often feel pressured to overcompensate for their impairment because of a deeply ingrained cultural belief that persons with disabilities are inherently inferior to their able-bodied counterparts.

1.2.2 Medical Model. The second model of disability, the medical model, was a direct consequence of an increased emphasis on rehabilitative medicine following the Civil War. As articulated by Longmore and Umansky (2001), the medical model is inextricably linked to all modern social arrangements regarding disability. This approach places almost exclusive emphasis on the responsibility of the individual to overcome his or her disability. Under this model, individuals with disabilities are culturally mandated to work as hard as possible to emulate the nondisabled norm. Our cultures' emphasis on the medical aspects of disability has direct consequences in terms of the ways in which we choose to allocate social and economic resources. By focusing on cure rather than care, we limit the monetary and interpersonal support available to individuals who choose to live in the community. The social or minority model of disability (see below) directly addresses these discrepancies by framing disability as a social construction rather than as an individual malady.

1.2.3 Social/Minority Model. The social model views persons with disabilities as belonging to a minority group in much the same way as other disempowered cultural groups (Olkin, 1999). As with any other minority group, social practice directly results in restricted access to economic and cultural institutions. A defining characteristic of minority status rests in the repeated experience of stigma and discrimination. Persons with disabilities share many commonalities with other minority groups. These include restrictions on reproductive rights, inadequate health care and socioeconomic resources, underrepresentation, and increased incidence of hate crimes (Olkin, 1999). Many people with disabilities have developed a rich cultural framework of shared history, common experience, artistic expression, and community. In fact, some persons with disabilities consider themselves to be bicultural, in that they must become experts at successfully navigating between disabled and nondisabled worlds.

1.2.4 New Paradigm of Disability. A fourth model of disability has recently been introduced. The New Paradigm of Disability (National Institute on Disability and Rehabilitation Research [NIDRR], 1999) maintains that disability is a product of interaction between characteristics of the individual and characteristics of the natural, built, cultural, and social environments. This approach argues that past conceptualizations of disability ascribe disability to the individual and underplay the interaction that occurs between various environments and the individual. Furthermore, according to this paradigm, disability is located on a continuum, which suggests an applied-social model that interrelates the impact of environmental factors (e.g., families, immediate environments, various systems, public policies, culture, and society) on participation, productivity, involvement, quality of life, and psychological adjustment of those affected by disability. Compared to the sociopolitical model, the New Paradigm of Disability acknowledges disability as impairment and searches for the interplay between individual and environmental factors.

Of these four models, the social model of disability uniquely addresses the needs of women with disabilities who experience trauma because of its emphasis on cultural oppression and collective responsibility. Thus, women with disabilities are able to put their experiences of trauma into a larger context of injustice and hopefully avoid the internalized self-blame that often follows a traumatic event. In addition, compared to the moral and medical models, the New Paradigm of Disability also allows more room for exploring trauma-related experiences by placing a high importance on environmental and social factors. Thus, for the purposes of this chapter, disability will be addressed from this heightened comprehensive perspective so that the important issues specific to stress and trauma can be viewed within a sociopolitical context and so that the interplay between impairment and environment can be examined more thoroughly.

2 STRESS, TRAUMATIC STRESS, AND POSTTRAUMATIC STRESS DISORDER (PTSD)

2.1 Stress

Stress is a multifaceted concept that has been defined in a variety of ways. Some researchers focus on daily hassles (e.g., waiting in lines; Wagner, Compas, & Howell, 1988); some focus on chronic stressors (e.g., unemployment; Avison & Turner, 1988); and others focus on major life events (e.g., death of a spouse; Holmes & Rahe, 1967). Stress has also been defined in terms of loss of valued resources, including objects (e.g., a car), conditions (e.g., marriage), personal characteristics (e.g., self-esteem), and energies (e.g., time) (Hobfoll, 1989). Thus, a discussion of the ordinary stressors experienced by women with disabilities could catalog the stressors that affect all members of society, and then we can highlight the increased risk for hassles (e.g., transportation difficulties), chronic stressors (e.g., higher risk of poverty), major life events (e.g., surgeries), or losses (e.g., depleted financial resources) that differentially affect women with disabilities.

Stress can also be thought of as a transaction in which environmental demands exceed the coping capacity of an individual (Lazarus & Folkman, 1984); that is, a given event, such as a needed home repair, may be deemed stressful by particular individuals depending upon whether they have the personal, financial, and other resources to effect the repair. Traditionally, when examining a mismatch between environmental demands and individual coping capacity, psychological theories focus on the deficits in individual coping capacity, thus resembling the medical model of disability. In contrast, ecological perspectives shift the focus to highlight environments as the sources of the difficulty and are, therefore, more compatible with the modern paradigm of disability.

In fact, the modern paradigm of disability, which focuses on functional limitations in social–ecological contexts and on social construction of disability as a minority status (Pledger, 2003) can, to some extent, be thought of as defining disability in terms of the added burden of stressors society imposes upon those with physical, cognitive, or emotional differences relative to those who do not possess such differences. In other words, environmental demands that are constructed to suit able-bodied individuals' capacities are the reasons other individuals are defined and experienced as disabled. From this perspective, the physical and social environments we create are mismatched to the needs and capacities of women with disabilities (e.g., impediments to mobility, transportation, self-care, social relatedness, work, leisure, and other aspects of self-determined living), resulting in a disproportionate stress burden among these women.

2.2 Traumatic Stress and PTSD

Traumatic stress is a particular category of stress that has also been subject to a variety of definitions over the years. The definition of a traumatic event employed by the *Diagnostic and Statistical Manual of Mental Disorders* (4th ed., Text Revision [*DSM-IV-TR*], American Psychiatric Association, 2000) contains both of the following elements: "the person experienced, witnessed, or was confronted with an event or events that involved actual or threatened death or serious injury, or a threat to the physical integrity of self or others" and "the person's response involved intense fear, helplessness, or horror" (p. 467). The experience of trauma increases risk for a variety of psychological syndromes, notably acute stress disorder and PTSD, but also other anxiety disorders such as generalized anxiety disorder (characterized by chronic worrying), mood disorders such as major depressive disorder, and substance use disorders such as alcohol abuse or dependence, in addition to other disorders. PTSD is characterized by a constellation of symptoms that are clinically significant and persist for at least a month, including reexperiencing symptoms (e.g., intrusive memories, dreams, distress when reminded of the event), avoidance symptoms (e.g., avoiding reminders, reduced activities, emotional detachment), and arousal symptoms (e.g., sleep disturbance, irritability, exaggerated startle). Acute stress disorder includes dissociative symptoms in addition to the symptoms of PTSD (e.g., impaired memory for the traumatic event, reduced awareness of surroundings) and is only applicable if symptoms begin within a month of the traumatic event and last between 2 days and 1 month (*DSM-IV-TR*, American Psychiatric Association, 2000).

The destructive impact of trauma arises from its extreme and disruptive nature. Risk of PTSD following trauma exposure varies depending upon a variety of factors, including the intensity and type of trauma as well as the exposed individual's emotional, physical, and social context before and after the traumatic event. Certain types of trauma seem to be associated with particularly high risk of PTSD. For example, the experience of rape has been found to be related to PTSD among roughly one third to more than one half of those exposed (*DSM-IV-TR*, American Psychiatric Association, 2000). Women who experience trauma appear to be at higher risk for PTSD than men, for reasons that are not fully understood but that may be related to biological factors and to gendered roles and identity, as well as to gender differences in types of trauma experienced (Saxe & Wolfe, 1999).

Individuals possessing supportive social networks and those who are in relatively good physical and mental health prior to the traumatic event are at reduced risk. Those who are physically ill, psychologically vulnerable, or socially isolated are at increased risk. Given these risk factors, trauma-exposed women with disabilities may be at higher risk for PTSD compared to trauma-exposed men and able-bodied individuals. In addition, the risk of psychological disturbance following a trauma is heightened when the trauma is followed by (or possibly precipitates) significant ongoing life events (Maes, Mylle, Delmeire, & Janca, 2001). This may be particularly relevant for women with disabilities, whose daily routines are particularly vulnerable to disruption, given their greater socioeconomic marginalization and their reliance on scarce resources, such as accessible transportation and facilities, and personal assistance providers to accomplish important personal and employment-related tasks (Nosek, 1990; Nosek et al., 2001).

Women with disabilities may experience a range of traumatic stressors, and the relationship between their traumatic experiences and their disability status may vary. For example, women with disabilities may have experienced trauma that predates the development of disability (e.g., childhood abuse predating a disabling illness or accident) that is concurrent with a transition to disabled status (e.g., a violent attack or motor vehicle accident that results in changed physical capacity) or that follows the experience of disability (e.g., a disabled woman is raped). In the last case, the occurrence of trauma may be independent of, or may flow from, her status as a woman with a disability. For example, a woman with disabilities may experience a traumatic traffic accident that is entirely independent of her disability. Or she may experience abuse at the hands of an intimate that would have been less likely to occur, or less severe, if she were not disabled. Or she may be singled out for trauma based upon her status as a disabled woman (e.g., the target of a hate crime).

3 TRAUMA AND WOMEN WITH DISABILITIES

Research on trauma and PTSD has been rapidly increasing, but women with disabilities are still underrepresented in this area of inquiry, and their unique risks and sources of resiliency have not been adequately documented. Below, we highlight four sources of trauma exposure that are particularly relevant for women with disabilities: medical mistreatment, abuse by personal assistants, sexual abuse, and hate crimes.

3.1 Medical Mistreatment

Nowhere is the depersonalization of a disabled women's body more significant than in the medical arena. The social imperative of bodily integrity can have devastating physical and emotional consequences for women with disabilities. For example, many disabled women have endured the trauma of "public stripping" (Blumberg, 1990). This practice entails a partially, or completely, unclothed individual being presented as a medical case to a room full of strangers. This event is sometimes referred to as "grand rounds" in a medical setting. These public examinations typically occur in large teaching hospitals and specialty clinics and are considered justifiable learning tools. According to Blumberg (1990), medical professionals often feel that "trivial" considerations, such as modesty, pale in comparison to the need to facilitate the exchange of medical knowledge. Although increased emphasis on patient rights has diminished this practice, it has not disappeared entirely. And, as a result of this practice, women with disabilities often leave such medical experiences with a sense of dissociation from their bodies and a sense of depersonalization from their selves.

The public objectification of a disabled woman's body can result in an internalized belief that the self is merely the sum of a medical condition (Crawford & Ostrove, 2003). Women with disabilities may mentally begin to separate themselves into parts and forget about other personal identities (e.g., spiritual self, roles as professionals, parents, lovers). A sense of dislike of her body may accompany this separation of the self. Given that an internalized sense of shame and self-loathing is often a precursor to mental health concerns, such as PTSD and major depression (Herman, 1992), women with disabilities may be prone to these mental health issues. Unfortunately, women with disabilities who have experienced such abuse by medical professionals may be reticent to seek future treatment with hopes of avoiding future medical mistreatment.

3.2 Personal Assistance Services (PAS) and Potential for Abuse

The PAS are defined as those tasks performed in order to assist an individual with a disability in performing any function that is related to self-directed living. Thus, PAS include assistance with a wide range of domains of functioning, including self-care and household care (e.g., toileting, bathing, cooking, medical self-management, or cleaning); cognitive tasks (e.g., scheduling); family and relational life (e.g., child-rearing activities, sexual positioning, or communication); and educational, employment, leisure, or community involvement (e.g., transportation) (Nosek, 1990; World Institute on Disability [WID], 1999). Government and insurance funding for PAS is variable and generally inadequate (WID, 1999), and many women with disabilities utilize unpaid PAS providers, including members of their families of origin, spouses, friends, and community members with whom barter arrangements are established (e.g., housing exchanged for PAS). A smaller but significant amount of PAS are provided by paid employees, who may be in full- or part-time, live-in or live-out arrangements. The PAS providers are often not screened for legal or employment history (Nosek, 1990; Saxton, Curry, Powers, Maley, Eckels, & Gross, 2001).

Although PAS are invaluable in the movement to reduce the social inequities experienced by women with disabilities by fostering their capacities for self-directed living, PAS also afford many opportunities for abuse toward women with disabilities. Abuse may take many forms, ranging from the types of verbal, physical, and sexual abuse that are consistent with abuse suffered by able-bodied women. However, there are additional forms of abuse that are particularly relevant for women with disabilities. For example, PAS providers may handle women with disabilities roughly and may leave individuals in painful, uncomfortable, confining, dangerous, or helplessness-inducing situations by failing to appropriately manage toileting, bathing, or medical needs, by removing access to mobility or other functional aids, by withholding medication or overmedicating, by leaving their posts, or by coming to work late or under the influence of drugs or alcohol. The PAS providers may engage in potentially inappropriate touching or other intimacies or may violate confidentiality (Saxton et al., 2001).

Factors in the relationships between PAS providers and women with disabilities that complicate the issue of protesting or reporting abuse are myriad. The PAS providers may intimidate women due to their ability to constrain mobility, interfere with communication, enforce social isolation, or perpetrate violence. The PAS providers may be in relationships with women with disabilities with ambiguous or complex boundaries due to the level of physical intimacy (e.g., dressing, bathing, toileting, sexual positioning) frequently involved in PAS. Emotional intimacy may be assumed or imposed by the PAS provider or may exist due to familial or sexual ties that predate the PAS relationship or that arise in the context of PAS relationships. The PAS providers may be stressed, tired, impulsive, poorly trained, or not well supported in managing their roles. Thus, situational or relational factors may increase risk for abuse (Saxton et al., 2001).

Some researchers suggest that women with disabilities are at particularly high risk of experiencing violence and abuse; others suggest that they experience similar rates of abuse but of a more chronic, long-standing nature than that experienced by able-bodied women or by men with disabilities (Nosek et al., 2001; Nosek et al., 1997; Waxman Fiduccia & Wolfe, 1999). They may be uniquely vulnerable to enduring long-term abuse for several reasons. First, due to their status as individuals with disabilities, they may have internalized even more pronounced forms of gendered norms of passivity, compliance, and other-focused coping. Second, women with disabilities may have little experience with nonabusive relationships and, thus, lack a frame of reference for defining ill treatment as abusive rather than normative, particularly when abuse is perpetrated in a subtle or ambiguous manner (e.g., rough handling, delayed responsiveness of the provider). Third, women with disabilities are often economically disadvantaged, which may result in the necessity to tolerate abusive situations. Finally, women with disabilities may be inexperienced employers and may have yet to develop skills related to that status (e.g., assertiveness, appropriate expectations, and limit-setting). These factors may reduce the likelihood that women with disabilities will promptly identify and protest abuse (Nosek et al., 2001; Saxton et al., 2001).

In the event that law enforcement personnel become aware that a woman with disabilities is potentially being abused, they may be poorly prepared to respond appropriately. Oftentimes, police lack training in disability issues and are unaware of the nature of PAS. Therefore, they may be ill equipped to evaluate abusive situations they encounter. Women with disabilities may be constrained in their abilities to pursue law enforcement interventions due to their vulnerability to retaliation and their reliance on the PAS provider for everyday needs. Given a lack of backup PAS, and the rarity of accessible social services, women with disabilities face the risk of being institutionalized if their PAS are jeopardized (Nosek et al., 1997).

3.3 Sexual Abuse

For women with disabilities, unique cultural circumstances may serve to compound the effects of sexual violence. Eighty percent of victims of sexual assault who have disabilities have been victimized more than once—and 50% have experienced sexual violence 10 or more times (Sobsey & Doe, 1991). Some of this repetitive incidence can be attributed to the increased reliance of women with disabilities on health care and other social service systems. Women with disabilities are much more likely than their able-bodied counterparts to experience violation by a health or social service provider (Nosek, 1995). If a perpetrator is providing PAS or other vital services, a survivor may feel like she must choose between physical subsistence and personal safety. For women who live in institutionalized settings, such "choice" may not be an option. Many of these women do not have control over their own staffing. Thus, the removal of an abusive staff member is dependent upon the degree to which a woman is able to vocalize her concerns and be believed. Negative social constructions of disability may undermine a woman's credibility when reporting an assault. Cultural notions of women with disabilities are predicated on images of helplessness, vulnerability, asexuality, and perpetual childlike innocence (Crawford & Ostrove, 2003; Haller, 2000; Pelka, 1997).

The perception that women with disabilities are sexless beings further solidifies our cultural denial regarding the prevalence of sexual assault in this population. Additionally, such depictions may restrict a disabled women's access to knowledge regarding what constitutes sexual violation. This lack of information can be particularly insidious, because the sexual abuse of disabled women often takes subtle forms. For example, disability-related sexual abuse may include being left naked or exposed for prolonged periods. This lack of respect for the dignity of women with disabilities is inextricably tied to the objectification and depersonalization of their bodies. As stated by Wendal (1996), our cultural obsession with bodily perfection as the expected norm can result in tacit acceptance of the mistreatment of disabled women.

3.4 Hate Crimes

Hate crimes are defined as actions directed at harming or intimidating individuals because of their membership in a defined group. Because of their nature, hate crimes are actually dual crimes, resulting in community-wide terror in addition to direct harm or threat to targeted individuals. Persons with disabilities are not consistently included in legislation directed at hate crimes; in fact, federal and many states' acts of legislation have excluded disability status as a hate-crime category (Sherry, 2003; Waxman, 1991). However, Waxman (1991) argued forcefully that much of the violence against persons with disabilities is hate-motivated rather than random. In fact, the higher rates of abuse and violence directed at members of this group are compelling evidence that much of this violence is based upon group membership. Indeed, she argued that society as a whole is complicit in perpetuating hatred toward this group, through tolerance of violence, negative portrayals of disability that equate physical difference with spiritual badness, and hostile or paternalistic attitudes that range from denying the competence, sexuality, and humanity of those with disabilities, to endorsing eugenics and even homicide. In addition, Waxman (1991) outlined the impact of dual status as a woman with a disability on rates of victimization. Women, already disproportionately affected by certain types of violence (e.g., rape), are at disproportionate risk when they also possess a physical difference. In fact, women with disabilities are not considered legitimate participants in the most gendered roles our society typically affirms for women (i.e., sex objects and child bearers), and they are not considered legitimately productive workers. Hate crimes are directed at those who are seen to illustrate stereotypes, as well as toward those who function outside of prescribed stereotyped roles, resulting in there being no way for women with disabilities to "play it safe," even if that were a goal.

Thus, women with disabilities are particularly likely to be targeted for hate (Waxman, 1991).

One way in which hate crimes against persons with disabilities may differ from hate crimes directed at other groups is that such violence may be carried out in public, by strangers (which characterizes a typical hate crime), or it may be carried out in private, by intimates who feel justified in abuse because of the devaluation of the individual's experiences and worth (Sherry, 2003; Waxman, 1991). However, even when violence is highly public and targets specific aspects of the individual's status as disabled (e.g., Waxman, 1991, cited the burning of a wheelchair ramp), law enforcement personnel hesitate to label it as other than random, or possibly even victim-provoked.

Sherry (2003) cited Federal Bureau of Investigation data on hate crimes that suggest that hate crimes against this group are fairly rare (133 such crimes recorded for the years 1997 to 2001). However, he critiqued these data based on the likelihood that there are numerous sources of inaccuracy inherent in the process of labeling crimes against persons with disabilities as hate crimes. First, he provided several reasons that hate crimes against individuals with disabilities may fail to be recognized as such: lack of reporting by victims; bureaucratic and administrative resistance to reporting; failure to recognize or to prosecute the crime as a hate crime; mislabeling hate crimes as abuse; ambiguities in the crime (e.g., when a victim and perpetrator have a preexisting relationship, the legal case that an act of violence is hate-motivated can be weakened); community resistance (e.g., reluctant witnesses); and failure to recognize that hate crimes may be committed by individuals who share group membership with the victim (e.g., individuals with disabilities may perpetrate hate crimes against other individuals with disabilities) (Sherry, 2003).

Second, Sherry (2003) outlined factors that may reduce the accuracy of reporting due to the failure to label victims as persons with disabilities. One problem may be the failure to report the victim's disability status due to the presence of a hidden or invisible disability, the victim's failure to report hate language, or the perception that the victim's disability will hinder prosecution. Another area of concern is the failure to recognize that disability status confers group membership; other identities, such as minority ethnicity, are more salient. Third, when a medical-model approach is utilized, disability status is reduced to an individual trait, and its existence as a sociocultural phenomenon is overlooked. Finally, the potential for hate crimes to be perpetrated by those who are known to the victim, or who are involved in providing services to individuals with disabilities, can mislead investigators who fail to recognize this phenomenon.

4 BARRIERS TO TREATMENT

The disabled community's reluctance to seek health-care-related services presents a significant obstacle to offering appropriate treatment to trauma survivors with disabilities. This reluctance may stem from negative past experiences in health care settings and lack of knowledge of where to seek trauma and abuse services when you are a woman with a disability. Additionally, finding service providers who are both culturally sensitive to disability issues and have expertise in trauma can be extremely challenging. As stated by Olkin (1999), the majority of mental health therapists have limited expertise in understanding the broader context of disability and in providing therapies that are more disability-affirmative oriented. In most states, individuals with disabilities are considered to be vulnerable adults, even if they are competent to direct their own lives (E. Tomas, personal communication, October 24, 2000). Thus, even if a trauma or abuse survivor is able to locate a disability-knowledgeable practitioner, this designation may force a clinician to report any specific incidence of abuse to the appropriate authorities. Obviously, such a report can have devastating consequences for a trauma or abuse survivor, particularly if she is dependent on the perpetrator for PAS or financial help. These laws are designed to protect individuals who are unable to make decisions about protecting themselves. However, for many women with disabilities, these regulations are yet another form of disempowerment.

Although philosophical and legislative factors affect access to services for women with disabilities, logistical barriers also play a large role. Architectural access for people with mobility impairments, sign language interpretation for some people who are deaf, Braille or print materials available in alternative formats, and PAS for individuals with varying disabilities may all be necessities in seeking services for women with disabilities. Without the opportunity to access services, the choice to seek assistance is removed for this population. Most shelters available to abuse victims do not meet standard accessibility to women with disabilities (Nosek et al., 2001), and subsequently, there are often few places to find assistance with coping with and escaping from repeated trauma situations.

With these barriers in mind, how are women with disabilities seeking support? Unfortunately, we do not clearly know the answer to this question. Women with disabilities, similar to the larger disability community, are forced to be resourceful and creative with their lives (M. Saxton, personal communication, August 27, 2003). In other words, it is thought that women with disabilities may use skills and relationships with others to help facilitate assistance when needed. For example, asking for guidance from other women with disabilities, seeking information from disability nonprofit organizations (e.g., centers for independent living), and posting questions on disability-focused listservs. The complicating factor of feeling victimized or abused may obviously interfere with one's ability to take immediate action. However, accessing resources used for other disability needs may, in fact, be of help to women with disabilities who are in need of information about trauma resources.

5 SUMMARY AND FUTURE DIRECTIONS

It is clear that definitions and explanations of disability and types of trauma affecting the lives of women with disabilities have not been fully explored or researched. The ways in which disability is framed obviously have an impact on the ways in which trauma-related experiences are conceptualized. Although we highlighted the various negatives and difficulties faced by women with disabilities, there is optimism about new research directions and attention paid to providing services.

Nosek, Howland, and Hughes (2001) delineated issues that should be considered by investigators endeavoring to conduct empirically sound research on abuse and women with disabilities. For example, these authors propose incorporating variables that assess increased vulnerability in research design, as well as using literature-based definitions that distinguish emotional, physical, sexual, and disability-related abuse. It is argued that by paying attention to study design, more accurate data will be gathered. In addition, given the unique issues around privacy and safety for women with disabilities, Nosek, Howland, and Hughes (2001) suggested that securing informed consent; maintaining confidentiality; and installing safety measures to protect study participants and project staff from retaliation are imperative when researching this population.

Acquiring more accurate data on the traumatic experiences of women with disabilities will help to lay a foundation to reach a better understanding of this population, provide better services for women with disabilities, and serve to launch new research directions to help inform future investigators as to how to comprehensively explore this topic. Continued discussion of this topic, at both academic and community levels, is vital to assist in empowering women with disabilities to lead lives that are filled with choice, freedom, and resources to lead an enriched quality of life.

REFERENCES

American Psychiatric Association. (2000). *Diagnostic and statistical manual of mental disorders* (4th ed., text revision). Washington, DC: Author.
Americans with Disabilities Act of 1990, Pub. L. No. 101-336, 42 U.S.C. § 12111, 12112.

Avison, W. R., & Turner, R. J. (1988). Stressful life events and depressive symptoms: Disaggregating the effects of acute stressors and chronic strains. *Journal of Health and Social Behavior, 29,* 253–264.

Banks, M. E. (2003). Preface. In M. E. Banks & E. Kaschak (Eds.), *Women with visible and invisible disabilities: Multiple intersections, multiple issues, multiple therapies* (pp. xxiii–xli). Binghamton, NY: Haworth.

Blumberg, L. (1990). Public stripping. In V. Shaw (Ed.), *The ragged edge* (pp. 73–78). Louisville, KY: Avocado Press.

Crawford, D., & Ostrove, J. M. (2003). Representations of disability and the interpersonal relationships of women with disabilities. *Women and Therapy, 26*(3), 180–194.

DeJong, G. (1984). Independent living: From social movement to analytic paradigm. In R. P. Marinelli & A. E. Dell Orto (Eds.), *The psychological and social impact of physical disability* (pp. 84–97). New York: Springer.

Haller, B. (2000). If they limp, they lead? News representations and the hierarchy of disability images. In D. O. Braithwaite & T. L. Thompson (Eds.), *Handbook of communication and people with disabilities: Research and application* (pp. 273–288). Mahwah, NJ: Lawrence Erlbaum Associates.

Hamiliton, K. W. (1950). *Counseling the handicap in the rehabilitation process.* New York: Ronald.

Herman, J. (1992). *Trauma and recovery.* New York: Basic.

Hobfoll, S. E. (1989). Conservation of resources: A new attempt at conceptualizing stress. *American Psychologist, 44,* 513–524.

Hohenshil, T. H., & Humes, C. W. (1979). Roles of counseling in ensuring the rights of the handicapped. *Personnel and Guidance Journal, 4,* 221–227.

Hohmann, G. (1975). Psychological aspects of treatment and rehabilitation of the spinal cord injured person. *Clinical Orthopedics, 112,* 81–88.

Holmes, T. H., & Rahe, R. H. (1967). The Social Readjustment Rating Scale. *Journal of Psychosomatic Research, 11,* 213–218.

Lazarus, R. S., & Folkman, S. (1984). *Stress, appraisal and coping.* New York: Springer.

Longmore, P., & Umansky, L. (2001). Disability history: From the margins to the mainstream. In P. K. Longmore and L. Umansky (Eds.), *The new disability history* (pp. 1–33). New York: New York University.

Maes, M., Mylle, J., Delmeire, L., & Janca, A. (2001). Pre- and post-disaster negative life events in relation to the incidence and severity of post-traumatic stress disorder. *Psychiatry Research, 105,* 1–12.

Nagi, S. Z. (1965). Some conceptual issues in disability and rehabilitation. In M. B. Sussman (Ed.), *Sociology and rehabilitation.* Washington, DC: American Sociological Association.

Nagi, S. Z. (1969). *Disability and rehabilitation: Legal, clinical, and self-concepts and measurement.* Columbus: Ohio State University.

National Institute on Disability and Rehabilitation Research. (1999). *NIDRR long-range plan.* Washington, DC: Office of Special Education and Rehabilitative Services.

Nosek, M. A. (1990). Personal assistance: Key to employability of persons with physical disabilities. *Journal of Applied Rehabilitation Counseling, 21,* 3–8.

Nosek, M. A. (1995). Sexual abuse of women with physical disabilities. *Physical Medicine and Rehabilitation: State of the Art Review, 9,* 487–502.

Nosek, M. A., Howland, C. A., & Hughes, R. B. (2001). The investigation of abuse and women with disabilities: Going beyond assumptions. *Violence Against Women, 7,* 477–499.

Nosek, M. A., Howland, C. A., & Young, M. E. (1997). Abuse of women with disabilities: Policy implications. *Journal of Disability Policy Studies, 8,* 157–175.

Nosek, M. A., & Howland, C. J. (1997). Sexual abuse and people with disabilities. In M. L. Sipski & C. J. Alexander (Eds.), *Sexual function in people with disabilities and chronic illness: A health practitioner's guide.* Gaithersburg, MD: Aspen.

Olkin, R. (1999). *What psychotherapists should know about disability.* New York: Guilford.

Pelka, F. (1997). *The ABC–CLIO companion to the disability rights movement.* Santa Barbara, CA: ABC–CLIO.

Pledger, C. (2003). Discourse on disability and rehabilitation issues: Opportunities for psychology. *American Psychologist, 58,* 279–284.

Saxe, G., & Wolfe, J. (1999). Gender and posttraumatic stress disorder. In P. A. Saigh and J. D. Bremner (Eds.), *Posttraumatic stress disorder: A comprehensive text.* Boston: Allyn & Bacon.

Saxton, M., Curry, M. A., Powers, L. E., Maley, S., Eckels, K., & Gross, J. (2001). "Bring my scooter so I can leave you": A study of disabled women handling abuse by personal assistance providers. *Violence Against Women, 7,* 393–417.

Sherry, M. (posted 2003, January 8). *Don't ask, tell or respond: Silent acceptance of disability hate crimes.* Retrieved August 7, 2003, from http://dawn.thot.net/disability_hate_crimes.html

Siller, J. (1963). Reactions to physical disability. *Rehabilitation Counseling Bulletin, 7*(1), 12–16.

Sobsey, D., & Doe, T. (1991). Patterns of sexual abuse and assault. *Sexuality and Disability, 9,* 243–260.

Wagner, B. M., Compas, B. E., & Howell, D. C. (1988). Daily and major life events: A test of an integrative model of psychosocial stress. *American Journal of Community Psychology, 16,* 189–205.

Waxman, B. F. (1991). Hatred: The unacknowledged dimension in violence against disabled people. *Sexuality and Disability, 9,* 185–199.

Waxman Fiduccia, B. F., & Wolfe, L. R. (1999). *Violence against disabled women* (Report). Washington, DC: Center for Women Policy Studies.

Wendal, S. (1996). *The rejected body: Feminist philosophical reflections on disability.* London: Routledge.

World Institute on Disability. (1999). *Personal Assistance Services 101: Structure, utilization and adequacy of existing PAS programs.* Oakland, CA: Author.

12

Heterosexism and Violence in the Lives of Lesbian Women: Implications for Mental Health

BATYA HYMAN

Living within the heterosexist culture of the United States constitutes a form of trauma that is rarely considered. The mental health of lesbian women is shaped by the unique intersection of violence across the life span with the trauma of living in a heterosexist society. Heterosexism is manifested at both individual and cultural levels. I discuss how the traumatic context created by heterosexism fosters the development of internalized homophobia and shapes the mental health of lesbian women. We must recognize that lesbians are not a homogenous group; there are significant within-group differences based on such factors as ethnicity, socioeconomic status, and age. These differences result in interlocking oppressions that influence mental health.

Lesbians experience violence across their life spans. I discuss the mental health implications of the victimization of lesbian adolescents within their homes, schools, and communities. I then examine lesbian women's experiences, reported retrospectively, of childhood physical and sexual abuse perpetrated by family members and others. The experiences of lesbian and heterosexual women are compared, and the impact on mental health is considered. Finally, I present findings about the impact of heterosexism, ageism, and racism on the mental health of older lesbians.

1 HETEROSEXISM, INTERNALIZED HOMOPHOBIA, AND MENTAL HEALTH

Heterosexism has been defined as the ideological system that denies, denigrates, and stigmatizes any nonheterosexual identity, form of behavior, relationship, or community (Herek, 1990). Heterosexism may be described as heterosexuals' prejudices against lesbian women and gay men, as well as the behaviors predicated on these prejudices (Herek, 1996).

"Cultural heterosexism, like institutional racism and sexism, pervades societal customs and institutions. It operates through a dual process of invisibility and attack" (Herek, 1996, p. 102). When people are identified as gay, they are subject to stigmatization and victimization by society. Examples of cultural heterosexism in the United States include the lack of legal protections for gays in the workplace, housing, and services; the military's "Don't Ask, Don't Tell" policy, which results in the dishonorable discharge of thousands of service people every year; and the failure to recognize lesbian and gay committed relationships.

1.1 Internalized Homophobia and Mental Health Outcomes

From the time American children are very young, they are socialized with the antihomosexual biases that are sanctioned by our culture (Gonsiorek, 1993a). Children internalize these idealized values learned from their society and culture. When these idealized values do not match their experience of coming out, internal conflict can ensue (Pearlin, 1993). They realize that society disapproves of them. Lesbians incorporate these negative feelings into their self-image, which results in internalized homophobia (personal homonegativity). Internalized homophobia is defined as a set of negative attitudes and affects toward homosexual features in oneself (Shidlo, 1994). Internalized homophobia can range from self-doubt to overt self-hatred (Gonsiorek, 1993b). Internalized homophobia can make lesbians feel that "the very center of their being is sick and disgusting" (Bobbe, 2002, p. 218).

Shidlo (1994) found that internalized homophobia explained a significant portion of "overall psychological distress, depression, somatic symptoms, self-esteem, and distrust" (p. 198). However, in the course of coming out, most lesbian women successfully navigate the threats to psychological well-being posed by heterosexism. They cope with the need "to reclaim disowned or devalued parts of themselves, developing an identity into which their sexuality is well integrated" (Herek, 1996, p. 107).

1.2 Minority Stress as a Consequence of Heterosexism

All lesbians do not experience heterosexism in the same way. Many lesbian women must integrate multiple identities. Greene (2000) stated that the African American community is perceived as homophobic by many of its lesbian members. She suggested that African Americans "may regard any sexual behavior outside of dominant cultural norms as reflecting negatively on African Americans as a group" (Greene, 2000, p. 245). African Americans view gays as affluent, white, and endowed with both skin color and class privilege. Therefore, many African Americans do not see how gays are oppressed. "Being gay is a chosen identity and inconvenience where being black is true hardship" (Greene, 2000, p. 20). People of color feel that a comparison of heterosexism and racism as oppressions trivializes the history of racial oppression (Greene, 2000). Given this, lesbians of color are less likely to be out. They are, therefore, less visible to white lesbian women. Additionally, lesbians of color may not take for granted that they will be welcomed into the white lesbian community without continuing confrontations with racism.

In healthy African American families, children learn to view themselves positively because of loved and trusted family members' positive response to them as African Americans. This process affirms and reinforces for children the most important aspects of membership in their ethnic group (Greene, 2000). African Americans and other families of color teach their children how to negotiate manifestations of racism. However, these families may be unable to teach them about how to negotiate homophobia. Lesbians and gay men must go outside of their families to develop an affirmative identity.

Unlike most other minority groups, lesbians are often not recognized as a legitimate minority group deserving of protections against discrimination. Lesbian stress is a form of minority stress. The stress that results from stigmatization often precipitates adverse life events over which the individual has no control (DiPlacido, 1998).

Mays and Cochran (2001) found a robust association between gay persons' experiences of lifetime and day-to-day discrimination and indicators of psychiatric morbidity. They suggested that extensive and destructive experiences of discrimination lie at the root of the somewhat greater prevalence of psychiatric morbidity among lesbians and gay men found in recent studies (Cochran & Mays, 1994; Fergusson, Horwood, & Beautrais, 1999).

2 MENTAL HEALTH IMPLICATIONS OF THE VICTIMIZATION OF YOUTHS

In this section, I discuss aspects of the coming-out experience that are shaped by heterosexism, stigmatization, and internalized homophobia. Studies of these concerns sample either males alone or males and females. I focus on reports of the experiences of lesbian youth who generally represent one third of study samples. The process of coming-out often increases vulnerability to victimization within families and school settings.

2.1 Coming-Out and Heterosexism

The biological, psychological, and social changes related to puberty are stressful for many teenagers, but lesbian and gay youths face even more difficult challenges. By age 12, children have learned that heterosexuality is natural and that lesbianism is shameful. Youths are attacked with epithets like "you're so gay," or "you're a fag." According to an American Association of University Women (AAUW) report, being called "gay" by others was deemed the most upsetting form of sexual harassment in schools (AAUW, 1993). D'Augelli (1998) argued that youths with homoerotic feelings have experienced a "developmental opportunity loss"; that is, they are unable to positively resolve the developmental dilemma of puberty with an age-appropriate expression and exploration of homoerotic social and sexual relationships. They have also experienced "self-doubt induced by cultural heterosexism." "Self-acknowledgment of homoerotic feelings, itself the end point of a complex developmental process, instigates other processes of identity consolidation that are fundamentally social" (D'Augelli, 1998, p. 191).

The internalization of a devalued identity can erode coping efforts. Savin-Williams (1994) found three major problem areas. Lesbian youths have school problems due to harassment from other students, leading to excessive absences, poor academic performance, and dropping out. Lesbian youths may run away from home, and some wind up homeless. Lesbian youths abuse alcohol, drugs, and other substances to cope with daily stressors and with facing the future as a member of a stigmatized group. We do not have reliable empirical evidence regarding the adult consequences of living one's adolescence and early adulthood in self-doubt, fear, and alienation from self.

2.2 Victimization in Families

Pilkington and D'Augelli (1995) found that more than one third of their lesbian, gay, bisexual (lgb) sample had been verbally abused by a family member, and 10% were physically assaulted by a family member because of their sexual orientation. Of those youths who were still living at home, one third of the lesbian youths who had disclosed their sexual orientation said that their mothers were verbally abusive; fathers were reported to be verbally abusive by 20 of the disclosed youths. Disclosed lesbian youths living at home were physically attacked by their parents—10% by mothers and 5% by fathers—more often than were the disclosed male youths—3% by mothers and 2% by fathers. Many reported fear of verbal or physical abuse at home.

2.3 Victimization in School

Garofalo, Wolf, Kessel, Palfrey, and DuRant (1998) used a representative sample of Massachusetts high school students to compare lesbian, gay, and bisexual identified youths with heterosexual students. One quarter of the lgb youths said they had missed school in the last month because of fear, compared to 5% of the non-lgb youths. One third of the lgb youths said they had been threatened with a weapon at school, compared to 7% of the other youths. Thirty-eight percent of the lgb youths were involved in fights at school, in contrast to 14% of the other students. And, half of the lgb youths reported property damage at school, compared to 29% of the other youths.

D'Augelli, Pilkington, and Hershberger (2002) studied 350 youths gathered from social and recreational groups for lgb youths located in the United States and Canada. The average age was 19 years old; only 7% were 14 to 17 years old. Forty-four percent of the sample was comprised of lesbian youths. The lesbian youths reported becoming first aware of their same-sex attraction at age 11, and self-labeled as lesbian at age 16. Current high school students were more open about their sexual orientation than college students were during their high school years. Students in high school reported higher overall victimization and verbal victimization compared to that experienced in high school by college students. Seven percent of the lesbian youths reported being assaulted due to their sexual orientation.

2.4 Victimization and the Mental Health Status of Youths

D'Augelli, Pilkington, and Hershberger (2002) sampled 350 high-school-aged and college-aged youths. On the Personal Homonegativity Scale, participants had overall positive views of their own sexual orientation. Ninety-four percent of the lesbian youths reported that they were glad to be lesbian. However, the researchers found that 25% of lesbians said they had sometimes or often thought of suicide. About half (48%) said their suicidal thinking was related to their sexual orientation. Over one third acknowledged a past suicide attempt. The earlier youths were aware of their same-sex feelings, self-identified as lgb, and disclosed their sexual orientation to others for the first time, the more they were victimized in high school. The overall number of years they had been out was also related significantly to increased victimization. In addition, the more open youths were about their sexual orientation in high school, the more they were victimized. Total victimization was related positively to mental health symptoms on the Brief Symptom Inventory and the Trauma Symptom Checklist.

Hershberger and D'Augelli (1995), employing an earlier sample of youths from recreation and social clubs across North America, found that positive adjustment in lesbian youths was associated with self-acceptance of their sexual orientation. A general sense of personal worth, coupled with a positive view of their sexual orientation, appeared to be critical for the youths' mental health. Even for youths who were fortunate to have family support and self-esteem, there existed a strong residual effect of victimization on mental health.

In the National Lesbian Health Care Survey (Bradford, Ryan, & Rothblum, 1994), mental health problems were common among the 17- to 24-year-old group. Sixty-two percent had received counseling. They most often reported concerns with family problems, depression, problems in relationships, and anxiety.

There is a disproportionally high incidence of suicide attempts among lesbian youths. Lewinsohn, Rohde, and Seeley (1996) noted that lifetime suicide attempt rates in studies of all high school students range from 6% to 10%. In the National Lesbian Health Care Survey (Hyman, 2000), one quarter of the young lesbians had made a suicide attempt. Herdt and Boxer (1993) found that 53% of the lesbian youths in a Chicago youth support group program had made a suicide attempt, compared with 20% of the gay male youths. Hershberger, Pilkington, and D'Augelli (1997) found that 42% of the 194 youths reported a past suicide attempt. Attempters were aware of their sexual attractions at an earlier age, were more open about their sexual orientation, had lower self-esteem, and showed more current symptoms. Those who attempted suicide were also more often victimized than were others. The strongest correlations with past suicide attempts were the loss of friends due to sexual orientation and low self-esteem.

Many lesbian youths cope with the consequences of victimization by themselves or with a close circle of friends. For some youths, attacks may lead to an unexpected disclosure of their sexual orientation. Some youths have families who are uncomfortable with their child's sexual orientation. For these families, the victimization may compound problems within the family (Boxer, Cook, & Herdt, 1991).

3 CHILDHOOD VICTIMIZATION AND MENTAL HEALTH

In this section, we review studies of the prevalence of child abuse in lesbian women. We also examine the consequences of child abuse in these women. Each study faces methodological limitations, which are presented. A significant limitation is the inability to recruit a sample that is representative of all lesbian women. Some studies discussed here employ large representative samples, with small proportions of lesbian and gay respondents. Others employ community-based convenience samples. Importantly, studies of lesbian women are not able to tap into the well of lesbians who are not out or who are out to only a select few people in their lives.

3.1 Prevalence of Child Sexual Abuse in Lesbians

During the 1980s, three studies examined the rates of child sexual abuse among lesbian women. Loulan (1987) studied 1,566 lesbians who were primarily white and middle class. Their ages ranged from 25 to 60 years. Thirty-eight percent of these women experienced sexual abuse prior to age 18. Russell (1983) interviewed 930 women in San Francisco. She did not ask the sexual orientation of the women; however, one may assume that a significant portion of her sample was lesbian. Thirty-eight percent of the women in her study experienced sexual abuse prior to age 18. Bradford and Ryan conducted the National Lesbian Health Care Survey (Bradford & Ryan, 1988). This diverse sample of 1,925 lesbians completed questionnaires. Thirty-two percent of these lesbian women reported child sexual abuse. Nineteen percent reported sexual abuse by relatives. These three studies reported correlations between childhood victimization and adverse psychological consequences—such as depression, anxiety, suicide attempts, poor self-esteem, difficulty trusting others, and alcohol and drug abuse—in the adult lesbian women (Klinger & Stein, 1996).

Recent research provides evidence of conflicting findings regarding the prevalence of child sexual abuse in lesbians when compared with heterosexual women. Some studies have found higher rates of child sexual abuse among lesbians (Hughes, Haas, Razzano, Cassidy, & Matthews, 2000; Lechner, Vogel, Garcia-Shelton, Leichter, & Steibel, 1993; Roberts & Sorenson, 1999). Others have found rates similar to those of women in the general population (Bradford et al., 1994; Brannock & Chapman, 1990; Peters & Cantrell, 1991; Rankow, Cambre, & Cooper, 1998; Weingourt, 1998). Differences in prevalence rates among both lesbians and women in the general population are likely due to variations in study methods and definitions, specificity and number of questions, and sample characteristics.

3.2 The Consequences of Child Maltreatment

Hughes, Johnson, and Wilsnack (2001) studied a sample of 63 lesbian and 57 heterosexual women. Only one third of the sample was European American, which differs significantly from the usual samples of lesbians who are white, middle-class, and well-educated. Lesbians were recruited through a variety of sources, including ads in newspapers as well as contacts within organizations and informal social networks and events. During the initial telephone contact, the lesbians were asked if they knew a heterosexual woman of the same race who had a job or role similar to their own, who might be willing to be interviewed. This technique was only partly successful, and one third of the heterosexual women were recruited in a manner similar to the lesbians. There were no significant differences between the lesbian and heterosexual women on demographic measures.

This research team administered the Health and Life Experiences of Women instrument to the fourth wave of subjects. This interview instrument was developed to gather data about the alcohol use and abuse behaviors of women, including those factors known to predict substance use, such as child sexual abuse. Sexual orientation questions were added to the instrument in 1996, and it is that data that the team reports.

In the Hughes, Johnson, and Wilsnack (2001) study, more lesbian (68%) than heterosexual (47%) women reported sexually abusive behavior occurring prior to age 18. In addition, more lesbian (37%) than heterosexual (19%) women reported that they perceived themselves as having been sexually abused as a child. There was a trend, though not significant, toward a greater number of lesbians reporting intrafamilial abuse.

Lesbians are assumed to be at heightened risk for alcohol abuse as a consequence of cultural and environmental factors associated with being stigmatized and marginalized (Hughes et al., 2001). Thirteen percent of the heterosexual women were lifetime abstainers; none of the lesbians were. Four percent of the heterosexual women were 12-month abstainers; 25% of the lesbians were. More lesbian (18%) than heterosexual (2%) women reported that they were in recovery. Forty-seven percent of the lesbians and 16% of the heterosexual women reported that they have wondered at some point in the past whether they might have a drinking problem. The researchers noted that the majority of lesbians in the study did not drink excessively or experience alcohol-related problems.

Child sexual abuse was associated with lifetime alcohol abuse, to a similar and significant degree, in both the lesbian and heterosexual women—a finding that supports results from research with women in the general population (Wilsnack, Vogeltanz, Klassen, & Harris, 1997). The rate of child sexual abuse among the lesbians in this study (25%) was similar to rates reported for lesbians in the National Lesbian Health Care

Survey (32%) (Bradford & Ryan, 1988) and in the Boston Health Project (21%) (Roberts & Sorensen, 1999).

Hyman (2000) investigated the relation between a lesbian woman's experience of childhood sexual victimization and her economic welfare as an adult. She analyzed data from the National Lesbian Health Care Survey (Bradford & Ryan, 1988) that gathered information from 1,925 participants about experiences of childhood victimization, adult health status, mental health status, and economic welfare. The child sexual abuse survivors reported a greater number of health and mental health problems than the other lesbian women. They were receiving treatment for a larger number of health problems. They reported higher rates of depression, anxiety, and attempted suicide. Survivors of intrafamilial abuse were more likely to have a history of mental health hospitalization.

Additionally, the survivors did not attain as much education as the others. They were less likely to work, less likely to work full-time, and less likely to choose high-status occupations. The child sexual abuse survivors also reported lower earnings. Estimation of the simultaneous equation model revealed that the experience of child sexual abuse adversely affected the health, mental health, educational attainment, and annual earnings of the survivors.

By shifting the emphasis from isolated aspects of a woman's life, such as her psychological functioning, to an integrated examination of the major spheres of her life, this model moves away from a simple cataloging of consequences toward a richer appreciation of how child sexual abuse affects several dimensions of the adult's functioning.

Hall (1999) conducted qualitative interviews with eight lesbian survivors of child sexual abuse. She found that the lesbian women described their identities as survivor and lesbian as a double secret to be kept. These women also reported a lack of sexual spontaneity with their partners. Three of the women reported being sexually assaulted by another woman during adulthood.

Tomeo, Templer, Anderson, and Kotler (2001) compared the incidence of childhood sexual abuse in 942 heterosexual and homosexual men and women. Four hundred and sixty heterosexual female students and 153 lesbians participated. Nearly all of the lesbians were recruited through gay-pride festivals. On average, the women were 30 years old and had 15 years of schooling.

Respondents were asked "did you ever have sexual contact with a ..." Of course, sexual contact and sexual abuse are not necessarily the same. Because the female victims in this study had a mean age of 13 at the time of sexual contact, and 68% of them were at least 12 years old, we are dealing with adolescent sexual contact. By definition, the perpetrators were at least 16 years old and 5 years older than the victims. Using these parameters, one quarter of the heterosexual women reported being sexually abused as a child; 24.3% by a man and 1.1% by a woman. Forty-two percent of the lesbian women reported molestation: 29% by men and 22% by women.

Tjaden, Thoennes, and Allison (1999) studied violence against children and adults in a nationally representative sample of same-sex and oppo-site-sex cohabitants, the National Violence Against Women Survey of November 1995 through May 1996. Participants were not asked their sexual orientation but were instead asked to identify whether they lived with someone of the same or opposite sex, as well as information about their past live-in relationships. A total of 8,000 women and 8,000 men were interviewed using a computer-assisted telephone interviewing system. One percent of all women surveyed (n = 79) reported they had lived with a same-sex partner "as a couple" at some time in their lives. Several screening questions were asked regarding sexual victimization, and a modified form of the Conflict Tactics Scale was used.

Differences between the opposite-sex cohabiting and same-sex cohab-iting female samples were noted. Same-sex cohabiting women tended to be younger than opposite-sex cohabiting women, a factor that may predispose them to higher rates of abuse. Same-sex cohabiting women also tended to have more education, more full-time employment, and somewhat higher incomes—factors that are inversely association with victimization.

The same-sex cohabiting women were nearly twice as likely as opposite-sex cohabiting women to report sexual assault as a minor (16.5% versus 8.7%). Same-sex cohabiting women were significantly more likely to report being physically assaulted as a child by an adult caretaker (59.5% versus 35.7%). Further, the physical abuse reported by same-sex cohabitants was more severe. Over half (53.2%) of the same-sex cohabiting women reported being physically assaulted as an adult compared to only 29.7% of the opposite-sex cohabiting women. Additional findings regarding domes-tic violence were presented.

Corliss, Cochran, and Mays (2002) investigated the prevalence and nature of childhood maltreatment experiences among lesbian, gay, and heterosexual adults. The self-administered questionnaire data were collected as part of the 1996 National Survey of Midlife Development in the United States. Parental maltreatment behaviors were adapted from three subscales of the Conflict Tactics Scale. Respondents were asked to self-identify as heterosexual (n = 2844), homosexual (n = 41), or bisexual (n = 32). Lesbian and bisexual women, 2.2% of the sample (n = 37), were grouped together for the purpose of analysis. The lesbian and bisexual women differed from the heterosexual women on two important demo-graphic factors: age and annual income. The lesbian and bisexual women were younger and earned more than the heterosexual women.

The rate of abuse by either parent was 43.6% for the lesbian and bisexual women and 30.9% for the heterosexual women. The lesbian and bisexual women reported more physical maltreatment by their mothers (32.8% versus 23.7%). The rate of major physical maltreatment by mothers was greater among the lesbian and bisexual women as well (22.8% versus 6.9%). The lesbian and bisexual women reported more physical maltreatment by their fathers (27.2% versus 18.6%). Again, the rate of major physical abuse by fathers was greater among the lesbian and bisexual women (15.1% versus 5.8%). The prevalence of major physical maltreatment by either parent was dramatically higher among the lesbian and bisexual group (33.6% versus 10.3%). Clearly, lesbian and bisexual women are more likely than heterosexual women to report childhood histories of parental maltreatment. These findings are supported by other research (Faulkner & Cranston, 1998; Garofalo et al., 1998; Saewyc, Bearinger, Heinz, Blum, & Resnick, 1998).

4 MENTAL HEALTH STATUS OF LESBIANS

We now take up three major studies that examine the factors that contribute to a lesbian woman's mental health status.

Hughes, Haas, Razzano, Cassidy, and Matthews (2000) compared the mental health functioning of lesbian and heterosexual women. The survey questionnaire was developed by an interdisciplinary team and was piloted in Chicago, Illinois. Nearly all data gathered were based on closed-ended questions. In order to collect a diverse sample of women, the research team asked lesbians who completed the survey to give a second copy to a heterosexual woman with a role as similar as possible to the lesbian's own. In one city, the women were given a small incentive for recruiting heterosexual work or role mates.

Rather than rely on one definition of sexual orientation or ask the women to self-identify, two questions were included in the survey instrument dealing with sexual attraction, sexual behavior, and sexual identity. This allowed the research team to define sexual orientation "more systematically" (Hughes et al., 2000). Based on this schema, 550 women were categorized as lesbian, 279 as heterosexual, and 33 as bisexual. The mean age of the sample was 42.5 years old. Seventy-six percent of the lesbians and 72% of the heterosexual women were European American, and 12% of the lesbians and 14% of the heterosexual women were African American. The same proportions of lesbian and heterosexual women (52%) reported living with a partner or spouse. Sixty-six percent of the lesbian women reported being in a committed relationship.

Both the lesbian and heterosexual women reported moderate levels of stress. Lesbians rated job, money, and overall responsibilities as the highest sources of stress. The only significant differences in the sources of stress between the two groups of women were that the heterosexual women rated children as the biggest source of stress, and the lesbian women rated sexual identity the highest.

The two groups of women were equally likely to report they had "ever been a victim of nonsexual physical violence" (45% and 41%). A family member was the most commonly reported perpetrator, especially a sex partner. The majority of these women reported that the physical violence occurred more than 5 years ago. Forty-one percent of lesbian women and 24% of the heterosexual women reported an experience of child sexual abuse before age 15 ($p < 0.001$). Fifty-six percent of lesbian women and 49% of heterosexual women reported depression as a reason for seeking therapy. Twenty-six percent of lesbian women and 20% of heterosexual women reported taking medication for a mental health problem. Most had taken antidepressants. Fifty-eight percent of the lesbian women and 52% of the heterosexual women reported at least one of these two indicators of past depression. There were significant differences between the lesbian (51%) and heterosexual women (38%) in the rates of suicidal ideation. Further, significantly more lesbians (22%) than heterosexuals (13%) reported prior suicide attempts.

Lesbians were significantly more likely to have received therapy or counseling (78% and 56%). The majority of both lesbian and heterosexual women who had sought therapy had done so during their 20s or 30s. In both groups, the most common reason for seeking therapy was for problems with a spouse or partner. Lesbians also reported problems with their sexual identity, suicidal ideation, sexual abuse, and problems related to substance use. Almost all of the lesbians and 70% of the heterosexual women reported having a female therapist as important. The same proportions of lesbian and heterosexual women (52%) reported living with a partner or spouse. Sixty-six percent of the lesbian women reported being in a committed relationship.

Lesbians were more likely than heterosexuals to report abstinence from alcohol during the prior 12 months (24% and 17%). This supports findings from other studies (Heffernan, 1998; Saulnier & Miller, 1997). Seventy-three percent of the lesbian women and 82% of the heterosexual women reported light to moderate drinking levels at the time of the study. The two groups were similar in their reports of at least one indicator of problem drinking during the past year. Significantly, 14% of the lesbians and 6% of heterosexuals indicated they sought help for alcohol or drug problems in the past. The study authors speculated that the lesbians' high rates of seeking mental health services may serve as a buffer against stress and the resulting depression.

The experience of coming-out may have influenced several of the study findings. The lesbian women reported suicide attempts at the ages of 15 to 19, during the years they may have self-identified as lesbian. Also, younger lesbian women were at highest risk for alcohol problems.

Perhaps age also influenced perceptions of stress. Would contemporary younger lesbian women who are maturing during the recent period of greater visibility of lesbians still rate sexual identity as the highest source of stress?

Matthews, Hughes, Johnson, Razzano, and Cassidy (2002) investigated the predictors of depression in a community sample of lesbian and heterosexual women. They employed data from the Hughes, Haas, Razzano, Cassidy, and Matthews (2000) study reviewed above to examine whether sexual orientation is a predictor of depressive symptoms, such as a history of seeking therapy, treatment for depression, a history of suicidal ideation, and a history of suicide attempts. They tested several assumed predictors of depression, including experiences of physical violence and child sexual abuse, perceived level of stress, global stress, lack of social support, and coping strategies.

Most of the women were white, were married, or were involved in a committed relationship, had more than a high school education, and were employed full time for pay. The median household income for both lesbians and heterosexual women was $36,000 to $50,999.

The lesbian and heterosexual women were equally likely to report being victims of nonsexual physical violence. Lesbian women were more likely than heterosexual women to report experiences of child sexual abuse (30% and 16%).

Overall mean scores on the global stress index were in the lower range and did not differ according to sexual orientation. The lesbian and heterosexual women all reported moderate to extreme levels of perceived stress. The only significant differences in sources of stress for the lesbian and heterosexual women involved children and sexual identity. The heterosexual women rated children as moderately or extremely stressful. The lesbian women rated sexual identity as moderately or extremely stressful.

More heterosexual women (6%) than lesbians (3%) reported an absence of social support. The use of positive coping strategies was low among both groups of women. Lesbians were significantly more likely to report never using talking as a coping strategy (46% versus 37%). Fewer lesbians (19%) than heterosexual women (25%) reported doing something fun when they were stressed or using exercise as a coping strategy (36% versus 43%). Equally few lesbian and heterosexual women reported confronting situations directly.

The logistic regression analyses successfully identified factors that contributed to each of the four depression variables: whether the woman ever sought counseling, whether the woman participated in counseling for depression, a history of suicidal ideation, and a history of suicide attempts. We are particularly interested in three of the explanatory factors: lesbian sexual orientation, high stress levels, and a history of child physical or sexual abuse. All three of these factors predicted each of the four depression variables with one exception: high stress levels did not predict a history of suicide attempts.

Lesbian sexual orientation was a significant predictor of all four depression measures. The researchers speculated that other factors not included in their models may in part account for the association between sexual orientation and depressive distress. "For example, self-esteem, internalized homophobia, level of social support, and religious attitudes and beliefs may be important variables that moderate or mediate the relationship between sexual orientation and depressive distress" (Matthews et al., 2002, p. 1137). Additionally, they stated that it is not clear whether the sexual orientation's power is conferred through the long-term chronic stress associated with membership in a stigmatized minority group or through more time-limited stressful life circumstances, such as coming-out.

Razzano, Matthews, and Hughes (2002) compared the use of mental health services by lesbian and heterosexual women. They employed data from the Wilsnack et al. (1997) study described above. The sample consisted of 63 lesbians and 57 matched heterosexual women. The average age of the women was 40 years old. Only 37% of the sample was European American. Twenty-eight percent were African American, 25% Latina, 7% Asian, and 3% American Indian. Fifty-seven percent were married or in committed relationships. Fifty-eight percent were working full-time for pay. There were no significant differences between lesbian and heterosexual women on variables such as anxiety, sexual problems, insomnia, problems with alcohol or drugs, behavioral problems of children, or relationship concerns.

Descriptive data analyses indicated significant differences in the proportion of lesbians (70%) compared to heterosexual women (44%) who reported any use of mental health services during the prior 5 years, as well as any use of substance-related services in the past 5 years (23% versus 4%). Contrary to other studies, no significant differences were found between lesbian and heterosexual women regarding their ability to obtain mental health services, past history of child sexual experience, past history of physical abuse, or current antidepressant use. Lesbians were significantly more likely than heterosexual women to seek services for reasons related to depression and sexual orientation.

5 MENTAL HEALTH OF LESBIAN ELDERS

D'Augelli, Grossman, Hershberger, and O'Connell (2001) studied a sample of lesbian and gay elders, ages 60 to 91. The elders completed a self-administered questionnaire that employed standardized measures. Two thirds of the sample had children. Ten percent reported mental illness or a mental health disability. Eighteen percent of these elders used medication for mental health treatment. The elders demonstrated high self-esteem and low personal homonegativity (internalized homophobia). This study examined the percentage of people in each elder's life who knew his or her sexual orientation. For 20% of the sample, fewer than 25% of the people in their lives were aware of their sexual orientation. For another 20%, between 25% and 50% knew their sexual orientation. For 22%, between 51% and 75% were aware of their sexual orientation. Thirty-seven percent were "out" to more than 75% of the people in their lives.

Their health, cognitive functioning, self-esteem, and loneliness predicted the current mental health of these elders. Internalized homophobia was not a factor. Their physical health, cognitive functioning, and percent of people who knew their sexual orientation predicted a change in their mental health in the past 5 years. Those who were out to more people demonstrated better mental health. This may be misleading, because mental health is also a predictor of physical health, and cognitive functioning may be a function of mental health. Whether these elders had ever thought about suicide was predicted by personal homonegativity (internalized homophobia), loneliness, and the percentage of people who were aware of their sexual orientation. As is true with heterosexuals, the gay people who lived with partners demonstrated better current mental health, higher self-esteem, lower probability of suicidal thinking, and less loneliness.

How do we understand the influence of heterosexism in the lives of this sample? These elders demonstrated low homonegativity or internalized homophobia. Nearly 60% of these gay people were "out" to more than half of the people in their lives. For years, gay mental health professionals have argued that being out, not the initial process of coming-out, improves mental and physical health. This appears to be true for this sample.

Fortunately, efforts are being made to address the potential isolation of older lesbian and gay elders. There is some evidence that elders are making plans for growing old (McFarland & Sanders, 2003), but we do not know how this planning process may affect their mental health. Senior Action in a Gay Environment (SAGE) provides extensive mental health services to the lesbian and gay residents of two Eastern cities. In addition, they provide a range of educational, social, recreational, community organizing, and public-outreach programs to combat ageism and heterosexism (Shankle, Maxwell, Katzman, & Landers, 2003). In one Northwest city, 550 older lesbians are discovering each other and developing projects together (Nystrom & Jones, 2003). This community-building effort may serve as a model for other communities.

6 CONCLUSION

Lesbian women are thought to be at greater risk for mental health problems than are heterosexual women (Bradford et al., 1994; Cochran & Mays, 1994; Hyman, 2000; Rothblum, 1994; Trippet, 1994). This is borne out by the studies reviewed here. Lesbians are believed to be affected by additional, unique risk factors, including the coming-out process, level of disclosure of sexual orientation, discrimination experiences, and chronic stress associated with being a member of a stigmatized minority group (Ayala & Coleman, 2000; Oetjen & Rothblum, 2000; Rothblum, 1990; Tait, 1997). Several of the studies reviewed here report similar findings. We need to learn more about the impact of living with multiple forms of minority stress.

Some researchers have found higher rates of childhood maltreatment among lesbians when compared with heterosexual women. Why might lesbian women be more likely to have a history of childhood physical and sexual abuse? Hughes et al. (2001) speculated that lesbian women may be more likely to acknowledge and disclose their sexual identity and other stigmatized statuses or experiences. Research shows that lesbian women are more likely to engage in therapy, which may increase their willingness to be open.

How do lesbian women come to terms with their experiences of childhood victimization? How does this childhood experience shape one's coming-out process and possibility of internalizing homophobia? Matthews et al. (2002) pointed out that past traumatic experiences, such as physical or sexual abuse, may add to the vulnerability of young lesbians who may be struggling with issues related to coming-out, and may increase the risk of suicide.

We need to expand our research with lesbian youth. More lesbian youth will, in the future, disclose their sexual orientation to others, and at earlier ages. As youths self-label earlier, they will experience greater vulnerability in unfriendly school settings. The increased visibility of lesbian and gay people in our society may open a new vista for lesbian youth. It may also stimulate a backlash. Will this endanger lesbian youths? We must think about the supports lesbian youths will need to have available to them in the coming years. Studies should be undertaken with today's youth and tomorrow's youth, because our environment is changing so quickly.

Additional issues in the lives of lesbian elders should be investigated. The current cohort of elders has aged since the Stonewall rebellion and the birth of the gay rights' movement in the summer of 1969. Some of these elders have talked about the impact of the gay-related historical events on their lives (Rosenfeld, 2003). The mental health of the baby boomer generation as it ages cannot be predicted at this time. However, the baby boomers are likely to be "out" to the people in their lives in the same or greater proportions. A greater percentage of the lesbian and gay baby boomer generation has probably sought mental health treatment, including medications.

The D'Augelli et al. (2001) study described above does not address the negative aspects of aging, including dependency, disability, and decline. Because of the longer life span of women, lesbians may be more likely to have surviving mates. The absence of a marriage license may mean the absence of documentation of the existence of a primary intimate relationship. Older people are often thought of as asexual. Older women may tell us about sexuality. We have little information about the family constellations of older lesbian women. Finding a partner is more difficult for older lesbians (Greene, 2000). Older lesbians may not have much family support. We need more information about the role adult children play in providing care to older lesbian women. Lesbians who are in financial need are at greater risk for social isolation and rejection. The incomes of lesbian women tend not to be commensurate with either their education or their experience. Older lesbians are five times as likely as other women to have financial problems (Greene, 2000). Certainly, this socioeconomic stress is likely to affect the older lesbian's mental health.

The studies reviewed here suffer from methodological limitations. As discussed earlier, we cannot collect a representative sample of lesbian women. In addition, the studies employ different definitions of lesbian, childhood maltreatment, stress, and mental health. Each study uses different measures of similar concepts. Many of these studies gather retrospective data regarding childhood victimization and adolescent experiences of violence and coming-out. We must consider how experiences during the intervening years have colored memories. We do not know now how self-identifying as a lesbian affects the perception of past experiences.

According to all of the studies reviewed here, most lesbian women exhibit mental well-being. In the course of coming-out, most lesbian women successfully navigate the threats to psychological well-being posed by heterosexism and internalized homophobia. They cope with the need "to reclaim disowned or devalued parts of themselves, developing an identity into which their sexuality is well integrated" (Herek, 1996, p. 107). DiPlacido (1998) commented that minority stress may lead to negative health outcomes among some members of sexual minorities, but we must remember that not all members of sexual minorities experience adverse physical and mental health consequences as a result of their minority status. Instead, many lesbian women demonstrate a kind of resilience found among many members of marginalized groups (Greene, 2000). One characteristic of resilient people, including abuse survivors, is their capacity to evoke affirming reactions from others (Hyman & Williams, 2001). The lesbian and gay community provides some of this support.

Most Americans now believe that lesbian women and gay men deserve civil rights and protections. The United States and Canada are engaged in heated debates about same-sex marriage. How will such changes in the climate shape heterosexism, minority stress, and the victimization of youths? And, how will these newly formed processes affect the mental health of lesbian youths, adults, and elders in the coming years? The increased visibility and political foothold of lesbian women and gay men provide an exciting new backdrop for new research.

REFERENCES

American Association of University Women Foundation. (1993). *Hostile hallways: The AAUW survey on sexual harassment in America's schools.* Washington, DC: Author.

Ayala, J., & Coleman, H. (2000). Predictors of depression among lesbian women. *Journal of Lesbian Studies, 4*(3), 71–86.

Bobbe, J. (2002). Treatment with lesbian alcoholics: Healing shame and internalized homophobia for ongoing sobriety. *Health and Social Work, 27*(3), 218–222.

Boxer, A. M., Cook, J. A., & Herdt, B. (1991). Double jeopardy: Identity transitions and parent–child relations among gay and lesbian youth. In K. Pillemer & K. McCartney (Eds.), *Parent–child relations throughout life* (pp. 59–92). Hillsdale, NJ: Lawrence Erlbaum.

Bradford, J., & Ryan, C. (1988). *National Lesbian Health Care Survey: Final Report.* Washington, DC: National Lesbian and Gay Health Foundation.

Bradford, J., Ryan, C., & Rothblum, E. D. (1994). National Lesbian Health Care Survey: Implications for mental health care. *Journal of Consulting and Clinical Psychology, 62*(2), 228–242.

Brannock, J. C., & Chapman, B. E. (1990). Negative sexual experiences with men among heterosexual women and lesbians. *Journal of Homosexuality, 19,* 195–210.

Cochran, S. D., & Mays, V. M. (1994). Depressive distress among homosexually active African American men and women. *American Journal of Psychiatry, 151,* 524–529.

Corliss, H. L., Cochran, S. D., & Mays, V. M. (2002). Reports of parental maltreatment during childhood in a United States population-based survey of homosexual, bisexual, and heterosexual adults. *Child Abuse and Neglect, 26,* 1165–1178.

D'Augelli, A. R. (1998). Developmental implications of victimization of lesbian, gay, and bisexual youths. In G. M. Herek (Ed.), *Stigma and sexual orientation: Understanding prejudice against lesbians, gay men, and bisexuals* (pp. 187–210). Thousand Oaks, CA: Sage.

D'Augelli, A. R., Grossman, A. H., Hershberger, S. L., & O'Connell, T. S. (2001). Aspects of mental health among older lesbian, gay, and bisexual adults. *Aging and Mental Health, 5*(2), 149–158.

D'Augelli, A. R., Pilkington, N. W., & Hershberger, S. L. (2002). Incidence and mental health impact of sexual orientation victimization of lesbian, gay, and bisexual youths in high school. *School Psychology Quarterly, 17*(2), 148–167.

DiPlacido, J. (1998). Minority stress among lesbians, gay men, and bisexuals: A consequence of heterosexism, homophobia, and stigmatization. In G. M. Herek (Ed.), *Stigma and sexual orientation: Understanding prejudice against lesbians, gay men, and bisexuals* (pp. 138–159). Thousand Oaks, CA: Sage.

Faulkner, A. H., & Cranston, K. (1998). Correlates of same-sex sexual behavior in a random sample of Massachusetts high school students. *American Journal of Public Health, 88,* 262–266.

Fergusson, D. M., Horwood, L. J., & Beautrais, A. L. (1999). Is sexual orientation related to mental health problems and suicidality in young people? *Archives of General Psychiatry, 56,* 876–880.

Garofalo, R., Wolf, R. C., Kessel, S., Palfrey, S. J., & DuRant, R. H. (1998). The association between health risk behaviors and sexual orientation among a school-based sample of adolescents. *Pediatrics, 101,* 895–902.

Gonsiorek, J. C. (1993a). Threat, stress, and adjustment mental health and the workplace for gay and lesbian individuals. In L. Diamant (Ed.), *Homosexual issues in the workplace* (pp. 243–264). Washington, DC: Taylor & Francis.

Gonsiorek, J. C. (1993b). Mental health issues of gay and lesbian adolescents. In L. D. Garnets & D. C. Kimmel (Eds.), *Psychological perspectives on lesbian and gay male experiences* (pp. 469–485). New York: Columbia University Press.

Greene, B. (2000). Beyond heterosexism and across the cultural divide: Developing an inclusive lesbian, gay, and bisexual psychology: A look to the future. In B. Greene & G. L. Croom (Eds.), *Education, research, and practice in lesbian, gay, bisexual, and transgendered psychology: A resource manual* (pp. 1–45). Thousand Oaks, CA: Sage.

Hall, J. (1999). An exploration of the sexual and relationship experiences of lesbian survivors of childhood sexual abuse. *Sexual and Marital Therapy, 14*(1), 61–70.

Heffernan, K. (1998). The nature and predictors of substance abuse among lesbians. *Addictive Behaviors, 23*(4), 517–528.

Herdt, G. H., & Boxer, A. M. (1993). *Children of horizons: How gay and lesbian teens are leading a new way out of the closet.* Boston, MA: Beacon Press.

Herek, G. M. (1990). The context of anti-gay violence: Notes on cultural and psychological heterosexism. *Journal of Interpersonal Violence, 5,* 316–333.

Herek, G. M. (1996). Heterosexism and homophobia. In R. P. Cabaj & T. S. Stein (Eds.), *Textbook of homosexuality and mental health* (pp. 101–113). Washington, DC: American Psychiatric Press.

Hershberger, S. L., & D'Augelli, A. R. (1995). The impact of victimization on the mental health and suicidality of lesbian, gay, and bisexual youths. *Developmental Psychology, 31*(1), 65–74.

Hershberger, S. L., Pilkington, N. W., & D'Augelli, A. R. (1997). Predictors of suicide attempts among gay, lesbian, and bisexual youth. *Journal of Adolescent Research, 12*(4), 477–497.

Hughes, T. L., Haas, A. P., Razzano, L., Cassidy, R., & Matthews, A. (2000). Comparing lesbians' and heterosexual women's mental health: A multi-site survey. *Journal of Gay and Lesbian Social Services, 11*(1), 57–76.

Hughes, T. L., Johnson, T., & Wilsnack, S. C. (2001). Sexual assault and alcohol abuse: A comparison of lesbians and heterosexual women. *Journal of Substance Abuse, 13,* 515–532.

Hyman, B. (2000). The economic consequences of child sexual abuse for adult lesbian women. *Journal of Marriage and the Family, 62,* 199–211.

Hyman, B., & Williams, L. (2001). Resilience in adult female survivors of child sexual abuse. *Affilia: Journal of Women and Social Work, 16*(2), 198–220.

Klinger, R. L., & Stein, T. S. (1996). Impact of violence, childhood sexual abuse, and domestic violence and abuse on lesbians, bisexuals, and gay men. In R. P. Cabaj & T. S. Stein (Eds.), *Textbook of homosexuality and mental health* (pp. 801–818). Washington, DC: American Psychiatric Press.

Lechner, M. E., Vogel, M. E., Garcia-Shelton, L. M., Leichter, O. L., & Steibel, K. R. (1993). Self-reported medical problems of adult female survivors of childhood sexual abuse. *Journal of Family Practice, 36,* 633–638.

Lewinsohn, P. M., Rohde, P., & Seeley, J. R. (1996). Adolescent suicide ideation and attempts: Prevalence, risk factors, and clinical implications. *Clinical Psychology: Science and Practice, 3,* 25–46.

Loulan, J. (1987). *Lesbian passion.* San Francisco, CA: Spinsters/Aunt Lute Books.

Matthews, A. K., Hughes, T. L., Johnson, T., Razzano, L. A., & Cassidy, R. (2002). Prediction of depressive distress in a community sample of women: The role of sexual orientation. *American Journal of Public Health, 92*(7), 1131–1139.

Mays, V. M., & Cochran, S. D. (2001). Mental health correlates of perceived discrimination among lesbian, gay, and bisexual adults in the United States. *American Journal of Public Health, 91*(11), 1869–1876.

McFarland, P. L., & Sanders, S. (2003). A pilot study about the needs of older gays and lesbians: What social workers need to know. *Journal of Gerontological Social Work, 40*(3), 67–81.

Nystrom, N. M., & Jones, T. C. (2003). Community building with aging and old lesbians. *American Journal of Community Psychology, 31*(3/4), 293–301.

Oetjen, H., & Rothblum, E. D. (2000). When lesbians aren't gay: Factors affecting depression among lesbians. *Journal of Homosexuality, 39*, 49–73.

Pearlin, L. I. (1993). The social context of stress. In L. Goldberger & S. Breznitz (Eds.), *Handbook of stress: Theoretical and clinical aspects* (pp. 303–315). New York: Free Press.

Peters, D. K., & Cantrell, P. J. (1991). Factors distinguishing samples of lesbian and heterosexual women. *Journal of Homosexuality, 21*, 1–15.

Pilkington, N. W., & D'Augelli, A. R. (1995). Victimizations of lesbian, gay, and bisexual youth in community settings. *Journal of Community Psychology, 23*, 34–56.

Rankow, E. J., Cambre, K. M., & Cooper, K. (1998). Health care-seeking behavior of adult lesbian and bisexual survivors of childhood sexual abuse. *Journal of the Gay and Lesbian Medical Association, 2*(2), 69–76.

Razzano, L., Matthews, A., & Hughes, T. (2002). Utilization of mental health services: A comparison of lesbian and heterosexual women. *Journal of Gay and Lesbian Social Services, 14*(1), 51–66.

Roberts, S. J., & Sorensen, L. (1999). Prevalence of childhood sexual abuse and related sequelae in a lesbian population. *Journal of the Gay and Lesbian Medical Association, 3*(1), 11–19.

Rosenfeld, D. (2003). *The changing of the guard: Lesbian and gay elders, identity, and social change.* Philadelphia, PA: Temple University Press.

Rothblum, E. D. (1990). Depression among lesbians: An invisible and unresearched phenomenon. *Journal of Gay and Lesbian Psychotherapy, 1*(3), 67–87.

Rothblum, E. D. (1994). Lesbians and physical appearance: Which model applies? In B. Greene & G. M. Herek (Eds.), *Lesbian and gay psychology: Theory, research, and clinical applications* (Vol. 1, pp. 84–97). Thousand Oaks, CA: Sage.

Russell, D. E. H. (1983). The incidence and prevalence of intrafamilial and extrafamilial sexual abuse of female children. *Child Abuse and Neglect, 7*, 133–146.

Saewyc, E. M., Bearinger, L., Heinz, P. A., Blum, R. W., & Resnick, M. D. (1998). Gender differences in health and risk behaviors among bisexual and homosexual adolescents. *Journal of Adolescent Health, 23*(3), 181–188.

Saulnier, C. F., & Miller, B. A. (1997). Drug and alcohol problems: Heterosexual compared to lesbian and bisexual women. *Canadian Journal of Human Sexuality, 6*(3), 221–231.

Savin-Williams, R. C. (1994). Verbal and physical abuse as stressors in the lives of lesbian, gay male, and bisexual youths: Associations with school problems, running away, substance abuse, prostitution, and suicide. *Journal of Consulting and Clinical Psychology, 62*, 261–269.

Shankle, M. D., Maxwell, C. A., Katzman, E. S., & Landers, S. (2003). An invisible population: Older lesbian, gay, bisexual, and transgender individuals. *Clinical Research and Regulatory Affairs, 20*(2), 159–183.

Shidlo, A. (1994). Internalized homophobia: Conceptual and empirical issues in measurement. In B. Greene & G. M. Herek (Eds.), *Lesbian and gay psychology: Theory, research, and clinical applications* (Vol. 1, pp. 176–205). Thousand Oaks, CA: Sage.

Tait, D. (1997). Stress and social support networks among lesbian and heterosexual women: A comparison study. *Smith College Studies in Social Work, 67*(2), 213–224.

Tjaden, P., Thoennes, N., & Allison, C. J. (1999). Comparing violence over the life span in samples of same-sex and opposite-sex cohabitants. *Violence and Victims, 14*(4), 413–425.

Tomeo, M. E., Templer, D. I., Anderson, S., & Kotler, D. (2001). Comparative data of childhood and adolescence molestation in heterosexual and homosexual persons. *Archives of Sexual Behavior, 30*(5), 535–541.

Trippet, S. E. (1994). Lesbians' mental health concerns. *Health Care Women International, 15,* 317–323.

Weingourt, R. (1998). A comparison of heterosexual and homosexual long-term sexual relationships. *Archives of Psychiatric Nursing, 12,* 114–118.

Wilsnack, S. C., Vogeltanz, N. D., Klassen, A. D., & Harris, T. R. (1997). Childhood sexual abuse and women's substance abuse: National survey findings. *Journal of Studies on Alcohol, 58,* 264–271.

Index